Military Power

Military Power

EXPLAINING VICTORY AND DEFEAT

IN MODERN BATTLE

Stephen Biddle

PRINCETON UNIVERSITY PRESS

PRINCETON AND OXFORD

Copyright © 2004 by Princeton University Press
Published by Princeton University Press,
41 William Street, Princeton, New Jersey 08540
In the United Kingdom: Princeton University Press,
3 Market Place, Woodstock, Oxfordshire OX20 1SY

Fifth printing, and first paperback printing, 2006
Paperback ISBN-13: 978-0-691-12802-3
Paperback ISBN-10: 0-691-12802-2

The Library of Congress has cataloged the cloth edition
of this book as follows

Biddle, Stephen D.
Military power : explaining victory and defeat in modern
battle / Stephen Biddle.
p.   cm.
Includes bibliographical references and index.
ISBN 0-691-11645-8 (acid-free paper)
1. Deployment (Strategy).   2. Offensive (Military science).
3. Defensive (Military science).   4. Military art and science—
History—20th century.   5. Military history, Modern—20th century.
I. Title.

U163.B53 2004
355.02—dc21   2003056325

British Library Cataloging-in-Publication Data is available

This book has been composed in Dante

Printed on acid-free paper. ∞

pup.princeton.edu

Printed in the United States of America

10   9   8   7   6

*The views expressed are the author's, and do not necessarily
represent positions of the U.S. Army, the Army War College,
or the Department of Defense.*

For Anna Emmaline Biddle

Contents

Preface

MANY NOW BELIEVE that war's future will be very different from its past. New technology, the end of the Cold War, and an emerging war on state sponsors of global terrorism all seem to presage a coming "revolution in military affairs" (RMA) with potentially sweeping consequences.

Change, of course, is inevitable. But so is continuity. And today's policy debate systematically exaggerates the former and slights the latter. In this book I argue that major warfare since 1900 has actually seen much less real change than most now suppose, and that the future, too, should bring far more continuity than many now expect. In fact, the real causes of battlefield success have been surprisingly stable since 1917–18 and are likely to remain so for at least the first decades of the twenty-first century. Expectations of a looming revolution in military affairs are both a serious misreading of modern military history and a dangerous prescription for today's defense policy: they could easily lead to an overemphasis on new technology or radical operational concepts that could weaken, not strengthen, the American military and undermine its ability to prevail on future battlefields.

Scholars, too, have misunderstood the nature of military power. Most international relations theorists focus on gross numerical strength: they see the weight of material resources as the heart of power in international politics. Others see a technological pendulum swinging warfare from offense- to defense-dominance, shaping international politics in the process. Many historians see the world wars chiefly as struggles of industrial production or technological innovation or both. None of these views, however, is sound. Real battle outcomes cannot be explained by materiel alone; in fact, material factors are only weakly related to historical patterns of victory and defeat. To understand the military underpinnings of international politics requires a systematic explanation of how material and nonmaterial factors interact to produce real combat outcomes.

This book provides such an explanation. I argue that a particular nonmaterial variable—force employment, or the doctrine and tactics by which forces are actually used in combat—is centrally important, shaping the role of material factors and often predetermining winners and losers. Moreover, I see the critical period of innovation in force employment occurring very early—on the western front from 1917 to 1918—with technological change since then serving mostly to increase the price of ignoring the lessons taught in the first decades of the twentieth century.

That force employment should matter is hardly news. To date, however, there has been no systematic, falsifiable account of just how this notoriously slippery variable affects combat outcomes, leaving explicit theories to more tractable material factors alone. I thus develop here a systematic account of force employment's role, then show that it holds up under aggressive testing.

To accomplish this, I use a variety of methods, ranging from careful historiography to formal theory, archivally based case research, large-n statistical analysis, and experimental testing using a Defense Department simulation model. This multimethod approach enables me to address "soft" variables like force employment in a rigorous way and offers a means of compensating for the weaknesses of individual methods taken alone.

Some of these methods are technically complex. The book is designed, however, to allow nontechnical, qualitatively oriented readers to grasp the central ideas and historical case analyses without grappling with mathematical detail as long as they are willing to read selectively and forgo some quantitative chapters. In particular, chapter 8 and the appendix present technical material that adds rigor and provides a more complete understanding of my claims, but they can be skipped by nonspecialists without missing the book's main arguments. Although specialists will want to confront the book in its entirety, nontechnical readers should exploit the book's organization to focus on the material of greatest interest.

I have benefited from the generous assistance of many helpful individuals and agencies, without whom this book would not have been possible. I would particularly like to thank the Smith Richardson Foundation, whose Junior Faculty Grant enabled me to spend the 1999 calendar year in writing and research; the University of North Carolina Department of Political Science, whose assistance extended the Smith Richardson grant to the entire year, and who offered an additional semester of research leave in fall 2000; and the Institute for Defense Analyses' Central Research Program, under which much of the foundational analysis was conducted. Dr. Victor Utgoff, my long-time mentor at IDA, was particularly instrumental both in helping me think through critical ideas and in securing funding for their early development; I owe him a special debt of thanks.

Richard Betts and Lynn Eden read the entire manuscript and offered comments both incisive and unfailingly constructive. Eliot Cohen, Conrad Crane, Mark Crescenzi, Peter Feaver, Michael Fischerkeller, Hein Goemans, David Herrmann, Wade Hinkle, Dustin Howes, Wayne Hughes, Craig Koerner, Richard Kohn, Stephen Long, Timothy McKeown, Raymond Millen, Ivan Oelrich, Michael O'Hanlon, Daryl Press, Alex Roland, Marco Steenbergen, Alex Vacca, and James Wirtz read selected chapters and offered helpful comments. Members of the University of Chicago Program in International Security Policy, the Columbia University Institute of War and Peace Studies, the Harvard University Olin Institute, the University of Pennsylvania International Studies Program, and the Princeton University Woodrow Wilson School of Public Affairs all heard presentations of the book's main argument and offered valuable input. Bruce Anderson, Jerome Bracken, Chris Christenson, Damon Coletta, Jeffrey Cooper,

Steven David, Colin Elman, Joshua Epstein, Bernard Finel, Ben Frankel, Charles Glaser, David Graham, Richard Harknett, Marshall Hoyler, Christopher Jehn, Lawrence Katzenstein, Chaim Kaufmann, Michael Leonard, Kier Lieber, Jack Levy, Sean Lynn-Jones, Thomas Mahnken, John R. Martin, Frederick Mayer, Brian McCue, H. R. McMaster, John Mearsheimer, Holger Mey, James Miller, Jesse Orlansky, Robert Pape, George Quester, James Ralston, Dani Reiter, Brad Roberts, William Schultis, Allan Stam, Tomoko Sugiyama, Richard Swain, Nigel Thalakada, John Tillson, Marc Trachtenberg, Robert Turrell, Stephen Van Evera, Eugene Visco, Volney Warner, Larry Welch, Caroline Ziemke, and Robert Zirkle offered formative input on related papers without which the book would not have taken the form it did. Katja Breidt and Dustin Howes provided able research assistance. The members of the 1998–2002 classes of the Columbia University Summer Workshop on the Analysis of Military Operations and Strategy (SWAMOS) deserve special thanks for their questions and enthusiastic critiques of the ideas presented here—one could not ask for a more stimulating intellectual community, or a more engaging summer home away from home. Finally, my wife, Tami Biddle, read much of the manuscript and provided a crucial sounding board for ideas, approaches, frustrations, and discoveries. I am grateful to all, but especially to her.

Abbreviations

ACR	armored cavalry regiment
ANOVA	analysis of variance
BEF	British Expeditionary Force
BW	biological weapons
CENTCOM	Central Command
CINC	composite index of national capability
COW	Correlates of War
CW	chemical weapons
DARPA	Defense Advanced Research Projects Agency
DU	depleted uranium
FFR	force-to-force ratio
FLER	fractional loss exchange ratio
FOFA	follow-on forces attack
FSR	force-to-space ratio
GPS	global positioning system
GWAPS	Gulf War Air Power Survey
IDA	Institute for Defense Analyses
IDF	Israeli Defense Forces
IR	international relations
JDAM	joint direct attack munition
KTO	Kuwait Theater of Operations
LER	loss exchange ratio
LIC	low-intensity conflict
MITL	man-in-the-loop
MORS	Military Operations Research Society
NATO	North Atlantic Treaty Organization
NCO	noncommissioned officer
NTC	National Training Center
OLS	ordinary least squares
OPFOR	opposition force
SAR	synthetic aperture radar
SOF	special operations forces
WMD	weapons of mass destruction

CHAPTER ONE

Introduction

WHAT CAUSES VICTORY and defeat in battle? Why do the winners win and the losers lose? What makes some campaigns bloody stalemates and others apparent cakewalks? How can states maximize their odds of winning and minimize their casualties? And are the answers changing in the information age? Will new technology or changing geopolitics transform warfare, creating new winners—and new losers—on the battlefields of the future?

These are life-and-death questions, and not just for soldiers. They affect everyone: from infantrymen on the battlefield to office workers in the World Trade Center to entire nations and peoples. German victories in Poland and France condemned millions of French and Polish Jews to the gas chambers in World War II. Soviet victories in 1944–5 consigned a generation of East Europeans to a Communist oppression that was spared those who were reached first by American and British armies. The trench stalemate of 1914–18 sentenced millions to deaths that a quicker victory would have averted and ruined economies across Europe. By exhausting some countries and embittering others, it shaped the subsequent politics of the twentieth century. Today's world would be very different if European generals had fought differently in 1914–18. Defeat in battle has meant occupation and a conqueror's rule for nations from France to Poland and from Japan to Indonesia. Today, swift victory in a war against fundamentalist terrorism could spare the lives of thousands—or millions—in the West and Islam; failure could bring consequences too horrible to contemplate.

With so much at stake, great effort has been spent on these questions. The answers, however, often fall short.

As recently as 1991, a massive effort using state-of-the-art methods and the nation's best analysts radically overestimated U.S. losses in the upcoming Gulf War. The prewar congressional debate hinged on casualty expectations; these were widely seen as the key to Congress's vote on the use of force. With so much at stake, no effort was spared to achieve realistic estimates: prominent academics, government analysts, and senior military officials gave testimony using methods ranging from computer models to historical analogies to professional military judgment. Virtually all were way off. Even the closest estimate overshot the actual casualty count by more than a factor of two. The next best missed by a factor of six. The majority were off by more than an order of magnitude; official estimates were reportedly over by at least that much; while some official projections erred by a factor of over 200.[1]

The pre-Gulf war debate was hardly unique, however. For over a century, soldiers and diplomats have analyzed military balances, yet the subsequent fighting has often surprised both sides. In 1914, for example, Europeans expected a short, decisive war of movement. None foresaw a nearly four-year trench stalemate—if they had, the war might never have happened.[2] In 1940 Allied leaders were astonished by the Germans' lightning victory over France. They had expected something closer to the trench warfare of 1914–18; even the victors were surprised, with most German planners expecting an extended war of attrition in France and the Low Countries.[3] In 1973 both Israelis and Arabs alike were stunned by the October War's staggering losses, which forced Israel to beg emergency aid from the United States and spurred a wave of postwar pronouncements that tanks were now doomed, given their apparent vulnerability to guided missiles.[4] By the mid-1970s, tanks were widely seen as dinosaurs, the next generation of obsolete weapon to follow the horse cavalry or the battleship. Yet this, too, proved wrong: by the mid-1990s, the M1 tank was widely hailed as an invincible "King of the Killing Zone" after its nearly casualty-free performance in the Gulf War.[5]

Academics have done no better. Military balance estimates are central to modern political science. Much of our current understanding of international politics rests on the assumption that state behavior is shaped by the threat of war and the pursuit of military capability. The empirical study of politics thus depends on measures of capability, which play a pivotal role in the war causation, arms racing, alliance formation, conflict duration, crisis escalation, or deterrence literatures, among others.[6] Yet the standard capability measures at the heart of all this are actually no better than coin flips at predicting real military outcomes.[7] An enormous scholarly edifice thus rests on very shaky foundations.

We must—and can—do better. But real improvement will require a new approach.

Today, most analyses are either rigorous but narrow, or broad but unrigorous. Mathematical models of combat, for example, are rigorous but typically focus on material alone: how many troops or weapons do the two sides have, and how good is their equipment?[8] By contrast, holistic assessments consider issues such as strategy, tactics, morale, combat motivation, or leadership as well as just materiel but treat these variables much less systematically. Real progress demands rigor *and* breadth: a systematic treatment of both material and nonmaterial variables, backed up with a combination of empirical evidence and careful deductive reasoning. Below I advance such an analysis for one key nonmaterial variable: force employment, or the doctrine and tactics by which armies use their materiel in the field.

I hold that a particular pattern of force employment—the *modern system*—has been pivotal in the twentieth century and is likely to remain so. I argue that since at least 1900, the dominant technological fact of the modern battlefield has been increasing lethality. Even by 1914, firepower had become so lethal that exposed mass movement in the open had become suicidal. Subsequent technological change has only increased the range over which exposure can be fatal. To perform meaningful military missions in the face of this storm of steel requires armies to reduce their exposure, and since 1918 the central means of doing so has been modern system force employment.[9]

The modern system is a tightly interrelated complex of cover, concealment, dispersion, suppression, small-unit independent maneuver, and combined arms at the tactical level, and depth, reserves, and differential concentration at the operational level of war. Taken together, these techniques sharply reduce vulnerability to even twenty-first century weapons and sensors. Where fully implemented, the modern system damps the effects of technological change and insulates its users from the full lethality of their opponents' weapons.

Not everyone can master it, however. The modern system is extremely complex and poses painful political and social tradeoffs. While some have been able to surmount these challenges and implement the modern system fully, others have not. Militaries that fail to implement the modern system have been fully exposed to the firepower of modern weapons—with increasingly severe consequences as those weapons' reach and lethality have expanded. The net result has thus been a growing gap in the real military power of states that can and cannot implement the modern system, but surprisingly little change over time in outcomes between mutually modern-system opponents.

The modern system is also essential to understanding the role of numerical preponderance in war. Many suppose that victory normally goes to the preponderant side. Without modern-system exposure reduction, however, armies cannot survive long enough to make their numbers tell. Superior numbers can be decisive or almost irrelevant depending on the two sides' force employment. This in turn means that states' relative economic, demographic, or industrial strength are poor indicators of real military power: gross resource advantages matter only if they can be exploited via modern-system force employment, and many states cannot do so.

If so, then to assess military power without taking force employment into account is to risk major error. Assessments focusing solely on materiel will radically overestimate well-equipped but poorly handled armies—such as the Iraqis in 1991—and underestimate poorly equipped but well-handled troops—such as the North Vietnamese in 1965–72. The same policy initiatives can have opposite effects depending on the two sides' force employment. Typical *ceteris paribus* cost-effectiveness analyses can thus be dangerously misleading: a new weapon can look wonderful when a non–modern system opponent is assumed but terrible if the enemy uses its forces differently, and neither assumption will hold true all the time. In fact, analyses considering materiel alone may be little better than blind guesses.

The results challenge a wide variety of standard views, ranging from current U.S. defense policy and common projections for future warfare to mainstream international relations (IR) theory and orthodox interpretations of twentieth-century military history. The defense debate is increasingly focused on technology; most assume that in the information age, superior technology wins wars, fueling growing pressure to speed modernization by spending less on training and readiness. Official analyses reinforce this trend: official models that focus on materiel and exclude force employment overvalue the former and undervalue the latter. Policy decisions informed by such models are thus likely to overspend on modernization and force structure and underspend on the readiness and training needed for sound force employment. Similarly, threat assessments based on the numbers and types of hostile weapons are likely to overestimate real capability for enemies with modern equipment but limited skills but underestimate militaries with older equipment but high skills. Ensuing intervention and use-of-force decisions could produce *over*confidence and overcommitment against ill-equipped but adept militaries but *under*confidence and unnecessary caution against enemies with state-of-the-art weapons but little skill in their use.

Projections of future warfare are now dominated by the claim that technology is creating a "revolution in military affairs" (RMA) in which the nature of military power is being transformed. In the future, it is held, long-range precision air and missile strikes will dominate warfare, ground forces will be reduced mostly to scouts, and the struggle for information supremacy will replace the breakthrough battle as the decisive issue for success. These views misunderstand the relationship between technology and force employment, however. Because RMA advocates misunderstand warfare prior to the 1990s, they misread the 1991 Gulf War as a radical departure; by projecting this mistake forward into the twenty-first century, they derive a case for a radical restructuring of U.S. defense policy that is neither necessary nor desirable.

For international relations theory, the weakness of simple material proxies poses serious problems. Military power plays a pervasive role in the study of international politics; in fact, much of modern IR theory amounts to a debate on its influence over state behavior. Yet all of this rests on very simplistic treatments of its nature and determinants. Theoretically, the literature relies on logically unsound, unitary notions of military capability that mask crucial tradeoffs. Empirically, the use of weak proxies undermines existing findings and suggests that the literature may have underestimated capability's effects relative to audience costs, signaling, or resolve. Analyses of deterrence, power distribution, and polarity rest on especially thin ice given the weakness of the measures used to represent capability. The mercantilist position in international political economy is based on the proposition that economic preponderance conduces to military power, yet the relationship between economic strength and real capability is much weaker than commonly thought. More broadly, much of the empirical and theoretical literature will need to be revisited in light of a more meaningful measure of real capability.

The received view of modern military history centered on technology for much of the postwar era. The World War I trench stalemate was seen as the product of the industrial revolution in the machine gun, new artillery, and mass munition production. World War II was seen as a war of movement brought on by the tank, the airplane, and the radio. Postwar conflict was seen as overshadowed by the atom bomb.[10] A more recent interpretation emphasizes preponderance: industrial coalition wars are held to turn on the size of the combatant economies, with victory going to the side that could outproduce the other, and with the conduct of operations taking a back seat to the battle for production.[11] I suggest, however, that force employment has played a more important role than either technology or preponderance for twentieth-century warfare. How forces are used is critical; to explain historical outcomes chiefly in terms of materiel is to misinterpret the major military events of the century.

The balance of this chapter supports these contentions in three steps. First, I define what I mean by military power, or "capability," and justify my choice. Second, I discuss how I will explain capability and present some of the limitations of my analysis. Finally, I outline the book's structure and provide a road map for what is to come.

What Is "Military Power"?

My focus is on the military dimension of power. It is important to be clear on its nature and limits. State power embodies "soft" persuasive or attractive elements as well as its "hard" or military component.[12] Nor does military power in itself guarantee success in war. Militarily weak but resolute states can prevail over militarily strong but irresolute ones. War outcomes are products of more than just military power alone.

Moreover, military power (or "capability") itself can mean different things in different contexts. Military forces, after all, do many things, ranging from defending national territory to invading other states, hunting down terrorists, coercing concessions, countering insurgencies, keeping the peace, enforcing economic sanctions, showing the flag, or maintaining domestic order. Proficiency in one or even several does not imply proficiency in them all: good defenders of national territory can make poor peacekeepers; forces that can defend national territory cannot necessarily conquer their neighbors.[13] For any one mission, moreover, "success" can be defined very differently by different actors. Defenders of national territory may all value low casualties, short wars, and complete restoration of the status quo, but these goals often conflict with one another, and different defenders value them differently at the margin. Some would trade higher casualties and a longer war for complete reconquest of lost territory; others would not.[14] Some would bomb an opponent for months to avoid losing friendly ground troops; others would invade quickly to shorten the war at the cost of heavier casualties.[15] If capability is the ability to succeed at an assigned mission, different states will thus assess capability very differently for the same forces—no single, undifferentiated concept of "military capability" can apply to all conflicts in all places and times.

Any analysis must therefore focus on a subset of the tasks militaries perform, which are in turn a subset of the elements of state power. For my purposes, I concentrate on the mission of controlling territory in mid- to high-intensity continental warfare, and I define its accomplishment via three interconnected criteria: the ability to destroy hostile forces while preserving one's own; the ability to take and hold ground; and the time required to do so.

Specifically, I define offensive military capability as *the capacity to destroy the largest possible defensive force over the largest possible territory for the smallest attacker casualties in the least time*; defensive military capability is conversely the ability to preserve the largest possible defensive force over the largest possible territory with the greatest attacker casualties for the longest time. As these criteria can be fulfilled in differing degree (and often conflict with one another), I offer a theory that explains casualties, ground gain, and duration as distinct but interconnected outcomes; I then discuss the interactions and tradeoffs among them in light of the proposed theory as a whole.[16]

My unit of analysis for this theory is the *operation*. An operation is a series of interconnected battles resulting from a single prior plan. The battles associated with the invasion of France and the German drive to the Channel in 1940, for example, comprise an operation (Operation FALL GELB), as do the battles associated with the American breakout from the Normandy beachhead beginning on July 25, 1944 (Operation COBRA).[17]

By "mid- to high-intensity conflict," I mean the middle part of a spectrum ranging from guerilla warfare at the low end to global thermonuclear war at the high end. "Mid-intensity" conflicts would include regional conventional wars such as the recent campaigns in Afghanistan, the Balkans, or Kuwait; the Arab-Israeli wars; the Sino-Vietnamese War; or the Indo-Pakistani wars. "High-intensity" conflicts are conventional world wars among the great powers. I thus exclude guerilla warfare at the low end, and mass destruction warfare involving nuclear, chemical, or biological weapons at the high end of the spectrum of conflict. By "continental warfare" I mean combat fought between military forces on or over major land masses. I thus exclude war at sea, and strategic bombing against civilian targets.

I thus seek to explain the outcomes of operations to control territory in mid- to high-intensity continental warfare. Why this focus? Is this just irrelevant "old thinking" in an era of counterterrorist warfare, ethnic conflict, coercive strategic bombing, and weapons of mass destruction (WMD)?

The answer is no. While major conventional war is only one among many important missions, it remains far more important than some now suppose, and it will be for the foreseeable future. It will also remain the most expensive mission to fulfill, it will remain the central purpose for the majority of the U.S. military, and it will continue to occur between other parties in other parts of the world.

In the emerging war on terrorism, for example, counterintelligence and police work against terrorists hiding in the shadows will be accompanied by periodic major warfare against states who harbor them. This is a central implication of the "Bush Doctrine," which holds states accountable for the actions of terrorists within their borders and uses the threat of major war as a central means of enforcing accountability.[18]

The recent campaign to destroy al Qaeda's sanctuary in Afghanistan, for instance, was precisely the kind of regional conventional war I examine here.[19] Contrary to popular perception, Afghanistan was neither a guerilla war nor simply long-range bombing. The Taliban regime sought to control territory and defend key geographic objectives, not merely to harass their enemies with hit-and-run tactics. And this struggle for territorial control involved substantial close combat on the ground between Western and allied Afghan infantry on one side, and opposing Taliban fighters who had eluded American surveillance and survived American air strikes on the other. The result was a series of surprisingly orthodox ground battles, as at Chapchall on October 23, 2001, Sayed Slim Kalay on December 2–4, Highway 4 on December 2–6, or Operation ANACONDA in March 2002.[20] The critical action in the war's northern phase, for example, involved a breakthrough battle near the village of Bai Beche on November 5, 2001, in which Taliban forces that had survived more than two days of preliminary American bombing were overrun, opening the door for the Northern Alliance's advance to Mazar-e-Sharif.[21] Until ANACONDA, the *American* role in the war was mostly bombing (and spotting targets for the bombers), but the war itself involved far more than just the American contribution. That contribution was critical, but its role was to strengthen allied ground forces to enable them to prevail in traditional close combat—the air strikes did not simply annihilate the Taliban or break their will to fight. New technology played an important role in Afghanistan—and its relative importance is a major theme below—but the war itself was precisely the kind of mid- to high-intensity struggle for territorial control on which I focus here.

Nor is it clear that direct U.S. military involvement in the war on terrorism will be mostly air power or small special forces teams. Any initially limited U.S. intervention will face powerful pressures to escalate if small-scale efforts prove insufficient.[22] And among America's most powerful escalatory threats is the ability to topple regimes by invading and taking political control of their territory—that is, by fighting and winning a major conventional theater war. Against regimes like Mullah Omar's, Saddam Hussein's, Bashar Assad's, or Kim Jong-Il's, this is the ultimate sanction. It threatens what they value most: their hold on power. And it is the single most credible threat one can direct at this value: few regimes can survive an American march on their capital. Even where this ultimate sanction is unused, its existence makes other coercive means more effective: it makes one's opponents consider one's ability to remove them by force if they ignore lesser threats. In Kosovo, the United States initially took this threat off the table only to regret it later; it would be a similar mistake now to assume that lesser threats will always suffice, and thus that America will never again have to wage a major theater war.

Major war is also the primary planning yardstick not only for U.S. forces, but for most world and regional powers. For most of the post–Cold War era, the U.S. military was sized and structured to win two, nearly simultaneous major regional conflicts; the Bush administration has modified this standard to winning one while holding the line in another, but the standard is still set in major-war terms.[23] Most of the U.S. military is oriented to this threat; by contrast, the special forces, which some now see as the vanguard of American military action, consume only about 1 percent of annual U.S. defense spending.[24] Many of the world's other major militaries are similarly oriented: India's, for example, is designed for major war with Pakistan or China; Pakistan and China must be ready for major war with India; Israel must prepare for major war with Syria or other Arab neighbors.

Nor are concerns with major warfare limited to great and regional powers, or wholly superseded by ethnic disputes, guerilla warfare, or other low-intensity conflicts elsewhere. The recent wars in Bosnia, Croatia, Eritrea, Zaire/Congo, Rwanda, Azerbaijan, and Kuwait were all mid- to high-intensity conflicts in which combatants sought to take and hold territory in conventional ways.[25] If war breaks out tomorrow in Kashmir or the Bekaa Valley, the fighting would not be low intensity. The conflicts I focus on here are hardly a thing of the past for anyone, and their centrality to U.S. interests makes them an appropriate place to start in understanding capability.[26]

I exclude countervalue strategic bombing chiefly because its dynamics are well studied elsewhere ("counterforce" violence is directed against hostile military forces; "countervalue" violence is aimed at hostile populations, economic centers, or political leadership).[27] Purely countervalue bombing is also less common than many think—and much less successful. To date, almost all strategic bombing has blended countervalue coercion with military counterforce to reduce an opponent's ability to wage war.[28] The latter is within my scope and has provided the overwhelming bulk of strategic bombing's actual historical impact. Whatever its intent, the primary result of Allied strategic bombing in World War II was to reduce Germany's war-making capacity.[29] Countervalue strategic bombing in Korea and Vietnam failed to bring political concessions directly; where it succeeded it was by reducing the target states' ability to wage a counterforce war effort.[30] In the Gulf War, strategic bombing was mostly counterforce in intent; limited countervalue bombing aimed at coercing Saddam by threatening his hold on power failed.[31] In Kosovo, NATO bombing combined countervalue strikes against Serbian leadership and economic infrastructure with counterforce missions against Serbian ground forces; Serbian concessions occurred only after NATO began preparations for a major land invasion of Kosovo.[32] In Afghanistan, early hopes that bombing Taliban leadership targets would yield concession-proved unrealistic. Strategic bombing has thus shown little ability to succeed via countervalue coercion, and recent experience in Kosovo and Afghanistan gives little reason to expect change any time soon.

Weapons of mass destruction (i.e., nuclear, chemical, and biological weapons) are a major threat and will become an increasingly common problem as technology proliferates. They are clearly an important issue for capability, but not the *only* important issue. Many states will either fail to acquire WMD or choose not to use them; conventional capability will thus remain important even as WMD proliferate.[33] Moreover, to understand WMD's military effects, one must explain conventional capability first. Regional mass destruction warfare would probably not shut down conventional operations by a great power: regional nuclear arsenals will probably be tiny for the foreseeable future, and most great powers train their troops to fight in chemical and biological environments.[34] The nature of the fighting would change, perhaps drastically, as the combatants seek to cope with damage incurred and reduce vulnerability to further attacks. But most do this by modifying their conventional-war methods for the special conditions of WMD (e.g., by spreading out troops and supporting infrastructure). To understand such measures' effects, one needs to understand the effects of dispersion, for example, on military outcomes generally. Without this, assessments rest on unnecessarily speculative ground. Understanding conventional operations alone is obviously insufficient to assess WMD, but it is a necessary precondition.

Finally, international relations theory rests on the empirical record of state behavior—its central function is to explain that behavior as we have observed it—and for modern interstate warfare, most of the empirical record concerns conventional continental counterforce. Of the forty-six twentieth-century interstate wars in the University of Michigan's Correlates of War dataset, for example, fully forty have been primarily conventional continental counterforce in nature.[35] If capability is an important contributor to state behavior, then the issues I address here are essential foundations for understanding the politics of international conflict.

METHODOLOGY

I explain capability in modern counterforce warfare using a combination of complementary methods. Social science has yet to provide a single perfect methodology; each of the major research traditions has important shortcomings taken alone. Each tradition also has important strengths, however. Taken together, a combination of contrasting approaches offers an opportunity to cover the weaknesses of each with the strengths of others, providing what Donald Polkinghorne has termed "methodological triangulation," and increasing our ability to tease knowledge from the imperfect data available to us.[36]

In particular, I combine close review of recent historiography with formal theory, case method, statistical analysis, and simulation experimentation. As for the first of these, historians are now developing a major reinterpretation of the two world wars (especially the first), focusing on the role of doctrinal adaptation for the wars' course and outcome.[37] This emerging view has important—but as yet largely unrecognized—implications, not just for the military history of the remainder of the twentieth century, but also for current defense policy and IR theory. Historical narrative, however, is an awkward medium for addressing such broader concerns. Its scope is typically limited narrowly to particular events. And natural-language narrative is ill-suited for sorting out the internal logic of complex, multivariate relationships, or for projecting trends into new situations where particulars differ from past events.

By contrast, formal theory, or the use of mathematical language to describe causal relationships, has advantages in sorting out the internal logic of complex, interconnecting claims. It also facilitates inference from observations of the past to conjectures about the future. Its specificity can strengthen policy prescription while disciplining thought. Formal theory alone, however, can be precise and specific but wrong—or, maybe worse, irrelevant where it abstracts away the real issues in the interest of mathematical clarity or tractability. I thus place the history first: formal language is used to generalize, systematize, and extend ideas drawn from serious historiography, harnessing deductive rigor to historically critical substance, and producing new ideas with important implications.

This new theory is tested using three different methods. First, I provide three detailed, archivally based case studies of actions fought under conditions chosen to provide maximum theoretical leverage. Small-n case method permits the depth of analysis needed to characterize variables, like force employment, that have not heretofore been included in large-n datasets. It also allows detailed process tracing to help distinguish real causation from mere coincidence. This depth of detail, however, makes it impossible to consider more than a handful of cases.

I thus complement the case studies with a series of large-n statistical analyses. The statistical findings speak to larger trends extending over a much wider body of experience. But since force employment has not been studied systematically, it is absent from available datasets and must thus be treated indirectly via enabling assumptions and proxy variables. Taken alone, the statistical results would offer at best a partial test; combined with case method, however, they enable methodological triangulation and the prospect of greater confidence than either could provide alone.

Both small-n case method and large-n statistics, however, are limited to battles already fought (and the peculiarities of surviving documentation). The future may differ from the past, and key details of past events may now be lost to history. Moreover, any ex post facto method—whether large or small n—faces a problem of selection on wars when testing theories of capability. The outcomes of interest here (casualties, territorial gain, combat duration) can be observed only in wartime. Yet "capability" exists as a potential in peacetime as well—in fact, many of its most important applications rest on claims about peacetime capability.[38] Deterrence, for example, is a product of peacetime capabilities.

International relations theories resting on capability must measure it in peacetime as well as wartime if its causal role is to be properly tested. But what if war is such an unusual special case that the relationship between capability and its causes is different there from what it is under normal, peacetime conditions? Perhaps, for example, states normally assess each others' capability in peacetime, determine likely winners and losers in advance, and avoid war by settling disputes in accordance with the mutually understood balance of power; if so, then war could occur only under unusual conditions wherein the "normal" determinants of capability were clouded by private information in ways that foreclosed peaceful settlement.[39] This would imply that all actual wars were outliers characterized by peculiar relationships among materiel, force employment, and capability—and thus that tests using only observations of actual warfare would be misleading for claims about capability in general (which pertain mostly to times of peace). While the severity of this problem is hard to gauge, it is a widespread conundrum in international relations scholarship on war, and one to which any ex post test of capability theories is inherently subject.

I thus complement ex post observation of real combat with a series of ex ante experiments using a Defense Department combat simulation, Janus, as a kind of laboratory, changing key features of a battle while holding all other aspects constant. This provides a unique ability to control for extraneous variation and observe whatever details of the (simulated) fighting may be of theoretical interest. And because experimentation creates new events under conditions chosen by the experimenter, it can create conditions of theoretical importance but historical rarity, allowing a theory's entire parameter space to be explored systematically, and freeing the analysis from dependency upon any special conditions thought to be unique to the wars states have actually fought. It can thus illuminate conditions that might be more characteristic of peacetime confrontations that do not escalate all the way to open warfare. The result is an unusually systematic form of counterfactual analysis. Any counterfactual, however, is simulation rather than reality. As such it lacks the verisimilitude of historical observation. In combination with multiple forms of empirical observation, however, it offers an important source of contrasting perspective.

Each method thus has strengths and weaknesses. None would be sufficient alone, yet each offers something unique and important. By combining them I thus exploit a wider range of potential insight and reduce the odds that my findings are artifacts of a given method's blind spots.

PLAN OF THE BOOK

Chapter 2 critiques the state of the art in capability assessment in greater detail, providing a more sustained case for the need for improvement. It also uses the particular shortcomings identified to suggest some properties needed in potential improvements. Especially, it shows why a focus on the tactical and operational levels of war is an especially promising approach.

Chapters 3 and 4 present the new theory. Force employment is central to this, but little studied by theoretical social scientists. Given this, I devote chapter 3 to a detailed exposition of the modern system as it emerged by 1918. Chapter 4 then assesses post-1918 technological change, variations in numerical preponderance, and their interactions with modern-system force employment.

The theoretical discussion in chapters 3 and 4 is entirely qualitative. While this conveys the key arguments, the formal presentation in the appendix is needed for a complete understanding of the details. The appendix presents a dynamic model of territorial gain, casualties, and duration as a function of force employment, technology, and preponderance. It then treats the model's *comparative statics* (its predictions for how capability changes with controlled variation in causal variables) with much greater rigor than the qualitative discussion in chapters 3 and 4 can provide.

Chapters 5 through 7 test this theory via three historical case studies of actions selected to provide maximum theoretical leverage for the claims in the new and orthodox explanations of capability. Chapter 5 examines Operation MICHAEL, the first of the German 1918 Spring Offensives. Chapter 6 considers Operation GOODWOOD, the penultimate Allied attempt to break out of the Normandy beachhead in July 1944. Chapter 7 explores Operation DESERT STORM, the Coalition offensive in the Persian Gulf War of 1991. MICHAEL and GOODWOOD present conditions of nearly ideal defense- and offense-dominance, respectively, in orthodox theories' terms. By contrast, the new theory predicts offensive success in MICHAEL and defensive success in GOODWOOD. The historical results correspond much more closely with the new theory's predictions than its orthodox competitors,' and under conditions that should have offered easy, unambiguous predictive successes for orthodox theories if the latter were correct. While this neither proves the new theory nor falsifies its competitors, the unusual conditions merit a greater shift in confidence than would otherwise be warranted from such a small sample of cases. In Operation DESERT STORM, by contrast, both the new and orthodox theories predict a Coalition victory. The reasons behind the prediction are very different, however, and by process tracing I show that the *way* the Coalition won was consistent with the new theory but inconsistent with orthodox views, in a case whose prominence in the public debate makes it especially important for any policy-relevant theory of capability.

Chapter 8 presents the statistical analysis. To mitigate the shortcomings of individual datasets taken alone, I use a combination of three different databases with contrasting coverage, units of analysis, and sources of potential error. The results show a strong, consistent pattern of greater correspondence between the data and the new theory than for its orthodox competitors; for this to hold across such diverse data sources offers significantly greater confidence in the findings than could be obtained from any one dataset alone.

Chapter 9 presents the simulation experimentation using the results of the joint U.S. Army, Defense Advanced Research Projects Agency, and Institute for Defense Analyses "73 Easting" project. The Battle of 73 Easting was a representative action from Operation DESERT STORM in which elements of the U.S. 2d Armored Cavalry Regiment struck the Iraqi Tawakalna Division on a stretch of featureless desert near a map reference line called 73 Easting. Immediately after the war, researchers were dispatched to the battlefield to collect a historically unprecedented mass of detailed data on the minute-by-minute activities of each participating tank, troop carrier, truck, or infantry team, which was then represented electronically in a modern combat simulation, Janus. I use the simulation to explore a series of seven controlled variations in technology and force employment, "refighting" the historical battle for each change in conditions and observing the resulting differences in combat outcomes. The experimental findings support the new theory but contradict both orthodox material-based theories of capability in general, and orthodox explanations of the Gulf War outcome in particular.

Chapter 10 concludes the book. It provides a more detailed summary of my main arguments and findings; most of the chapter, however, develops their implications for scholarship and policy and contrasts these with the views now typically held on the basis of current understandings. I argue that these contrasts are quite sharp, and that neither scholarship nor policy can be conducted on a sound basis without a more systematic consideration of force employment and its role in military power.

A Literature Built on Weak Foundations

THIS CHAPTER argues that an enormous range of scholarship and policymaking rests on ideas about capability, yet this intellectual foundation is too weak to bear the weight. To do this, I first review existing ideas and trace their influence. I then critique them both theoretically and empirically. I conclude by showing how the results point to force employment at the tactical and operational levels of war as the best avenue for improvement.

IDEAS ON THE DETERMINANTS OF CAPABILITY

Existing ideas fall into three broad classes: numerical preponderance, technology, and force employment.

Numerical Preponderance

Napoleon once said that "God is on the side of the big battalions," summarizing concisely the preponderance explanation of military capability.[1] Many believe that states with larger populations, larger or more industrialized economies, larger militaries, or greater military expenditures should prevail in battle. This association of victory with material preponderance underlies the widespread perception that economic strength is a necessary precondition for military strength; that economic and military power are fungible; that economic decline leads to military weakness; and that economic policies merit co-equal treatment with political and military considerations in national strategy making.[2] These perceptions are fundamental to the orthodox treatment of power in international relations theory.[3] They are at the heart of hegemonic transition theory and the debate over relative gains stemming from international cooperation, and they define much of the realist/mercantilist position in international political economy.[4] These beliefs also hold powerful policy implications for debates over the defense budget, the trade deficit, competitiveness, and long-range threat assessment for states like China, India, Russia, Germany, or Japan.

Most preponderance arguments claim only that numerical superiority determines capability; some, however, offer elaborations. It is sometimes held, for example, that force *density* matters rather than just force size: the higher the "force-to-space" ratio, the greater the defender's relative advantage, and vice versa.[5]

Others impute threshold effects via "rules of thumb." The most common holds that successful attack requires at least a 3:1 local superiority; some require a 1.5:1 theaterwide advantage.[6]

These elaborations are rarely clear enough to be tested, however. In particular, most are vague on the intended unit of account. Many 3:1 and 1.5:1 rule proponents, for example, think these ratios should compare quality-adjusted "combat power" rather than simple troop strength, yet few say how to make the adjustments.[7] Most force-to-space analysts compute troops per linear mile of frontage, then argue that low density creates gaps through which attackers can maneuver; yet the former cannot establish the latter. Only troops per *square* mile speaks to the likelihood of gaps: 100,000 troops on a 500-km front could yield a gap-free defense if concentrated forward at a depth of only 20 meters, but a gap-riddled one if spread over 10,000 meters depth—yet each yields the identical ratio of 200 troops per linear kilometer of front. The literature, however, is devoid of such measures. While specialists debate the proper counting rules, both the public debate and the scholarly literature thus rely heavily on simpler measures of gross preponderance per se: the greater A's numerical superiority over B, the greater its relative capability.

Technology

After preponderance, the most influential ideas on capability concern technology. Views on its role fall into two schools, systemic and dyadic.

SYSTEMIC TECHNOLOGY THEORY

The first focuses on the gross "state of the art" in the international system at any given time, rather than the particulars of individual states' holdings. For systemic theorists, the difference between the era of the tank and the era of the horse, for example, is the key, not which side's tanks are better than the other's. Offense-defense theory is the best known of these views. It holds that changing technology shifts the relative ease of attack and defense (the "offense-defense balance") for all states in the international system. Prior to 1914, for example, it mattered little how any single state was armed—the machine gun made attack impossible for anyone, it is held. When tanks shifted the balance back to attack, this gave anyone who took the offensive an important edge; states' particular holdings were less important than their choice to attack or not in an era of offensive advantage. For systemic technology theorists, technology's main effect is thus not to strengthen state A relative to state B—it is to strengthen *attackers* over *defenders* (or vice versa) regardless of who attacks and who defends. If technology favors the defense, then A loses if it attacks B, but B also loses if it attacks A.[8]

This view has been very influential for IR scholarship. Offense-defense theory offers political science's chief understanding of technology's role in international security. It has been widely used to explain war causation, arms racing, alliance formation, crisis behavior, and international system structure.[9] It has been used to illuminate historical events such as the origins of the First World War and the outbreak of ethnic fighting in the former Yugoslavia.[10] It has played a role in the debate over relative gains in international political economy,[11] and it has recently been advanced by some as a means of respecifying—or replacing— orthodox neorealism.[12]

It has also played an important policy role. Arms control negotiations, for example, have long relied on the same logic that underpins offense-defense theory. From the 1932 World Disarmament Conference to the 1989 Conventional Forces in Europe Treaty to post–Cold War discussions of arms control for the Mideast, East Asia, or southeastern Europe, arms control has repeatedly sought to limit technologies seen as "offensive" or destabilizing, while permitting those seen as defensive.[13] Similar foundations undergird U.S. policy for military restructuring in Bosnia and have been central to U.S. nuclear arms control for over thirty years.[14] Most recently, an important element in the Revolution in Military Affairs thesis is the claim that a transnational information revolution is transforming the mode of civil economic production, and with it, the nature of war.[15]

DYADIC TECHNOLOGY THEORY

The second school holds that technology's effects are mainly dyadic, not systemic: if A enjoys a technological edge over B, then A prevails—whether A attacks *or* defends. Whereas systemic technology theorists see technology as favoring attack or defense across the international system, dyadic theorists see its chief effect as favoring individual states over others, depending on their particular holdings.

Many U.S. defense planners see capability chiefly in dyadic technological terms. In the Cold War, U.S. policymakers chose not to compete with the Soviets numerically, but to "offset" their superior numbers with smaller but technologically superior U.S. forces.[16] Today, superior technology is widely seen as essential for containing U.S. losses, feeding growing pressure for faster modernization to maintain or extend U.S. leads over likely opponents.[17]

The formal models that support this planning combine a dyadic treatment of technology with a powerful role for preponderance. The causal foundation for most official combat models is provided by Lanchester theory.[18] Frederick William Lanchester was a British engineer who in 1916 proposed a simple system of differential equations for predicting the outcomes of aerial dogfights. Lanchester's equations consider both numerical strength and technology, the latter via each side's attrition coefficients (i.e., the number of opposing weapons each friendly weapon could kill per unit of time).[19] In Lanchester theory, systemic changes that raise or lower both sides' coefficients together can neither change losers into winners nor alter either sides' losses in a fight to the finish; only a change in A's coefficient relative to B's can accomplish this.[20] Lanchester theory thus treats technology dyadically: only the two sides' relative holdings matter; unilateral advantage is more important than systemic change. Lanchestrian outcomes, however, are not driven solely by technology. In Lanchester's "Square Law," which underlies most official models, outcomes are actually much more sensitive to proportional changes in preponderance than technology. Lanchester's original equations have subsequently been adapted to many forms of warfare and extended in multiple directions; all, however, treat technology dyadically, and most display greater proportional sensitivity to preponderance than to technology.[21]

Though influential, neither systemic nor dyadic technology theories have been extensively tested empirically. Offense-defense theory has long suffered from a lack of systematic empirical work.[22] Official capability models are almost wholly untested empirically. Most models in widespread use by the Defense Department are far too complex for determinate testing: the Joint Chiefs of Staff's TACWAR model, for example, uses more than a thousand independent variables, almost none of which are included in standard historical databases, making systematic empirical work effectively impossible.[23] Attempts to test simplified versions have been inconclusive; in more than a dozen studies dating back to the 1950s, the basic Lanchester equations have generally failed to correspond with available historical data, but since modern models use extended versions of the equations, this failure has usually not been considered decisive.[24]

Force Employment

It seems intuitive that force employment should matter, and subjective assessments have long incorporated it. Military staffs, for example, routinely consider nonmaterial factors such as tactics, doctrine, skill, morale, or leadership in their net assessments and war plans. The French in 1914 concluded that the Germans would not invade Belgium because German reserve divisions ostensibly lacked the skills for offensive action, leaving the Germans without the forces for such a wide turning movement.[25] The Germans in 1940 assessed their prospects against France in light of a detailed review of likely French and German force employment.[26] Prewar qualitative analyses of likely U.S. casualties in 1991 often turned on assessments of U.S. and Iraqi doctrine, experience, and morale.[27] The track record for such judgments, however, is poor: German reserves proved sufficient to invade Belgium in 1914; the French collapse in 1940 surprised both sides; and even the most experienced military observers nonetheless overestimated U.S. Gulf War losses by a factor of two to ten or more.[28]

A logical route for improving on a record of flawed judgments is to be more systematic and theoretically rigorous, allowing implicit assumptions about cause and effect to be tested against explicit evidence and building thereby a more reliable body of theory. Yet explicit theories of capability typically exclude force employment.

Official modelers usually consider it too hard to measure and too multidimensional to theorize. Instead, they focus chiefly on representing particular weapon types and numerical balances, often in tremendous detail, usually with a single, officially sanctioned military doctrine "hardwired" into the model's mathematics as an enabling assumption. This, of course, masks force employment's importance by treating it as a constant—and risks serious error if force employment and materiel interact, as I argue below that they do. Where official models make explicit provision for force employment, they often use "man-in-the-loop" (MITL) techniques wherein real military officers directly input movement or firing orders. MITL, however, produces results idiosyncratic to the officers involved, making it difficult to replicate findings or compare the effects of differing weapon programs or force levels on a consistent basis. Alternatively, decision making can be built into the model via explicit rule sets ("if losses reach 60 percent, withdraw," for example). Results, however, are typically very sensitive to the specific decision thresholds established and can easily produce unstable or counterintuitive results as complex arrays of artificially stark decision variables interact under changing conditions.[29] Though modelers have long recognized that nonmaterial factors matter, and though critics have periodically called for less materially focused models, no systematic, formal model of force employment has gained general acceptance.[30] On the contrary, attention is now focused mostly elsewhere: ongoing efforts to develop a new generation of theater models focus on capturing the effects of new information technologies and deep precision strike systems for Lanchester attrition coefficients; no innovations in the treatment of force employment are contemplated.[31]

International relations theorists mostly ignore force employment. Many simply assume that states will use materiel "optimally," hence the materiel itself is the only important variable.[32] Classical realists like Morgenthau and Knorr touched briefly on strategy as a component of power but focused chiefly on preponderance and offered no testable treatment of either.[33] Standard empirical databases contain no information on how military resources were used, even where capability per se is ostensibly addressed.[34]

A few have addressed force employment explicitly. The most important to date include John Mearsheimer's use of an "attrition-blitzkrieg" strategic dichotomy to explain conventional deterrence, and Allan Stam's, Dan Reiter's, and D. Scott Bennett's use of a similar "attrition-maneuver-punishment" schema to address war duration, victory, and defeat.[35] These are major improvements on the materially determinist treatments of capability in the literature at large. Yet they represent first steps rather than conclusive resolutions. "Attrition" and "blitzkrieg/maneuver," for example, only scratch the surface of potentially meaningful distinctions in force employment; military doctrinal publications and military historiography consider an enormous array of other variations in the ways states have used their military forces. The characterization of any given military as attrition or blitzkrieg/maneuver, moreover, is necessarily a subjective judgment, rather than an objective measurement. And this subjective judgment can be difficult to render without risking artificiality. Few real doctrinal publications explicitly prescribe anything like attrition as Mearsheimer or Stam define it; in practice, attrition is difficult to separate from a tautological characterization of failure or unimaginative conduct as opposed to the success and ingenuity of maneuver.[36] While this scheme offers a valuable point of departure, much thus remains to be done.[37]

While force employment is often believed to be important, few analyses thus account for it in any systematic way. It is one thing to suppose that force employment must matter somehow—it is another to say *how* in a way that could inform policy or further research and could be tested objectively against evidence. Unlike preponderance or technology, there is yet no significant body of existing thought that would do this for force employment.

ASSESSMENT

So there are differing views, each intuitively plausible but none of which can be considered empirically proven. This raises a number of dilemmas for scholars and policymakers whose work rests on assumptions about capability.

Theoretical Concerns

To begin with, the two main views imply mutually inconsistent policies and conflicting understandings of international politics. Defense planners cannot maximize technological sophistication and numerical preponderance simultaneously. Quality and quantity trade off: for a constant defense budget, the more we spend on force structure, the less we can spend to modernize equipment, ceteris paribus. It thus matters which is the stronger determinant, and how they interact. Simply to suggest that both matter is little help to policy planners, who need to know *how much* and in *what way* they each matter in order to make sound decisions.

For academics, the technology and preponderance schools imply very different theories of international relations. If technology really does create similar incentives for attack or defense across the state system, then security or insecurity will tend to be mutual, widespread, and relatively independent of the balance of power: eras of offense-conducive technology will enable many states to attack successfully but not to defend themselves; preponderant forces will offer little guarantee of security; military preparations will be viewed suspiciously; arms races will be triggered easily, and these will often spur preemptive attack. Conversely, eras with *defense*-conducive technology will enable many to defend but few to attack; preponderant forces will be unnecessary for security; arms races will be fewer and less energetic; and preemption infrequent. In this view, power balancing is thus no more likely to yield peace than war, and deterrent buildups are either superfluous (when defense has the advantage) or dangerous (when offense does); the security dilemma and the spiral model of conflict will then offer the key insights into the nature of international politics.[38]

By contrast, if preponderance is the key to capability, then security will be a function of the local balance of power; preponderant states will be secure, but smaller ones vulnerable; and buildups will more often be effective and necessary for self-defense. Under these conditions, the distribution of power and the *deterrence* model of conflict will be the better lenses for understanding state behavior. These diametrically opposite views of politics rest critically on an underlying difference of assumptions about the nature of military capability—to ignore the interaction of technology and preponderance and which is relatively more important is thus to beg central questions for international relations theory.

Finally, this exclusive focus on materiel leaves out a major, intuitively plausible variable: force employment. At best, this reduces our ability to explain variance in real capability. Worse, it means the current literature is probably biased in its treatment of the variables it does address: unless force employment is wholly uncorrelated with preponderance or technology, analyses that leave it out will systematically mispredict their effects. The more important force employment is, the worse the bias, and the greater the consequences for both policy and scholarship.

Empirical Anomalies

Second, the historical record poses a number of important anomalies for either of the main views. While a complete empirical analysis must await the detailed presentation in chapter 8, I review here a few illustrative inconsistencies to suggest the scale and nature of the problem.

Perhaps the most prominent example involves the 1991 Persian Gulf War. As noted above, state-of-the-art assessment methods overestimated U.S. casualties in the Gulf by up to a factor of two hundred or more. The scale of this surprise led to widespread dissatisfaction with available models. Many took the huge margin of error to mean that the nature of warfare itself had changed in 1991, signaling a revolution in military affairs and invalidating the orthodox approach to capability assessment. In fact, however, the Gulf War was just an unusually salient example of a longstanding problem: since at least 1900, materiel has never been a reliable predictor of actual military outcomes.

NUMERICAL PREPONDERANCE

A broader look can be had by considering the data on numerical preponderance and military outcomes found in the University of Michigan's Correlates of War (COW) dataset.[39] Table 2.1 uses these data to evaluate several commonly used measures of numerical preponderance as predictors of victory and defeat in twentieth-century wars. Where the preponderant side won, the case is scored as a predictive success; otherwise, the case is scored a failure. Of course, this is

TABLE 2.1.
Material Preponderance as Predictor of Victory and Defeat in War, 1900–92

	Fraction of Cases Predicted Correctly	Significance Level for Rejecting Null Hypothesis of No Explanatory Power	Number of Cases for Which Data Are Available
GNP	0.62	0.13	13
Population	0.52	0.33	44
Military personnel	0.49	0.50	43
Military expenditure	0.57	0.16	35
Composite Index of National Capability*	0.56	0.19	45

*The Composite Index of National Capability (CINC) measures a state's proportional share of six resources deemed militarily consequential: military personnel, military expenditure, steel/iron production, energy consumption, total population, and urban population. The higher a state's share of the global totals, the higher its CINC score. See, e.g., Stuart A. Bremer, "National Capabilities and War Proneness," in J. David Singer, ed., *The Correlates of War* (New York: Free Press, 1980), vol. 2, pp. 63–66. The CINC is very widely used in empirical IR: for a review, see Richard L. Merritt and Dina Zinnes, "Alternative Indexes of National Power," in Richard Stoll and Michael Ward, eds., *Power in World Politics* (Boulder: Lynne Rienner, 1989), pp. 11–28. The analysis here drops missing components when at least one component of each category (military, economic, and demographic) is available; where there are no data for either component of a given category, the war is dropped.

an imperfect test: victory in war is not the same as victory in operations per se (my unit of analysis here). Yet the intuition behind the materialist conception of military power draws little distinction between wars and operations—where preponderant material is thought to win wars, it is ostensibly by winning battles. If preponderance theory is right, table 2.1 should thus show an important correlation between materiel and victory.

The results, however, show a weak relationship. On average, flipping a coin would predict the outcome 50 percent of the time; a powerful theory should outperform a coin toss by a wide margin. Yet none of the five indicators predicted more than about 60 percent of the cases, and the indicator with the best apparent performance, GNP, is one for which very little data is available: its result is based on a sample of only about a dozen cases. In fact, one measure, military personnel, actually *under*performed a coin toss with only 49 percent accuracy. More formally, for none of the five indicators can one reject the null hypothesis of no explanatory power at customary significance levels.

Of course, "winning" and "losing" says nothing about the magnitude of victory or the costliness of defeat, and for wars (rather than operations) it entails more than just capability as I define it: asymmetries in stakes or resolve, for

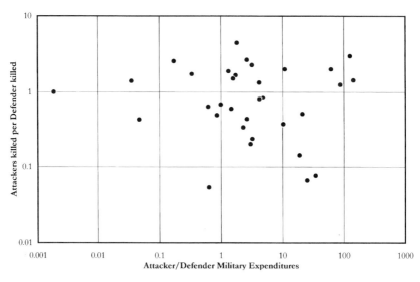

Figure 2.1. Preponderance in Twentieth-Century Warfare. Materiel preponderance as predictor of loss exchange ratios, 1900–92

example, can defeat even highly capable states. More fine-grained or tightly focused measures of capability, however, show similarly weak results.

Figure 2.1 shows the relationship between one common measure of preponderance (military expenditures) and the loss-exchange ratio (LER), a finer-grained measure of capability widely used by defense analysts. The LER is the number of attackers killed per defender killed; ceteris paribus, the higher the LER, the more capable the defender and vice versa. The LER not only measures relative magnitudes along a continuous scale (rather than simply a dichotomous "win-lose"), it also focuses more closely on questions of battlefield capability per se, with less risk of misrepresenting an inferior political stake as inferior military capacity. Data are drawn from the COW dataset. If preponderance were a powerful determinant of capability, we should see a strong negative correlation between preponderant military expenditures and the LER: the more the attacker outspends the defender, the more the fighting should favor the attacker and the fewer attackers should die per defender casualty.

The results, however, show no meaningful relationship at all. Data points are scattered apparently at random; the anticipated negative correlation is nowhere to be found. More formally, one cannot reject the null hypothesis of no relationship between military expenditures and loss-exchange ratio at any customary significance level. Similar results obtain for the other four measures of preponderance in table 2.1 and for a wide variety of other, continuous-variable indicators of military capability in addition to just the loss-exchange ratio.[40] Data on individual battles, rather than wars, yield no stronger results. All told, the data show no support for a simple assumption that preponderance predetermines capability.[41]

TECHNOLOGY

Technology poses similar anomalies. To begin with, lethality and speed, the traits most analysts focus on, do not predict casualty or advance rates. From 1900 to 1990, weapon platforms' nominal speed increased by more than a factor of ten, yet armies' average rate of advance remained virtually constant at levels little changed since Napoleon's day.[42] Weapon lethality has grown progressively for more than a century: crew-served weapon range and net penetrativity grew by more than a factor of ten between 1900 and 1990.[43] Yet average casualty rates actually *fell* more than 60 percent over the same interval.[44]

The specific claims of the systemic or dyadic technology schools also face difficulties. Systemic technology theorists hold that periodic shifts in prevailing technology induce secular shifts in the relative ease of attack and defense. Analysts differ in the time periods they assign to these shifts, but for the twentieth century most would hold that the first quarter-century (1900–24) was the most defense-dominant; the second (1925–49) was more offense-conducive; the third (1950–74) was still more offensive for nonnuclear states; while the fourth (1975–99) was more defensive than the third.[45]

Figure 2.2 considers this claim by plotting the mean frequency of attacker victory in war by quarter-century using the COW data. The results show little of

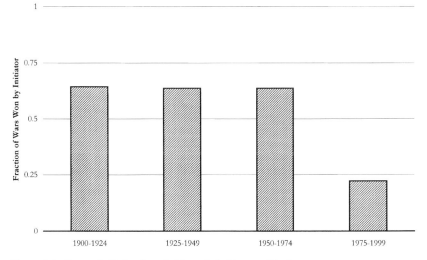

Figure 2.2. Systemic Technology in Twentieth-Century Warfare

the periodic, epochal transitions the systemic technology view predicts. In fact, the data show no meaningful change of any kind for the first seventy-five years after 1900, with only the 1975–99 period departing from the norm of attackers winning about two-thirds of the time.[46] Similar results obtain for a variety of continuous-variable indicators of capability in addition to just the win-loss rate.[47] Nor are the results sensitive to the particular periodization one adopts: a variety of alternative schema yield similar results.[48] Nor does it help to combine the preponderance and systemic technology views: statistical analysis to control for the effects of preponderance yields no improvement in explanatory power.[49] At best, offense-defense theory thus faces a significant body of contradictory evidence.

The dyadic technology school fares little better. No systematic data have ever been collected on the role of technological advantage in war outcomes.[50] To obtain an initial perspective, I have compiled data on the major weapon systems employed in sixteen interstate wars fought between 1956 and 1992.[51] As an index of relative sophistication, I use the weapons' date of introduction: the more recent the introduction, the more sophisticated the system, ceteris paribus. For each war, I compute a mean date of introduction for the tank and fighter/ ground attack aircraft types in service for the respective combatants, weighted by the number of weapons of each type in each arsenal. I then average the state's score for tanks with its score for aircraft, obtaining a crude estimate of that state's overall technological sophistication. By subtracting the attacker's score from the defender's, I thus obtain a measure of the technological asymmetry between the two sides, denominated in average years by which the defender's weapon technology lags behind the attacker's.[52] For such a measure, the dyadic technology school would predict that the side with the more sophisticated weapons (i.e., the higher index score) should prevail.

Table 2.2 summarizes this predictor's performance. The results indicate that by this measure, technological superiority is no better than a coin flip for predicting victory and defeat: of the sixteen wars for which data are available, only eight were won by the technologically superior side.

TABLE 2.2.
Dyadic Technological Superiority and Victory and Defeat in War, 1956–92

		Actual		
		Initiator Win	Initiator Loss	
Predicted	Initiator Win	3	6	9
	Initiator Loss	2	5	7
		5	11	

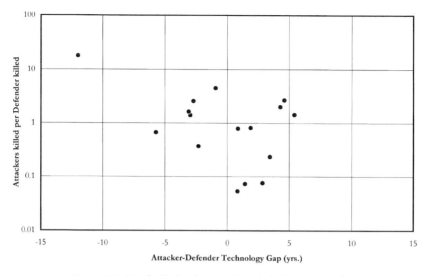

Figure 2.3. Dyadic Technology in Twentieth-Century Warfare

Nor do finer-grained measures show any strong relationship. Figure 2.3 plots the attacker:defender loss exchange ratio against the attacker's technological edge (the attacker's index score minus the defender's). Positive values for the latter indicate superior attackers; negative values are superior defenders. If dyadic technology were a powerful determinant, one would expect a strong negative correlation here: the greater the attacker's technology edge, the more the fighting should favor the attacker and the fewer attackers should die per defender casualty. The results, however, are ambiguous at best. A weak negative correlation might be present but cannot be confirmed statistically and reflects a single outlier's effects: without the Gulf War (-12, 18), any relationship disappears completely.[53]

Of course, this is a crude measure. Only tanks and fighter/ground attack aircraft are considered, and not all weapons introduced the same year are equally sophisticated.[54] If technology were centrally important, however, then even a coarse measure like this one should show at least *some* meaningful correlation with capability. Yet it does not.

Implications

This critique poses two important implications. First, orthodox treatments of capability are insufficient. The standard views are intuitively plausible but imply contradictory theories and policies and face important empirical inconsistencies. There is important room for improvement.

Of course, the standard treatments are very simple, and above I treat them mostly in isolation. It may not be surprising that real capability is more complicated, and left-out variable bias may account for some of the more egregious failures in the univariate assessments above. Yet simple, mostly univariate notions are exactly the way capability is typically treated in the published literature.[55] If such simple proxies have so little to do with real battlefield outcomes, then both the public debate and the empirical literature in international politics are built on very unreliable foundations.

Second, the nature of the problems offers guidance for finding solutions. It suggests, for example, that a new explanatory variable is probably needed. Many of the empirical findings are counterintuitive: casualty rates fall even as weapons become more lethal; attackers win no more often with tanks and aircraft than they do with machine guns and footsoldiers; outnumbering an opponent offers so little advantage that it cannot be statistically distinguished from flipping a coin as a predictor of victory and defeat. This is strongly suggestive of left-out-variable bias: ignoring a causally important variable can make included variables behave strangely.[56]

An obvious candidate for this left-out variable is force employment. It is intuitively important, but mostly overlooked in the analytical literature. It is probably related to preponderance and technology but not perfectly covariant with them: many armies will try to adapt their methods to changing technologies and numerical balances, but not all adapt the same way or at the same pace. In principle, force employment could thus account for the failures of preponderance or technology taken alone.

Finally, the nature of the anomalies offers guidance for *how* force employment should be treated, focusing analytical attention within the sprawling question of how military force can be used in war.

In particular, the operational and tactical levels of war offer the most direct route to resolving the empirical anomalies above.[57] Grand strategy and military strategy, organizational adaptability, administrative skill, or politicomilitary coordination are all clearly important. Operations and tactics, however, are more proximate to realized capability—many of the effects of grand strategy or institutional structure can best be understood via their effects on preponderance, technology, and operational/tactical force employment. Moreover, the anomalies above probably cannot be explained *without* considering the operational and tactical levels of war.

Grand strategy, for example, makes its effects felt largely via its influence on preponderance and technology. Unlike military strategy, operations, and tactics, which govern the use of materiel, grand strategy is largely about creating materiel. Central grand strategic tasks include denying allies to one's opponent and securing them for oneself, providing the economic basis for a large war effort while denying resources to one's opponents, or ensuring domestic political support for mobilizing resources.[58] For capability, these effects are ultimately felt as changes in the balance of forces engaged. Grand strategy also shapes technology. It influences states' priority for technical sophistication relative to other goods, and their ability to realize that priority by molding economic performance. Again grand strategy is important, but its effects are felt as changes in fielded weapon technology. For my purposes, explicit treatment of grand strategy is thus unnecessary as long as its material fruits are assessed directly.[59]

Nor would grand strategy be *sufficient* to explain capability. Materiel alone correlates poorly with observed capability. Yet if grand strategy is chiefly a root cause of material advantage, then it will also correlate poorly with capability.[60] To account for the observations above requires some additional, nonmaterial factor—and force employment at the operational and tactical levels offers just such a possibility.[61]

None of this means that grand strategy, organizational adaptability, or politico-military integration are unworthy of study: preponderance and technology are clearly important for both policy and scholarship, and their determinants are thus clearly important. Preponderance and technology are not the *only* determinants of capability, however—in fact, an exclusive focus on them alone yields serious error. Given this, analysis of their root causes is insufficient for understanding capability and can be set aside for my purposes as long as their effects in realized preponderance and technology are taken fully into account.

Force employment at the operational and tactical levels thus offers an especially promising avenue. But how is it to be characterized? And what are its effects? I turn to these questions in chapter 3, the modern system of force employment.

CHAPTER THREE

The Modern System

MY CENTRAL CLAIM is that force employment is a powerful—and explicable—determinant of capability. But which aspects of force employment are most important? Commanders make hundreds of decisions in war; doctrinal manuals fill thousands of pages with prescriptions and instructions—which warrant theoretical attention? And how do these prescriptions affect capability? By what process does force employment interact with preponderance and technology to produce military outcomes?

To answer these questions I look to the First World War. This conflict introduced the central problem of modern warfare: how to conduct meaningful military operations in the face of radical firepower. And by the end of the war, an answer appeared that has remained central to great power military doctrines through more than eighty years of subsequent warfare.

I argue that by 1918, a process of convergent evolution under harsh wartime selection pressures had produced a stable and essentially transnational body of ideas on the methods needed to operate effectively in the face of radically lethal modern weapons. These new methods focused on reducing exposure to hostile fire and enabling friendly movement while slowing the enemy's. Taken together, they broke the trench stalemate in 1918 and defined the standard for successful military operations throughout the post-1918 era. The resulting *modern system* of force employment, however, is extremely difficult to implement in its entirety; some states have mastered it, but others have not. The result has been wide variation in actual force employment, with decisive consequences for success and failure in battle.

The modern system that emerged from this crucible thus offers special leverage for understanding capability. The purpose of this chapter is to describe it, to show how its advantages made it a uniquely powerful response to modern firepower, and to show how its disadvantages have prevented many states from implementing it even so. This discussion is set in the context of the early twentieth century, numerically balanced armies that gave rise to the modern system; in a sense, I hold technology and preponderance constant and analyze the effects of varying force employment. Given this foundation, the following chapter considers post-1918 technological change and numerical variance and shows how the modern system has retained its importance in the face of sweeping technological and numerical change. The resulting, qualitative theory is formalized in the technical appendix, providing a systematic model of capability.

I assemble this foundation in four steps. First, I review a series of profound technological changes in the late nineteenth century that transformed warfare and defined the problem of firepower as the key issue for subsequent operations and tactics. Second, I trace the responses of Western militaries to this problem in the First World War and show that these responses reveal a convergent evolution on a broadly similar body of techniques, the modern system of force employment. Third, I explain how and why the modern system worked and show how it enabled armies to function in the face of potentially annihilating firepower. Finally, I present the organizational and political difficulties of implementing the modern system and argue that these have prevented many states from adopting it, giving rise to wide variance in actual force employment.

INDUSTRIALIZATION, FIREPOWER, AND THE PROBLEM OF
 TWENTIETH-CENTURY WARFARE

The industrialization of European economies in the mid-nineteenth century brought a complex of developments with major implications for the conduct of war. In particular, the introduction of mass production, the substitution of machine for animal power, and dramatic improvements in metallurgy, agriculture, administration, and public health led to enormous increases in the size and firepower of armies by 1914.[1]

In 1812 the French Grande Armee numbered about 600,000 men and was the second largest army in Europe; by 1914 the French Army numbered over 1.6 million men yet had fallen to third largest.[2] In 1812 muzzle-loading brass cannon could fire one 12-pound ball 1,000 yards every 30 seconds; by 1914 steel breechloaders could fire more than twice as many 18-pound shells to ten times the distance in less than 20 seconds.[3] A Napoleonic infantry battalion of 1,000 men with smoothbore flintlock muskets could project 1,000 rounds to an effective range of 100 yards twice a minute; a bayonet charge by a comparable formation would thus receive about 2,000 rounds before reaching its target, or about 2 shots fired at each soldier.[4] By 1916 an infantry battalion with 1,000 magazine rifles and 4 machine guns could project over 21,000 rounds to distances of over 1,000 yards every minute.[5] An assault by a comparable unit could absorb over 210,000 rounds in the time needed to close, or more than 200 per targeted soldier—an increase of more than two orders of magnitude. As a result of the enormous increase in iron and steel production over this period, the massive armies of the twentieth century could be equipped with such weapons on a monumental scale. French iron and steel output grew by more than a factor of 15 between 1815 and 1914, enabling France to deploy by 1914 a multimillion-man army capitalized to a level that Napoleon could never have dreamed: in 1815 the French army deployed around three crew-served weapons per thousand soldiers; by 1918 the figure had grown to more than thirty.[6]

In an era of continuous fronts, this new firepower—what Ernst Junger called the "storm of steel"—posed radical challenges.[7] How could armies survive the storm of steel long enough to accomplish meaningful military missions? While survival on the attack was especially problematic (how could one cross the fire-swept ground to advance on the enemy?), survival on the defense was no trivial matter either. Defenders could dig into the ground for protection, but even thoroughly dug static positions could be blasted out by the new artillery given time. The garrisons of Belgium's state-of-the-art frontier fortresses discovered this in August 1914, when the Germans' new 420-mm siege howitzers reduced their steel-reinforced, six-foot-thick concrete bunkers to rubble in a few hours, burying the occupants inside.[8] German trenches in 1917 suffered obliterating artillery barrages of literally atomic magnitudes: the ten-day Allied bombardment before Messines in July 1917 dropped about 1,200 tons of explosives—in nuclear parlance, more than a kiloton, or more explosive power than the U.S. W48 tactical nuclear warhead—on every mile of German defensive frontage.[9]

Nor was the expansion of firepower restricted to the years prior to World War I—in fact, it has been an ongoing, defining characteristic of modern warfare. Between 1900 and 1990, average artillery range increased by a factor of more than twenty; small arms rate of fire increased by a factor of three to four; weapons payload and unrefueled range for ground attack aircraft increased by more than a factor of six; and the distance at which antitank guns could penetrate 200 mm of rolled homogeneous armor plate increased by a factor of sixty.[10] Of course, as guns became more powerful, armor protection increased in response. The trend in the modern gun-armor race, however, has strongly favored the gun. As an illustrative example, the weighted mean lethal range for the armor-penetrating weapons in a U.S. armored division when fired against the tanks in a representative opposing division increased by a factor of ten between 1945 and 2000.[11]

THE EMERGENCE OF THE MODERN SYSTEM

This tremendous, ongoing increase in lethality defined the central problem of modern tactics: how to survive the hail of metal long enough to perform meaningful military missions. How was this problem solved?

Many suppose that the initial answer lay in defensive entrenchment (defenders, unlike attackers, could protect themselves by digging in), and that the ultimate answer lay in technology—the arrival of the tank to break the stalemate that resulted from mutual entrenchment. In fact, neither assumption is correct. Entrenchment alone proved insufficient to protect defenders from the nuclear-scale firepower directed at them by 1917. And the tank proved neither necessary nor sufficient to break through entrenched defenses.

Instead, the real answer lay in force employment: the emergence of the modern system. Its significance for the history of the First World War lies in its crucial role in breaking the trench stalemate on the western front.

Its larger significance, however, lies in its stability over time (the subject of chapter 4) and its transnational nature. Exposed to the same problem, radical firepower, each of the European great powers eventually arrived at essentially the same solution. This convergent evolution suggests that the pattern of force employment embodied in the modern system is not merely idiosyncratic or happenstantial but instead represents a fundamental property of modern warfare.

The process of trial and error that drove this convergent evolution began well before 1914. Early, if partial, exposure to the new lethality in the Boer War of 1899–1902 and the Russo-Japanese War of 1904–5 triggered extensive debates in all European militaries over how to respond. Two broad approaches emerged almost immediately. The first used cover and concealment to reduce the attackers' exposure while advancing; the second used suppressive fire to keep the defenders' heads down while the attackers were exposed. Even before the Boer War had ended, for example, British tactics had shifted from massed attacks in line to "open order" advances by short rushes, making use of the terrain to conceal dispersed attackers prior to brief dashes in the open from one covered position to the next. During periods of exposure, artillery and rifle fire would suppress defensive positions to keep them from firing.[12]

Two problems emerged, however. First, the required infantry movements proved very hard to control. Dispersion put more distance between leaders and led, making it hard for the former to keep their troops moving. Units could find cover but tended to remain there too long; attacks then lost momentum, degenerating into desultory small arms exchanges at extended range as more and more troops went to ground and resorted to fire rather than movement. This gave defensive artillery time to extinguish the stalled attack before it could close on the objective.[13]

Second, it proved very hard to control the needed suppressive fires without leaving the shooters too exposed to survive defensive counterfire. The key issue here was artillery support, which alone could provide the needed volume of fire. Artillery can fire directly over "open sights" (that is, shooting with a flat trajectory at targets the gunners can see themselves), or it can fire *indirectly* (that is, shooting over intervening obstacles with an arced trajectory at targets the gunners cannot see). Direct fire is easier to control, since the gunners can see both the targets and their own infantry, making it much simpler to maintain suppressive fire until the infantry had almost overrun the target, then lifting the fire at the last minute to avoid fratricide. Direct fire, however, required the guns to move well forward and thus exposed them to defensive counterfire. Indirect fire, by contrast, allowed the guns to move to safer positions in the rear but greatly complicated fire control since the gunners could no longer see the battle they supported. Indirect fire required forward observers who could see the targets to communicate firing instructions back to the blind gunners in the rear; this in turn made it much harder to maintain accurate suppressive fire over the target until the last minute, since delayed, garbled, imprecise, or interrupted messages could result in either a fatal gap in suppressive coverage (if the fire lifted too soon or fell long) or fratricide (if the fire lifted too late or fell short).[14]

When the war began in August 1914, these difficulties led to slaughter. Suppressive fire was either inaccurate or unavailable; without it, assault units either were massacred in the open or became pinned down behind cover and were eventually wiped out by hostile artillery. Germany's attempt to evade French defenses by marching through Belgium thus bogged down short of Paris; France's attempt to break through German defenses in the Battle of the Frontiers yielded trivial ground gains for horrifying casualties. By Christmas the front had ossified into a continuous line of trenches from the North Sea to the Swiss border.[15]

This failure induced a rapid change in tactics. Prewar thought emphasized infantry as the primary arm of decision, with artillery as a secondary supporting weapon. By March 1915 this was completely reversed. Artillery would now destroy entrenched defenses outright via massive preparatory barrages, with the infantry advancing afterward merely to mop up the dazed survivors and take possession of their smashed trenches. As the French put it, *"l'artillerie conquiert, l'infanterie occupert"*: the artillery conquers, the infantry occupies.[16] This was meant to overcome the problems of fire control and maneuver control by decoupling fire from maneuver and deemphasizing the latter: if artillery could not be controlled precisely enough to suppress defenders while assault teams maneuvered, then perhaps it could annihilate defenders on its own from safe positions in the rear while friendly infantry simply stayed out of harm's way.[17]

The new tactics proved little better. Preparatory barrages reached extraordinary intensity: the seven-week-long bombardment before Passchendaele in June 1917 consumed some 4.3 million shells (or the industrial output of 55,000 workers for a year at a cost of 22 million pounds, just short of the cost of the entire Home Army in 1914) yet failed to produce breakthrough.[18] Contrary to popular impression, however, such barrages were not utterly futile. One would assume that nuclear-scale firepower could batter down a defense, and in fact it could. As early as 1915–16, crushing Allied barrages at Neuve Chapelle and the Somme had demonstrated that entrenchment alone could not preserve a field defense: garrisons exposed to such punishment suffered prohibitive losses, and as the Allies lengthened their barrages it became evident that static trenches could not hold ground against them. In fact, by 1917 Allied offensives routinely took the defenders' forward positions in the initial assault.[19] The reason the midwar artillery offensives failed was not that they failed to crush static defenses—it was that the defenders had learned to abandon static defenses in favor of a new reliance on depth, reserves, and counterattack.

Against such new defenses, midwar attackers could take ground, but they could not hold it. Defenders who could tell the time and place of attack from the weeks-long offensive barrages now used the time to mass reserves and defensive artillery in depth behind their initial trench system, which was increasingly seen as expendable and whose garrison was thinned to strengthen the mobile reserves in the rear. These defensive reserves then struck the unsupported, overextended attackers with an artillery barrage of their own. The same offensive inability to coordinate artillery fire and infantry maneuver that had doomed 1914's tactics now crippled their successors in 1915–17: the infantry that had advanced into the defender's trench system following the initial preparatory barrage was now on its own without effective supporting fire. The defender's counteroffensive barrage and ensuing infantry advance thus threw the unsupported attackers back to their own lines.[20]

Either side could thus advance as far as a preplanned artillery program could carry it, but neither could go any farther, and neither could hold its gains against counterattack. The result resembled a form of war on a tether: the battle was actually quite fluid, but movement was limited to the reach of the preparatory artillery barrages on either side. Massive midwar offensives at the Somme, Verdun, Passchendaele, or the Chemin des Dames thus yielded no meaningful change in either side's positions.

Gradually, however, a new system of tactics emerged that replaced the prewar emphasis on infantry and midwar emphasis on artillery with a combined arms approach in which infantry and artillery cooperated as co-equals. In the new approach, surprise was restored by restricting the preparatory artillery program to a brief but intense "hurricane barrage" designed not to destroy but merely to suppress the defenses. This temporary suppressive effect was exploited by independently maneuvering infantry teams armed with hand grenades and portable light machine guns; these were trained to exploit covering terrain to find their own way through hostile defenses via the path of least resistance. These independently maneuvering assault teams were much better able to sustain their advance through the depths of a hostile defense; as the brief barrage denied the defender advance warning of the time or place of attack, defenders found it much harder to amass sufficient reserves in time to repel the attack before it broke through.[21]

In fact, the new system was not really new: it represented a return to prewar ideas on the combination of suppression and maneuver to enable an advance in the face of the new firepower. But whereas the prewar armies were unable to master the technical problems associated with fire and maneuver control, by 1918 the intricacies of controlling indirect fires and coordinating them with small-unit infantry movement had finally been worked out. Over the long months of stalemate, a process of hard trial and error had gradually hammered out the systems of "scientific" gunnery and improved small-unit leadership and training needed to make the prewar ideas work.[22]

The new methods were recognized and accepted by each of the Western armies by the beginning of 1918, though variations in the rate of retraining and doctrinal diffusion within the respective militaries brought differences in the speed and completeness of their implementation. By mid-1917 Germany had mastered modern system defense. Full implementation of modern system offensive methods came later, but between December 1917 and March 1918 Germany established a system of specially organized schools and retrained over fifty divisions in the new techniques; the instructors in these schools were themselves employed as infantry in the 1918 Spring Offensives that followed the retraining.[23] Britain accepted but never fully implemented elastic defense: the conversion of British defenses to the new methods was only beginning when they were shattered by the German Spring Offensives (see chapter 5). Similarly, Britain accepted the new offensive methods, which were reflected in formal British training and doctrinal publications; implementation began late, however, and again was disrupted by the battlefield crises of March to June. By the end of the war, some British units (especially the Canadian and Australian Commonwealth divisions) had achieved considerable proficiency; others lagged behind.[24] France, like Britain, accepted the new techniques and tried to implement them but encountered difficulty in converting actual battlefield behavior to the new standard. By the Second Battle of the Marne in July, French defenses had finally been deepened and made more elastic, but French offensive force employment never fully reflected the new standards.[25] By the end of the war, however, formal doctrine in each of the European great powers had come to reflect a consistent modern system canon, each was in the process of retraining their forces to implement it, and each had made substantial progress in implementing major components of that doctrine in the field.

As it was adopted, the nature of the fighting on the western front changed dramatically. The final year of the war saw a series of unprecedented offensive successes. The Germans unveiled the new offensive methods in their Spring Offensives of March to June 1918. After forty months in which neither side had reached the opponent's artillery, the Germans now overran the entirety of the prepared defenses before them three times in succession: at the Second Battle of the Somme (March 21–April 9), the Battle of Lys River (April 7–29), and on the Chemin des Dames (May 27–June 6).[26] The Allies applied the new methods in their counteroffensives at the Second Battle of the Marne in July, at Amiens in August, and in the Hundred Days offensives of September to November that ended the war.[27] Although the Germans managed to contain these attacks short of breakthrough, the Allied gains progressively levered the Germans out of the entirety of their prepared positions in West, eventually driving them back over open ground on a more than 200-mile front, and capturing more than 10,000 square miles of German-held territory in the process. In fact, 1918 as a whole saw more than 13,000 square miles change hands in some eight months of fighting, vastly more than in the preceding forty months of continuous warfare.[28] The trench stalemate that had begun by November 1914 had thus ended by March 1918.

What about the tank? Many today see tank technology as the key that unlocked the stalemate; First World War officers are often pilloried for their conservatism in failing to see this sooner. Yet the army that first broke the stalemate was almost devoid of tanks: the German attackers in Operation MICHAEL, the first of the 1918 Spring Offensives, deployed exactly nine tanks in support of a million-strong assault.[29] Nor were tanks sufficient to produce breakthrough for armies that had them in quantity. In the First World War, tanks had neither the range nor the reliability to produce decisive battlefield effects, and the intense heat, noise, and fumes of 1918-era tanks limited crew endurance to at most a few hours of intense fighting.[30] Nor were early tanks immune to hostile fire: German antitank gunnery improved radically following their initial exposure to massed tanks at Cambrai in 1917, and by mid-1918 German artillery posed a severe threat to Allied tanks. Taken together, tanks' mechanical unreliability, vulnerability, and crew exhaustion made for very heavy loss rates in 1918. At Amiens, for example, only 6 of the 414 Allied tanks that opened the battle on August 8 were still operational on the 12th.[31] By November 4, only 37 operable tanks remained in the entire British army to support the war's final assaults.[32] Whatever its ultimate potential, the tank in 1918 was too unreliable, too hard on its crews, and too vulnerable to be a war-winning weapon. The stalemate was broken by March 1918, but tank technology was not the reason.[33]

How much of this transition can be attributed to the adoption of modern-system force employment? Most of it can, I argue. My purpose in this chapter is not to sustain this claim, however—I test the thesis laid out here in chapters 5 through 9, and chapter 5 in particular evaluates the role of force employment in ending the trench stalemate in much greater detail. For now, it is enough to note that the correspondence between the modern system's adoption and open warfare's return to the western front was suggestively close—and thus the mechanisms by which modern-system force employment might have brought this about warrant close attention before turning to the systematic theory testing below.

WHY WAS THE MODERN SYSTEM SO EFFECTIVE?

What made these methods able to overcome machine guns, barbed wire, and quick-firing artillery? Many think such weapons predetermined stalemate;[34] how could mere changes in force employment have brought open warfare in the face of such firepower? More broadly, how does the modern system work, and what made it so effective in early-twentieth-century warfare? To answer these questions, I consider modern-system offensive tactics, defensive tactics, defensive operations, and offensive operations in turn.

Offensive Tactics

The key elements of modern-system offensive tactics are cover, concealment, dispersion, small-unit independent maneuver, suppression, and combined arms integration.

Cover and concealment deny defenders visible targets. The new weapons could project great quantities of steel, but they still needed targets to aim at, and an unblocked line of flight from the barrel to the target. Concealment thwarts the former; cover thwarts the latter.

Both are widely available, even where the terrain is apparently flat and open. The earth's surface is extremely irregular. Hills, gullies, slopes, vegetation, buildings, fences, or walls radically reduce defenders' lines of sight—especially for defenders with their eyes at ground level (as are trench dwellers' when peering over the parapet to fire).[35] Less than two feet of net elevation difference can conceal a prone soldier from a machine gunner dug in with the barrel at ground level. Few of us can keep our entire front lawns under observation from true ground level; the much less regular surfaces of rural battlefields thus offer an enormous amount of potential cover, and especially so after artillery has added shell holes to the natural variation in the terrain. Even virgin land, however, offers ample cover to attackers trained to find it: in the North German plain, more than 65 percent of the ground within 1,000 meters is invisible to a typical weapon position; in the more rolling, broken terrain of the Fulda Gap, more than 85 percent is invisible.[36]

Dispersion and independent small-unit maneuver made this cover usable by breaking up large formations and allowing subunits to find their way forward by sprinting between terrain features. The small, irregular folds in the Earth that account for most cover cannot conceal thousand-soldier formations advancing in thick skirmish lines; to make the most of the potential inherent in the ground, small groups or even individuals must move separately, and at rates determined by the local terrain rather than the progress of their neighbors. The platoons or sections that made up the basic maneuver elements by 1918 could thus exploit the ground effectively for cover; the companies and battalions that preceded them could not.

Even when units are seen and fired upon, dispersion reduces vulnerability by putting fewer targets in the blast radius of any given shell, or in the beaten zone of any given machine gun. A 100-soldier infantry company advancing in a skirmish line on a 200-meter front, for example, can be wiped out by a single battalion volley from hostile artillery; dispersed over a 1,000-meter front and a 200-meter depth, the same unit might suffer less than 10 percent losses.[37] With maximum use of cover, this reduction in defensive artillery effectiveness is even greater: if only part of the company is spotted and the artillery is thus misdirected against an element rather than hitting the centroid of the formation, losses might be reduced to as little as 5 percent.[38]

Even the most dispersed units, however, using the most covered approach routes, eventually have to cross patches of open ground; modern-system tactics reduce the frequency, duration, and consequences of such exposure, but they cannot eliminate it altogether. Suppressive fire must thus be added to cover, concealment, and dispersion.

Suppression reduces attackers' exposure by forcing opponents to take cover. Whereas destructive fire is meant to kill, suppressive fire is not—it merely keeps the defender from firing while other attackers maneuver into position to kill. Defenders forced to duck, to cower in deep dugouts, or to reposition to an unspotted location cannot fire in the meantime, and thus their weapons, whatever their nominal lethality, are temporarily harmless.

Suppression's central advantage is its tremendous efficiency relative to destructive fires against dug-in targets: even in 1977, to destroy a dug-in infantry platoon required over forty rounds of 155 mm howitzer fire; to suppress the same position can require fewer than four.[39] The destructive barrage at Messines in 1917 required 383,000 rounds per mile of front to pulverize the German trenches; the suppressive barrage at Amiens the following year used fewer than 43,000 per mile, or about 10 percent as many.[40] This in turn restored surprise to the battlefield: suppression, unlike destruction, could be achieved without weeks-long bombardments that gave away the point of attack.

Combined arms integration reduces net vulnerability by teaming together weapon types with contrasting strengths and weaknesses. In 1918 the key combination was between infantry and artillery.[41] Artillery can project massive volumes of fire over great distances, but those very distances reduce its accuracy. Its remove from the line of contact means that it needs assistance from forward observers to locate targets, and its immobility limits its capacity to keep up with an advance. Infantry, by contrast, is limited to the weapons and ammunition that individual soldiers can carry—hence its firepower potential is much smaller than artillery's. Infantry fire, however, is more accurate; infantry can find their own targets for immediate engagement; and infantry weapons can be transported as rapidly as the advance itself. Employed separately, artillery and infantry each have fatal limitations. Inaccurate artillery fire can only destroy entrenched, distributed point targets by expending enormous amounts of time and ammunition, thereby giving away the attack's location and allowing the defender to counterconcentrate. Accurate infantry cannot carry enough ammunition to maintain suppressive fires long enough to cover their own advance over more than short distances. Used together, however, they cover one another's weaknesses. Suppressive artillery fire can keep the defenders' heads down while the infantry closes, enabling the infantry to conserve ammunition for the final gap between the lifting of the artillery and their arrival at the objective, where their accuracy will allow them to destroy the targets with aimed fire from point-blank range.[42]

Taken together, this yields a tactical system wherein a brief "hurricane barrage" suppresses defenses while small units work their way forward independently, using local terrain for cover and providing supplementary suppressive fires of their own to keep defenders' heads down during brief periods of exposure. Without advance warning from a week-long artillery preparation, defenders have far less time to move reserves to the battlefield and are thus forced to defend initially with whatever local garrison happens to be holding the affected positions. Attackers seek to overwhelm these initially outnumbered local defenders, then maintain the attack's momentum into depth by arranging extemporaneous suppressive fires while on the move.[43]

The resulting offensive tactical system is very effective but has a number of important drawbacks. Two loom especially large: complexity and speed limitation.

OFFENSIVE TACTICS AND COMPLEXITY

Modern-system offensive tactics are extremely complex and demand high levels of training and skill to be implemented properly. To make the most of cover and concealment, for example, each of the hundreds to thousands of local commanders in a mass army must fashion their own unique plans for movement and disposition based on the vagaries of local conditions. Most terrain types offer cover, but useable dead ground is often irregularly shaped, irregularly distributed, and widely varying in size. To make the most of it requires careful scouting, custom tailoring of movement orders, and individual siting of fighting positions to fit the peculiarities of units' immediate surroundings. Troops cannot simply be laid out in standard, textbook formations and marched toward the objective, or deployed in formulaic cookie-cutter defensive layouts.

Proper use of suppressive fire requires tight coordination between widely separated, moving units and multiple commanding officers. To protect moving assault units, suppression must be maintained until the last possible minute but lifted in time to allow the assault to overrun the objective without taking casualties from friendly fire. Sightings of enemy weapons must be communicated to distant supporting units, and suppressive fire redirected as intelligence is developed. As units move forward, artillery must eventually cease firing and advance to maintain coverage; if support is not to be lost in the meantime, these moves must be coordinated with both neighboring batteries and forward maneuver elements. Since the pace of an assault varies unpredictably with local terrain or unanticipated enemy action (e.g., discovery of minefields), maintaining continuous suppression thus requires a complex combination of planning, adaptation, and efficient communications among harried commanders at many different echelons.[44]

Dispersion and independent small-unit maneuver make it harder for leaders to see and communicate with their troops even as they increase the demands on those officers to exercise independent leadership functions. At the same time, they challenge morale and combat motivation by putting more distance between the soldiers themselves, reducing the power of group reinforcement to motivate individual behavior.[45]

Combined arms tactics impose very high orders of complexity. Commanders must know the respective pros, cons, conditions for effective employment, maintenance needs, training procedures, and resupply requirements of a whole range of unique (and individually complex) weapons. The closer the integration is to be, the more junior the officers that must hold this knowledge. Great care must be taken to keep weapons of such different mobility within mutual supporting distance as they move over changing terrain and encounter unexpected obstacles or hostile resistance, and to prevent fratricide (especially when combining rapid maneuver with remote firepower from artillery or aircraft). Finally, the troops themselves often require special training in methods for cooperative operations.[46]

By contrast with the Napoleonic maneuver of massed formations or the 1914–17 methods of unsupported advances in thick skirmish lines, modern-system offensive tactics are thus much more complex. While effective if implemented properly, they demand high levels of skill from both troops and leaders.

SPEED LIMITATIONS

Modern-system tactics are best described as a moderate-tempo system. While they shorten battles dramatically relative to the ponderous, artillery-dominated methods that preceded them, they nevertheless preclude attackers from advancing as fast as their feet or their vehicles might carry them. In fact, modern-system attackers can almost never use the maximum speed of their conveyances except in administrative movements away from contact, and in brief sprints between cover in forward areas.

To reach their conveyances' maximum speeds, attackers must travel in vehicles (if available), on roads, in column formations, without frequent halts or delays. Effective use of cover and concealment, however, requires attackers to leave exposed roadways and travel cross-country over often-circuitous routes and difficult ground, to disperse into smaller formations better suited to the available dead space, and to dismount vehicle-borne infantry in order to exploit their ability to use vegetation and small terrain features for cover. To find useable cover requires careful advance scouting of the ground and the enemy's dispositions, yet such reconnaissance can be very time-consuming. To suppress enemy fire often requires artillery support, yet it takes time to develop a fire plan, coordinate it with movement orders to preclude fratricide, then fire the necessary rounds; extensive artillery support often requires time to build up and move the required ammunition and supplies. Combined arms tactics cover for the weaknesses of individual arms acting alone but reduce the attack to the speed of the slowest arm (which is often the speed of dismounted infantry).

Modern-system tactics thus create a sharp tradeoff between speed and losses: attackers can reduce exposure, and thus their losses, but only by slowing their net rate of advance when in the presence of the enemy. Of course, even this is still much faster than the glacial pace of an offensive designed to destroy a dug-in defense by artillery alone—but it is much slower than the pace the attackers' equipment could afford them (even when that equipment was no more advanced than the infantry's shoe leather).

Offensive Operations

Even with their drawbacks, modern-system offensive tactics still enable well-trained attackers to close with and destroy defended positions in the face of heavy fire. But then what? How can this be exploited to defeat an opposing state and conquer its territory?

Modern system operations employ one or the other of two broad approaches to this end: limited aims "bite-and-hold" offensives, and breakthrough-and-exploitation attempts. Neither is unique to the modern system; both concepts long predated the twentieth century. Post-1900 conditions and modern-system defenses, however, brought important modifications in both traditions.

BREAKTHROUGH AND EXPLOITATION

Breakthrough and exploitation is designed to induce systemic collapse of a defense while fighting through only a fraction of it directly. Heavily capitalized mass armies require an elaborate infrastructure to sustain them in combat. Soldiers must be fed, clothed, and if possible sheltered; weapons must be supplied with the mountains of ammunition they now expend every day; horses must be supplied with fodder; vehicles must be supplied with fuel and lubricants; tens of thousands of pieces of complex mechanical equipment must be maintained and replaced when damaged or destroyed. Moreover, the activities of this sprawling mass of personnel and materiel must somehow be coordinated over continental distances in the pursuit of some sort of plan—the task of commanding and controlling such far-flung hordes demands an intricate system of command posts and communications nodes to keep information and instructions flowing efficiently. Rapid movement of the forces themselves, let alone their supplies, requires a transportation network of roads and railways sufficient to move these virtual cities from place to place quickly. Without these things, armies can continue to fight—and often do—but their performance falls dramatically when they are denied the essential support and coordination that distinguishes an army from an armed mob. The objective of breakthrough and exploitation is thus to gain access to the rear areas over which this supporting infrastructure is distributed, destroy it, and in the process render the great mass of the defender's forward forces incapable of fighting at full efficiency.[47]

Breakthrough-and-exploitation operations do this by concentrating the invader's forces disproportionately against a small portion of the defender's lines. By using the initiative to concentrate forces at a point while accepting risks elsewhere, attackers can amass a large local numerical advantage at that point while yielding a much smaller disadvantage elsewhere. For example, by accepting a modest 2:3 disadvantage over 550 kilometers of a 600-kilometer frontier, an invader who concentrates on a 50-kilometer breakthrough sector can obtain more than a 4:1 advantage at that key point, even if the defender's forces are numerically equal to the invader's overall. In fact, even outnumbered invaders can create a large local advantage on a chosen frontage if that frontage is narrow: an invader at an 8:10 theaterwide disadvantage can still obtain almost a 4:1 local superiority by concentrating against a 25-kilometer front while defending at a 2:3 disadvantage over the remaining 575 kilometers of frontier.[48]

This local preponderance is used to punch a hole through the defender's pre-pared positions at that point. Once the hole is punched, reserves are poured through the gap and into the relatively undefended area behind the prepared po-sitions. Freed of the need to penetrate prepared defenses, these reserves can safely accelerate, overrunning and destroying defensive infrastructure at a rapid pace, and encircling or isolating large sections of the defender's forward forces, most of whom will not have been heavily engaged heretofore. In this way the in-vader undermines the entire defense's effectiveness while fighting through only a part of it directly. Faced with the loss of essential command and support func-tions, some armies lose composure and collapse as organized bodies. Others fight on once encircled and isolated, but do so with radically reduced per-capita effect-iveness and can often be overwhelmed in detail even by invaders whose forces are smaller but which retain their full effectiveness and freedom of maneuver.

Breakthrough and successful exploitation is thus an important special case for capability: *it enables invaders simultaneously to take an entire theater's terrain, to do so quickly, and to limit casualties.* In fact, breakthrough is the only condition where this is possible. Limited aims offensives (and contained breakthrough attempts), by contrast, pose inherent tradeoffs among the respective dimensions of capabil-ity: ground gain is typically proportional to losses and time; to restrict losses or end the battle sooner, the attacker must forgo otherwise achievable ground gains.[49] While exploitation is not always sought, when attained it thus conveys unique and extraordinary capability. (And this in turn makes its prevention para-mount for defenders: see below.)

Differential concentration and operations against an opponent's supply lines and communications are hardly unique to the modern system, having played a central role in war since at least the sixteenth century.[50] By contrast with offen-sive tactics (where the modern system was a radical departure), modern-system offensive operations are thus largely an adaptation of traditional methods. This is not to say that there are no important differences, however. In particular, the emergence of deep elastic defenses spurred the development of what would ulti-mately become offensive "deep battle" doctrine in the interwar years.

Deep battle called for the use of longer-range offensive elements to disrupt defenders' ability to move resources in the rear, both by striking moving forces themselves and by disrupting the command functions needed to direct their movement.[51] Elastic defenses depend on such movement for their effectiveness; as these defenses became more common, attackers naturally sought means of interdicting this movement. Unlike the rest of the modern system, deep battle had not reached maturity by 1918, even conceptually. Its basic elements, how-ever, had begun to appear in the war's final offensives, and the concept itself had begun to emerge at least in outline.

By 1918, for example, aircraft were being used to isolate intended break-through zones by destroying selected transportation nodes and attacking defen-sive reserves as they moved toward the threatened point. The effectiveness of these efforts was mixed, but both the Germans and the British made systematic efforts at air interdiction in their 1918 offensives.[52] The British went a step further in their plans for renewed offensive action in 1919 had the Germans not sued for peace. Colonel J.F.C. Fuller's "Plan 1919" emphasized the coordinated use of aircraft and fast-moving light armored units to destroy defensive command and logistical systems throughout the depths of the defense as a means of inducing paralysis and preventing effective defensive response to breakthrough.[53]

While interwar military developments in Germany and the Soviet Union would add important definition and conceptual maturity to these early notions, deep battle had thus made at least an appearance by the end of the war. Deep battle, however, is the only element of twentieth-century breakthrough and exploitation operations new to the modern system: differential concentration, disruption of communications and supply, and encirclement of enemy forces precede not just the modern system but even the twentieth century itself. Deep battle, moreover, is a supporting rather than a primary element in the modern system: deep attacks have historically been designed to facilitate the action of penetrating ground forces, not to substitute for them.[54] By contrast with offensive tactics, modern-system breakthrough and exploitation operations are thus more a story of continuity and adaptation than one of discovery and departure.[55]

LIMITED AIMS

Limited aims "bite-and-hold" operations, by contrast, are not designed to break through in themselves. Rather, they are intended to exploit the temporary advantage conveyed by differential concentration to seize important terrain or major sections of the defender's prepared positions. This positional advantage could then be used in subsequent offensives; if these can be mounted before the defender can construct additional prepared defenses to the rear of the lost ground, then the attacker can eventually lever the defender out of its entrenchments and onto open ground, where subsequent offensive action can be much more effective.

The advantage of limited aims operations is that they avoid overextension and thus reduce the attacker's vulnerability to counterattack. Deep defenses concede initial gains and depend on counterattack to regain the lost ground; if counterattacks can be defeated, invaders can progressively advance without the defender restoring the original front. Breakthrough attempts, however, tend to create opportunities for such counterattacks. An attacker trying to break through is engaged in a race against the defender's arriving reserves: the initial advantage provided by differential concentration will erode over time as the defender shifts reserves from elsewhere in the theater to match the attacker's concentration, so if the attacker is too slow in penetrating, the defender will have time to cancel the invader's initial numerical advantage and breakthrough will become much harder. For an attacker to spend time preparing conquered positions for defense, or to withhold troops to defend lengthening flanks, is to slow the penetration and thus risk losing the race. Moreover, against deep defenses breakthrough will usually demand an advance beyond the range of supporting artillery; to delay while the artillery repositions forward will often forfeit the critical time advantage and foreclose any hope of breaking through, hence many attackers simply press the advance beyond effective artillery range. Aggressive pursuit of breakthrough thus leaves attackers overextended if the defender can assemble sufficient counter-attack forces in time. Limited aims attacks, by contrast, terminate early, allowing attackers to consolidate gains, reorganize forces, and prepare the newly occupied ground for defense before defenders can mount effective counterstrokes. At the price of forgoing breakthrough, limited aims operations thus increase invaders' odds of defeating counterattacks and holding onto initial ground gains.[56]

LIMITED AIMS, LIMITED PAYOFFS, AND RISK

As with tactics, modern-system operations also have drawbacks. While limited aims offensives, for example, are often lower risk than breakthrough attempts, they also promise lower payoffs if successful. The promise of breakthrough is that an initial investment in hard slogging will be repaid by an opportunity for rapid exploitation at much lower cost thereafter; limited aims attacks forfeit such opportunities. Moreover, a successful exploitation can often knock a defender out of the war in a single operation, as it did in Germany's invasions of Poland and France in 1939–40, and in Israel's wars against the Arabs in 1956, 1967, and 1973. Limited aims attacks, by contrast, typically leave the opponent in the field, risking a long war with uncertain consequences. While limited aims promise lower risk in the near term, the ultimate risk in a long war may be far greater.

TRADEOFFS BETWEEN BREAKTHROUGH AND EXPLOITATION

The demands of breakthrough and exploitation can also come into conflict when modern-system methods are taken to extremes. Narrow modern-system frontages, for example, enable attackers to amass greater local preponder-ances through differential concentration; this enhances attackers' ability to break through. The narrower the frontage, however, the fewer the roads available through the penetration corridor for moving and supplying the exploitation forces.[57] Fewer roads mean slower commitment of the reserve through the breach once created; they also mean slower movement of supplies, and a smaller sustainable exploitation force (or a shorter distance over which a large force can be sustained).[58]

This is compounded by increased vulnerability to counterattack during the breakthrough attempt itself. A counterattack against the flank of a very narrow penetration corridor need only advance a short distance before cutting through the supply routes needed to sustain the offensive spearhead. To stop counter-attacks short of such a modest advance requires significant flank defenses, whose deployment depth further chokes the available supply channel through the pene-tration corridor, and whose resupply needs further tax the available road capacity.

An attacker's ability to manufacture local preponderance via differential concentration is thus not unlimited. Narrow fronts offer important advantages, but fronts cannot be narrowed infinitely without posing unsolvable logistical problems for the subsequent exploitation.

EXPLOITATION AND COMPLEXITY

A final limitation is the complexity of successful exploitation. To exploit a breakthrough deeply enough and quickly enough to induce systemic collapse in a defense requires quick, independent decision making by local commanders in lead units, and an ability to cope with the unexpected on the fly without detailed guidance from higher command. In exploitation, the modal combat action is the meeting engagement, where both attacker and defender are moving at the time of contact; preplanned maneuvers or rigidly scripted responses are of little use in such a fluid environment. Events move too quickly for extensive staff analysis or promulgation of detailed formal orders; an ability to improvise from partial instructions is critical to success. Such operations put a premium on judgment, mental agility, and individual initiative at all levels of command and are thus more demanding than slower, set-piece actions prior to breakthrough.

Defensive Tactics

Against modern firepower, simply digging in is insufficient—static defenses have been fatally vulnerable since at least 1917. Instead, the more fluid conduct of modern system defense demands much the same exposure-reduction tactics of cover, concealment, dispersion, suppression, combined arms, and independent small unit maneuver that modern system attackers require, albeit adapted to the particular problems of the defense.

Cover and concealment, for example, are essential to prevent attackers from concentrating their firepower on known defender locations. Geometrically arranged, quasi-permanent trench lines are easily surveyed from the air and permit attackers to build plans around known locations for at least the initial defenses they will encounter in the early stages.[59] By contrast, irregular, camouflaged locations often offer superior protection by trading the cover of formal trenches for concealment.[60]

Just as important, however, is limiting the *attackers'* ability to exploit cover by providing interlocking fields of fire. Most natural cover is directional: a tree stump or a low rise blocks fire from ahead, but not from the sides, for example. If a point can be fired upon from only a single direction, the ground will thus provide much more usable cover (or "dead space") to an attacker. If each point before a defensive line can be fired upon from multiple directions, the amount of dead space can be reduced significantly. By siting adjoining weapons so that each can fire across the others' fronts (i.e., by interlocking their fields of fire), defenders can thus complicate the attacker's task of finding cover and concealment.[61]

Dispersion via depth reduces losses to hostile artillery; in the process, it mandates greater small-unit independence for defending infantry and encourages those defenders to maneuver rather than to fight from fixed locations. Small, spread-out defensive units are usually incapable of stopping an assault wave alone; if the defenders stand fast and fight to the last cartridge, they will often die where they stand. If, on the other hand, defenders fight just long enough to force the attackers to seek cover, maneuver evasively, and bring supporting fires to bear, then the defenders break contact and withdraw, they induce nearly as much delay as a fight-to-the-finish would provide, yet with much lighter losses.[62] The movement this requires, however, risks exposure and thus demands cover and suppression, just as offensive tactics do.[63]

Finally, combined arms are as important to defenders as to attackers. While twentieth-century weapons are extremely lethal, they each have significant limitations. Machine guns, for example, can saturate an open area with fire given sufficient ammunition—no matter how rapidly an attacker tries to move through the beaten zone, a continuously firing machine gun can stop almost any size force the attacker pushes into that area. Machine guns, however, are flat-trajectory, direct-fire weapons: they require a clear line of sight between the shooter and the target and can be blocked by intervening obstacles.[64] Attackers able to use the terrain for cover and suppress the machine gun's fire during brief sprints between obstacles can thus work their way forward and eventually overrun unsupported machine guns. Mortars and artillery, on the other hand, can fire over intervening obstacles and engage targets they cannot see. Indirect-fire systems can kill attackers sheltering behind terrain obstructions; typically, however, their rates of fire are much slower, and their fire is much less accurate. Unless the defender's artillery is very numerous (and unsuppressed by counter-battery fire), attackers who move quickly and deny the artillery a massed, identifiable target can thus transit a defensive barrage zone before the barrage can kill more than a fraction of them. Working together, however, machine guns and artillery cover for one another's weaknesses. Machine guns slow the attackers' movement by forcing them to take cover; while this may not kill many of them directly, it pins them down and exposes them to gradual attrition by defensive artillery. In effect, direct-fire systems suppress offensive movement, giving the slower indirect-fire systems time to destroy the attack in detail.[65]

DEFENSIVE TACTICS AND COMPLEXITY

Like other aspects of the modern system, its defensive tactics are more complex than their predecessors. Cover and concealment require nearly as much attention to local topography for defenders as attackers. Soil excavated in digging positions must be hidden or removed to avoid giving away locations; covered retreat routes must be identified to enable units to withdraw without exposing themselves to fire from numerically superior attackers in the process; positions must be custom-sited to minimize dead space. Artillery fire plans must be carefully coordinated to enable close-in attackers to be targeted without killing defenders by friendly fire.[66] Combined arms requires greater levels of knowledge in both the employment and the support and maintenance of the various weapons needed. At all levels, for both attackers and defenders, the modern system is thus a complex doctrine that demands high levels of proficiency for proper implementation.

Defensive Operations

The key elements of modern-system defensive operations are depth, reserves, and counterattack. These methods were developed to thwart midwar artillery offensives but proved essential for meeting mature modern-system attacks as well.

The key operational problem for defenders facing modern-system attack is to buy time for responding to differential concentration. This was hardly pivotal against the artillery offensives of 1915–17: weeks-long bombardments advertised the point of attack and provided ample time to shift forces from elsewhere in the theater, canceling the attacker's initial numerical edge.

The modern-system shift to brief, hurricane barrages, however, restored surprise to the battlefield, denying defenders advance warning as to the attack's location. This enabled attackers to begin the assault before defenders could even the local odds. Attacks with modern-system tactics and local numerical superiority could advance in spite of defensive firepower; unless defenders could reduce the attacker's numerical edge in time, this advance would break through the defense and threaten systemic collapse of the defender's theater position.

As it happened, however, the defensive depth that was adopted to thwart destructive artillery in 1915–17 also provided defenders the time they needed to counterconcentrate in 1918. It did so by exploiting the inherent drawbacks of modern-system offensive tactics. For attackers, defensive depth increases the distance they must travel to break through, but it also reduces the density of the defenses they must penetrate. If attackers could accelerate dramatically against these lighter defenses, they could travel farther in the same time, and depth would thus give defenders no added time to react. Modern-system attackers, however, cannot accelerate dramatically without a radical increase in casualties, even against light opposition.[67] Even a handful of defenders armed with modern weapons can take a terrible toll of massed attackers caught in the open, hence even light defenses can compel attackers to take time-consuming evasive measures to survive. Light defenses cannot *halt* such attacks—numerically superior modern-system attackers can overwhelm light defenses given the time—but can *slow* them dramatically simply by compelling them to use the modern system. This in turn meant that deep, modern-system defenses could extend the attacker's period of slow, furtive movement, delaying the onset of breakthrough and its consequent offensive acceleration, and providing time for even distant reserves to reach the critical battlefield.

Defensive depth also increases those reserves' effectiveness once they arrive, again by exploiting the inherent shortcomings of modern-system offensive

methods. Modern-system tactics are complex and unforgiving. Properly implemented they are very powerful, but if their manifold moving parts are not properly coordinated, the result can easily be lethal exposure to defensive firepower.
Attackers are typically best able to provide this coordination near their line of
departure, where the benefits of advance planning and careful staging are closest
at hand. As attackers advance into depth, however, formations begin to break
down; units move onto unfamiliar, unscouted terrain; contact with supporting
artillery tends to loosen; defensive maneuver creates obstacles unanticipated by
prebattle reconnaissance; leaders become too busy with immediate crises for adequate reporting to higher command, while others become casualties and are
replaced with less-experienced soldiers with less-extensive familiarity with the
mission and the units' situation; losses cause imbalances in the weapon mix available in the forward assault teams; subunits lose their way and fall out of position. The further an attack travels, the less tightly coordinated its parts thus
become—and the less effectively such harried units can execute the complex bal-
let of modern-system tactics. A deep defense that compels an attacker to penetrate many kilometers before breaking through thus progressively erodes the
attack's power as it advances into depth—above and beyond the direct effects of
casualties in the attacker's ranks. This *entropic effect* of depth thus increases the
defensive reserves' ability to halt the attack once they arrive.[68] By contrast with
shallow, non–modern-system defenses that must stop the attack well forward or
suffer breakthrough, deep elastic defenses defer the decisive battle until a time
and place where the attacker's ability to exploit modern-system tactics will be reduced, and where the defender's incoming reserves are thus likely to be at their
greatest relative advantage.[69]

Of course, to exploit these advantages, the defender must have enough reserves to move. Here, too, the defensive methods developed in 1915–17 proved
essential, in particular by shifting the balance of forward and reserve forces in
favor of the latter. Defenders deployed near the front lines can be pinned in place
by light "fixing attacks" at little cost to attackers.[70] Even outnumbered attackers
away from the critical sector can thus often hold forward defenders in front of
them, making those defenders unavailable for prompt counterconcentration.
Defenses with most of their troops deployed in their forward sectors can thus be
denied the wherewithal to counterconcentrate, leaving them unable to halt a
modern-system attack even if the defenses are nominally deep and the attacker's
progress is slow. Defensive reserves located well to the rear, by contrast, are
much harder for attackers to pin down and thus are more readily available for
counterconcentration. By reorienting defenses away from heavy forward garrisons
and toward greater reliance on reserves deployed to the rear, modern-system defensive methods thus provide the wherewithal for counterconcentration, as well
as giving those reserves time to reach the threatened sector, and a better chance
to halt the attacker once they get there.

Finally, this combination of time, wherewithal, and entropic reduction of
offensive efficiency make it much likelier that defensive counterattack will

succeed in regaining lost ground. An attack that has struggled forward over broken ground and gradually lost coordination and is then struck in unprepared positions by a counterstroke from a large body of fresh troops can often be thrown back with smaller losses to the counterattacker than the original attacker had suffered in the initial assault.[71]

Ironically, it is often easier for defenders to give ground away and retake it later than to try to hold it continuously from the outset. Differentially concentrated modern-system attackers can rarely be halted at their departure line by the initial garrison of a forward defense—and attempting to do so only traps so many troops forward that defenders are left without the means to halt the attack after it overruns the forward positions.

OPERATIONAL DEPTH AND COMPLEXITY

Depth, reserves, and counterattack are very effective if done right, but doing them right is more difficult than implementing a static defense. Depth, for example, disperses troops; like dispersion on the attack, this complicates command and control, increases the burdens on junior leaders, and challenges morale among troops who may feel dangerously isolated. Morale can be especially hard to maintain in the forwardmost positions, which are both thinly garrisoned and too close to the enemy to be reinforced before a major attack would overrun them. Soldiers often know this yet must stay and fight at least long enough to break the attack's momentum. This requires either conscious self-sacrifice or the ability to conduct a fighting withdrawal under pressure. Withdrawal under fire is among the most technically demanding maneuvers in modern land warfare; conscious self-sacrifice in defense of an untenable position requires a very high order of discipline and motivation.[72]

Modern-system defensive operations also require much more movement than static, forward defenses. Garrisons of prepared positions conduct fighting withdrawals; reinforcements are moved in large numbers over great distances; counterattack forces must be massed and committed against key points on the invader's flanks. These movements must be conducted under the threat of air attack, or at night under blackout conditions. To get the necessary thousands of moving parts to the proper destinations under such conditions demands efficient planning and staffwork lest the result be chaos and massive, vulnerable traffic jams at key road junctions or rail depots.[73] The net result is a more complex operation than a simple, static defense-in-place from massed forward positions.

WHY DOES FORCE EMPLOYMENT VARY?

If the modern system is so effective, then why don't all states adopt it? Why does force employment vary? The reason is that the modern system poses difficult political and organizational problems that prevent many states from implementing it.

Defense in depth, for example, requires states to yield territory early in hope of regaining it later by counterattack. This is systematically unpopular with residents of border areas and is often unattractive more broadly for states whose border conflicts are matters of wide nationalist concern. Through most of the Cold War, NATO declaratory doctrine precluded defense-in-depth because German political sensitivities made such a policy impossible.[74] Other states' small size (such as Israel) or outlying natural resources (such as France) make defense in depth unattractive by virtue of what it would give up early in a conflict even if the public were otherwise willing to accept it.[75]

Defense by counterattack can be politically problematic for states with strong domestic pacifist groups or fearful neighbors. The training, organization, and force structure needed for counterattack is hard to distinguish from that needed for invasion. Domestic antiwar groups often find such preparations objectionable. Neighboring states often interpret them as evidence of threatening intentions and may respond with arms buildups or hostile alliances. Given this, status quo powers can be unwilling to incur the domestic or international political costs of preparing for counterattack. In the postwar era, for example, both Germany and Japan have had great difficulty justifying offensively oriented force postures and training in the face of domestic opposition from antiwar groups. In NATO, counterattack-oriented doctrinal proposals generated sharp criticism from liberals in many member states, as in the debates over Follow-on Forces Attack (FOFA) and the American adoption of AirLand Battle in the 1980s.[76] For Japan, all but strictly defensive military preparations have been harshly criticized by neighbors like Korea or China who remember World War II and remain skeptical regarding Japan's longer-term motives.[77]

The modern system also requires extensive independent decision making by junior officers and senior enlisted personnel; for social and political reasons, many states are unwilling to tolerate such autonomy for so many individuals. In police states, for example, to adopt such methods would often be to trade future military effectiveness for immediate overthrow.[78] In class-based societies, upper-class officers are often unwilling to trust their lives and reputations on the courage or judgment of lower-class non-commissioned officers (NCOs).[79] In ethnically divided societies, cleavages along ethnic or racial lines often divide military units and make officers and men, or neighboring subunits, unwilling to trust comrades whom they cannot directly see or control.[80]

Among the most serious drawbacks of the modern system is its tremendous complexity, and the high levels of skill it therefore demands in soldiers and officers. Not all armies can provide such skills.

Short-service conscript militaries, for example, often lose soldiers to civilian life before they can master all the necessary tasks. Yet domestic political or economic conditions often mandate short-service conscription systems. In interwar France, for instance, civilian leaders felt threatened by the political power of a large professional military and thus imposed a conscription system with service terms of only twelve months. While the French high command recognized the modern system's importance, they did not think it could be mastered by a draftee army. They consequently adopted simpler tactics and operations that they thought were within the competence of their allotted personnel.[81]

Civil-military conflict can inhibit skill development in other ways, too. In autocracies, the threat of political violence by the military creates powerful incentives for civilian interventions that reduce the military's ability to develop professional expertise. Such interventions can include frequent rotation of commanders and purges of the officer corps; suppression of horizontal communications within the military; divided lines of command; isolation from foreign sources of expertise or training; exploitation of ethnic divisions in officer selection or unit organization; surveillance of military personnel; promotion based on political loyalty rather than military ability; or execution of suspected dissident officers.[82] Such techniques can be effective barriers to coup d'état, but they systematically discourage soldiers from focusing on disinterested technical expertise, and they make such expertise hard to obtain for those few who seek it anyway.[83]

Social or cultural constraints can also interfere with the development of skill. Many have argued that Arab cultures, for example, encourage rigidly hierarchical organizational structures and extreme deference to authority. Status is associated with distance from one's subordinates, and hands-on mastery of technical detail by superior officers is discouraged.[84] This tends to interfere with honest assessment of problems and promotes artificiality in training, as mistakes are too rarely acknowledged and thus too rarely rectified. It limits officers' knowledge of the technical requirements for maintaining and employing their equipment. And it constrains the flexibility and small-unit initiative so important for the modern system.

Conflicting funding priorities can also inhibit skill development. States with powerful military-industrial complexes, for example, face political pressures to spend scarce resources on weapon production rather than training. Alternatively, some militaries themselves prefer to divert money away from training and readiness and into equipment modernization. Training is expensive but perishable. Senior officers concerned with their long-term legacy and anxious to fund long-lived capital equipment investments thus have an incentive to transfer resources away from expensive, short-half-life activities like training and into development of a new generation of weapons.[85] States who see themselves as unlikely to fight in the near term are especially likely to respond to this incentive. Such policies can leave militaries undertrained in war, however. Conflicts can emerge much more suddenly than planners anticipate: British defense budgets, for example, were planned using the "Ten-Year Rule" (a planning assumption that there would be no major war for at least ten years) from 1919 until 1933[86]—yet World War II broke out in 1939. And rebuilding military skills once lost can be a slow process: the U.S. Army is not generally thought to have recovered the proficiency it lost after Vietnam until the mid-1980s.[87]

The skills required to implement the modern system properly are thus difficult to obtain, and many states have failed to acquire them. Insufficient skill is therefore an important barrier to the exercise of modern-system force employment.

More broadly, a wide range of political, cultural, and organizational factors pull states away from modern-system military doctrines, and the relative strength of these factors differs widely across states. Politically unstable autocracies face different doctrinal incentives from those faced by stable democracies; domestic political pressures vary in strength and nature from state to state; ethnically fractious states confront different tradeoffs from those confronted by homogeneous or harmonious ones. If doctrine were determined entirely by military considerations, then these varying nonmilitary pressures would be irrelevant and all states would be driven to adopt similar force employment along modern-system lines. But since real doctrines are the product of a complex interaction between military and nonmilitary influences, real doctrines thus vary widely both from state to state and within states over time as the relative balance of political, organizational, and military pressures changes.[88] The net result is wide variance in force employment across the international system as a whole.

CHAPTER FOUR

The Modern System, Preponderance, and Changing Technology

BY 1918, Germany, Britain, and France had thus identified an essentially common doctrinal solution to the problem of radical lethality. This solution, the modern system, proved hard to implement, but where fully exploited it shielded armies from the storm of steel and enabled effective operations on an otherwise impossibly lethal battlefield.

But what does 1918 have to do with today? Technology has changed dramatically, and troop strengths have varied widely since then. Does none of this matter?

Technology and preponderance do matter. Their role, however, is different—and smaller—than typically assumed. And even today, this role is bound inextricably to the force employment principles forged on the western front between 1914 and 1918.

The reasons lie both in the nature of modern technology and the nature of the modern system. The modern system works by exploiting properties of military technology that have changed little since 1918 and are changing only slowly today. It thus damps the effects of technological change: modern-system militaries are far less exposed to the effects of increasing lethality, speed, and sensory acuity than are non–modern-system forces. This in turn means that the modern system has actually grown more important over time: technological change is increasing the vulnerability of non–modern-system forces much faster than modern-system ones, yielding an ever-growing gap in real military capability between the two.

Preponderance, by contrast, requires modern-system exposure reduction for numbers to have any decisive effect. Modern weapons are so lethal that exposed, non–modern-system forces become cannon fodder. For numbers to tell requires modern-system force employment.

This chapter makes this case in four steps. The first section considers post-1918 technological change and its differential effects on modern-system and non–modern-system forces. The second section treats preponderance and its consequences. The third section considers the prospects for radical change in the future, specifying bounding conditions for the new theory's applicability. The final section summarizes qualitatively the resulting theory and its key predictions for modern warfare. (This theory is formalized as a mathematical model of capability in the appendix.)

Technological change since 1918 has had three main effects: continued increases in firepower and lethality; greater mobility over longer distances; and the ability to see, communicate, and process information in greater volumes over larger areas. I consider each major change in turn; I conclude the section by considering dyadic technological imbalance as a special case.

Increased Firepower

Many now argue that long-range, precision-guided weapons have revolutionized warfare, demanding radically new doctrines and tactics.[1] Yet sharp lethality growth is nothing new: it gave rise to the modern system in the first place and practically defined twentieth-century warfare thereafter. Precision-guided weapons are thus an extension of a very longstanding trend, and this trend has progressively increased the modern system's importance.

This is because weapon lethality, while increasing against all targets in absolute terms, has grown much faster against massed targets in the open than dispersed targets in cover. Over time, this difference in growth rate has steadily widened the difference in vulnerability between massed, exposed targets and dispersed, covered ones. This difference is central to modern-system tactics, which are designed to exploit the Earth's surface complexity to provide cover and concealment via dispersion. The net result has thus been to afford modern-system militaries an increasing edge in relative vulnerability as weapons have grown more lethal.

Flat-trajectory, direct-fire weapons like rifles, machine guns, or tanks, for example, have become increasingly lethal against exposed targets, but even the heaviest tank guns still have negligible effectiveness against targets in cover. Some types of light or shallow barriers can be penetrated by modern high-velocity kinetic energy rounds, but solid earth in proper thickness can stop even the M1A2's 120-mm depleted uranium ammunition; the chemical-energy warheads used on antitank missiles can be thwarted by even light cover.[2] In fact, penetrable concealment like foliage can be as effective as solid earth if it blocks the shooter's view of the target, denying the shooter knowledge of the target's approach or a useable aim point for engagement.[3] While modern direct-fire weapons can thus kill targets in the open faster and at much greater ranges, targets sheltered behind slopes or hidden among the rubble of destroyed buildings are little more vulnerable to a 2001 M1A2 tank than to a 1918 Mark IV.

Artillery has likewise seen great increases in range and munition lethality since 1918, but again the increase has been much greater against exposed targets. The U.S. 8-inch self-propelled howitzer of the 1970s, for example, had twice the range of the 105-mm howitzer of 1942; against exposed targets, each 8-inch round had more than seven times the lethal area. Against targets in cover, by contrast, the increase in lethal area from the 1942 ordnance to that of 1972 was less than a factor of 1.5.[4] More important, both weapons' real impact was limited primarily by target acquisition, and improvements in target acquisition against covered targets have lagged far behind those for targets in the open.

Artillery targets are acquired in three main ways. First, ground-based forward observers spot targets, communicate their locations back to the firing batteries, and may adjust their fire. Observer performance has improved since 1918,[5] but ground-based spotters are ultimately limited to line-of-sight target acquisition. The same field-of-view restrictions that limit direct-fire weapons against covered modern-system targets also limit ground-based spotters, limiting in turn the artillery they direct.[6]

The second means of artillery target acquisition is to detect hostile fire (especially by enemy artillery) and use it to infer the shooters' locations. The earliest such methods were flash and sound ranging, which date from 1915.[7] More recently, radars have been used to detect the fired shells in the air; by observing the shells at several points in their flight, their trajectory can be computed and used to deduce the shooter's location.[8] Such radars can thus thwart cover and concealment (since the shells become visible even where the shooters do not), but only against high-trajectory shooters (whose shells rise high enough to be seen), and only after they fire. Flat-trajectory, direct-fire weapons are thus immune, and artillery can escape real detection by shifting positions after firing ("shooting and scooting"), or by husbanding undetected silent guns for surprise use at key moments.[9] Sensing hostile fire is thus only a partial answer to modern-system cover and concealment.

Aircraft provide the third means of artillery target acquisition, though this function has often been eclipsed by air forces' role as direct weapon-delivery platforms. Aircraft have obviously become radically more effective since 1918 in all roles. Typical ground-attack ranges have increased by a factor of ten; payloads have increased by a factor of more than one hundred; the weapons themselves have become much more effective via precision guidance; and aerial reconnaissance and target acquisition now exploit a wide range of improved sensors.[10] Against massed targets in the open, these changes now enable aircraft to destroy whole brigades or divisions of ground forces by themselves in a matter of hours given air supremacy.[11]

Some of this tremendous improvement extends even to targets in cover. Small folds in the Earth do not obstruct vision or fire from the air. This reduces the net availability of useable shelter and increases lethality even against opponents who use modern-system exposure reduction.

Yet the *rate* of lethality increase against concealed modern-system targets is still far less than against massed targets in the open. This is so for three reasons: (1) even against aircraft, much cover remains for armies able to exploit it; (2) aircraft are transient observers, making it much harder to ensure that fleeting moments of modern-system exposure are caught before the targets are again under cover; and (3) natural cover and technical countermeasures interact—modern-system armies able to exploit the former make it much easier for the latter to thwart new surveillance and precision strike technologies. These points are important enough to warrant amplification.

COVER FROM AIR ATTACK

First, although some types of cover are less effective against aircraft, some are *more* effective, while others affect air and ground observation equally. For much of the twentieth century, for example, two of the most common forms of cover—darkness and foul weather—have been more effective against aircraft than against ground troops. Ground weapons suffer reduced lines of sight at night or in fog but are otherwise battleworthy. Most combat aircraft, on the other hand, were ineffective at night and grounded by bad weather until at least the 1980s.[12] Even in 1999, few aircraft could find ground targets through cloud cover.[13] Fog dims infrared contrast and reduces laser ranges, and rain disrupts radar performance at millimeter wave frequencies.[14] Such conditions are very frequent in much of the world. Darkness occurs every day everywhere short of the Arctic Circle; foul weather is nearly as common. In Europe, for example, ground attack aircraft can expect to be blinded by 80–100 percent cloud cover about 40 percent of the time.[15] Ground fog occurs about one morning in four in the spring and lasts an average of more than five hours.[16] Over the seventy-eight days of NATO's recent air campaign in Kosovo, cloud cover exceeded 50 percent more than 70 percent of the time.[17]

Forests, jungles, and buildings, moreover, are opaque to both air and ground observers and are likely to remain so for the foreseeable future. Current radar, infrared, and optical sensors are all blocked by foliage or masonry.[18] Electronic emissions from forests and towns can be sensed, but this rarely allows targeting more than just the emitter itself.[19] New low-frequency wideband radars may eventually penetrate foliage, but this program is in its early stages. If the technology proves feasible, countermeasure-resistant, and practical, a fielded military system could still be a generation away.[20] Remotely delivered unattended ground sensors might detect targets in forests or towns but have limited ranges and must be used in quantity for extensive coverage. For the foreseeable future, cost will restrict them to use in limited areas.[21] In theory, small special forces teams can infiltrate into sight of targets in forests or towns and then radio coordinates to aircraft for attack, but not if their targets prevent them from penetrating into such close proximity. A proper modern-system defense with interlocking fields of fire from concealed firing positions, an outpost zone oriented to defeating infiltration, and substantial depth, for example, would prove difficult to destroy in this way. A workable target acquisition system, moreover, would need an effective munition to threaten targets in wooded or built-up areas; foliage-penetrating terminal guidance could well prove more challenging than surveillance, while urban areas pose difficult masking problems for weapons descending on normal trajectories.[22]

Urban and forested cover is very common in most of the world. More than 40 percent of Germany's land area, for example, is forested or built up.[23] Almost one-third of Poland is forested; Estonia is 44 percent wooded; Hungary, 19 percent; Bosnia, 39 percent; China, 14 percent; South Korea, 65 percent.[24] The continental United States is 30 percent wooded and 6 percent urban.[25] Mideastern deserts, of course, have little woodland, but much of the geostrategically meaningful land area is urban, and these urban areas can be very large. Baghdad alone, for example, stretches over more than 300 square kilometers.[26]

This cover, moreover, is often distributed in small, widespread patches that facilitate short sprints from one to another. On the GOODWOOD battlefield of 1944 in Normandy, for example, over 80 percent of all 1-km grid squares now contain at least some forest or urban cover (though only 26 percent of the total land area is covered). Even if continuously observed from directly overhead, a dismounted modern-system ground unit working its way across the battlefield from Bretteville-sur-Laize to the coastal port of Ouistreham (28 kilometers as the crow flies) could remain under cover more than 85 percent of the time by selecting a circuitous route designed to minimize exposure.[27]

The recent wars in Kosovo and Afghanistan demonstrate that such cover remains important even against modern, high-technology air power. In 1999, for example, Serb ground forces in Kosovo may not have been capable of full modern-system implementation, but without a NATO ground threat they could still keep most of their heavy equipment under cover or in close proximity to civilians most of the time. As a result, seventy-eight days of NATO bombing comprising tens of thousands of sorties killed at most a few hundred Serb ground force targets.[28]

In Afghanistan, unskilled indigenous Afghan Taliban were incapable of exploiting cover and thus were extremely vulnerable to precision air power, but better-skilled al Qaeda fighters were much more successful in using cover to reduce their exposure. At Bai Beche on November 5, 2001, for example, a mostly al Qaeda defensive force subjected to nearly three days of intensive American bombing nevertheless survived in sufficient strength to drive back the initial advance of General Abdul Rashid Dostum's Northern Alliance cavalry.[29] Along Highway 4 on December 4–6, al Qaeda defensive positions hidden among culverts and in burned-out vehicles along the roadside remained undetected by any American surveillance system until they fired upon and turned back the advance of American-allied Afghan troops.[30] Al Qaeda counterattacks at Sayed Slim Kalay and Arghestan Bridge closed to small-arms range of American and allied forces before being detected, much less fired upon.[31] At Operation ANACONDA in March 2002, less than half of the al Qaeda fighting positions ultimately discovered on the battlefield were known to American forces prior to ground contact, in spite of an intensive prebattle reconnaissance effort using the latest in sophisticated surveillance technology. In fact, most fire received by U.S. forces in ANACONDA came from initially unseen, undetected al Qaeda fighting positions.[32]

Neither al Qaeda nor the Serbs were skilled enough for full modern-system implementation. The Serbs benefited from the absence of any NATO ground threat and could thus hide without needing to defend ground—a much easier job than waging a modern-system defense against a skilled ground attack. Al Qaeda fared much worse against skilled American and Canadian infantry than they did against less-proficient Afghan troops, and even against indigenous Afghan opposition, al Qaeda's inability to master the modern system in its entirety was instrumental in their rapid expulsion from Afghanistan following the American intervention.[33] Neither case shows the modern system fully at work. But both cases provide enough of a window into the problem of cover against modern air power to suggest that the natural complexity of the Earth's surface is still sufficient to degrade aerial targeting when exploited properly: where Serb and al Qaeda fighters were properly covered, they could not be annihilated from the air alone.

TRANSIENCE OF AERIAL OBSERVATION

The second major constraint on air effectiveness against modern system targets is the nonpersistence of aerial observation. Ground defenses are continuously present; they can thus maintain continuous surveillance of terrain and fire immediately at any target that becomes visible, even briefly. Aircraft, by contrast, are rarely numerous enough to maintain a continuous presence over the entire battlefield.[34] Ordinarily they patrol intermittently or respond to calls from others' target acquisition. Ground targets thus normally enjoy periods where the sky is clear of aircraft—in fact, the sky is often more clear than not, even in intense fighting. Modern-system forces can thus often wait to move from cover to cover until the sky is clear; if the movements are short, they can often be completed before air attacks can arrive.

In the Gulf War, for example, the Coalition deployed the most powerful air armada ever assembled, yet even the Iraqis managed to move a five-division blocking force of some six hundred tanks and six hundred other armored vehicles into position astride the U.S. Seventh Corps axis of advance without decisive losses en route. The Iraqis likewise moved a multibrigade counterattack into close combat with the marines at Burqan without significant losses en route, as well as moving a battalion across the border into Khafji unscathed.[35] Iraqi units caught in the open were badly mauled, but some managed to initiate and complete movements before coalition air power could respond—and this in a war where the coalition enjoyed complete air supremacy, where cover was unusually scarce, and where the enemy was hardly capable of the full modern system regimen. Had coalition air forces been overhead at the time, each of these units would probably have been destroyed before arriving; because air forces are inherently nonpersistent, however, it was possible for even large units to survive periods of exposure and complete tactically significant movements.

In Afghanistan in 2001–02, al Qaeda fighters quickly learned to retreat into cover when allied aircraft were overhead, then emerge to fire, move, or conduct resupply after the aircraft had departed. In Operation ANACONDA, for example, al Qaeda fighters' habitual movement from hiding into firing positions upon the departure of allied aircraft eventually prompted American infantry to time their own mortar fire to catch them in moments of exposure en route.[36] Even in the twenty-first century, aerial nonpersistence thus limits air forces' ability to destroy elusive modern-system targets before those targets find cover.

COVER-COUNTERMEASURE INTERACTION

The third factor retarding air effectiveness against modern-system targets is the interaction between cover and technical countermeasures. Better sensors and weapons spur development of countermeasures. These include decoys, obscurants, jamming, spoofing, hardening, signature suppression, and active defenses, inter alia. All have long been deployed to protect high-value air and naval targets, and all are now being applied to protect ground-force targets like tanks and armored personnel carriers against precision-guided air and missile-delivered weapons.[37] Massed, moving tank columns in the open, however, present multiple signatures and are thus exposed to such a wide range of seeker types that it will be nearly impossible to spoof or suppress or obscure them all simultaneously and continuously. By restricting the variety and degrading the effectiveness of hostile sensors, however, cover, concealment, and dispersion greatly ease the countermeasures' task. In the open, seeker technology has been winning the detection / counterdetection race, in large measure due to the effectiveness of multispectral sensing and data fusion techniques in thwarting countermeasures implemented singly.[38] In cover, the reduced variety and strength of signatures make it possible for feasible technical countermeasures to gain the upper hand. Moreover, routine use of natural cover enables ground forces to focus countermeasure use on temporary protection during brief periods of unavoidable exposure. Expendable obscurants like exothermic chaff or multispectral smokes, for example, are potentially very effective across a range of frequency bands, but continuous expenditure poses impossible logistical demands.[39] Militaries able to exploit natural cover to limit their exposure to brief windows can make such expendable countermeasures tactically feasible. Similarly, modern-system cover enables decoy and jammer use to focus on key times and places rather than being diffused across entire battlefields and entire armies. In effect, technical countermeasures thus work like suppressive fires: they do not permanently defeat hostile shooters (or seekers); rather, they temporarily shield modern-system subunits during brief sprints from cover to cover.[40]

So none of the major lethality increases since 1918, whether in direct-fire, artillery, or air-delivered weapons, has been as effective against covered as exposed targets. Of course, lethality against dispersed targets in cover has not stood still, nor will it. But the *rate* of lethality increase has been much slower than for exposed targets and will remain so in the foreseeable future. Unless lethality against dispersed targets in cover reaches annihilating levels—which it will not any time soon—the resulting gap in effectiveness gives modern-system militaries a powerful—and growing—edge over non–modern-system opponents.

Does this mean that an army of today could simply mimic German tactics from 1918 and survive against today's weapons? Of course not. Nor does it mean that sensors are no more effective against concealed targets in 2002 than they were in 1918: finding even half the defenders on a battlefield like Operation ANACONDA's is surely an important improvement over older technology. Neither does it mean that modern air power is not an extremely powerful weapon or an extremely valuable asset: it clearly is both.

What this analysis *does* mean is that the principles today's armies must use to survive are the same as 1918's, albeit implemented more aggressively, and that if implemented aggressively, these principles can still allow armies to survive modern firepower in sufficient strength to conduct meaningful military missions. Firepower alone—even twenty-first-century firepower—is not enough to defeat an opponent who can exploit modern-system exposure reduction. Firepower is critically important, but its main effect has been to allow militaries who can combine it with modern-system ground force employment to punish the mistakes of non–modern-system opponents with increasing severity. Firepower is a part of effective military power; it is not the answer in itself. And it is a component whose role can be understood only in interaction with force employment.

Cover, concealment, dispersion, suppression, combined arms, and independent small-unit maneuver are thus the keys to survival on any post-1900 mid- to high-intensity battlefield. In 1918, however, these techniques were needed only in the few hundred to few thousand yards from the front line in which troops were routinely exposed to hostile fire. Behind that zone, troops could be moved more or less freely in the open. As weapon ranges grew, the depth over which modern-system tactics were needed grew as well. Similarly, the more lethal the weapons, the shorter the period of exposure one can survive while sprinting from cover to cover, and the more aggressively one must maximize the covering potential of the available terrain. This in turn demands greater dispersion, more careful attention to adequate suppressive fires, and more thoroughgoing integration of the diverse arms needed to provide this. Technology thus affects force employment, but its effect is not to overturn the modern system—on the contrary, it demands ever more complete implementation of modern-system methods as weapons have grown more lethal.[41]

Increased Mobility

What about increasing speed and mobility? Have these undermined the modern system since 1918? Certainly today's forces are far more mobile than 1918's: whereas the foot soldier of 1918 could manage perhaps 6 kilometers per hour in an assault and 25 kilometers a day in an unopposed forced march, by 1940 the German Pzkw IIIe tank could make 40 kilometers per hour on roads (18 across country), and travel up to 175 kilometers without refueling, while the U.S. M1A1 tank of 1991 could reach 67 kilometers per hour on roads, with an unrefueled range of 465 kilometers.[42] With the helicopter in the 1960s, transport speeds increased by perhaps another factor of four to five, while fixed-wing aircraft can reach destinations hundreds of kilometers away in minutes.

Many have seen these mobility increases as revolutionary. The tank in particular is often seen as having restored movement to the western front, and as the catalyst for the German "blitzkrieg" offensives of 1939–41.[43] Others see the helicopter as a radical break from the past or highlight the airplane's ability to overfly battle lines and reach previously safe targets deep behind the front.[44]

Yet as noted in chapter 3, the tank was at most a secondary factor in the 1918 campaign that ended the trench stalemate. Tanks were essentially absent from the German Spring Offensives and were increasingly scarce in Allied armies after the initial battles of the Hundred Days, as combat losses and mechanical breakdown removed more and more of them from the field. While helpful, tanks were thus neither necessary nor sufficient to break the stalemate—modern-system tactics played a more essential role.

Of course, tank technology improved dramatically after 1918, and tanks have been joined by many other new high-speed platforms, including armored personnel carriers, self-propelled artillery, helicopters, and transport aircraft. Have these mobility improvements made the modern system less necessary?

On the contrary, post-1918 increases in nominal speed, like those in firepower, have *increased* the modern system's importance, especially for defenders at the operational level. Modern-system defensive operations are designed to compel attackers to slow down in order to survive, and to extend this period of furtive movement into depth, affording defenders time to respond. This offensive speed reduction lies at the heart of modern-system defense and is relatively insensitive to the nominal speed of the attacker's platforms: faster platforms allow only minor increases in penetration rates through a deep defense. Deep modern-system defenses thus limit attackers' ability to use the increasing speed that technology has provided them.

Why is penetration rate so insensitive to platform speed for modern-system defenses? The answer has to do with the demands of modern-system *offensive* tactics. As noted in chapter 3, these impose strict limits on an attacker's rate of advance, and few of these limits bear any direct relationship to the potential speed of the attacker's conveyances. For example, modern-system offensive tactics require careful scouting and reconnaissance (both before and during the battle), and thorough pre-attack planning to enable maximum coordination between maneuver units and fire support. In fact, much of the time there is no evident movement toward the enemy at all—staffwork, planning, prepositioning, reconnaissance, and rehearsals are largely invisible to the observer but are critical for effectiveness and can often account for more time than the actual assault.[45] The assault itself must then await completion of any preliminary artillery preparation or airstrikes. Minefields and defensive barriers must be located and breached, preferably before exposing the assault force to hostile fire. All are time-consuming but important functions, all have a major impact on the elapsed time needed to complete an attack, yet none has anything to do with the rated speed of tanks or supporting vehicles, and none can be appreciably speeded by faster weapon platforms per se. Once the final assault begins, full exploitation of combined arms synergy demands that tanks be accompanied by dismounted infantry; if this synergy is not to be lost, the tanks' pace cannot exceed the foot soldiers', no matter how fast the tanks. The modern system thus imposes an array of speed limitations that have little to do with the nominal mobility of the tanks, troop carriers, helicopters, or aircraft that support the attack.

These constraints, however, become much less severe if the attacker breaks through. Because exploitation forces operating behind the enemy's main positions are less likely to encounter dug-in defenders (and can often bypass those they do find), they have less need for time-consuming exposure reduction. This enables attackers *in exploitation* to accelerate to take full advantage of their platforms' maximum speed and range without suffering crippling losses. Planning cycles can be greatly compressed. Command can be exercised by brief, fragmentary orders communicated on the fly. Artillery support is less necessary; minefields and barriers are more rarely encountered; infantry can remain mounted. Units can often move on roads in column. Helicopters and airborne infantry can be rushed forward to great depths at acceptable risk. Not only can the platforms themselves move much more rapidly under such conditions, but their speed also accounts for much more of the total rate of advance (since there is much less time spent sitting still while preparatory activities unfold). In exploitation, rate of advance is thus much more sensitive to nominal platform speed than during breakthrough—and realized exploitation speed has thus increased rapidly as technology has increased nominal platform speed since 1918. This in turn has progressively increased the consequences of breakthrough—and thus the premium on preventing it via modern-system defensive operations even at the cost of an initial sacrifice of ground.

Fixed-wing aircraft and long-range missiles, on the other hand, are potentially major exceptions: they can safely overfly ground defenses and strike deep behind enemy lines rapidly without prior breakthrough.[46] Nor is their speed constrained by a need for modern-system exposure reduction: the full speed of aircraft and missiles can be realized over the battlefield with or without breakthrough. In fact, either one can reach a breakthrough's ultimate aim—enemy infrastructure— without fighting through hostile ground defenses at all. If so, why bother with breaking through? Why not go straight to the real target? As air and missile technology have improved, does this obviate the need for breakthrough in the first place—or will it anytime soon?

The answer is no. Modern missiles and aircraft can reach any target any-where, but to render modern-system force employment irrelevant they would also need the ability to *destroy* any target anywhere. For the foreseeable future this will remain out of reach, for the reasons discussed above: against a modern-system opponent, aircraft and missiles are too susceptible to cover and conceal-ment, and too transient a presence.

What deep strike by modern aircraft or missiles *can* do to a modern-system opponent is to slow its movement in the rear and reduce its command efficiency. Deep strikes can compel opponents to resort to modern-system movement tech-niques even for out-of-contact movements well behind the front. They can also compel modern-system opponents repeatedly to rebuild destroyed bridges or cratered roadways, and to clear remotely emplaced minefields before using roads or trails. Each can substantially increase the time it takes defenders to counterconcentrate, or the time it takes attackers to move supplies or replace-ments forward at the point of attack—though none can halt hostile movement completely.[47] Deep strikes can compel opponents to hide and disperse fuel and ammunition stockpiles. This slows resupply and depresses hostile operating tem-pos, though it can rarely halt operations entirely. Deep strikes can compel hostile command posts to limit their emissions, to remove antennas and generators to remote locations, to use landlines or couriers, to change locations frequently, and to practice skip-echelon techniques to replace those who get killed anyway.[48] This can reduce hostile commanders' efficiency, flexibility, and responsiveness, though it cannot usually prevent command from being exercised.[49]

Of course, against *non*–modern-system opponents, deep strikes can do much more: exposed movements can be shut down; concentrated supply dumps in the open can be destroyed outright; command can be paralyzed by some combina-tion of physical destruction and electronic jamming. Against non–modern-system opponents, deep-strike systems can thus increasingly substitute for orthodox breakthrough, and do so from a war's outset. This in turn is once again widening over time the gap in real capability between militaries that can implement the modern system and thus preserve their ability to move and communicate (even if more slowly than before) and those that cannot. Greater mobility, like heavier firepower, is thus increasing the premium on modern-system force employment.

Improved Information Technology

Has new information technology made the modern system obsolete? Certainly "C4ISR," as it is now called (for command, control, communications, comput-ers, intelligence, surveillance, and reconnaissance), has improved dramatically since 1918. Communications have progressed from 1918's primitive field tele-phones, runners, signal flares, and pigeons to the directional burst-mode radios and fiber optic networks of 2001. Intelligence gathering in 1918 was mostly by biplane observers whose reports awaited their return, and whose accuracy was limited by their inability to pinpoint their own locations over hostile territory. Today, radar, infrared, electro-optical, acoustic, and seismic sensors collect real-time data of great precision over tremendous distances. An opponent's own communications and radar signals provide critical information on the location of hostile emitters. In fact an "information revolution" is widely held to be transforming both the civil economy and the conduct of war, and many now see information technology as decisive.[50] One might suppose that this explosion of information collection, processing, and communications technology would invalidate tactics developed in an era as information-poor as 1918, and hence that the modern system would no longer be relevant in today's data-rich environment.

Yet it is easy to exaggerate information technology's role in war, especially amidst the hype now associated with information's role in the civil economy. While information technology is always important, it is only decisively important against non–modern-system militaries.

To see why, it is useful to distinguish several distinct functions of military information. To a first approximation, it can be seen as an enabler for mobility (by permitting far-flung movements to be coordinated and directed); an enabler for firepower (by providing targeting information for long-range weapons like aircraft, missiles, and artillery); and a contributor to operational planning (by providing intelligence on enemy whereabouts and intentions). In the first two of these, information improvements have had much the same effects as the improvements in mobility and firepower they facilitate; since the latter have increased the modern system's importance, so the enabling information improvements have, too.

As a contributor to operational planning, on the other hand, information could in principle have very different effects. For operational planning, broad surveillance information, rather than precise targeting data, is enough: if one knew that the enemy had massed in the general vicinity of Wadi al Batin and would strike there, this would justify moving the reserve to that sector, even if the locations of individual enemy tanks could not be pinned down. This kind of broad surveillance information is, in principle, easier to obtain than precise targeting data—and if obtained with sufficient reliability, could undermine the modern system at the operational level.

This is because modern-system differential concentration and defensive depth are premised on the assumption that attackers will use the initiative to concentrate at a point before defenders can react. This in turn requires defenders to buy time for counterconcentration by deploying in depth. Foreknowledge of the point of attack that allowed defenders to predeploy there would make differential concentration impossible, thus obviating the need for depth in the defense. If so, modern-system *tactics* might still be needed, but modern-system *operations* would be obsolete.[51]

Have post-1918 information improvements provided this kind of foreknowledge? No, for at least three reasons. First, surveillance information, while easier to obtain than targeting data, has never been perfect and is unlikely to be any-time soon. Even traditional intelligence-gathering always provided a fair amount of information, even against modern-system militaries: one cannot mass thousands of soldiers and weapons against a point and remain utterly invisible, even before twenty-first-century eavesdropping gear. What the modern system can do, however, is create ambiguity. If one cannot see everything, if the locations of individual elements are never certain, and if many are hidden at any given moment, then a deployment's precise contours can be blurred. Together with sophisticated use of decoy vehicles, phantom radio networks, and dummy emitters to create false information for today's high-volume collectors to collect, the result is inevitably some degree of ambiguity as to a force's true whereabouts and intentions.[52]

Second, these ambiguities give rein to cognitive and organizational distortions that can produce error even from apparently ample surveillance data. There is a large literature on surprise in war.[53] Among this literature's central findings is that surprise is usually *not* due to a lack of information per se—it results from organizational and cognitive factors that cause true but ambiguous information to be misinterpreted or mishandled. Most victims of surprise had information that, in retrospect, ought to have alerted them to the time and place of attack. Intelligence agencies, however, are barraged with information—some true and relevant, most true but irrelevant, some false, all ambiguous. Most of this information, moreover, is classified and must be compartmented to protect the sources and methods used to gather it. Compartmentation creates organizational complexity and necessarily limits information flow. The greater the volume of data handled and the larger the number of compartments created by diversity of collection methods, the greater the complexity. In such an environment, more information can make things worse as easily as better. Separating wheat from chaff in often huge volumes of incoming material is among the intelligence analyst's most important jobs, but more powerful sensors collect more chaff as well as more wheat—and do so via multiple channels that may reside in different parts of the organization. In such a setting, information overload is a growing problem—collecting more data increases the load and thus can often make this problem worse.

Moreover, the people within these complex organizations must interpret these data against a backdrop of prior expectations, hopes, and fears. These predispose all decision makers to see what they expect to see, or want to see, in ambiguous data; the emotional stress, danger, and fatigue of war reinforce this tendency.[54] In November 1950, for example, Harry Truman and the Joint Chiefs of Staff thought North Korea was all but defeated and victory finally in hand. Though Chinese prisoners had been taken as early as November 13, and although intelligence reports showed indications that the Chinese were preparing to intervene in force, this evidence was discounted against the strong expectation that the war was all but over. When the Chinese then launched a massive offensive beginning on November 25, overstretched American forces were thus taken by surprise and overwhelmed, spurring the longest retreat in American military history.[55] In Operation ANACONDA in March 2002, commanders staring at live video footage from American Predator reconnaissance drones saw al Qaeda figures maneuvering on Takur Ghar mountain but misinterpreted these as Americans because this is what they had expected to see.[56] Opponents who play on this problem by fashioning deception and concealment efforts around analysts' preconceptions magnify the difficulties. Because the Germans expected the D-Day invasion to take the shortest route via the Pas de Calais, it was easier for Allied deception to persuade them that phony divisions opposite Calais were real, in spite of indications that the Allies were actually massing well to the south.[57]

Intelligence is thus not just the physics of sensors and fiber optics—accurate perception is as much (or more) a matter of organizational and cognitive "software" as it is the "hardware" of radars and computers. And it is far from clear that better hardware will so overwhelm the human software constraints as to banish surprise from war. On the contrary, many of the sociologists who study the role of information technology in real human organizations fear that more information is making the problem worse, not better.[58] A modern-system military able to render its activities ambiguous and play to its opponent's predispositions can thus deny that opponent complete foreknowledge and preserve the possibility of surprise. This in turn means that differential concentration and defensive depth will remain important as hedges against that possibility.

The third reason why post-1918 information improvements have not undermined the modern system is that logistical constraints keep most defenders from exploiting even as much surveillance data as they have traditionally gotten—more data, even *perfect* data, would do nothing to overcome these. That is, even if attackers did somehow lose the ability to surprise defenders, few defenders would be able to exploit this so thoroughly as to forgo defensive depth—and attackers would still profit from differential concentration.

Defenders need considerable lead time to meet an offensive. From the time when the point of attack becomes clear, they must plan the movement of large masses of troops, move them, and prepare them for combat in their new positions.[59] This poses two contradictory problems. If the point of attack is identified too late, defensive reaction cannot be completed in time. But if knowledge comes too early, a defender who commits to a point, reaches it, and digs in there can be outmaneuvered by an attacker who uses the initiative to change the point of attack while pinning the defender's now-misdeployed forces in place with a secondary effort on the original front—leaving the now-committed defender without a reserve to adapt to the change. This timing is extremely difficult to fine-tune, and for reasons having little to do with inadequate knowledge of attacker intentions. Attackers often, for example, delay unexpectedly at the last minute: by some accounts, the Germans delayed their invasion of the Netherlands in 1940 as many as twenty-nine times before crossing the border on

May 10.[60] Even if the defender reads the attacker's true intentions perfectly up to the very minute the defender must commit, the defender thus still risks being drawn into overcommitment if they try to meet the attack in advance: if the attackers themselves do not know that they will delay until the last minute, the defender cannot possibly know any sooner, yet defenders have to commit long before the attacker moves if they are to be ready to fight in time on the key sector, and once committed they can be held there by pinning attacks using a fraction of the attacker's strength. Given these logistical constraints, defenders often choose instead to hold back from committing their reserves even when they think they know the intended point of attack.[61] A critical advantage of depth is that it enables defenders to do this without risking breakthrough in the meantime: by buying time while forcing the attacker to commit to a deliberate offensive at a particular point in order to gain ground, defense-in-depth thus enables defenders to distinguish feints from the real thing, and to wait until the *attacker* is fully committed before consigning the reserve to a particular front. Better information on attacker intentions is thus unlikely to change these dynamics; for logistical reasons, defenders often know more than they can afford to act upon, and the modern system plays a critical role in allowing them the time they need to act on the knowledge they have.[62] Even with more information, it is thus likely that modern-system defensive depth and reserves will remain necessary at least for the foreseeable future.

The information revolution is hardly irrelevant—it is a major component of the ongoing lethality increase at the dawn of the twenty-first century, and this increase is producing much higher casualties in non–modern-system militaries. But new information has not threatened modern system militaries to nearly the same degree, and this difference in vulnerability is increasing the gulf in real military capability between the two over time. Better information, like greater firepower and mobility, is thus rendering the modern system more, not less, important.

Dyadic Imbalance in Firepower, Mobility, or Information

The discussion above focuses on systemic technological change. But what about dyadic imbalance? Can superior weapons trump force employment? In principle, they have to. If one side were literally invulnerable but the other not, then technological advantage alone would be decisive. M1A2 tanks against flintlock muskets would be a technologically determined slaughter.

In practical terms, however, the margin of supremacy needed to trump force employment has never been available in the post-1900 era, and is unlikely to become so anytime soon. Competitive pressures give all states incentives to innovate technologically or to copy others' equipment. As a result, the actual asymmetry in fielded technology is rarely decisive. The 1991 Gulf War, fought between the world's only superpower and a developing state, posed the greatest measured technology gap of the postwar record, yet even here only twelve years separated the average introduction date of American and Iraqi weapons. None of the other post-1956 conflicts for which data are available display even a six-year average gap, and the median asymmetry is less than three.[63]

Nor is the near future likely to be radically different. Key precision guidance and information technologies are already diffusing through the international system. Even today, modern terminally guided top-attack antitank weapons are already available on the international arms market for anyone with the money and the inclination, as are laser-guided bombs, cruise missiles, antiradiation missiles for air defense suppression, jammers, multispectral obscurants, and decoys, to name but a few.[64] Commercial satellites now offer to any buyer image resolution fine enough to identify individual automobiles from outer space, and still better imagery is coming.[65] Data processing for communications and battle management is getting cheaper and faster every year, with an ever-widening range of international vendors available from which to choose.[66] The United States now enjoys a commanding lead in each of these technologies, but its ability to preserve today's margin indefinitely is less clear, especially as the civilian economy becomes a more important source of military technological innovation, and as globalization speeds the spread of civilian technology.[67]

How big a gap, though, is needed to induce decisive effects? The answer depends on force employment. The modern system can compensate for substantial technical inferiority. Suppression, for example, can reduce hostile firing rates by a factor of seven or more;[68] cover and concealment can reduce the enemy's effective range by multiple kilometers.[69] This is equivalent to at least ten to twenty years of technological progress, or as much as twice the greatest actual asymmetry on record.[70] Modern-system militaries can thus overcome even very superior weapons in the hands of non–modern-system opponents.

Conversely, non–modern-system militaries are fully exposed to their opponents' weapons. Against exposed targets, superior weapons can have much more decisive effects—especially when wielded by a modern-system force that can protect itself from preemptive fires. It is when *neither* side uses the modern system, however, that dyadic technology comes into its own. A modern-system military will often defeat a non–modern-system opponent even without superior weapons—technical superiority makes victory more one-sided but is neither necessary nor sufficient in itself. When *both* sides are exposed, however, marginal differences in the quality—or quantity (see below)—of their weapons becomes decisive.[71]

When *both* sides use the modern system, on the other hand, neither side is exposed to the full, proving-ground potential of their opponent's technology. Two-sided modern-system warfare displays a powerful tendency toward contained offensives with modest territorial gains that grow linearly with casualties and duration. To overcome this tendency and induce either breakthrough or zero ground gain would require extraordinary weapons effects; the inability to exploit a technology's full potential against such opposition makes this unlikely.

This is not to say that superior technology is irrelevant: even here, better equipment helps. But it helps only on the margin. High capability along all three dimensions of territory, casualties, and time requires breakthrough or the utter shattering of an attack at its line of departure, and neither extreme is likely when both sides use the modern system.

What about warfare with grossly mismatched air forces? The United States has several times faced opponents with little or no air capability, and many expect this to be increasingly common. The virtual absence of a major branch of modern military organization can belie the nominal age or sophistication of an opponent's weapons overall; is one-sided command of the air sufficient to trump force employment and determine outcomes in itself?

Certainly air supremacy is a major asset and conveys important advantages—especially when combined with modern-system ground operations. This combination was decisive in Afghanistan in 2001–02, where unchallenged American air power teamed with sizeable and generally capable ground forces to defeat the Taliban.[72] Predominant air power can make an enormous difference in an otherwise balanced ground confrontation.

Air supremacy also has important limitations, however. In Afghanistan, America's allies were usually their enemies' equals tactically, but not always. Where allied Afghan ground forces were tactically overmatched—that is, where al Qaeda's grasp of modern-system methods exceeded America's allies'—even unopposed precision air power often proved insufficient. At Arghestan Bridge on December 5, 2001, for example, repeated assaults by an untrained Pashtun militia faction failed to take dug-in, covered, and concealed al Qaeda defensive positions in spite of heavy American air support; only when better-trained troops took over the offensive did the objective fall.[73] In the opening action of Operation ANACONDA, Muhammed Zia's hastily trained Afghans were pinned down and ultimately thrown back by heavy fire from well-entrenched al Qaeda defenders in the ridge-lines around Shirkankeyl, notwithstanding American precision air strikes.[74] In both cases the al Qaeda defenders enjoyed a significant skill advantage that even very one-sided American air power was unable to trump.

Even so, the al Qaeda defenders in these actions took heavy casualties from air attack (as did German trench garrisons under Allied artillery barrages on the western front). The Afghan attackers at Arghestan Bridge and ANACONDA, moreover, were under pressure to move quickly; had the offensives been delayed for more extensive preliminary air attacks, they would presumably have fared better. Given enough time, one-sided pounding from the air can eventually wear down any defense—even a modern-system one. And the weaker the surviving defenses, the less predominant the attacking ground force need be to prevail, and the smaller their losses in doing so. Against modern-system defenses, however, even twenty-first-century air power cannot bring victory *quickly*. This makes it impossible for combatants with air supremacy to escape the tradeoff between time and territorial gain or casualties. In fact, it can take months for an unsupported air campaign to induce even 20–30 percent attrition on even a moderately well-concealed opponent, as NATO discovered in its seventy-eight-day air campaign in Kosovo in 1999.[75] Radically asymmetrical air forces are thus a special case of the more general relationship between technological asymmetry and capability in modern-system warfare: it certainly helps, but it cannot provide simultaneous high capability on all three dimensions against a modern-system opponent.[76]

PREPONDERANCE AND THE MODERN SYSTEM

Preponderance also matters, though again its effects differ radically with force employment. Taken alone, superior numbers help, but they are neither necessary nor sufficient for success.

Preponderance is unnecessary because modern-system attackers can break through a non–modern-system defense without it. Even numerically inferior attackers can manufacture local advantages via differential concentration; with modern-system exposure reduction, such advantages are enough to take ground. Against a shallow, forward, non–modern-system defense, this local advantage can be exploited before the defender can counterconcentrate, enabling the invader to rupture the defense and gain access to the defender's crucial infrastructure behind the front.

Nor is preponderance sufficient. Modern weapons are so lethal that even a handful can wipe out much larger formations if the latter are caught in the open and fail to suppress hostile fire. A 1915 machine gun could fill the space in front of it with 400–600 bullets per minute for as many minutes as it had ammunition; a single gun could slaughter whole battalions if they tried to rush it in the open.[77] A single 155-mm howitzer can kill any exposed infantry over an area of more than four football fields in just two minutes; massing more troops in the area would only raise the toll.[78] A single 1960s-era M60A1 tank can destroy ten to fifteen T62s in just five minutes if the latter are caught halted in the open within 1000 meters.[79] In principle, even such enormous firepower can eventually be saturated with more targets than the shooters can kill, but the costs are staggering. Few states are willing to lose twenty to hundred or more of their own soldiers for each of their opponent's, and few armies can consistently motivate troops to such suicidal self-sacrifice.[80] In practical terms, armies that cannot reduce their exposure thus cannot compensate by saturating their opponents' firepower with sheer numbers. Without modern-system exposure reduction, even very preponderant forces thus cannot survive long enough to make their numbers tell.

Moreover, even with modern-system exposure reduction, offensive preponderance cannot create breakthrough against a modern-system defense. At the tactical level, modern-system defenses are very powerful; even modern-system attackers require local superiorities to advance against a modern-system defender. Depth and reserves, however, enable modern-system defenders to erase attackers' local numerical advantages via counterconcentration. This means that attackers must eventually mount assaults at local force balances no greater than their theaterwide edge; only the largest invaders outnumber defenders by enough to advance against a modern-system defense without a boost from differential concentration. Modern-system defensive operations also saddle attackers with flank-defense costs that increase with the depth of advance. Extremely preponderant attackers may be able to advance even without differential concentration, but even they must still defend the flanks of this advance against counterattack. Large defensive reserve withholds and the time afforded by defensive depth enable modern-system defenders to threaten counterattack against any part of these flanks, which in turn requires attackers to defend them in their entirety. The longer the flanks, the greater the troop diversion this requires, and the longer the advance, the longer the flanks. If the defense is deep enough, eventually any attacker can be halted by this ever-increasing overhead cost.[81]

Nor can *defensive* preponderance preclude ground loss to a modern-system *attack*. Differential concentration combined with modern-system offensive tactics allow almost any attacker to take *some* ground while the defender redeploys. Against a modern-system defense, attackers cannot take enough ground quickly enough to break through, but the defensive elasticity that prevents breakthrough is bought at the price of forward defenses that are too weak to stop a preponderant, differentially concentrated modern-system attack cold in its tracks. The only way to hold a modern-system attacker to zero ground gain would be to predeploy everywhere, simultaneously, a forward defense large enough to stymie the largest force the attacker could mass against any one point alone. To do this would require an enormously preponderant defense: against an attacker who concentrated half its forces against 10 percent of the theater frontage, a defender would require a theaterwide numerical advantage of nearly 3:1 to succeed in this way.[82] In practical terms, modern-system attacks can be contained, but they cannot be denied some ground gain, regardless of the defender's troop strength.

This is not to say that preponderance is irrelevant, however. At the margin, superior numbers always help—whatever one's force employment, more troops are better than fewer (though the benefit can be trivially small for non–modern-system armies). For modern-system militaries who can reduce their exposure, preponderance enables attackers to extend their territorial gains, grinding their way further through a defense.

This is especially significant where both sides use the modern system. Breakthrough is typically impossible against a modern-system defense, but the more preponderant the attacker, the longer a contained advance can be sustained before defensive counterconcentration can halt it. A very preponderant attacker can eventually push even an unbroken modern-system defender out of the theater if the numerical imbalance is large enough. Without breakthrough, this advance comes at a price in casualties and prolonged fighting, but where both sides use the modern system, only preponderance can provide large offensive territorial gains—and preponderance is often the determining factor in such conflicts.

The above pertains mostly to the force-to-force ratio (FFR); what about the force-to-space ratio (FSR)? Here, too, the same basic logic applies. Low FSRs offer attackers an opportunity, but to exploit the opportunity requires modern-system exposure reduction.

Measured as troops per linear kilometer, a low FSR increases the local FFR attackers can obtain at the point of attack. Measured as troops per square kilometer, a low FSR offers attackers gaps through which to maneuver against the defenders' flanks and rear.[83] Both can help a modern-system attacker at the margin.[84] But if the attacker instead maneuvers en masse in the open, neither advantage can survive the withering firepower of modern weapons. Even the highest local FFR will rarely saturate the killing power of an unhindered defender. And even a very porous defense will rarely be so vaporous as to allow a massed, exposed attacker to reach its objectives without coming under fire. If modern defensive weapons are allowed to fire at their full, proving-ground potential, then their density over the ground will be of secondary import. Attackers simply cannot walk into shooting galleries and expect to survive, whatever the density of the defense, and whatever their own preponderance—for either a low FSR or a high FFR to matter, attackers must find a way to reduce the proving-ground lethality of their opponents' weapons, and this requires the modern system.

So preponderance cannot ordinarily trump force employment. Preponderance always helps, ceteris paribus, but it rarely overcomes disadvantageous force employment choices. Does this mean that the same dispositions would suffice against any attack, however preponderant—or that the same offensive methods would suit regardless of an attacker's numbers? No: modern-system principles are needed regardless of preponderance, but the worse the numerical imbalance, the more aggressively one must implement those principles to avoid disaster. Consider defensive depth. Depth is a tradeoff for defenders: the deeper the defense, the lower the risk of breakthrough but the lighter the forward defense at any given point, and thus the more ground an attacker can take before being halted by counterconcentration. To minimize attacker ground gain, defenders need enough depth to preclude breakthrough, but depth beyond that minimum yields unnecessary territorial gains. The less preponderant the attacker, the less ground the attack can take before being halted, and thus the less depth is needed to ensure against breakthrough. Astute defenders will build in a substantial cushion, defending in more depth than they think literally necessary in order to ensure against miscalculation. Still, a defender at numerical parity will typically need less depth than one outnumbered by 2:1. In general, the modern system's strengths are bought at the price of disadvantages in important (if ultimately secondary) qualities: defensive reserves (much like depth) reduce the odds of breakthrough yet enable a contained attacker to take more ground; offensive exposure reduction comes at a price in speed; differential concentration yields higher local FFRs at the point of attack but creates vulnerabilities to counterattack elsewhere. The more dangerous the situation, the less one can afford to entertain secondary ambitions and the more one must accept the modern-system's disadvantages in order to secure its central virtues. Hence the worse the numerical odds, the more completely the modern system must be implemented—and vice versa.

PROSPECTS FOR CHANGE

While the relationships I outline above have been stable since 1900, they are not eternal.[85] After all, the modern system itself is a response to a particular complex of technological changes in the mid to late nineteenth century; presumably it can be overturned by some comparably sweeping technological changes somewhere in the post-twentieth-century future. What would be required, and is it forthcoming any time soon?

The key requirement would be the capacity to make terrain irrelevant. The complexity of the Earth's surface, the opacity of much of its cover to sensors, the cluttered, intermingled nature of the background it creates for surveillance, and the ability of terrain to obstruct fire are what create the potential for modern-system force employment to defeat firepower and slow movement. If it really did become possible to see and destroy anything on the Earth's surface regardless of cover or concealment or intermingling, then force employment would lose much of its importance, and either superior technology or numerical preponderance would come to dominate continental warfare.[86]

Some believe that such transparency is near at hand: RMA advocates such as retired Admiral William Owens, former vice chairman of the Joint Chiefs of Staff, claim it will soon be possible to see and destroy anything in a 200-by-200-mile area.[87] I have argued above that this is unlikely anytime soon, given the opacity of much cover to even developmental sensor types, the problems of intermingling and collateral damage in urban areas, and the opportunities that cover provides to facilitate technical countermeasure use.

Yet this conclusion rests on the properties of known technologies and programs now at least under development. The great majority of the latter are intended to improve weapon and sensor effectiveness against massed targets in the open (especially at night and in adverse weather);[88] a systematic shift in priorities toward covered, concealed, intermingled targets might eventually produce significant improvement. For the foreseeable future (perhaps the next ten to twenty-five years), there is little basis to expect this. In the longer term, however, more is possible—and at least the possibility of transparency to the degree that Adm. Owens describes cannot be ruled out sometime later in the twenty-first century.

Two points seem clear, however. One is that the only technical development that could fundamentally undermine the theory here would be one that made terrain transparent to vision and fire—this is the key criterion bounding the theory's temporal applicability. The second point is that this is unlikely to happen soon. For the foreseeable future, the relationships presented here should remain critical to real military capability.

SUMMARY OF THE NEW THEORY

A complete formal specification of the logic above is presented in the appendix; here I summarize the results graphically and qualitatively to facilitate discussion in the testing chapters to follow. In particular, table 4.1 outlines the theory's key predictions qualitatively; Figures 4.1 through 4.3 summarize important interactions graphically using results from the formal version of the theory in the appendix.

Figure 4.1 plots one dimension of capability, attacker territorial gain, as a function of systemic technological sophistication for three different force employment combinations: modern-system attack vs. non–modern-system defense; two-sided modern-system use; and modern-system defense vs. non–modern-system attack.[89] In each case, only modest deviations from modern-system norms are considered, and only at the tactical level; greater departures would produce quick breakthrough or shut-down offensives, masking the effects of further technological change.[90] The results show graphically the effects described qualitatively above: technology drives a wedge between the real capability of modern-system and non–modern-system militaries. For 1910-era technology, moderately non–modern-system tactics hurt: attackers gain twice as much ground against non–modern-system defenders; defenders yield half as much ground to non–modern-system attackers. By the 1940s, however, the effect is much greater. Now a moderately non–modern-system defense yields twelve times the ground of a modern-system one; non–modern-system attackers gain only 8 percent as much ground as modern-system ones; the two differ by a factor of 143. By 2000 the difference has ballooned to a factor of more than 2,000. Between modern-system opponents, on the other hand, systemic technological change has little effect: on balance, territorial gain rises then falls slightly, but the net consequence of ninety years of technological change is less than a 15 percent difference in ground gain. Moreover, technology has precisely opposite effects depending on force employment: for one-sided modern-system use by attackers, systemic technological change powerfully benefits offense; for one-sided modern-system use by defenders, the very same technologies powerfully benefit defense.

Figure 4.2 presents a similar analysis for dyadic technological imbalance, plotting attacker territorial gain as a function of the difference between the mean introduction date of the attacker's and defender's weapons (positive values mean

TABLE 4.1.
Central Predictions

	Attacker:	
	Modern System *(low exposure/moderate closure rate;* narrow frontage)*	*Non–Modern System* *(exposed/high closure rate; broad frontage)*
Defender: Modern System (deep, large reserve withhold; low exposure)	Contained Offensive: • attacker, defender casualties moderate; increase with territorial gain • moderate territorial gain, limited by attacker preponderance • potentially long campaign duration • little sensitivity to technology • moderate sensitivity to preponderance *Dimensions of capability trade off; limited sensitivity to materiel*	Contained Offensive: • very high attacker casualties; very low defender casualties • low territorial gain • short campaign duration • attacker casualties increase rapidly with advancing technology • little sensitivity to preponderance: prohibitive attacker numerical advantage required to prevail *High-to-very-high defensive capability; low-to-very-low offensive capability; how low/high depends on technology*

Non–Modern System (shallow, small reserve withhold; high exposure)	Breakthrough:
	• low attacker casualties
	• exploitation prospects improve with advancing technology
	• if exploitation succeeds:
	  ▪ very high defender casualties
	  ▪ very large territorial gains
	  ▪ very short campaign
	• if exploitation fails:
	  ▪ high defender casualties
	  ▪ territorial gains proportional to preponderance
	  ▪ moderate campaign duration
	• little sensitivity to preponderance: inferior attacker can prevail
	
	Low-to-very-low defensive capability; high-to-very-high offensive capability; how low/high depends on technology
		Conditionally Contained Offensive:
		• casualties, territorial gain, campaign duration sensitive to technology, preponderance
		  ▪ if marked numerical, technological imbalance, then attrition, territorial, duration outcomes favor superior side
		  ▪ otherwise, high defender but very high attacker casualties; low territorial gain; potentially long duration
		  ▪ casualties increase with territorial gain, duration
		  ▪ duration increases with territorial gain
		  ▪ breakthrough possible if attacker materiel very superior, but exploitation unlikely
		
		Dimensions of capability trade off; significant sensitivity to materiel

*"Closure rate" or "assault velocity" can be used as an index of achievable exposure reduction in offensive tactics. Modern-system exposure reduction is time-consuming, hence high-velocity, high-closure-rate tactics imply high exposure: see the appendix.

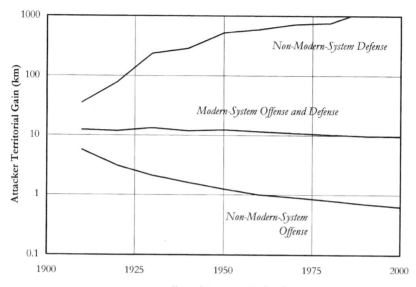

Figure 4.1. Effect of Systemic Technology

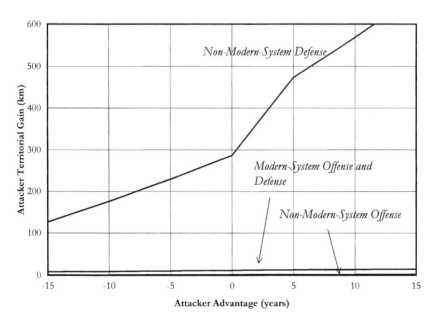

Figure 4.2. Effect of Dyadic Technology

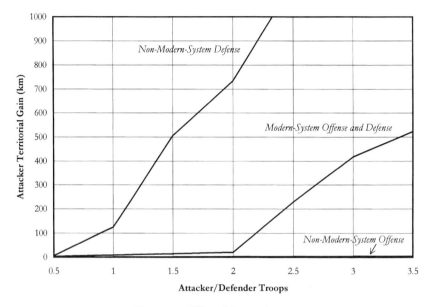

Figure 4.3. Effect of Preponderance

superior attackers, negative values mean superior defenders).[91] Results are given for the same three force employment combinations as figure 4.1. Superior technology always helps: the slopes of all three curves are monotonically positive. The advantage, however, is minor for non–modern-system militaries. Even a fifteen-year edge—greater than the United States enjoyed over Iraq in 1991—can add only a few hundred meters to the territorial gain of a non–modern-system attacker fighting a modern-system defense. Where superior technology comes into its own is in punishing the mistakes of a non–modern-system opponent: the same fifteen-year attacker edge more than doubles territorial gain when modern-system attackers use it against non–modern-system defenders. Like systemic technology, dyadic technology is thus important mostly in interaction with force employment: the more severe the technological imbalance, the more severe the consequences of non–modern-system behavior.

Finally, figure 4.3 considers preponderance, plotting territorial gain as a function of the theaterwide ratio of attacker:defender troop strength for the same three force employment combinations.[92] Preponderance, too, always helps: the slopes of all three curves are monotonically positive. Again, however, the effects are minor for non–modern-system attackers against modern-system defenses: a factor-of-seven increase in preponderance yields only a few kilometers of additional ground gain. Conversely, for non–modern-system defenders against modern-system attackers, offensive preponderance is catastrophic: ground gain rises by a factor of more than three hundred over the same interval. Preponderance's effects are thus radically different as a function of force employment—it can be decisive or almost immaterial as a function of even the modest, exclusively tactical-level variations considered here.

Of course, the ideas presented above are but informed conjectures pending systematic empirical testing. To begin the process of testing, chapter 4 thus turns to the first of three historical case studies: Operation MICHAEL, the German offensive in the Second Battle of the Somme.

CHAPTER FIVE

Operation MICHAEL—The Second Battle of the Somme, March 21–April 9, 1918

HOW DO THE RESPECTIVE THEORIES fare against the evidence? In this chapter I present the first of three case method tests. Operation MICHAEL, the German offensive in the Second Battle of the Somme, fought on the western front between March 21 and April 9, 1918, is a case with special leverage for the theories under study here. The results, which tend to corroborate the new theory but contradict the orthodox alternatives, thus warrant a greater shift in confidence than would typically be possible from a single case study.

I develop this argument in six steps. First, I discuss the problem of selection bias in case method research and motivate my selection of Operation MICHAEL as an Ecksteinian critical case for theories of military capability, which mitigates the potential for bias. Second, I outline briefly the main events of the case. Third, I develop values for the key independent variables associated with the competing theories. Fourth, I compare the battle's actual outcome with the respective theories' predictions given these values, assessing the relative fit between prediction and observation. Fifth, I consider two other explanations of the battle's outcome that have played prominent roles in its historiography. Finally, I conclude with a summary assessment of the case's implications for the theories under study.

WHY MICHAEL?

Case method poses a danger of selection bias: a theory's success (or failure) in a small sample might be an artifact of having chosen misleading or unrepresentative cases. How do we know that a theory's performance in a selected case is a valid test of its merits for the larger universe of cases generally? One way to mitigate such bias is to adopt Harry Eckstein's method of *critical-case* analysis: by picking cases with extreme values on the key independent variables, one creates conditions where theories should be at their strongest (or weakest), making it unusually illuminating if a theory fails to perform as expected. A *most-likely* case is one where extreme values put a theory on its strongest possible ground—if it is going to be right anywhere, it should be right here. For such cases, a valid theory should fail very rarely; if we nevertheless observe failure, this surprising result warrants a greater loss of confidence in the theory than would a single disconfirmatory observation under less ideal conditions. Conversely, a *least-likely* case is one where extreme values make the theory unusually unlikely to succeed—even if the theory were generally valid, under such unfavorable conditions it might well fail anyway. For such cases, we would expect weak theories to be overwhelmed by confounding effects; if we nevertheless observe successful prediction, this surprise would warrant a greater gain of confidence than would a single confirmation under less extreme conditions.[1]

Operation MICHAEL provides both a most-likely case for orthodox theories of capability and a least-likely case for the new theory, making it an especially useful test. In particular, it provides a very close fit to what preponderance and orthodox offense-defense theorists would consider ideal defense-dominance. It was fought virtually without tanks and with very limited contributions from ground attack aircraft, by armies consisting basically of infantry and artillery. The attacker was burdened with one of the least offense-favorable force ratios of a war known for its infamous defensive stalemates. If a combination of technology and numerical imbalance were ever going to preclude successful attack, it should have been here.[2] If orthodox theories fail to predict the outcome under conditions so strongly matched to those they describe as the paradigm of defensiveness, then the case poses an unusually strong challenge to their validity.[3]

Conversely, Operation MICHAEL provides a difficult hurdle for a theory emphasizing force employment. The new theory predicts offensive success in March 1918: as I will show, the British deployed a forward, shallow, exposed defense that the Germans struck with a low-exposure, modern-system attack. Yet the technology and numerical balance were so apparently defensive here that it would not be surprising if these effects were to overwhelm the offensive influence of the two sides' force employment—even if the latter really *were* the single best explanation under ordinary circumstances. On the contrary, what would be surprising is if force employment proved determinant even under conditions as apparently adverse as March 1918. MICHAEL thus offers a *least-likely case* for the new theory: to hold under conditions as apparently unfavorable as these provides a stronger corroboration than a single case study could otherwise provide. The fit between the case's specific characteristics and the nature of the theories under test thus enables a challenging test from a single case and helps mitigate the danger that selection bias will taint the results.

Finally, MICHAEL is intrinsically interesting for the history of the First World War and twentieth-century military affairs generally. World War I was a watershed in the history of modern warfare, and the German Spring Offensives were perhaps the pivotal event of the last year of the war. The Second Battle of the Somme broke the three-year trench stalemate on the western front and inaugurated an eight-month period in which more ground changed hands than in the rest of the war in the west put together. The battle thus had a major influence on the final outcome of the conflict. As Martin Middlebrook put it, "21 March 1918 was the beginning of the end of the First World War. When the German

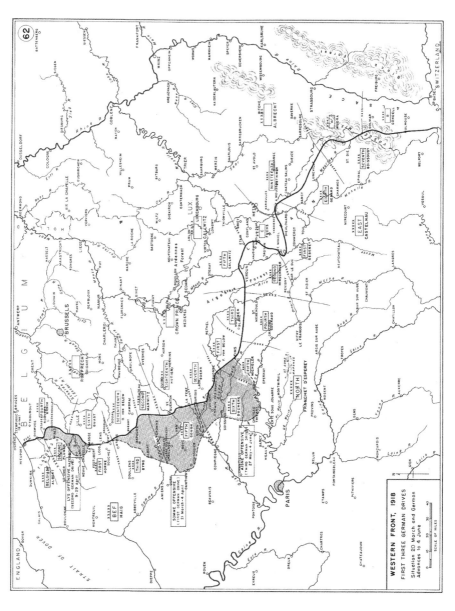

Map 1. Operation MICHAEL in the theater of war, spring 1918

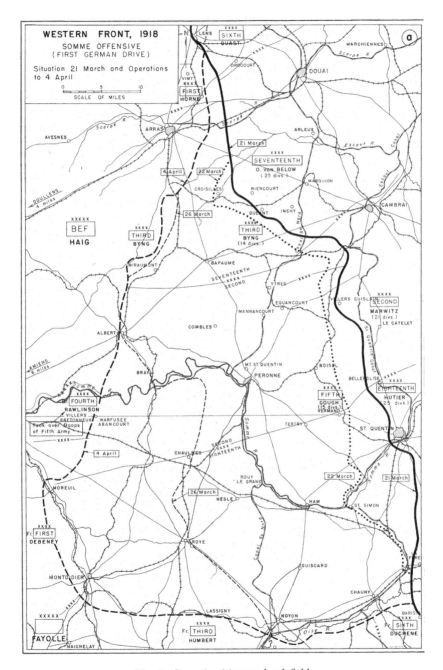

Map 2. Operation MICHAEL battlefield

storm troops crossed the shell-battered remnants of the British front line a few minutes before 10 A.M. that day, they set in motion a chain of events that was to end the war."[4] The Second Battle of the Somme was thus a central event for modern military history. While my primary purpose is to use the case to shed light on theory, it is thus also a valuable opportunity to use theory to shed light on an important case.

OVERVIEW OF EVENTS, MARCH 21 TO APRIL 9, 1918

The Second Battle of the Somme was the first of what would be four major German offensives in the spring of 1918.[5] This represented a major shift in German strategy in the west, which had been largely defensive following their defeat on the Marne and the ensuing race to the sea in 1914.[6] Two key events led the Germans to reevaluate this course by the end of 1917. On April 2, 1917, the United States had declared war on Germany following the German announcement of unrestricted submarine warfare on February 1. The subsequent failure of the submarine campaign to strangle Britain meant that Germany would eventually face the combined power of Britain, France, and the United States, while facing an increasingly constrictive Allied naval blockade, and with an Austro-Hungarian ally of ever-weakening military potential. On December 16, however, the Treaty of Brest-Litovsk took Russia out of the war, freeing more than forty German divisions for potential use on the western front.[7] With diplomatic options stalemated following the election of David Lloyd George on a total victory platform in Britain, Germany concluded that its only choice was to attack in the west: "[I]n 1918 Germany would decide the issue of the war with an offensive victory in France before the Americans arrived in force. It was the Schlieffen Plan again: a gamble under acute pressure of time, making use of a temporary superiority of numbers that in itself was far from overwhelming."[8]

To implement this policy, Germany planned to begin as soon as the weather would permit with an attack by three armies (the Seventeenth, Second, and Eighteenth) against the southern wing of the British Expeditionary Force on a fifty-mile front between Arras and La Fere. After breaking through, the attackers were to drive northwest, rolling up the British front from south to north, splitting the British and French armies, and compelling the British to fall back onto the Channel ports.[9]

The British forces opposite this attack comprised the southernmost two of the four British armies in France, under the overall command of Field Marshal Sir Douglas Haig. On the extreme right was the Fifth Army under General Sir Hubert Gough; to their left was the Third Army under General Sir Julian Byng. Haig's plan was to stand on the defensive, with a priority on defending the Channel coast against a direct attack, which might sever the army from its communications with Britain. If attacked in the south, Haig intended the Third and Fifth armies to hold their ground. If they could not, they were to withdraw slowly to the line Peronne-Somme River-Crozat Canal (some five to ten miles behind their initial positions), which was to be "held at all costs."[10]

The offensive began at 0440 with a five-hour barrage by 6,473 German guns. At 0940, the German infantry assault commenced, led by specially trained *stosstruppen* or "storm troopers." By midnight, these units had reached the final prepared defenses in the Third Army sector and had broken through the prepared defense on a roughly 2,000-yard front in the Fifth Army zone.[11] Withdrawn overnight by Gen. Gough to an unprepared position on the Crozat Canal, the Fifth Army proved unable to hold and was driven into a general retreat by the morning of March 23. The Third Army followed suit, and for the first time since 1914, open warfare returned to the western front.[12]

The British retreat degenerated quickly into a near rout, as units whose entire military experience had been trench-bound suddenly found themselves in a war of movement, albeit one conducted at the speed of walking infantry.[13] This withdrawal continued in considerable disorder for more than a week, during which time a three-mile gap opened between the British right and the French left.[14] The apparent danger of a separation between the British and French armies, and the associated loss of composure in the respective Allied headquarters, led to a series of high-level conferences resulting eventually in the establishment of a single supreme Allied commander in Ferdinand Foch.[15]

In the meantime, however, the German offensive had begun to lose impetus. Under the combined pressure of attrition, physical exhaustion, and the gradual accumulation of British and French reserves in the threatened sector, the German pursuit finally ground to a halt on March 28. A series of renewed drives between March 29 and April 4 gained little ground in exchange for heavy German losses, and on April 5 Ludendorff canceled further offensive action in the sector, effectively ending the first of the German Spring Offensives.[16]

INDEPENDENT VARIABLES

How do these events compare with the respective theories' predictions? To answer this question, I first characterize the battle in terms of the key independent variables of technology, numerical imbalance, and force employment.

Weapon Technology in Operation MICHAEL

Weapon technology in MICHAEL was typical of the First World War and afforded the German attackers no meaningful edge over the British defenders.

The formal version of the new theory characterizes technology via the mean date of introduction for the two sides' major weapons systems (see appendix). By this measure, the Germans and British were nearly indistinguishable in

MICHAEL, with scores of 1908.7 and 1908.9, respectively. These values are little different from those for typical battles of the great stalemate. The average introduction dates for weapons used in the First Battle of the Somme in July 1916, for example, were 1908.9 for the British attackers and 1907.2 for the German defenders.[17]

Nor does MICHAEL's technology look attacker-favorable when approached in orthodox theory's terms. Dyadic technology theorists would certainly find little in March 1918 to account for a German breakthrough. Not only were the introduction dates for the two sides' weapons almost the same, but their more detailed performance characteristics also tended to balance out. By 1918, German field artillery outranged comparable British guns by about 3,000 yards, but in heavy artillery the British 60-pounder gun and 6-inch howitzer enjoyed a range advantage of some 6,500 yards over the standard German 15-cm howitzer and 21-cm mortar.[18] German trench mortars were more mobile than the British Stokes Projector, but British hand and rifle grenades were generally thought to be superior to their German counterparts following the introduction of the improved No. 5 Mills Bomb, the No. 23 Mills Rifle Grenade, and the No. 24 Rifle Grenade early in 1916.[19] German heavy machine guns proved more effective in combat than did British weapons, but this was more a matter of tactics and training than of weapon quality per se.[20] The British Lewis light machine gun was lighter than the German Model 08/15 (31 pounds vs. 43) but less well suited to sustained firing; nevertheless, German troops with access to captured Lewis guns often preferred them to the Model 08/15.[21] In both armies, light machine guns were standard issue at the platoon level by 1918.[22] Technology is never identical for any two armies, but it is hard to see any difference in March 1918 that would imply an important advantage for the Germans.

Systemic offense-defense theorists, by contrast, point not to local imbalances but to broadly shared levels of prevailing technology and the characteristic or dominant weapon types these imply. For the first half of the twentieth century, tanks, ground-attack aircraft, artillery, and infantry small arms are usually seen as the dominant weapons; the first two are said to conduce to offensive advantage, and the latter two to defensive advantage. In these terms, World War I is usually seen as the defining example of technologically determined defense-dominance given its domination by infantry and artillery; in these respects Operation MICHAEL was a typical First World War engagement.

Certainly MICHAEL was fought between infantry- and artillery-rich armies. Of the 111 divisions engaged, 108 were infantry, the remaining three being British cavalry.[23] Moreover, since a World War I cavalry division had only one-third the manpower of an infantry division, in rough "division equivalent" terms over 99 percent of the major maneuver units were infantry.[24] These maneuver units were lavishly supported by artillery. In fact, by 1918 over 25 percent of total combat manpower in the BEF were in the artillery.[25] For Operation MICHAEL, this represented a force of 2,686 field and heavy artillery pieces in the Third and

Fifth Army inventories, with about 1,400 short-range trench mortars in forward positions.[26] The Germans opposite them fielded a total of 6,473 guns and about 3,500 trench mortars.[27] World War I is sometimes described as an "artillerist's war," and the two armies in the Second Battle of the Somme were well supported by artillery even by World War I standards.[28]

By contrast, tanks were few in number and primitive in technology; moreover, the few tanks present for MICHAEL were held overwhelmingly by the British defenders, not the German attackers. The Germans deployed a grand total of nine tanks in support of a seventy-four-division offensive, five of which were captured British vehicles.[29] The British defenders had more than the German attackers, but even they deployed a tiny number in absolute terms. The Third and Fifth armies together disposed of some 370 tanks, parceled out in small groups of about 36 vehicles each. In theory, these were to be held in reserve for possible use in local counterattacks.[30] Few, however, saw any action, and there is no evidence of their having played a significant role in the battle.[31]

Moreover, even where present in quantity, the tank in 1918 was hardly a mature technology. As noted in chapter 4, First World War tanks had neither the range nor the reliability to produce decisive battlefield effects, and the intense heat, noise, and fumes of 1918-era tanks limited crew endurance to at most a few hours of intense fighting. By 1918, moreover, German antitank gunnery posed a severe threat to British tanks. Taken together, tanks' mechanical unreliability, vulnerability, and crew exhaustion made for very heavy loss rates in 1918.[32] As John Terraine put it: "It is clear that both mechanically and humanly, the tank of 1918 was not a war-winning weapon."[33]

Aircraft, by contrast, were present in considerable numbers on both sides. The Germans concentrated some 730 airplanes behind their offensive frontage, while the Royal Flying Corps opposed them with about 580 machines.[34] Like the tank, however, aircraft played a marginal role in Operation MICHAEL, for three reasons. First, poor flying weather kept both air forces on the ground during the early, decisive phase of the battle. Second, technology for ground attack— the form of airpower generally considered offensive in the literature—was extremely primitive in 1918 and incapable of decisive impact even where the weather permitted flight operations. And third, the net effect of airpower in MICHAEL, while marginal, clearly favored the British defenders, not the German attackers. It thus cannot explain the success of the German offensive, even if it were otherwise a powerful or important weapon in 1918.

As for the first of these points, a dense fog kept both sides' aircraft grounded until early afternoon on the crucial opening day of the offensive. By the time the fog had cleared and the first sorties were launched, German infantry had already overrun more than a third of the entire defensive system.[35] Perhaps more important, as a result of this the troops on the ground had already become so intermingled that neither air force proved able to bring much fire to bear.[36] Over the successive days, aircraft did gradually become more involved, but the success of the infantry advance continued to interfere with the application of airpower. The Germans, for example, were hampered by the need to move airfields forward to keep up with the unprecedented pace of the advance, and they found it increasingly difficult to find suitable airfield sites as that advance carried them into terrain that had been furrowed for trench warfare.[37] The British, meanwhile, faced difficulties of their own in moving their operations back to avoid being overrun.[38]

Even when the combatants managed to get airplanes into the air and over a recognizable target, the technology available for direct ground attack was too primitive to provide decisive effects.[39] The primary purpose of aircraft in World War I was reconnaissance—not direct attack of ground targets, which represented at best a secondary or even tertiary mission. In particular, aircraft had become an almost indispensable element of the artillery targeting system by the middle of the war. The battle to establish control of opposing airspace was considered essential to a successful attack by 1918, but this was because it provided the means of effective artillery employment (especially counterbattery fire), *not* because it opened the opponent to direct attack from the air.[40] A few aircraft were designated as "bombers," but their limited payload and poor accuracy made them marginal contributors to ground operations.[41] Instead, the great majority of ground attack activity consisted of uncoordinated strafing by nonspecialist aircraft, which was widely judged far less effective than artillery spotting in influencing the ground war.[42]

Finally, even where airpower did make itself felt, the larger contribution was made by the British defenders, not the German attackers. By the end of the battle, the British had established virtual air superiority and had begun to use it to harass exposed German infantry packed along roads in the rear, behind the line of contact.[43] In fact, the most commonly discussed effect of airpower in the battle is the frequent mention in German accounts of the impact of British strafing against German march columns late in the battle.[44] If anything, then, airpower may have been a marginally *defensive* weapon in the Second Battle of the Somme. As a whole, however, it is unlikely that aircraft in general had any major effect on the outcome—and especially on the crucial initial penetration, which occurred before either air force became significantly engaged.

Neither of the two main technological innovations often suggested as causes for the breakdown of the great stalemate—tanks and ground-attack aircraft—were thus meaningful contributors in March 1918. The net result was a technology mix little different from that of the preceding three years of trench warfare.

Numerical Imbalance in MICHAEL

The numerical balance in Operation MICHAEL fell well short of the standard rules of thumb used by preponderance theorists to predict offensive success. In fact, the German attackers in March 1918 enjoyed significantly smaller numerical advantages than had Allied attackers in the worst failures of the great stalemate.

For the new theory, the key numerical balance is the ratio of attacker:defender troop strength in the theater of war (the theaterwide "force to force ratio," or FFR; see the appendix). By this measure, the western front balance in March 1918 was about 1.17:1.[45] By contrast, the theaterwide balance in January 1915 was 1.56:1; in 1916 it was 1.33:1; in 1917 it was 1.29:1.[46] The Germans in 1918 thus faced one of the war's most attacker-averse theater numerical balances.

Orthodox preponderance theorists often consider local (as well as theater-wide) balances, balances of particular weapon types (for World War I, especially artillery), and the relationship between these balances and various rules of thumb for offensive adequacy.[47] In none of these terms was MICHAEL's FFR very offense-conducive.

The Germans concentrated a total of sixty-three assault divisions behind their fifty-mile attack frontage (in addition to eleven "positional" divisions considered incapable of offensive action and not assigned to the attack). These were disposed in three waves of thirty-two, eighteen, and thirteen divisions, respectively. Artillery support consisted of 6,473 guns (2,508 of which were heavy caliber) and 3,532 trench mortars. The British Third and Fifth armies opposite this front deployed a total of twenty-seven divisions, of which twenty-one were "on-line" (that is, in prepared defensive positions), and six were in corps- or army-level reserve. In addition, four of the eight British GHQ reserve divisions were located behind the Third and Fifth Army sectors. British local artillery amounted to 2,686 guns (976 heavy) and about 1,400 trench mortars.[48]

These dispositions imply a local FFR of 2.0:1 (i.e., 63:31) in total divisions opposite the attack frontage. If one instead counts only initially engaged divisions (i.e., British "online" and German first wave: those actually in contact at the outset), the local FFR comes to only 1.5:1 (32:21).[49] The local artillery balance, on the other hand, is higher—2.4:1 in guns (and 2.6:1 in heavy caliber pieces), and about 2.5:1 in trench mortars.

To put these figures in context, figure 5.1 depicts the ratios of total divisions opposite the attack frontage, and engaged divisions opposite the attack frontage, for an illustrative sample of major offensives between mid-1915 and early 1918.[50] With the sole exception of Operation MICHAEL, all the data shown represent successful defenses. In fact, these battles include such infamous stalemates as Verdun, the First Battle of the Somme, and Passchendaele. Yet the local FFR for MICHAEL is the second smallest value of any given here—less than *half* that of Verdun in 1916 (i.e., 2.0:1 as opposed to 4.25:1 in total divisions, and 1.5:1 as opposed to 3.25:1 in engaged divisions), and less than 60 percent of the First Somme FFR (3.7:1 and 3.1:1, respectively).

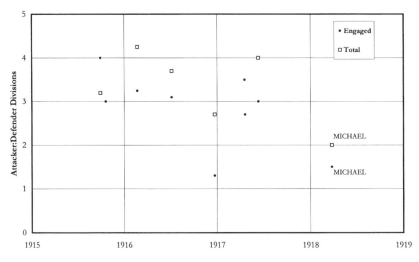

Figure 5.1. Local Force-to-Force Ratios, World War I

Figure 5.2 provides a similar sample of artillery ratios for mid-1915 to early 1918. Again, all values prior to MICHAEL represent successful defenses. The results suggest that while MICHAEL's artillery ratio (2.4:1) was not the very lowest of the war, it was far from the highest and in fact is well below the mean of the available data (3.0:1). By World War I standards, the March 1918 artillery

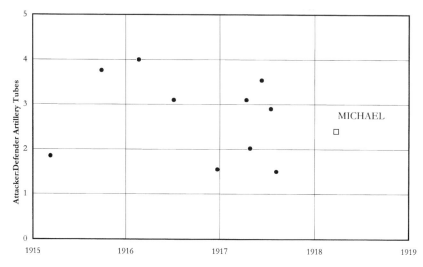

Figure 5.2. Local Artillery Balances, World War I

imbalance was unremarkable: smaller, for example, than that which produced stalemate in the First Battle of the Somme (3.1:1), and only 60 percent of the artillery imbalance at Verdun (4:1).[51]

In strict numerical terms, the two sides were thus unusually closely matched in March 1918. But were there significant imbalances in the quality of the troops behind these numbers? In effect, would quality differences produce a higher FFR in net "combat power" terms than that suggested by their numbers alone?[52]

The answer is no. German troops were generally somewhat better skilled, but only in a small subset of the German Army was the difference in skill an important one, and this subset was far too small to make much difference in the aggregate FFR. In particular, the Germans' army-level *stosstrupp* battalions were made up of specially equipped, specially trained, elite assault troops. These hand-picked specialists were used as instructors prior to the offensive and led the initial attack on March 21. But while clearly superior to either army's regular infantry, the *stosstrupp* battalions comprised only a tiny fraction of the total German forces taking part in the battle: there were not enough of these troops to allocate even a single company-size *sturmblock* to all of the first-wave assault divisions.[53]

Given this, the elite storm troopers' contribution to the gross overall "combat power" available to the attackers could not have been large enough to make a meaningful difference in the FFR. Even if each of these *sturmblocks* was equal in effectiveness to as many as ten times its number of regular infantry, for example, the resulting FFR in "divisional combat power equivalents" would still be less than 2.6:1 for total formations opposite the point of attack, or 2.4:1 for online formations.[54] Even these upper bounds are still well below the mean of the available data for 1915–17.

The remainder of the German Army, while on balance better trained and led than the British Expeditionary Force (BEF), did not enjoy nearly the degree of superiority embodied by the elite *stosstrupp* battalions. Of course, it is difficult to assess the magnitude of the difference quantitatively. It should be noted, however, that the German troops that had failed—with the advantage of a much greater numerical superiority—in Falkenhayn's offensive at Verdun in 1916 were also generally better trained and led than their opponents.[55]

In comparative terms, MICHAEL's FFR was thus unusually modest. It was also well below any of the standard rules of thumb. The best-known of these, the 3:1 rule, holds that at the point of attack, attackers require three times the defender's strength to succeed.[56] Even the upper bound, "quality-adjusted" local FFR of 2.6:1 here is well below this threshold; the ratio of online divisions at the point of attack (1.5:1) is only half the required value. An alternative rule of thumb holds that across the theater as a whole, attackers need 1.5 times the defender's strength to succeed.[57] Here, too, the theaterwide FFR of 1.17:1 is well below the threshold. However one counts and whatever one's standard, the FFR in Operation MICHAEL was very low.

FORCE-TO-SPACE RATIOS

Some preponderance theorists (and a few offense-defense theorists) empha-size troop density, or the "force-to-space ratio" (FSR). For those who consider it, low values are held to favor attackers.[58] In MICHAEL, however, the defender's FSR was higher than many of the most successful defenses of 1915 to 1917 and was certainly not low enough to preclude successful defense.

To see why, first recall that a force-to-space ratio, like a force-to-force ratio, can be measured in many ways. Not only can "force" be measured in any of the ways considered above, but "space" can be measured in linear units of frontage (e.g., miles or yards) or square units of area (square miles or square yards).

These alternative measures of "space," moreover, have very different proper-ties. Linear units of frontage, for example, are convenient for describing the total number of defenders that will encounter an attacker on a given sector. A linear measurement, however, cannot determine a defender's "porousness," or the likelihood of gaps or holes in the defense. This is because linear units yield the same FSR for a single division holding a four-mile front in a single trench line (yielding few gaps), or one division holding the same four-mile front but distrib-uted over one hundred successive lines in depth (yielding many gaps). Square units of area, by contrast, are well suited for assessing gaps, but poorly suited to determining the total number of defenders opposing an advance on a given frontage. One division per square mile, for example, could mean a single divi-sion's worth of troops opposite a one-mile attack frontage, disposed over one mile of depth; or it could mean *five* divisions of troops opposite the same one-mile front, disposed over five miles of depth.

The literature, paradoxically, uses mostly linear units of measure but tends to emphasize porousness (or the availability of "continuous fronts") in its causal logic.[59] To provide the broadest possible perspective, I present both linear and square measures below, but the differences are important to the conclusions drawn for the battle here.

As for the values themselves, at the theater level the Allies' 165 divisions and 15,182 artillery pieces (again excluding the Americans) held a front some 325 miles long in March 1918, stretching from the North Sea near Ostend to the Vosges Mountains in the south.[60] This implies a theaterwide FSR of 0.52 divi-sions and 47 artillery tubes per mile.

These forces were not evenly distributed, however. Haig had preferentially allo-cated the BEF to defend the channel coast, leaving its southern wing less strongly held. The Third and Fifth armies thus together defended a front of 70 miles with a combined force of 30 infantry and 3 cavalry divisions, for a local FSR of 0.44 total divisions per mile.[61] Of these forces, 21 infantry divisions were committed forward in prepared positions (the remainder being in corps, army, or GHQ re-serve). Though dispositions varied, their average depth on March 21 was under 4,500 yards.[62] This implies a local force to space ratio of 0.30 forward divisions per linear mile, or 0.12 forward divisions per square mile, at the point of attack.

The Third and Fifth armies' 2,686 artillery pieces, while nominally assigned to the two armies' frontage as a whole, were disposed centrally enough to concentrate their fire on the subset of that frontage subject to attack on the 21st; the density of defensive artillery able to fire on the attack was thus about 54 tubes per mile of assault frontage.[63]

But how should these values be interpreted? Standard rules of thumb are less established for FSRs than for FFRs. Nevertheless, Basil Liddell Hart, perhaps the best-known force-to-space ratio theorist, estimated that 0.17 to 0.25 forward divisions per linear mile at the point of attack was sufficient for successful defense in World War I.[64] By Liddell Hart's criterion, the MICHAEL FSR (0.30 forward divisions per mile at the point of attack) was thus well above the minimum.

Alternatively, one could compare these FSRs with those of other World War I defenses. Figure 5.3, for example, compares the theaterwide FSR in divisions per linear mile for March 1918 with those of January 1915, 1916, and 1917. The Allied 1918 value of 0.52 is the highest of the three, fully twice that of German defenses in 1915 (0.26 divisions per mile).

Figure 5.4 provides an illustrative sample of forward divisions per linear mile locally at the point of attack for major battles between 1915 and 1918.[65] With the exception of MICHAEL, all the data shown correspond to successful defenses. FSRs for the successful, pre-1918 defenses fall into two rough groups. A set of seven 1917 values between 0.4 and about 0.6 correspond to the Germans' late war Wotan and Flandern positions (e.g., the campaigns of Arras, Passchendaele, and the Nivelle Offensive). The remainder lie between about 0.1 and 0.25 and

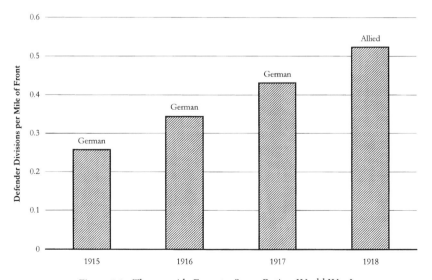

Figure 5.3. Theaterwide Force-to-Space Ratios, World War I

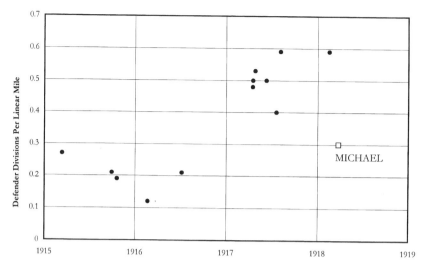

Figure 5.4. Local Force-to-Space Ratios, World War I (Linear)

correspond to battles such as Verdun, the First Battle of the Somme, Neuve Chapelle, and the First Battle of the Aisne. The value for MICHAEL is lower than for the first group, but higher than for the second—and greater than the mean for the data as a whole.

Figure 5.5 compares forward divisions per *square* mile at the point of attack for an illustrative sample of major battles between 1915 and 1918.[66] Again, all

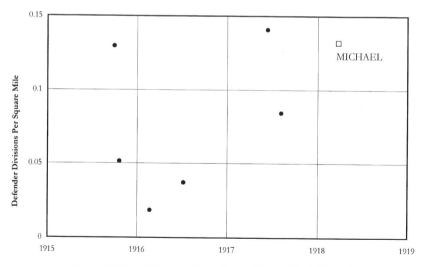

Figure 5.5. Local Force-to-Space Ratios, World War I (Square)

data prior to 1918 represent successful defenses. Yet MICHAEL represents the third highest value shown and is fully 50 percent higher than the mean for the available data (i.e., 0.13 versus 0.08). In square units of area, MICHAEL was thus a higher FSR than even such late-war stalemates as Passchendaele (0.08), while it was *three times* denser than the German defense in the First Battle of the Somme (0.04), and fully *six times* the density of the French defense at Verdun (0.02).

Finally, figure 5.6 provides a sample of defensive artillery tubes locally per mile of assault frontage for major battles between 1915 and early 1918.[67] All data prior to 1918 again represent successful defenses. Here, as in forward divisions per linear mile, Operation MICHAEL (at 54 tubes per mile) is lower than the German 1917 values (which range from 63 in the Battle of the Scarpe to 92 for Passchendaele) but higher than the 1916 and 1915 values (with the exception of Neuve Chapelle in March 1915). Here, however, MICHAEL is slightly below the mean for the available data (60 tubes per mile).

What, then, do these results mean? In effect, the Allies deployed a theater force larger than that of any preceding western front defense but chose to leave the frontage between Arras and La Fere more thinly guarded than elsewhere.[68] The consequence of this was a local FSR at the German point of attack that was still higher in square units of area than even the Germans' late war Wotan and Flandern positions, was higher in linear density than the defenses that defeated the Allied attacks of 1915 and 1916, but was lower than the linear densities of the German 1917 defenses, both in divisions and in artillery tubes.

How important is it that German 1917 linear densities were higher than those opposite MICHAEL? Recall that the real meaning of any linear density estimate is

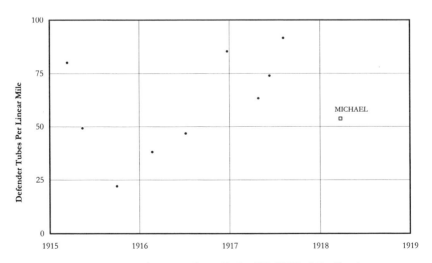

Figure 5.6. Local Force-to-Space Ratios, World War I (Artillery)

its consequences for the total number of defenders opposite a given attack frontage. A low linear density means fewer defenders in the path of any given assault; a high linear density means more defenders opposite the attack. A low linear density defense thus offers attackers an opportunity: by concentrating assault forces on a narrow front, an attacker can create an overwhelming local force to *force* ratio at the point of attack when the defender's linear force to *space* ratio is low. In March 1918, however, the Germans largely forfeited this opportunity. Ludendorff's unusually wide, fifty-mile attack frontage diluted Germany's modest resources, with the result that the local FFR, as shown above, was among the lowest of the war.[69] A 1917-magnitude linear FSR at the point of attack would have made the local FFR even lower, but the military consequences of the linear density the British actually attained were thus quite modest.

Of course, a very low FSR could be problematic even without a large local FFR if it created gaps through which attackers could gain access to the defensive rear. But the best measure of this is square units of area—not linear units of frontage—and the British density in divisions per square mile was in fact unusually *high* by World War I standards.[70] The British defense in March 1918 was significantly less porous than standard German practice of 1917 and in any case was far from insufficiently dense to provide for successful defense.

Overall, Operation MICHAEL thus posed a highly defense-favorable numerical balance. By comparison with the First Battle of the Somme, for example, MICHAEL was conducted at a lower theaterwide FFR (1.17:1 in divisions, as opposed to 1.33:1); a lower local FFR in online divisions (1.5:1 vs. 3.1:1), total divisions (2.0:1 vs. 3.7:1), and artillery (2.4:1 vs. 3.1:1); and a higher FSR in theaterwide divisions per linear mile (0.52 vs. 0.34), local divisions per linear mile (0.30 vs. 0.21), local divisions per square mile (0.12 vs. 0.04), and local artillery tubes per linear mile (54 vs. 47).[71] For preponderance theorists, the Germans should thus have been stopped cold in their tracks in March 1918.

Force Employment in MICHAEL

In MICHAEL, the Germans implemented the modern system very thoroughly at the tactical level and to some degree at the operational level as well; the British, however, failed to implement modern-system methods either tactically or operationally.

OFFENSIVE TACTICS

MICHAEL brought mature modern-system offensive tactics to the western front. The Germans dispersed their formations; made extensive use of terrain for cover and concealment; dispensed with destructive artillery fires and substituted a brief, predicted "hurricane barrage" designed for chiefly suppressive effects; used combined arms techniques to provide local suppressive fires to supplement the artillery program; and allowed subunits to maneuver independently along

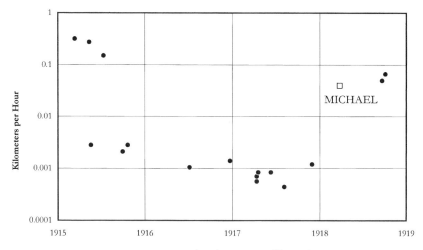

Figure 5.7. Assault Velocities, World War I

the path of least resistance rather than tying the movement of all to the progress of the slowest.[72] The net result increased aggregate assault velocity dramatically relative to the artillery offensives of the midwar period, but without reaching the extremely high closure rates of the infantry-predominant tactics of 1914–15.

This characterization is summarized in figure 5.7, which plots net offensive closure rate for an illustrative sample of major offensives.[73] At Neuve Chapelle or Aubers Ridge in spring 1915, for example, artillery preparations could be as short as 30–45 minutes, producing a net closure velocity as high as 0.3 kilometers per hour.[74] By June 1917, however, the nineteen-day barrage at Passchendaele reduced net closure velocity to an astounding 0.0004 kilometers per hour.[75] By contrast, the new German techniques provided a net closure rate of about 0.04 kilometers per hour in March 1918—an increase of about two orders of magnitude relative to June 1917, but still well below the early-war pace of 0.1–1 kilometers an hour typical of early 1915.

OFFENSIVE OPERATIONS

MICHAEL was hardly a theaterwide frontal offensive, but neither did it exploit differential concentration as aggressively as it could have. Ludendorff's fifty-mile assault frontage was in fact among the widest of the war and significantly exceeded the minimum for effective logistical support. Artillery ranges in 1918 were limited to four to five miles beyond the line of battle, and effective ranges against fleeting targets were far less; a frontage as narrow as ten to fifteen miles could thus ensure a resupply corridor of several miles width free of interference from hostile artillery. A wider frontage improves security from counterattack, but British doctrine made little provision for the large-scale counterstrokes needed to pose a major threat (see below); even a much narrower frontage would have sufficed. By comparison, western front offensives in 1915–17 had typically been launched on frontages of five to fifteen miles: at First Ypres in April 1915, for example, the Germans had used a five-mile front; at Loos in September 1915, the British used a six-mile front; at the First Battle of the Somme in July 1916, the frontage was fourteen miles; at Passchendaele in July 1917, it was fifteen miles.[76] Even in their 1918 offensives, Allied frontages were little wider than in 1917: for the Meuse-Argonne offensive of September 1918, the frontage was twenty-five miles; at Saint Mihiel, it was thirty-five.[77] MICHAEL was thus launched on a front more than twice as wide as most preceding offensives, and wider by half than most attacks mounted after it. As noted above, this broad frontage reduced Germany's achievable local numerical advantage; even so, by concentrating on 50 miles of the 325-mile theater frontier, the Germans still reaped benefits from differential concentration: Germany's local FFR of 2:1 in total divisions committed was about twice the theaterwide balance of 1.17:1.

DEFENSIVE TACTICS

British defensive tactics used modern-system principles much less effectively than did contemporary German defenses. By 1917, German defenders had recognized that permanent, interconnected trench lines offered cover but sacrificed concealment: prebattle aerial reconnaissance could map such fixed positions in great detail, making their locations known to the attacker and greatly increasing their vulnerability. Prior to Allied infantry assaults, German trench garrisons thus dispersed into shell holes or other expedient cover, denying the Allies knowledge of their locations and adding concealment to cover.[78] By contrast, British defenders in March 1918 made no systematic effort to disperse from their fixed emplacements when attacked. Instead, British forward garrisons fought from trench lines whose locations were well known to the Germans, and through which the Germans could thus maneuver on the basis of extensive pre battle reconnaissance.[79]

Moreover, the quality of that prebattle reconnaissance was enhanced by the particular siting of the British trench lines. Most of the British positions on the Somme were located on forward slopes, exposing them to continuous direct surveillance from German forward observation posts to a depth of several thousand yards across much of the German assault frontage. When the Germans withdrew to the Hindenberg Line in 1917, they systematically sought out reverse slopes for their principal deployments.[80] This not only shielded their main defenses from view by British ground observers, it also provided clear lines of sight into much of the British positions opposite them for German observers dug in along the crests. When the Germans shifted to the offensive in spring 1918, this topography now made for ideal prebattle reconnaissance in the attack: assault units could survey much of the ground between their jump-off points and their initial (and in some cases, intermediate) objectives from observation posts in their own forward trenches.[81] The British were thus exposed to continuous German observation in the weeks before the battle.[82] Combined with the British garrison's strict reliance on fixed, permanent positions, this afforded the Germans an ideal opportunity to identify the great majority of British battle positions prior to the attack.[83]

DEFENSIVE OPERATIONS

British defenses on the Somme in March 1918 were far shallower and more forward oriented than contemporary German practice. Early in the war, German defensive preparations were sometimes as little as a single trench line with wire obstacles to its front and a total depth of less than 500 yards. This was quickly increased to a system of two to three lines, interconnected by communication trenches and reaching as much as 6,000–7,000 yards deep by the end of the year. By late 1917, German positions extended to as many as seven to eight individual trench lines, with the rearmost positioned as far as 20,000 yards from no man's land.[84]

The British defensive system opposite MICHAEL, however, consisted of only four to five trench lines, the deepest of which averaged less than 4,500 yards from no man's land.[85] GHQ's instructions on preparation for defense, issued December 14, 1917, had specified a system of three "zones"—forward, battle, and rear.[86] Army and corps defense plans further specified that these zones were to contain a total of twelve trench lines, color coded by zone for reference.[87] The deepest (green) line of the rear zone was to average almost 16,000 yards behind the British front.[88] At the time of the order, however, only three of these lines were in existence, and these were the forwardmost of the planned twelve.[89] Construction proceeded throughout the winter, but by March 21 only the forward zone was complete as designed. The battle zone comprised in places as few as two of its planned six lines, and the rear zone was no more than a blueprint. Overall, the deepest of the completed lines averaged less than 4,500 yards from no man's land.[90]

As a result, the depth of the prepared defenses actually available to the British in March 1918 corresponded roughly with typical German practice of about mid-1915 (fig. 5.8).[91] British practice was thus almost three years out of date at the time of the battle and provided less than one-half the depth of typical late-war German defenses.

British reserve allocations likewise approximated German practice of mid-1915. Like defensive depth, reserve allocations also increased progressively over the course of the war. At Neuve Chapelle in 1915, the German defenders committed twenty-three of twenty-nine available infantry companies forward to the line of initial contact—a reserve fraction of only 21 percent. By early 1917, this

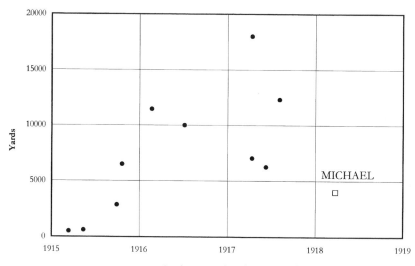

Figure 5.8. Depth of Prepared Defenses, World War I

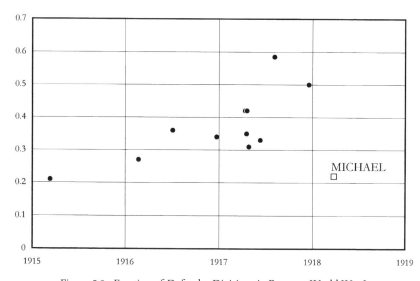

Figure 5.9. Fraction of Defender Divisions in Reserve, World War I

fraction had increased to a typical value of 30 to 40 percent, while by the end of the year it was not uncommon for German defenders to withhold as much as 50 to 60 percent of their available forces in mobile reserve (fig. 5.9).[92] In March 1918, however, the British committed forward fully twenty-one of the twenty-seven divisions under Third and Fifth Army command, with only six withheld in either corps- or army-level reserve—a reserve fraction of only 22 percent.[93] The result was one of the more forward-oriented defenses of the war.

Given these characterizations, how does MICHAEL's outcome correspond with the respective theories' predictions? Orthodox theories predict a contained offensive here: the numerical balance fell well short of the usual rules of thumb for offensive success and compared poorly with the failed offensives of the great stalemate; the Germans enjoyed no meaningful technological edge; and the dominant weapon types were still the infantry and artillery of 1915–17. Under such conditions, an attacker should be unable to breach a prepared defense.

The new theory, by contrast, predicts breakthrough: a tactically modern-system attack struck a non–modern-system defense. In terms of the formal model in the appendix, the theory predicts that an offensive with an assault velocity of 0.95 km/day and a frontage of 80 km (50 miles) will break through a defense with a depth of 4 km, a reserve withhold of 0.2, a reserve velocity of 100 km/day, and an exposure fraction of 0.5.[94] The new theory also holds, however, that breakthroughs with 1910-era technology will be difficult to exploit: the absence of deep-strike systems or high-speed, long-range vehicles should make it difficult for attackers to destroy enough defensive infrastructure to bring down the theater defense as a whole before the defender can stabilize a new front somewhere to the rear.

In fact, the battle produced an offensive breakthrough. The German attackers breached the rearmost British trench line by midnight of the first day's fighting on the Fifth Army front, and by 3 P.M. of the second day on the Third Army front.[95] By March 23, the Germans had overrun the entirety of the British prepared defenses across the whole fifty miles of their attack frontage, with the surviving defenders in full retreat over open ground.[96] As John Terraine described the second day: "The British line was breached, the Germans poured through. It was no longer a question of assault; it was pursuit."[97]

This result was literally unprecedented in almost four years of continuous warfare on the western front. Never before had an attacker reached the defensive gun line; yet by midnight of March 22, the Germans had captured more than 530 British artillery pieces.[98] Operational forward airbases were taken under German fire on the first day of battle; Number 5 (Naval) squadron was forced to abandon its aerodrome at Mons-en-Chausee by shellfire before noon on the 21st.[99] In a single day, over twenty thousand British troops were captured, untold quantities of supplies and ammunition were overrun, and some forty-seven battalions of British infantry simply ceased to exist.[100]

Yet this breakthrough failed to produce a decisive exploitation. Instead, the two armies staggered westward some forty miles in an enormous, often intermingled mass—the retreating British unable to form a coherent defense to halt the German pursuit, the Germans unable to administer a final coup de grace.[101] Casualties mounted: the breakthrough itself had been accomplished at the cost of about 40,000 German dead and wounded (out of the perhaps one million men in the Seventeenth, Second, and Eighteenth armies); by the end of the battle, German losses had reached almost 250,000.[102] Allied losses were scarcely fewer: about 39,000 on the first day, and some 240,000 for the battle as a whole.[103] Eventually, the pursuit simply ground to a halt, caused as much by simple German exhaustion as by British counteraction. As Winston Churchill put it: "The actual fighting gave place to the painful toiling westward of two weary armies; and when the retreating British were sufficiently reinforced to come to a general halt, their pursuers found themselves not less exhausted, and far in front of their own artillery and supplies."[104]

While the resulting advance was unprecedented by western front standards—and far from trivial in any context (a forty mile advance into Germany from the east today would capture Berlin)—it thus did not end the war. In fact, with time on the Allies' side, the failure of the Spring Offensives to win the war outright was effectively the death knell for Germany in the conflict as a whole.

The key outcome of the battle thus tends to corroborate the new theory and contradict the orthodox views: the Germans broke through but failed to exploit decisively. What about the *process* by which this outcome came about, however? Does the *way* in which the battle unfolded match the expectations of any of the theories under study?

For orthodox theories, their underdeveloped causal mechanisms complicate process tracing, but little of the available logic fits the events here. Offense-defense theory, for example, treats infantry, machine guns, and artillery as defense-conducive because it assumes that armor protection is needed to advance against automatic weapons and shrapnel shell. Though one might suppose that Ludendorff's failure to exploit could offer partial support for this claim, the theory's underlying logic is focused on the problem of breakthrough, not exploitation, and cannot explain an infantry attack's ability to survive an advance across fire-swept ground, break through, yet fail to bring down a defense. Orthodox offense-defense theory would expect the German infantry to have been mown down in no man's land, and the attack to fail because it could not take ground. This was not the way the battle unfolded.

Of the several varieties of preponderance theory, Lanchester's Square Law embodies the clearest causal logic.[105] That logic implies, however, that the numerically superior side should impose far more casualties than it suffers, and that attrition results in intense combat should quickly diverge, with the stronger side growing progressively stronger and the weaker side becoming ever weaker.[106] Casualties in the Second Battle of the Somme, however, were about equal on the two sides, notwithstanding the Germans' local numerical superiority. Moreover, the trajectory of casualties over time shows little apparent change: the ratio of German to Allied losses during the initial breakthrough was about 1.03:1; the final casualty ratio was still only 1.04:1. This is difficult to square with the dynamic instability and disproportionate effects of numerical imbalance in Lanchester theory, regardless of the presence or absence of breakthrough.

For the new theory, by contrast, important elements of the battle's conduct fit, though some points of divergence can also be found. The new theory's dynamic structure sees continental operations as races between penetration and counterconcentration; the central purpose of defensive depth and reserves is to buy the time and wherewithal needed to counterconcentrate. The reason that shallow, forward defenses are ineffective is that they enable attackers to breach the prepared defense before sufficient reserves can arrive. In MICHAEL, the shallow, forward British defense had precisely this effect. Of the twenty-four divisions of Allied reserves ultimately committed to the Second Somme front, fewer than five arrived in time to contest the breakthrough itself; the other nineteen arrived after the British had abandoned their prepared positions and were retreating over open ground.[107] The shallowness of the British defense thus enabled the Germans to rupture the British position before more than 80 percent of the Allied reserve could reach the battle, an outcome consistent with the new theory's causal logic.

Central to the new theory's analysis of offensive tactics is the claim that modern-system methods permit even unarmored attackers to advance over fire-swept ground against prepared defenses without debilitating losses. MICHAEL presents just such an advance. An essentially tank-free modern-system infantry attack overran more than 320 square km of prepared, barbed-wire-fronted entrenchments in the face of plentiful machine gun and artillery fire with losses of less than 10 percent of the troops engaged in the first-wave divisions.[108] This, too, is consistent with the causal mechanism proposed in chapters 3 and 4.

The formal model that implements the new theory offers a number of additional process-tracing opportunities. The model's computed duration and casualty predictions are restricted to contained offensives; if one scales the results down to reflect only the effort involved in penetrating prepared defenses en route to a breakthrough, it becomes possible to evaluate additional predictions here. In particular, for the conditions described above, the model implies that breakthrough would require roughly eight days of fighting; that differential concentration would enable the Germans to deploy some 2,400,000 total troops at the point of attack; that German losses in breaking through would exceed 125,000; that British losses in the breakthrough phase would approach 100,000; and that the attacker to defender loss exchange ratio (LER) would be about 1.3 for the breakthrough effort.[109] In fact, the Germans had completed the breakthrough by March 23, after about two days of fighting; hence the model overestimates the required duration by about six days. The Germans actually chose to mass only a million troops for the offensive; hence the model overestimates German troop strength at the point of attack by about a factor of 2.4. German losses in breaking through totaled 39,929; hence the model overestimates German casualties by a factor of three. British breakthrough casualties totaled about 38,512, making the actual breakthrough LER about 1.04.[110] The model thus overestimates British losses by a factor of 2.5, but it gets the LER about right.

While the formal model predicts the key outcome (i.e., the breakthrough) well, and while it closely approximates the historical casualty ratio, the magnitudes of several important quantities are thus significantly overestimated. The model's failure to anticipate the Germans' modest troop allocation to MICHAEL is due in part to its implicit assumption that attackers undertake major theater offensives singly; Ludendorff, by contrast, planned from the outset for a series of four such attacks, and he husbanded his forces accordingly.[111] Historians have criticized this choice: Corelli Barnett, for example, has argued that Ludendorff unnecessarily diluted an already modest offensive surplus by splitting it among multiple efforts, and that he should have concentrated his forces more aggressively.[112] The model assumes an approach closer to Barnett's. The model's overprediction of casualties stems in part from its assumption that the attacker would expose more forces to battle at the point of attack, and in part from two simplifications in its treatment of tactics: it uses a linear formulation for the relationship between casualties and velocity (a nonlinear form would better capture the modern system's ability to reduce attacker losses via time-consuming combined arms and fire-and-movement techniques, but at the cost of a more complex model), and it ignores defensive withdrawal (which yields ground but lowers defensive casualties). The simplifications inherent in modeling make some divergence between prediction and observation inevitable; my choices here have been to keep the model as simple as possible by focusing on central predictive outcomes, but this choice comes at the cost of greater divergence elsewhere.

ALTERNATIVE EXPLANATIONS OF THE GERMAN BREAKTHROUGH

How does the argument above compare with existing historical explanations of the German breakthrough? In fact, many historians of the battle cite some combination of German offensive doctrine, shallow British defensive preparations, and British inattention to defensive doctrine as important causal factors.[113]

The most common explanations, however, are substantially at odds with the analysis presented above. In particular, ever since the publication of the British Official History in 1935, the standard view of the battle has been that the British were overwhelmed by "Mist and Masses," that is, by the effects of a heavy morning fog the day the offensive was launched, and by sheer German numerical superiority.[114] This view, however, is seriously flawed.

German Numerical Superiority

The British official historian, Sir James Edmonds, argued that the British Army was seriously understrength as the result of Lloyd George's deliberate decision to deny Haig the manpower needed to launch another British offensive in spring 1918. In combination with the Germans' eastern reinforcements, and Haig's agreement to accept an additional twenty miles of French defensive front in December 1917, the result was held to be a dangerously overextended British defense that was simply overwhelmed by the weight of the German masses.[115] This view has been widely endorsed by subsequent historians and persists in various forms through much of the historiography of the battle.[116]

As stated, this argument is inconsistent with the actual balance as detailed above: neither the local FFR nor FSR was adverse here by World War I standards. Indeed, the local force-to-force ratio was among the least attacker-favorable of any major offensive of the war.[117]

It remains, however, to deal with an important subargument of the general Edmonds thesis, namely, that British troops were not evenly distributed across the attack frontage—and especially, that the southern wing of Fifth Army's front was much weaker than the rest of the British defense. As a result, it is argued, the Germans were able to overwhelm Fifth Army, then use their success in the south to turn the flank of the otherwise solid Third Army, unhinging the position overall and forcing a general retirement.[118]

In fact, Fifth Army *was* weaker than the Third (by thirteen divisions to fourteen) and did hold a longer front (forty-two miles as opposed to twenty-eight).[119] It is far from clear, however, that even Fifth Army faced an especially difficult numerical imbalance. The FFR across its front was still only 2:1 (in forward divisions) to 2.5:1 (in forward plus reserve divisions), which would still be the second lowest values among those in figure 5.1. The Fifth Army FSR was about 0.26 forward divisions per mile, which would still fall between the two groups of values in figure 5.4.

Moreover, Edmonds' argument hinges on the proposition that Fifth Army's defense proved significantly less resilient than Third Army's (a difference that can then be explained by reference to the greater numerical odds facing the Fifth Army). Yet there was very little difference in the Germans' actual progress on the two army fronts on the crucial first day of the battle. For both, the battle zone had been penetrated on a narrow frontage by the Germans on the afternoon of the 21st.[120] In the north, however, this gap was sealed off by repeated local counterattacks from forces ranging in size from as few as two platoons to as many as two battalions.[121] In the south, no attempt was made to counterattack and restore the position, even though as many as three battalions of fresh, previously unengaged infantry were available opposite the breach.[122] Gough subsequently pulled his southernmost corps out of its last prepared positions and redeployed them some 6,500 yards to the rear along the bank of the Crozat

Canal.[123] As a result, the front-line trace for the morning of the second day shows the Fifth Army yielding about three miles more than the Third Army, but this distinction is thus due almost entirely to Gough's decision to withdraw, versus the Third Army's decision to counterattack—rather than being the inevitable result of vastly superior German forces in the south.

Fog

The second argument attributes the breakthrough to a heavy fog on the morning of the attack. From dawn until as late as noon in some places, the battlefield was covered by a dense white mist, reducing visibility to as little as 200 yards. As a result, the effective range of British small arms fire was substantially reduced, visual direction of defensive artillery got harder, and it became possible in places for German infantry teams to infiltrate unseen between British forward positions.

Of course, the fog also posed difficulties for the German attackers—command and control were greatly complicated by the poor visibility, units became scattered and lost direction, and artillery observation aircraft were grounded, limiting artillery support to preplanned targets and a rigidly programmed creeping barrage.

On balance, however, low visibility hurts defenders more than attackers. Attackers are very vulnerable while closing with the defense. Low visibility, by reducing their exposure during this period of vulnerability, thus reduces the single greatest threat to a successful assault—a benefit that outweighs the disadvantages of harder command or fire support coordination.

Given this, many historians have concluded that poor visibility from the morning fog was the primary cause of the German breakthrough.[124] In fact, this argument appeared within days of the battle itself in the form of appendices to the war diaries of at least ten of the British divisions engaged.[125] It was quickly picked up by the British press and subsequently formed the second pillar of Edmonds' explanation of the German success.[126] While by no means universally accepted, the notion that fog made the breakthrough possible has nevertheless become a major part of the historiography of the battle.[127]

This argument, however, is also seriously flawed. While reduced visibility certainly favored the attacker, its effects were neither necessary nor sufficient to explain the breakthrough.

WAS FOG A SUFFICIENT CONDITION FOR THE GERMAN BREAKTHROUGH?

Many First World War offensives were conducted under foggy weather, yet for almost four years, none broke through. Fog is very common in northwest Europe. On average, it can be expected about one morning in four during the early springtime, lasting an average of almost five hours.[128] Indeed, it would be hard to conduct an offensive on the western front *without* eventually encountering fog and mist sufficient to curtail visibility. To cite just a few examples, the

British offensive at Neuve Chapelle in March 1915 was launched under a "dense white mist"; large stretches of the First Somme and Verdun campaigns in 1916 were fought in fog; the "battles of the Scarpe" following the initial assault at Arras in April 1917 were fought under periodic morning mists heavy enough to cut lines of sight; and the infamous Passchendaele offensive in October 1917 was shrouded in fog and rain.[129] Yet none broke through.

Moreover, a variety of other means for obscuring defender lines of sight had existed—and were widely exploited—prior to 1918, yet none produced break-through. Night attack, for example, is in many ways similar to the effects of fog.[130] Yet night offensives as early as 1915 at Festubert, or as late as 1917 at Arras, failed to break through.[131] Artificial smoke, a manufactured fog, had been used en masse as early as Loos in 1915.[132] In fact, by 1918 smoke shell was considered a major ammunition type for the ubiquitous British Stokes Projector, the most common Allied trench mortar.[133] Smoke screens had been used in the French offensive in Champagne in 1915, the First Somme campaign in 1916, or Arras and Passchendaele in 1917, to name just a few.[134] Indeed, the Germans fired smoke shell in their artillery preparation for Operation MICHAEL.[135] With the exception of MICHAEL, however, none of these attacks broke through.

The reasons that neither fog nor smoke nor night is sufficient in itself for breakthrough are threefold. First, while they can reduce defensive lines of sight, they cannot eliminate them. Attackers must eventually close with defenders, and even in a dense fog this means they will eventually become visible, and thus exposed to fire from stationary, usually concealed defenders, while the very reduction in visibility can make the defenders' concealment more effective. On balance, lower visibility still helps an attacker, but not to an unlimited degree.

Second, reduced visibility conveys this advantage on defensive counterattack-ers as well as the initial attacker. A defense trained to counterattack aggressively (like the Germans'—and unlike the British) can thus appropriate much of the advantage of fog or night action for themselves, and use it to restore defensive integrity.

Finally, and most important, fog (and smoke) are transient. Eventually, the air clears and the defenders' sight is restored. A key advantage of defense in depth is that it ensures that the attacker will still be within the defended zone when this happens. Shallow defenses, by contrast, make it possible for attackers to breach the defense in a single blow, before a morning's fog has burned off, or an artificial smoke screen has cleared.[136] In Operation MICHAEL, the Germans crippled the British defense on the morning of the first day, while the fog was still heavy; few other First World War defenses were shallow enough to be undermined so quickly.

WAS FOG A NECESSARY CONDITION FOR THE GERMAN BREAKTHROUGH?

Nor was fog a necessary condition. Indeed, the fourth Spring Offensive, the Battle of the Chemin des Dames, produced a breakthrough without the benefit of fog or mist.[137] Similarly, the infantry offensives of Tannenberg in 1914 and Megiddo in 1918 broke through defenses under clear skies.[138]

What *is* necessary is that cover of some sort be provided to reduce the attackers' vulnerability. As suggested above, however, that cover need not be fog. It could be smoke, darkness, or, as in the Spring Offensives, a combination of suppressive fire, cover, and concealment.[139] There is no reason to require that cover take the form of fog for an infantry attack to succeed, and there is little basis for a claim that fog on the morning of the attack was responsible for the German breakthrough on March 21.

CONCLUSIONS AND IMPLICATIONS

For a single case study, MICHAEL thus offers unusually strong evidence. The case offers an extreme example of what should have been defense-dominant technology and numerical imbalance. Yet the attacker broke through. This is consistent with the new theory's predictions for the British defenders' shallow, forward, non–modern-system force employment and the German attackers' modern-system use of cover, concealment, and combined arms. With the deck stacked against a force employment explanation by such extreme technology and numerical odds, corroboration in Operation MICHAEL is thus a particularly significant outcome.

Nevertheless, the new theory does not perfectly match the case: the formal model fails to anticipate Ludendorff's unwillingness to commit his entire strength to a single effort, and it overestimates German losses and campaign duration. It correctly anticipates the defender's inability to counterconcentrate, however, as well as the German infantry's ability to advance against 1918 firepower, and of course it is consistent with the central outcome of breakthrough without decisive exploitation. By contrast, orthodox theories fit neither the key outcome nor the details of its conduct or dynamics.

The new theory thus outperforms the orthodox alternatives in a case where one should reasonably have expected the opposite. While no single case can ever validate a theory, this does establish a degree of correspondence between the new theory and an important example of real warfare; it shows a closer correspondence for the new theory than the orthodox alternatives in a critical case; and it thus offers grounds for shifting our confidence in the respective theories.

In addition, though, MICHAEL also suggests that the new theory can be helpful in reaching a deeper understanding of real historical events. Operation MICHAEL was a central event in modern military history; the new theory provides a plausible, consistent interpretation of the reasons behind its outcome, and this theory presents a more successful explanation than the "Mist and Masses" view so prominent in the historical literature. More broadly, the analysis above implies that the great stalemate was broken neither by new technology nor by American intervention nor by the sheer exhaustion of war-weary armies, views widely held in the historiography of the war.[140] Neither technology nor numerical imbalance succeeds as an explanation of an offensive breakthrough in the face of a morally unbroken defense in MICHAEL; new methods of force employment offer a more effective account. While an analysis of MICHAEL cannot in itself prove that this explanation holds for all the 1918 offensives, the result is strongly suggestive of a powerful role for force employment in deciding the battles that ended the war. The analysis here thus does more than use a case to shed light on theory—it shows that the theory can shed new light on an important case.

CHAPTER SIX

Operation GOODWOOD—July 18–20, 1944

THIS CHAPTER PROVIDES a further test of the new theory with a case study of Operation GOODWOOD, the penultimate Allied attempt to break out of the Normandy beachhead in July 1944. In particular, I argue that if orthodox theories were correct, then GOODWOOD should have been a dramatic offensive success—by contrast with MICHAEL, systemic technology and numerical imbalance here were as *offense*-dominant in orthodox terms as any in the twentieth century. The new theory, by contrast, predicts offensive failure: a non–modern-system attacker struck a modern-system defender. In fact, the British offensive did fail, and the details of how and why again provide corroborative evidence for the new theory and disconfirmatory evidence for orthodox views.

As in chapter 5, I present the case in six steps. First, I motivate its selection as an Ecksteinian critical case. Second, I outline the main events. Third, I develop values for the key independent variables. Fourth, I compare the battle's actual outcome to the respective theories' predictions given these values, assessing the relative fit between prediction and observation. Fifth, I consider other prominent explanations for the battle's outcome. I conclude with a summary assessment of the case's implications for the theories under study.

WHY GOODWOOD?

Like MICHAEL, GOODWOOD offers an Ecksteinian *most-likely* critical case for key orthodox theories, and a *least-likely* case for the new theory.[1] As I demonstrate below, GOODWOOD combined one of the heaviest concentrations of tanks and ground-attack aircraft in history with a major numerical advantage for the British attackers at both the theater and the local level. If preponderance or systemic technology were ever to predetermine offensive breakthrough, it thus should have been here.[2] If orthodox theory fails to predict the outcome under conditions so strongly matched to those it describes as the paradigm of offensiveness, then the case poses an unusually strong challenge to its validity.[3]

Conversely, GOODWOOD presents a difficult hurdle for a theory emphasizing force employment. The new theory predicts a contained offensive: as I argue below, the Germans deployed a deep, reserve-oriented, modern-system defense that the British struck with a high-exposure, non–modern-system attack. Yet the technology and numerical balance here were so apparently offensive that it would not be surprising if this were to overwhelm the defensive influence of force employment—even if the latter really *were* the single best explanation of capability under ordinary circumstances. On the contrary, what would be surprising is if force employment proved determinant even under conditions as apparently adverse as those of July 1944. Operation GOODWOOD thus offers a *least-likely case* for the new theory: to hold under conditions as apparently unfavorable as these provides a stronger corroboration than a single case study could otherwise produce. GOODWOOD's particular characteristics thus enable a challenging test from a single case and help mitigate the danger that selection bias will taint the results.

OVERVIEW OF EVENTS, JULY 18–20, 1944

The D-Day landings of June 6 provided the Allies an initial lodgement on the European continent, but it had proven much harder than expected to advance inland in the weeks following the invasion. On the Allied left, a series of British offensives at Tilly sur Seulles, Villers Bocage, Operation EPSOM, and Operation CHARNWOOD had gained little ground at the cost of heavy casualties; on the right, the Americans were making slow progress through heavy bocage country.[4] As days turned into weeks and as growing congestion on the beaches began to restrict the Allied buildup, fears grew that the Normandy campaign might be bogging down into another western front trench stalemate.[5] To avert this, British Gen. Bernard Montgomery, commanding Allied ground forces in Europe, conceived two major operations, codenamed GOODWOOD and COBRA, to breach the Germans' primary defenses and open an avenue for a high-speed advance out of the Normandy peninsula toward Paris.[6]

The first of these, GOODWOOD, was to employ a seven-division force under British Second Army commander Lt. Gen. Sir Miles Dempsey against a 15-km frontage south and east of Caen. Four infantry divisions (the 2nd and 3rd Canadian, and 3rd and 51st British) were to secure the shoulders of the advance and drive the Germans back from the banks of the Orne River and the southern suburbs of Caen. The main effort, however, was to be a three-division armored corps (the VIIIth), which was massed on a front of less than three kilometers and ordered to penetrate through the Germans' rearmost prepared defenses on the Bourguebus Ridge.[7]

The German defenses opposite this attack comprised remnants of three battered infantry divisions (the 272nd, 346th, and 16th GAF) and three panzer divisions (the 21st, 1st SS, and 12th SS) of the German LXXXVI and I SS Panzer Corps, under the overall command of Gen. Heinrich Eberbach. Eberbach's forces, all radically understrength save the 1st SS, were disposed in a series of fortified farming villages dotting the gently rolling fields south and east of the city; elements of the 272nd were dug in among the ruins of the southern suburbs of Caen.[8]

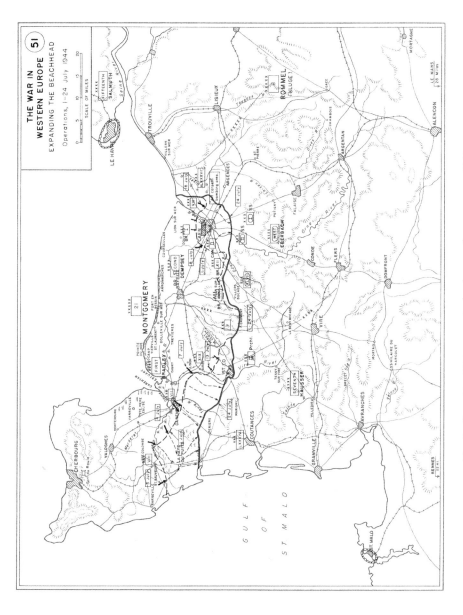

Map 3. Operation GOODWOOD in the theater of war, summer 1944

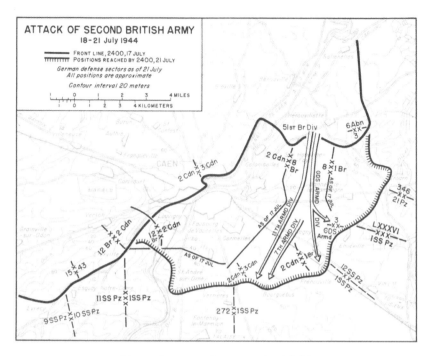

Map 4. Operation Goodwood battlefield

The battle began with one of the most intense preparatory bombardments in history. Beginning at 0530 on July 18, more than 4,500 aircraft of RAF Bomber Command and the U.S. Eighth and Ninth Air Forces carpet-bombed the German defenses with more than 7,900 tons of ordnance. Together with a further 800 tons of shells from the massed guns of three corps' worth of artillery, and naval gunfire support from the monitor *Roberts* and two Royal Navy cruisers, this crushing barrage struck the German positions with the explosive power of more than eight one-kiloton tactical nuclear warheads in a span of only three hours.[9]

The ensuing ground attack made rapid early progress, as the massed British armor overran or bypassed the shattered remnants of the German forward positions. Soon, however, the assault began to lose impetus as the attackers encountered surviving German antitank positions in the villages of Cagny and Emieville. As German reserves arrived at the scene, resistance stiffened. By the end of the first day, the British advance had slowed to a crawl well short of the Bourguebus Ridge. Renewed efforts to penetrate over the course of the following two days made negligible progress, the offensive grinding to a dead halt by midday on the 20th with the Bourguebus Ridge still in German hands, and the German rearward defenses intact. By 1600 on July 20, a torrential rainfall turned the battlefield to mud, leading the British to call off offensive operations, and ending Operation Goodwood.[10]

How do these events compare with the respective theories' predictions? To answer this question, I first characterize the battle in terms of the key independent variables of technology, numerical imbalance, and force employment.

Weapon Technology

In orthodox theories' terms, systemic technology in GOODWOOD should have favored attack over defense; the specific defender here lacked any dyadic technical edge sufficient to overcome this systemic effect.

Systemic offense-defense theorists point to tank and ground-attack aircraft prevalence as key indicators of offensive advantage. In July 1944 the combatants in Normandy deployed two of the most tank- and ground-attack-aircraft-heavy forces in history. The British attackers amassed a force of 1,277 tanks (738 medium and 189 light in VIII Corps, plus another 350 medium tanks supporting the four infantry divisions) and over 4,500 aircraft in support of a 118,000-soldier offensive.[11] The Germans deployed between 118 and 319 tanks and up to several hundred aircraft in support of some 29,000 defending troops.[12] The British figure for aircraft per supported soldier is probably an all-time high for a major ground attack; by comparison, the Coalition air forces in the 1991 Gulf War deployed fewer than 1,800 combat aircraft in support of a 540,000-soldier ground force, yielding a ratio less than one-tenth of GOODWOOD's.[13] GOODWOOD's figures for tanks per capita, while not necessarily an all-time high, were still very high indeed. The British attackers deployed about twice as many tanks per capita as either the attackers or defenders at El Alamein in 1941, for example; over three times more than either the Germans or the Russians at Kursk in 1943; and over ten times more than the German invaders of France or Russia in 1940 and 1941. Even the German defenders at GOODWOOD deployed more tanks per capita than had the attackers at Alamein, Kusk, or the invasions of France and Russia.[14] In terms of spatial distribution, the armor massed for GOODWOOD was among the highest concentrations in recorded history: with over 900 tanks on less than a 3-km front, GOODWOOD presented more than twice as many tanks per kilometer as even the highest-density sector at Kursk, the largest tank battle of World War II in total numbers of machines engaged.[15] Even the 1991 Gulf War failed to provide spatial concentrations of armor anywhere near GOODWOOD's: at the Battle of 73 Easting, for example, fewer than seventy American armored vehicles advanced on a 15-km front, for an armor density less than one-one-hundredth of GOODWOOD's.[16] By any measure, GOODWOOD was thus extremely rich in the weapon types considered most offense-conducive by orthodox offense-defense theorists.

The *dyadic* technological balance, moreover, was close to parity, but across the entire range of weapon types it probably offered a slight edge to the British over the Germans. More specifically, in the new theory's terms, the average date of introduction for the German weapons used in the battle was around 1940.3; for the British, about 1942.2 (see appendix).[17]

This characterization differs from many historians', who often highlight the superiority of the Germans' Pzkw V Panther and Pzkw VI Tiger tanks over the British Shermans and Cromwells in Normandy.[18] The Panther and the Tiger were indeed far better weapons than the Sherman or the Cromwell[19]—but this comparison alone is far from the whole story. Panthers and Tigers, for example, comprised a minority of the German Army's tank holdings in 1944 and provided only about a third of the German armor present on the GOODWOOD battlefield.[20] The most common German tank at GOODWOOD was the Pzkw IV, which had been introduced in 1937 and, though modified extensively by 1944, was still marginally inferior to either the Sherman or the Cromwell at the time of the battle.[21] The balance of the German armor at GOODWOOD was provided by eighty-six turretless assault guns; fifty of these were remanufactured expedients created by mounting German 75-mm antitank guns on obsolete French tank chassis that had been captured in 1940; while helpful, these ersatz armored vehicles were no match for the Sherman or the Cromwell in technical sophistication.[22] While a few of the Germans' tanks were markedly superior, most were actually less capable than their British counterparts.

Tanks, moreover, were only one of the major weapon types with an important role in the battle. In antitank guns, for example, the German 88-mm antitank gun was perhaps the most efficient of the war, but here too, the 88 comprised only a portion of the German holdings; the more common 75-mm PAK was little better than the British 6-pounder, and notably inferior to the British 17-pounder.[23] German machine guns were generally thought superior to Allied equivalents, but Allied rifles were superior, and Allied howitzers, heavy guns, and ammunition were generally higher quality than their German counterparts.[24]

Arguably the most important weapon type at GOODWOOD, however, was the airplane. Not only was air power chiefly responsible for the devastating preparatory barrage on the morning of the 18th, but it also provided both an ongoing interdiction effort that radically complicated German reserve movements in the rear, and regular close air support that greatly augmented Allied firepower during the battle. By 1944, Allied aircraft were markedly superior to their German counterparts in all major roles. For example, the P-51 Mustang, the chief Allied air superiority fighter, outperformed the German FW 190 (the most advanced, but not the most common, fighter in Luftflotte 3) in range, speed, and rate of climb. The P-47 Lightning, the most common Allied fighter-bomber, outperformed the ground-attack versions of the FW 190 in range, speed, and payload—in fact, the P-47's maximum bomb load exceeded the FW 190's by more than a factor of three.[25] The Allied Lancaster and Halifax heavy bombers that contributed so much to the aggregate tonnage dropped on the Germans on July 18 had no real competitors in the Luftwaffe. The Germans' heaviest bomber in widespread service, the Do 217, carried a bomb load less than one-third of the Lancaster's to a 30 percent shorter range.[26]

At most, then, the Germans could claim superior machine guns and a major technical edge in the most advanced one-third of their tank fleet. In artillery, aircraft, and the majority of the tanks actually employed in GOODWOOD, Allied weapons were technically superior to the Germans'. A narrow focus on two tank models, the Panther and the Tiger, thus provides a misleading picture of the technological balance overall. Even if tanks really were the queen of the bat-tlefield and the essential arbiter of victory and defeat—which contradicts the combined arms principles underlying either side's formal military doctrines at the time—the overall tank balance was itself less one-sided than often portrayed. But, of course, tanks alone are not the only important weapon class. Looking across weapon classes, the British probably enjoyed a slight technological advan-tage over the Germans, though the balance differed by weapon class and reached decisive magnitude for few if any of those classes.

Numerical Imbalance

The numerical balance in GOODWOOD well exceeded the standard rules of thumb used by preponderance theorists to predict offensive success. In particu-lar, the Allies enjoyed an extraordinarily high theater and local force-to-force ratio; the German force-to-space ratio, though not unprecedentedly low, was nevertheless well below that of many other, failed, World War II defenses. Taken together, these values imply an unambiguous prediction of offensive break-through for orthodox preponderance explanations of capability.

FORCE-TO-FORCE RATIOS

Theaterwide, total Allied troop strength in Normandy reached 1,000,000 on July 4, and 1,452,000 by July 25;[27] assuming roughly constant arrivals, this implies an attacker strength of about 1,300,000 on July 18. German troop strengths are harder to pin down. Prior to the invasion, German ground force strength in France and the low countries totaled about 1,097,000 troops in fifty-seven divi-sions.[28] By July 18, twenty-three of these divisions were fighting in Normandy (with the others tied down defending coastlines elsewhere) and had suffered over 100,000 casualties, few of which had been made good by replacements.[29] This implies a sur-viving strength of around 340,000 troops in Normandy by the time of Operation GOODWOOD, or a theaterwide FFR of 3.8:1 in orthodox theory's terms.[30]

This ratio is well in excess of any normally applied standard for offensive ade-quacy. The usual rule of thumb for theaterwide FFRs needed for successful at-tack is 1.5:1; the GOODWOOD figure is more than twice this value.[31] In fact, the July 1944 theater imbalance actually exceeds the usual rule of thumb for *local* FFRs, which is only 3:1.[32] The GOODWOOD theater FFR exceeds that for the German invasion of France in 1940 by more than a factor of four. It is nearly three times that of the German invasion of Russia, more than twice that of the German invasion of Poland, and exceeds even the Soviets' margin of preponderance over Finland in 1939.[33] The Allies thus enjoyed a truly crushing theater numerical advantage in Normandy by July 1944.

In addition to theaterwide balances, orthodox theorists often consider local FFRs, and balances for particular weapon types (for World War II, especially tanks). Counting rules, however, are often much more ambiguous for local balances. This is because the definition of "local" can vary from historian to historian, and the different definitions can yield very different results.

To illustrate this problem, table 6.1 presents local FFRs for a variety of intuitively plausible counting rules (or definitions of "local" forces). The results vary by a factor of more than seven for troop counts, and by a factor of more than fourteen for tanks. These variations stem from the peculiarities of the two sides'

TABLE 6.1.
Local FFR as a Function of Counting Rules[†]

	Local Force-to-Force Ratio for:	
Counting Rule	Troops	Tanks[††]
Forward divisions, VIII Corps corridor	22.7	82.7
Forward divisions, Second Army assault frontage	10.2	16.3
Forward divisions engaged on July 18, VIII Corps corridor	15.2	55.1
Forward divisions engaged on July 18, Second Army assault frontage	9.2	12.6
Forward and corps/army reserve divisions, Second Army assault frontage	3.0	5.9

[†]Troop counts are ration strengths, per the treatment in orthodox theory. Dempsey's radically narrow VIII Corps frontage complicates local FFR calculation, as both attackers and defenders on the flanks of this frontage could readily fire across its entire width. Moreover, German subunit boundaries are not known with sufficient precision to place subunits unambiguously within or outside such a narrow front (or even to establish with certainty which subunits could fire into VIII Corps' front and which were out of range). On the other hand, British attacks on the VIII Corps corridor's shoulders presumably occupied flanking defenders' attentions to some degree. I thus allocate German units against frontages for local FFR calculation by computing troops/km and tanks/km overall for I SS and LXXXVI Corps' 26 km front, then allocating 15/26 of this total against the 15 km Second Army frontage, and 2/26 of this total against the 2 km VIII Corps frontage. Data are derived from TDRC-7725, pp. A-4 to A-5, A-7; TDRC-5041, p. 6; NA RG242, T-313-420, KTB PzW 15.7.44, Anlage 135; KTB PzW 10.7.44, Anlage 105; TDRC-5041, pp. 6, b-1; Sweet, *Mounting the Threat*, pp. 55, 112; BOHN, pp. 333, 535. Note that troop data are for holdings at division level and below; as British corps and army slices far exceeded Germany's in 1944, the results are thus conservative for the scale of British numerical advantage.

[††]The figures below count only medium and heavy tanks, thus excluding the 189 light tanks available in the three British armored divisions (Sweet, *Mounting the Threat*, p. 112).

dispositions and plans. Dempsey's forces were not distributed uniformly over the Second Army's assault frontage; in particular, the three tank divisions of VIII Corps, the British main effort, were concentrated on a very narrow 2-km subset of an overall frontage of more than 15 km for the offensive as a whole.[34] This was intended to provide maximum preponderance at the critical point; supporting attacks to either side were expected to fight with a lesser numerical edge.[35] The FFR thus differs as a function of whether one focuses on the sector of main effort (the VIII Corps corridor) or the entire attack frontage. In addition, VIII Corps proved unable to get all three of its divisions into action on the first day as planned (delayed by traffic congestion in the assault corridor, the 7th Armored Division saw little combat until the second day of the battle);[36] if one excludes 7th Armored from the British total, one likewise obtains a different figure for the initial "local" FFR at the point of attack. Finally, much of the German combat strength in the area was in mobile reserve behind the front.[37] Defensive reserves are often excluded from "local" FFR calculations precisely because their mobility makes it possible for them to fight in many possible places, rather than on any particular frontage. The Germans, however, had anticipated a British offensive in the vicinity of Caen and had placed their reserves nearby to facilitate rapid commitment should such an offensive occur; the proximity of these mobile reserves might lead some to count them as part of the "local" German forces initially deployed at the British point of attack, yielding yet another figure.

How, then, should the local balance be assessed? Three points bear noting.

First, none of these counting rules yield local FFRs lower than 3:1 for troops, or 5.9:1 for tanks. All these variations thus imply balances that meet or well exceed the usual 3:1 rule of thumb for offensive adequacy at the point of attack. In fact, if we focus on the main effort in the VIII Corps corridor (as Dempsey intended), the British numerical advantage was staggering: more than 22:1 in troop strength, and more than 80:1 in tanks. By the 3:1 rule's terms, any reasonable counting rule thus yields a prediction of offensive breakthrough here.[38]

Second, GOODWOOD's local FFR is unusually high when compared with other Second World War actions using comparable counting rules. Figures 6.1 and 6.2, for example, present illustrative data for local FFRs in total forces (engaged and reserve) across the entire assault frontage for a variety of World War II operations.[39] Of the counting rules given in table 6.1, this is the least likely to favor the British at GOODWOOD relative to other Second World War experience (since the German defenders at GOODWOOD had atypically large reserves in the immediate vicinity of the assault frontage, and since the British main effort comprised only a tiny fraction of the assault frontage overall). Yet the ratio of troop strengths at GOODWOOD (3:1) is still the fifth highest of the 25 data points given in figure 6.1 and is almost 50 percent above the mean value for the data as a whole (2.1:1). The ratio of tank strengths at GOODWOOD (5.9:1) is the third highest of the 16 data points in figure 6.2 and is almost twice the mean of the data (3.1:1).

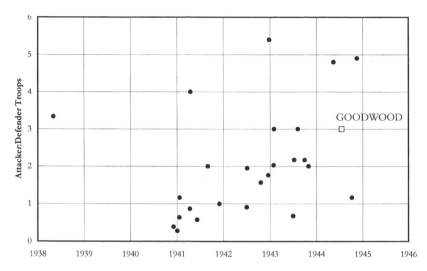

Figure 6.1. Local Force-to-Force Ratio, World War II (Troops)

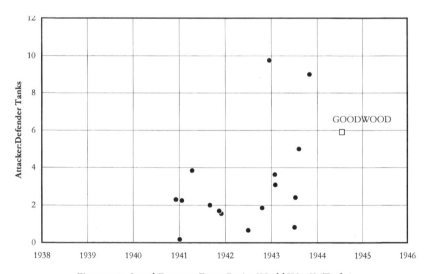

Figure 6.2. Local Force-to-Force Ratio, World War II (Tanks)

Third, none of these figures take account of the Allies' crushing numerical superiority in the air. Allied aircraft contributed about eight kilotons of firepower to the attackers at GOODWOOD, whereas the German Luftwaffe was essentially absent from the fighting.[40] At a minimum, this suggests that the ground force comparisons in table 6.1 are conservative with respect to the degree of aggregate numerical preponderance available to the British.

Whether by a rule of thumb or by comparison with other experience, and whether by theaterwide or local measures, the FFR at GOODWOOD was thus well above the normal thresholds used for predicting breakthrough.

FORCE-TO-SPACE RATIOS

Some preponderance theorists (and a few offense-defense theorists) emphasize troop density, or the force-to-space ratio. For those who consider it, high values are held to benefit defenders.[41] GOODWOOD's FSR, while not the lowest of the war, was far from high enough to preclude successful attack.

FSRs, like FFRs, are sensitive to the counting rules used, and, as noted in chapter 5, one of the most important distinctions concerns linear units of frontage and square units of area. Just as the British FSR in MICHAEL differed widely when measured in troops per linear kilometer as opposed to troops per square kilometer, so the German FSR in GOODWOOD looks very different by the two counting rules.

In particular, the Germans deployed about 1,100 troops per linear kilometer of front locally at the GOODWOOD point of attack (if one includes the mobile reserves to the rear of the prepared defenses, a counting rule that tends to elevate the GOODWOOD FSR relative to other World War II experience), and 20 forward troops per square kilometer.[42] To place these figures in context, figures 6.3 and 6.4 present a representative sample of linear and square local FSRs for other Second World War actions.[43] The results put GOODWOOD just above the average FSR in linear units of frontage (i.e., 973 troops/km), but far below it in square units of area (629 troops/km^2).[44]

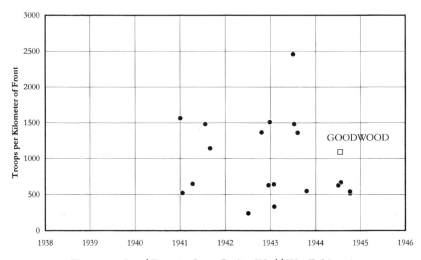

Figure 6.3. Local Force-to-Space Ratios, World War II (Linear)

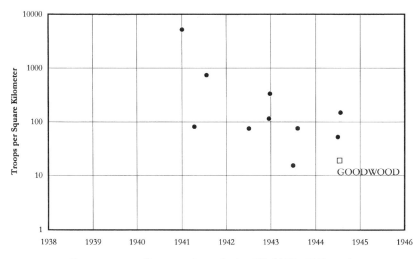

Figure 6.4. Local Force-to-Space Ratios, World War II (Square)

To interpret these figures, recall from chapter 5 that linear force-to-space ratios matter mainly as permissive conditions for high local force-to-force ratios: linear FSRs describe only the total number of defenders that attackers eventually encounter in penetrating the defense; if this figure is small, the attacker gets an opportunity to create a large local FFR by massing a large assault force at the point of attack. So the Germans' relatively large linear FSR matters chiefly because it reduced the Allies' local FFR. Yet the FFR here was very high even so: the Allies' theaterwide preponderance was so massive that they could overmatch even a fairly numerous local defense with greatly superior numbers, hence the effect of a high linear FSR was largely counteracted.

By contrast, square units of area better represent the primary causal logic of most force density arguments. Defenses with few troops per square kilometer are said to present gaps through which attackers can maneuver, and to provide fewer defensive weapons within reach of any given assault wave at any given point; taken together, these effects are supposed to enable attackers to destroy such defenses in detail. By this logic, however, the GOODWOOD defense was actually rather porous in Second World War terms. While there were many defenders opposite the British attack, they were spread over a tremendous depth, leaving them sparsely arrayed on the ground at any given point within the defended area. In fact, in square units of area, the GOODWOOD FSR was only half that of the German defenses opposite Operation COBRA, where the Americans broke through the following week.[45] If the logic of orthodox force-to-space arguments were a powerful explanation of combat outcomes, GOODWOOD should thus have been a penetrable defense by comparable World War II standards.[46]

Force Employment

In GOODWOOD, the British failed to implement the modern system at the tactical level and provided a rare example of a too-narrow assault frontage in a breakthrough attempt at the operational level. The Germans, by contrast, implemented the modern system very thoroughly at both the tactical and the operational levels.

OFFENSIVE OPERATIONS

Two aspects of British offensive operations warrant noting here. First, in its actual conduct, GOODWOOD was a breakthrough attempt and not a limited aims attack. Much has been written regarding Montgomery's intentions for GOODWOOD. His defenders characterize his plan as a limited-aims attack meant solely to pin German armor in place opposite Caen in preparation for a subsequent effort on the Allied right in Operation COBRA.[47] Montgomery's critics see this as a post hoc rationalization meant to conceal failure in an attempted breakthrough.[48] Either way, though, Dempsey and the Second Army officers who actually planned and directed the offensive clearly thought their mission was to break through German lines and exploit toward Falaise.[49] Whether they misunderstood Montgomery or not, the operation that resulted was a breakthrough attempt, not a limited aims attack. By observing it, we can thus shed important light on breakthrough battle dynamics, whatever Montgomery may have intended beforehand.

Second, Dempsey's plan called for a remarkably narrow assault frontage. Though the nominal frontage for the three participating corps (I and VIII British and II Canadian) was about 15 kilometers, the great majority was allocated to the supporting attacks by the four infantry divisions. The critical sector allocated to VIII Corps' three armored divisions—the units actually assigned to break through the German defense—was only 2 kilometers wide.[50]

This was among the narrowest frontages assigned to a three-division armored corps in the entire war. By way of comparison, the three Panzer divisions of the German XIX Corps that broke through the French defenses at Sedan in 1940 advanced on a 30-km front; at Alamein in 1941, the British 1st and 10th Armoured divisions each had nearly as wide a frontage as the entire VIII Corps at GOODWOOD; and the three-division mobile reserve echelon for the American offensive at COBRA that immediately followed GOODWOOD attacked on an 8-km front, or about four times that of British VIII Corps.[51]

This narrow assault frontage helped ensure a high local FFR, but in exchange it posed a number of important problems. The front was so narrow that enfilading fire from German positions on either flank could sweep the entire penetration corridor, interfering with British resupply and reducing British freedom of maneuver.[52] The narrow frontage forced the British to echelon the three armored divisions one behind the other, rather than bringing all three into action simultaneously.[53] Perhaps most important, it created serious congestion in the British assembly areas and approach routes. This delayed commitment of the 7th and Guards Armoured divisions, neither of which was fully exploited on the first day of the battle, and restricted access to any units not placed near the head of the British columns. As Dempsey had arranged the columns with tanks forward and supporting arms to the rear, this made proper combined arms coordination much harder.[54]

OFFENSIVE TACTICS

The British attackers at GOODWOOD systematically failed to exploit modern-system cover, concealment, dispersion, suppression, small-unit independent maneuver, and combined arms integration. Instead, British armor simply rolled forward in dense, exposed waves. British infantry advanced in the open and tended to bunch up when taken under fire. Neither made much effort to use terrain to cover their advance.[55]

Nor did the two maneuver branches support one another in any sustained way. British armor-infantry cooperation had been consistently poor throughout the Normandy campaign.[56] At GOODWOOD, this longstanding problem was exacerbated by the particulars of Dempsey's plan. Much of the infantry nominally intended to support the tanks had been placed too deep in the congested march columns to get forward in the battle's early stages.[57] Those who did became bogged down almost immediately in clearing the villages of Cuverville and Demouville less than 2 kilometers beyond the jump-off line.[58] The associated British armor meanwhile continued to advance, leaving the infantry behind and thus quickly producing an unsupported, nearly tank-pure offensive once the assault moved more than 2 kilometers into the depth of the German position.[59]

The British systematically failed to coordinate movement and suppressive fires after about midmorning of the opening day. The sheer magnitude of the carpet bombing left most of the surviving defenders *hors de combat* during the battle's early stages.[60] By 1100, however, the Germans had begun to recover and dig themselves out.[61] In principle, combined arms fire-and-movement should then have been employed to maintain suppression while the attackers continued to advance. Yet British suppressive fires were now all but unavailable. The attack had by then moved beyond the reach of the British batteries on the northern side of the Orne River, and the congestion in the march columns had kept the artillery from moving forward into supporting range.[62] Late in the day an attempt was made to arrange for a second saturation bombing against German antitank positions on the Bourgebus Ridge, but the massive air effort earlier in the day had left Allied air forces unable to respond quickly to a new mission. Smaller-scale close air support missions were flown and proved instrumental in defeating German counterattacks on the afternoon of the first day and thereafter, but sustained suppressive fires of the kind needed to screen an extended advance in massed formations over open ground were unavailable.[63]

Part of the reason for such exposure was Dempsey's radically narrow assault corridor. Much of the problem lay deeper, however. Most British units simply lacked the training, skills, and low-level initiative needed to implement modern-system tactics, whatever the assault frontage. Pre-invasion training, for example, had been undemanding and unrealistic, and once units reached France they found themselves in constant offensives with little time for in-theater retraining.[64] Noncommissioned and junior officer quality was a particular problem: aggressive junior leaders who tried to urge their units forward courted dangerous exposure under prevailing methods. Their disproportionate causualty rate, combined with rapid promotion of talented survivors, left small units chronically short of skilled, experienced leadership.[65] Without this, independent small-unit maneuver in dispersed, combined arms formations was simply too challenging to master. As one experienced infantry officer explained: "Look, all that I can do with my men, the sort of men I have, is to persuade them to get out of their holes in the ground, march up to the objective, dig a hole there, and get into it."[66] This was a far cry from the kind of initiative, professional skill, and tactical judgment needed to implement the modern system.

The net result was thus an exposed, massed, nearly tank-pure assault pressing forward rapidly without waiting for its infantry or supporting suppressive fires. This produced rapid closure but rendered modern-system casualty reduction impossible. In the new theory's terms, British tactics yielded a net velocity of 10–20 kilometers per day—a figure more than twice that of the subsequent American offensive at COBRA.[67]

DEFENSIVE OPERATIONS

German defenses at GOODWOOD were disposed in depth with a very large fraction of total troop strength withheld in mobile reserve. As in the First World War, the Second saw a similar progression from shallow early dispositions toward deeper defenses as the conflict wore on. This progression is illustrated in figure 6.5.[68] In 1940–41, for example, defenses with as little as 3–5-km depth were common. By 1943, defenders more often deployed to depths of 5–10 km, and by mid-1944, depths of up to 15 km had become commonplace.

At GOODWOOD, Eberbach's defenses extended over a depth of fully 16 kilometers, comprising four distinct belts of interlocking positions. The forwardmost consisted of the remnants of the 16th Luftwaffe Field Division, whose infantry was dug in among the ruins of the villages of Cuverville and Giberville, within some 2–3 km of the British front lines.[69] The second belt was held by the two panzer-grenadier regiments of the 21st Panzer Division, stiffened by a battalion of the division's Panzer regiment (deployed around Sannerville), the 503rd Heavy Tank Battalion (dug in near Emieville to its south), and the 200th Assault Gun battalion (deployed around Demouville to its west). Taken together, this belt spanned about 6 km and extended to a distance of about 9 km from the British front lines.

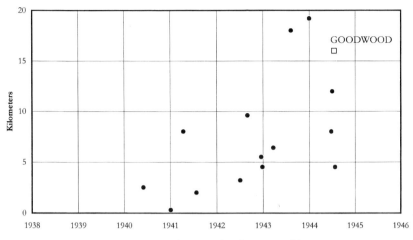

Figure 6.5. Depth of Prepared Defenses, World War II

The third belt consisted of a line of dug-in antitank guns and artillery supported by the 21st Panzer Division's Reconnaissance and Engineer Battalions (serving as infantry), which together were deployed along and behind the crest of the Bourguebus Ridge, some 10 km from the front. The fourth belt was made of elements of the 1st and 12th SS Panzer Divisions. Assigned as mobile reserves, these units were nominally in assembly areas from which they were to move before fighting, but given their proximity to the anticipated axis of a major forthcoming British offensive, their positions were prepared to enable them to serve as a rear defense line if necessary and extended to a total depth of some 16 km from the initial line of contact.[70]

This position was thus unusually deep by even late Second World War standards. In fact, it constitutes the third deepest value of the fifteen data points presented in figure 6.5, the second highest of the 1944–45 data, and more than twice the median value of the data overall (7.2 km).

Eberbach's defense was also unusually reserve-heavy. Though only four of Panzergruppe West's thirteen divisions were in reserve, these four divisions held a disproportionate fraction of the panzergruppe's overall strength. More than 70 percent of the combat manpower in the five divisions directly opposite the GOODWOOD assault frontage, for example, was held by the two reserve divisions in the sector (i.e., 1st and 12th SS). Across the entire theater, roughly 45 percent of German combat manpower was withheld in mobile reserve by July 18.[71]

To put these reserve allocations in context, figure 6.6 presents values for an illustrative set of Second World War operations.[72] Of the eleven values shown, GOODWOOD (0.73) is the highest single figure, more than twice the median (0.24)

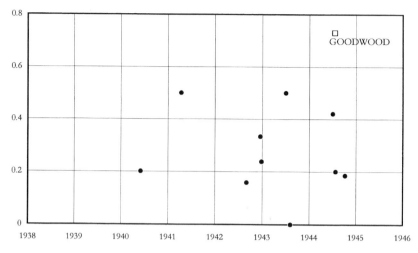

Figure 6.6. Fraction of Defender's Troops in Reserve, World War II.

and more than two standard deviations above the mean (0.31) of the data overall. By World War II standards, the Germans thus withheld an unusually large fraction of their overall troop strength in mobile reserve.

DEFENSIVE TACTICS

The Germans at GOODWOOD made very effective use of modern-system defensive tactics. In particular, their prepared positions were extremely well covered and concealed, and their reserve movements made aggressive use of exposure-reduction techniques to reduce their vulnerability to Allied air attack.

Throughout the Normandy campaign, German defenders were adept at camouflage. At times, Allied tanks advanced to within as little as 20–30 meters of concealed German armored vehicles without detecting them.[73] Few German fighting positions could be detected until their occupants opened fire. One result of this was the great difficulty Allied tactical intelligence encountered in mapping German positions prior to attack: at GOODWOOD, for example, British intelligence underestimated the depth of the German dispositions by about a factor of two.[74]

German units were also adept at concealing their movements, especially from air attack. German reserve movements were subject to extraordinary interdiction efforts: the Allies enjoyed complete air supremacy in Normandy and devoted tens of thousands of sorties to ground attack missions over the course of the campaign. In June alone, over 67,000 attack sorties were flown against German ground force targets in France.[75] Yet the Germans proved able to move more than twenty-one divisions over many hundreds of kilometers from other parts of France, the Low Countries, Poland, and elsewhere into the Normandy theater over the course of the six weeks between the invasion and Operation GOODWOOD.[76] Though these units suffered losses in transit, these losses were typically far smaller than those suffered from Allied ground fire once they arrived in theater.[77] Had their movements been conducted in the open against such a massive air campaign, few would have survived to reach their destination. The key to the Germans' ability to move such masses over such great distances in the face of an unprecedented interdiction effort was their exploitation of a wide range of measures to reduce their exposure en route in exchange for reduced speed.

In particular, German units moved only in darkness and foul weather; they avoided main roads; they traveled in very small units by circuitous routes to take maximum advantage of natural overhead cover; they observed strict radio listening silence when moving; and they systematically scanned the skies before leaving cover to make sure no Allied aircraft were overhead—only when the skies were clear did they initiate movement in the open. During daylight hours they sheltered in railway tunnels, forests, orchards, and towns, hiding rather than moving. Whenever and wherever units stopped, they dug in and provided expedient overhead camouflage.[78]

Taken together, these techniques were very effective in allowing large German units to move into and within the Normandy theater, but they radically lengthened the travel time required for such redeployment. The 9th and 10th SS Panzer divisions, for example, traveled 1,300 km from Poland to Lorraine in only four days; the subsequent journey from Lorraine to their assembly areas in Normandy, by contrast, was conducted under threat of Allied air attack and took twice the time to cover about one-fourth the distance.[79] More broadly, in the new theory's terms, German reserve redeployments in Normandy were conducted at an average net velocity of about 30–40 km/day—or about one-third the nominal, no-interdiction rate.[80]

Modern-system exposure reduction thus imposes important penalties: it cannot be accomodated without major reductions in velocity. But the alternative of exposure in exchange for speed can be costly against even a 1944-era interdiction effort. As an illustration, in August the Germans were forced to move in the open during daylight to escape from the Falaise Pocket. An Allied encirclement threatened to cut off some twenty-one German divisions that had failed in the Mortain counterattack, and the German command faced the choice of allowing these forces to be surrounded and annihilated by Allied ground forces if they moved cautiously, or exposing them to Allied air attack if they moved rapidly to escape the pocket.[81] They chose the latter, and the result was slaughter: in a few days of massive air strikes, the Germans lost some ten thousand vehicles and guns in the attempt to escape the pocket, comprising perhaps as much as 80 percent of the materiel that began the move.[82] For most of the campaign, however, and for the duration of Operation GOODWOOD in particular, German tactics were characterized by modern-system cover and concealment—where necessary at the expense of speed.

OUTCOME AND SIGNIFICANCE

Given the characterizations above, how does the battle's outcome correspond with the respective theories' predictions? Orthodox theories predict break-through here: GOODWOOD was among the most tank- and ground attack aircraft-rich actions of the century; the German defenders enjoyed no net technological edge; and the numerical balance both exceeded the usual rules of thumb and compared favorably with other Second World War experience. The new theory, by contrast, predicts a contained offensive: an exposed, tactically non–modern-system attack struck a mature modern-system defense. In the terms of the formal model developed in the appendix, the new theory predicts that an offensive with an assault velocity of 10 km/day and a frontage of between 2 and 15 km will fail to break through a defense with a depth of 16 km, a reserve withhold of 0.45, a reserve velocity of 35 km/day and an exposure fraction of 0.[83] The model further predicts that the attacker will gain about 4.4 km of ground, that the operation will come to a halt after about a half a day of fighting, and that attackers' casualties will greatly exceed the defenders'.[84]

The actual historical results are much more consistent with the new theory than the orthodox alternatives. Rather than an extremum of offensive success, as orthodox theories predict, GOODWOOD produced a contained offensive that pe-tered out with a net ground gain of only about 8–10 km.[85] Attacker losses were modest in troops but extremely high in tanks: the British lost 400–500 medium tanks, or nearly half of the Second Army's initial strength, and more than one-third of all the British armor on the continent at the time.[86] In fact, the results were so disappointing that it led some in Allied command councils to talk of Montgomery's dismissal.[87] As Eisenhower put it: "it had taken more than 7,000 tons of bombs to gain seven miles and the Allies could hardly hope to go through France paying a price of a thousand tons of bombs per mile."[88] For per-haps the most tank-heavy engagement in history to have produced such a dra-matic fizzle with such attacker-preponderant numbers is an important challenge to orthodox theories of capability.

By contrast, the new theory is mostly consistent with the historical results. Most important, it correctly predicts defensive containment in spite of radically offense-favorable materiel. Its estimated ground gain is also within 4–6 km of the historical outcome, and its estimated duration is a close approximation of the time at which the British offensive ground to a halt.[89]

There are also several points where the formal model and the historical out-come diverge, however. In particular, the model implies that the attacker will concentrate about 200,000 combat assault troops at the point of attack and will lose the great majority of these.[90] In the actual battle, the British concentrated more than 118,000 soldiers for GOODWOOD, but fewer than 50,000 of these were combat assault troops (i.e., the riflemen and tank crews who closed with the de-fense), and of these, only about 11 percent (5,537) were killed or wounded.

Moreover, on the critical VIII Corps frontage the British concentrated only about 14,500 actual combat assault troops, suffering 1,818 casualties.[91] The model thus overestimates both the size of the British assault force at the point of attack and, especially, its casualties.[92]

What accounts for these discrepancies, and how serious a challenge to the theory are they? Most of the divergence stems from two simplifying assumptions that conflict with peculiarities of the British dispositions at GOODWOOD. When these peculiarities are taken into account, the model's casualty predictions come into much closer alignment with the historical outcome, suggesting that the theory's underlying causal logic is broadly consistent with the case even if some of its simplifying assumptions are not.

First, the model assumes that attackers mass their forces for a single theater offensive, with other sectors left quiet. As in MICHAEL, however, the attackers in July 1944 actually planned for several nearly simultaneous operations: COBRA was to follow GOODWOOD by only a few days, hence available forces had to be divided between the two efforts. In addition, the Allies in Normandy conducted frequent minor offensives along much of the theater frontier throughout June and July, siphoning forces away from the major efforts in GOODWOOD and COBRA (and before that, from the offensives in EPSOM or CHARNWOOD).[93] By dividing forces among multiple efforts, the Allies thus chose to commit many fewer troops to each than the model assumes.

Second, the model's casualty calculations assume that forces at the point of attack have the same tank:infantry balance as those away from it—the model makes no provision for an attacker choosing to leave its infantry off the battle-field.[94] By contrast, Dempsey did just this: his unusual choices of assault frontage and march-column organization meant that the Britons doing the actual fighting on the critical sector at GOODWOOD were mostly the armored sub-components of the assault forces as a whole—the infantry elements were stuck in traffic jams and missed most of the decisive early fighting.[95] Tank units have many fewer soldiers than comparable infantry formations and thus place many fewer personnel at risk: a British tank battalion (or "squadron") in July 1944, for example, had only about one-fourth the soldiers of a British infantry battalion.[96] Moreover, tanks' armor protection means that many of the personnel at risk can escape a stricken vehicle alive and thus survive the loss of the tank itself: on average, only two of the five crewmembers of a Sherman tank were killed or wounded per tank knocked out.[97] Tank units thus tend to suffer far fewer personnel casualties than comparable infantry units. At GOODWOOD, this produced radically disparate figures for British tank and personnel loss rates—about 50 percent for tanks, but only 11 percent for troops—and this in turn produced an unusually low personnel casualty rate for such an unsuccessful offensive.[98] The model, by making no provision for an attacker leaving its infantry out of the fight, thus overestimates the personnel losses to be expected from a formation of VIII Corps' size and exposure.[99]

If one controls for these differences between the model's assumed troop alloca-tions and the actors' actual choices, much of the discrepancy between predicted and observed casualties goes away. In particular, if one treats the attacker's and defender's local forces at the point of attack as exogenous variables, sets their values at the historical levels (rather than computing them endogenously as the model does), focuses on the forces actually deployed on the critical VIII Corps corridor, and assumes that the British forces actually exposed to fire are chiefly ar-mored subunits with one-fourth the manpower at risk, then predicted casualties fall to values much closer to the actual historical result.[100] Specifically, predicted attacker casualties in the VIII Corps sector come to 3,370 (as opposed to the ac-tual 1,818); ground gain comes to 2 km (as opposed to the actual 8–10), and dura-tion comes to 0.2 days (as opposed to the 0.5 days it took for the British to reach their maximum depth of penetration in the actual event).[101]

As in chapter 5, the simplifications inherent in modeling again make some di-vergence between prediction and observation inevitable. Rather than seeking to account for the peculiarities of theater commanders' troop allocations, I have in-stead chosen to focus on what I believe to be the central dynamics of theater-level warfare and to abstract out such details as secondary. No theory can ever account for all details of particular cases, but the underlying causal dynamics of the new theory are nevertheless broadly consistent with the facts of the case, as indicated by the correspondence obtained when controlling for the specific histori-cal dispositions as noted above. And most of the key historical outcomes—i.e., breakthrough vs. containment, attacker ground gain, and conflict duration—are predicted well even with the model's simplifying assumptions as to the particular geographic distribution of the two sides' forces in July 1944. On balance the re-sult is thus a much closer fit than orthodox theories provide.

ALTERNATIVE EXPLANATIONS OF THE BRITISH FAILURE TO BREAK THROUGH

How does the argument above compare with existing historical accounts? Many historians cite some combination of German defensive depth and tactical skill, poor British combined arms coordination (especially, poor armor-infantry coop-eration), and congestion arising from Dempsey's narrow assault frontage.[102] This was also how the Germans themselves explained the outcome in their own after-action analyses in the days following the operation.[103]

Several prominent explanations, however, are at odds with the analysis above. Some, for example, cite superior German technology, especially tanks.[104] Yet, as I argue above, only in two tank models, the Pzkw V Panther and Pzkw VI Tiger tanks, did the Germans enjoy a meaningful edge. To explain British failure in these terms is not just to overlook most of the weapon types used in the battle, and especially aircraft; it is also to overlook most of the *tanks* actually used in the battle (since Panthers and Tigers comprised a minority of the German armor at

GOODWOOD). In fact, the attack had largely ground to a halt before either the Panthers or the Tigers had become heavily engaged; though the latter helped apply the coup de grace, most of the crucial early killing was done by towed anti-tank guns prior to the main tank units' arrival on the battlefield.[105] Weapon technology in GOODWOOD is simply a much larger issue than duels between Tiger and Sherman tanks. And the effects of any of the weapons involved were powerfully influenced by the two sides' tactics—especially the British armor's exposure and the near absence of supporting infantry, artillery, and close air support from the assault. The German antitank guns that created so much havoc, for example, would have been extremely vulnerable either to British infantry or to British sup-pressive artillery if these had been available in the critical times and places.[106] It is easy to overemphasize tank duels in battles like GOODWOOD precisely because the British left everything else behind, but this was hardly due to technological inferi-ority. While the Panther and the Tiger were clearly superior tanks, there is little reason to believe they were necessary or decisive for the outcome.

Others suggest that German defenders were simply too numerous for the British to defeat; by striking the German front where it was strongest, Montgomery had taken on too large an opponent to break through.[107] The Germans had indeed made an effort to strengthen the Caen front, partly because it offered the best of-fensive terrain for the Allies, partly because Germany had received intelligence indications that the British would in fact attack there, and partly because the Germans wanted to launch an offensive of their own there as soon as conditions permitted.[108] But even so, the local FFR at GOODWOOD hardly precluded success-ful attack. As shown above, Allied forces in Normandy were so large that they could radically overmatch even the heaviest section of German defenses in July 1944. The GOODWOOD FFR and FSR were both unusually offense-conducive by comparison with other World War II experience. The local FFR met or exceeded the standard rules of thumb for offensive success by almost any plausible count-ing rule. The British offensive did not fail for lack of sufficient numerical prepon-derance.

A few have argued that inaccurate bombing by the American Eighth and Ninth air forces allowed too many Germans to survive in their target areas, lead-ing to unnecessarily heavy losses when the British tanks reached the (deeper) tar-gets assigned to these aircraft.[109] Yet there is little evidence that German casualty rates differed significantly across U.S. and RAF target areas. Cagny, for example, was struck with 650 tons of bombs by RAF Bomber Command, yet the crucial 88-mm guns survived to decimate the 2nd Fife and Forfars and 5th Guards Armoured Brigade when these appeared in midmorning.[110] Instead, the chief problems with the carpet bombing were twofold. First, the German defense was simply too deep: key German antitank positions (especially those on the Bour-guebus Ridge and beyond) were outside the bomb carpet, and thus could not be destroyed by it, however accurate its delivery.[111] Second, the exposed, tank-pure British units that conducted the assault were extremely vulnerable to even tiny parties of surviving Germans.[112] No preliminary barrage—even multikiloton efforts like the carpet bombing at Goodwood—can ever destroy the entirety of a properly dug-in defense. Carpet bombing can cause terrific casualties, but some defenders will still survive. If poor attacker tactics present those few survivors with exposed, unsupported targets in the open, then attacker losses will be heavy regardless of the effort devoted to preliminary fire preparation. Fires alone cannot create breakthroughs; only a tightly integrated combination of fire and movement using combined arms can enable progress at acceptable losses against a well-handled defense.

Alternatively, some argue that the offensive actually succeeded.[113] After the battle, Montgomery claimed he had never sought to break through, but merely to hold the German Panzer divisions in place around Caen and "write down" their armored strength, thereby easing the task for Bradley's subsequent offensive in Cobra. This position proved highly controversial, in part due to the highly ambiguous nature of Montgomery's own communications prior to the battle. His defenders, however, continue to hold that the attack was never meant to break through and in fact succeeded in keeping most of the German armor on the Allied left. Yet, as noted above, Dempsey and Goodwood's actual planners clearly sought to break through, whatever Montgomery's (ambiguously stated) actual intentions.[114] As such, Goodwood can be judged on its merits as a failed breakthrough attempt; whether this should detract from Montgomery's reputation is a question I leave to others.

Finally, some argue that the British offensive was overcautious; had it been more "thrustful," it could have punched through the German defense before the Germans had recovered from the carpet bombing.[115] The British offensive did in fact fail to keep pace with the creeping barrage laid down by the artillery following the carpet bombing.[116] This failure presumably led to unnecessary casualties. Insufficient boldness, however, can hardly explain the failure of perhaps the single greatest massed tank charge in history. The German antitank guns in Cagny, Four, Soliers, and the Bourguebus Ridge that wiped out the exposed tanks of 11th and Guards Armoured Divisions had survived the carpet bombing untouched and were beyond the range of the creeping barrage; they would have been just as lethal if reached a bit sooner. In fact, the "overcautious" argument has it precisely backward: the problem with the British offensive was that it threw caution to the winds, deliberately courting a highly exposed advance in order to move more quickly. It was hoped that surprise and boldness, in conjunction with a massive bombing raid, would enable a massed armor force to overrun German defenses before they could react. Its problem was that it sacrificed any chance for proper combined arms integration or cover and concealment in the interests of speed, denying the lead armored units the dismounted infantry they needed to deal with concealed, dug-in antitank guns and quickly outrunning the reach of the suppressive artillery available to them from the batteries on the north side of the Orne. If bold handling of massed armor were ever going to create a breakthrough by shock action alone, it should have been here; the fact that such a massive phalanx of armor instead impaled itself on antitank guns it could neither see nor counter provides an important object lesson in the limits of exposed, unsupported tanks on the modern battlefield.

CONCLUSIONS AND IMPLICATIONS

For a single case study, GOODWOOD thus offers unusually strong confirmatory evidence for the new theory, and unusually strong disconfirmatory evidence for orthodox views. The case offers an extreme example of what should have been offense-dominant technology and numerical imbalance, yet the attack ground to a halt after an advance of less than 10 km, losing nearly a third of all the British armor on the continent in the process. This is consistent with the new theory's predictions for the Germans' deep, well-concealed modern-system defense and the British attackers' exposed, non–modern-system attack. With the deck stacked against a force employment explanation by such extreme technology and numerical odds, corroboration in GOODWOOD is thus a particularly significant outcome. Nevertheless, the new theory does not perfectly match the case: the formal model fails to anticipate the Allies' multiple nearly simultaneous offensives, and it overestimates British personnel losses. It correctly anticipates the attackers' inability to break through, however, as well as the duration of the British advance, its rough depth of penetration, and the gross scale of German losses. By contrast, the orthodox theories fit neither the battle's key outcome nor the details of its conduct or dynamics. The new theory thus outperforms the orthodox alternatives in a case where one should reasonably have expected the opposite. While no single case can ever validate a theory, the results do establish a degree of correspondence between the new theory and an important example of real warfare; they show a closer correspondence for the new theory than the orthodox alternatives in an Ecksteinian critical case; and they thus offer grounds for shifting our confidence in the respective theories.

Operation DESERT STORM—January 17–February 28, 1991

THIS CHAPTER PROVIDES a final case method test in Operation DESERT STORM, the Coalition offensive in the Persian Gulf War from January 17 to February 28, 1991. I argue that the details of DESERT STORM's conduct contradict orthodox theories' implications, while sustaining the new theory's. The Gulf War has proven powerfully influential for today's defense debate. Yet the war's main lesson for most observers—that technology is now decisive—is inconsistent with the war's actual conduct. The Coalition's radically low loss rate in the Gulf cannot be explained without considering force employment—and its nonlinear *interaction* with technology—as the new theory provides but orthodox analyses lack.

I develop this argument in six steps. As before, I begin by motivating my selection of DESERT STORM as a case study. Unlike chapters 5 and 6, however, I include here an early discussion of the historical outcome to be explained and its importance in order to clarify the case's theoretical role. Second, I outline the main events. Third, I develop values for the key independent variables. Whereas this theoretical characterization comprised the bulk of the MICHAEL and GOODWOOD cases, here my primary attention is on the next two parts of the argument: an assessment of the contrasting theories via a combination of process tracing and subunit analysis; and a consideration of other explanations of the DESERT STORM outcome. I conclude with a summary assessment of the case's implications for the theories under study.

WHY DESERT STORM?

Unlike MICHAEL and GOODWOOD, DESERT STORM is not a critical case in Eckstein's terms. As I demonstrate below, the Coalition attackers enjoyed superior numbers, technology, *and* force employment. The gross outcome—breakthrough—is thus overdetermined. Yet the case is not indeterminate. The key lies not in the theories' gross predictions for breakthrough or containment, but in their divergent causal accounts of *why* and *how* the Coalition broke through. The respective theories provide very different reasons for expecting a breakthrough, implying contrasting and observable implications for the way in which the fighting ought to have unfolded. By comparing these implications with the war's actual conduct, one can distinguish stronger from weaker accounts of the same basic outcome.

Breakthrough and containment, moreover, are not the only relevant outcomes. In fact, DESERT STORM's most important single feature is not that the Coalition broke through, but that *it won with an unprecedentedly low loss rate.* In less than six weeks, 795,000 Coalition troops destroyed a defending Iraqi army of hundreds of thousands for the loss of only 240 attackers.[1] This loss rate of fewer than one fatality per 3,000 soldiers was less than one-tenth of the Israelis' in either the 1967 Six-Day War or the Bekaa Valley campaign in 1982, less than one-twentieth of the Germans' in their blitzkriegs against Poland or France in 1939–40, and about one-one-thousandth of the U.S. Marines' in the invasion of Tarawa in 1943.[2] Whereas breakthrough per se is theoretically undemanding given 1991's preponderance and technology, breakthrough at a historically unprecedented low loss rate is much more challenging to explain. And orthodox methods generally failed to do so before the war.[3]

This startlingly low loss rate has had important policy consequences. In fact, it made the Gulf War a shaping event for defense planning today in much the way the painful defeat in Vietnam came to shape U.S. planning in the 1980s. U.S. forces are now sized and structured against a Gulf War yardstick. New doctrines, weapons, and organizations are assessed in simulations of updated Gulf Wars. Acceptable casualty levels are judged against a 1991 benchmark.[4] In fact, the war changed the whole course of American military thought—the revolution in military affairs thesis that now dominates the defense debate is a product of the radically surprising nature of the DESERT STORM loss rate. Though the RMA thesis had been presented before the war, few were persuaded. The Gulf War's stunning loss rate acted as a catalyst, however, and in less than four years a wholly new vision of future warfare had become conventional wisdom in Washington. This now-conventional view—indeed, the entire set of underlying assumptions on technology that underpins today's defense planning—rests on a particular understanding of the reasons for the 1991 loss rate. Understanding this loss rate thus has profound intrinsic importance for the current debate, above and beyond the case's value for testing theories of capability.

The outcome to be explained here is thus the *way* the Coalition broke through, and in particular, its ability to do so with a historically unprecedented low loss rate. This outcome is important in its own right, and it also provides critical methodological leverage in distinguishing the relative validity of the respective theories. As such, the case offers a challenging test even without providing an Ecksteinian critical case.[5]

OVERVIEW OF EVENTS, JANUARY 17–FEBRUARY 28, 1991

The war began with a massive six-week air campaign. This quickly crippled the Iraqi air defense system and destroyed key elements of their command and control network. There followed more than a month of effectively uncontested, round-the-clock pounding of ground targets across Iraq and over the entire depth of the Kuwait Theater of Operations (KTO).[6]

As the air war unfolded, Coalition ground forces secretly redeployed from east to west. By February 23, the Coalition had positioned two corps on the Iraqis' extreme right flank. The Iraqis were disposed with twenty-six conscript infantry divisions deployed forward in a prepared defensive belt. Behind them were nine higher-quality army mechanized divisions, with eight elite Republican Guard divisions located well to the rear.[7]

The Coalition ground invasion began the morning of February 24, when lead elements of two U.S. Marine divisions entered the Iraqi defensive belt near the coastal highway. The main effort, however, was on the far left, where the Coalition VII and XVIII Corps soon followed with a massive single envelopment of the Iraqi forward defenses. This "left hook" quickly collapsed the Iraqi right wing and opened a clear path across the Iraqi rear toward the Republican Guard.

Progress was rapid. Iraqi conscripts offered little resistance and surrendered in large numbers as Coalition forces overran the forward defenses. By February 26, Kuwait City had been reached, and three heavy divisions of the Coalition VII Corps were massed for a direct assault on the Republican Guard.

Beginning on February 26, VII Corps drove through the Guard from west to east. Unlike the infantry at the border, however, the Guard fought back. By then the surviving Iraqis in the KTO were attempting to withdraw via Basra; perhaps three Guard and another three army heavy divisions had been maneuvered into blocking positions in an attempt to keep their retreat route open.[8] The result was the heaviest fighting of the campaign as they met the Coalition's heaviest forces head on.

For some forty-one hours, a series of battles were fought as VII Corps overran the Iraqi blocking force. Initial contact was made on the afternoon of February 26 by the U.S. 2d Armored Cavalry Regiment (ACR), which struck the Iraqi Tawakalna Division on a stretch of mostly featureless desert near a map reference line called "73 Easting"; the ensuing engagement thus became known as the "Battle of 73 Easting." Launching an immediate assault, 2d ACR's lead troop of nine M1 tanks and twelve M3 Bradleys subsequently destroyed the entire defensive position in front of them, hitting thirty-seven Iraqi T-72s and thirty-two other armored vehicles in about forty minutes. The two adjoining troops immediately followed suit. Before stopping to regroup, these three U.S. cavalry troops had in fact overrun and wiped out an entire Republican Guard brigade.[9] Subsequent Iraqi counterattacks were beaten off with heavy losses, leaving a total of 113 Iraqi armored vehicles destroyed at the cost of one U.S. Bradley lost and one crew member killed by Iraqi fire (with a second vehicle loss attributed to fratricide). Some 600 Iraqi casualties were removed from the battlefield.[10]

The other actions followed a similar pattern. The largest of these, the Battle of Medina Ridge, pitted the 2d Brigade of the U.S. 1st Armored against the 2d Brigade of the Medina Luminous Division. In forty minutes of fighting, the

U.S. brigade annihilated the Iraqi armor in place, took 55 Iraqis prisoner, and killed another 340. No U.S. casualties were suffered.[11] At Objective Norfolk, two battalions of the U.S. 1st Infantry Division destroyed more than 100 armored vehicles of the Iraqi Tawakalna and 12th Armored divisions for the loss of two U.S. Bradleys.[12] In the Battle for Wadi Al Batin, a battalion of the U.S. 3rd Armored Division wiped out an Iraqi brigade, killing more than 160 armored vehicles while losing less than a half dozen of its own.[13]

By the morning of February 27, the Iraqi blocking force had been effectively wiped out. In all, VII Corps destroyed as many as 1,350 Iraqi tanks, 1,224 armored troop carriers, 285 artillery pieces, 105 air defense systems, and 1,229 trucks. VII Corps itself, by contrast, lost no more than 36 armored vehicles to enemy fire and suffered a total of only 47 dead and 192 wounded.[14]

INDEPENDENT VARIABLES

Weapon Technology

Weapon technology in DESERT STORM strongly favored the Coalition.[15] Though Iraq fielded the best weapons Saddam's oil money could buy, American technology in 1991 was still markedly superior. The U.S. M1A1's compound armor, depleted uranium ammunition, and 120-mm gun gave it a penetration range advantage of more than a kilometer over the Iraqis' Soviet-made T-72s and T-55s, and the M1's thermal sights afforded an even greater margin in target acquisition.[16] U.S. counterbattery radars enabled even outranged American guns to win artillery duels by directing counterfire against Iraqi artillery before the first Iraqi round had even reached the ground.[17] U.S. Global Positioning System satellite receivers allowed American units to navigate over trackless deserts where Iraqi forces were unable to travel.[18] Perhaps most important, U.S. surveillance, precision guidance, and air defense suppression technologies gave American air power radical new lethality against exposed ground targets that the Iraqis could not remotely match.[19] In the new theory's terms, the average date of introduction for the U.S. weapons used in DESERT STORM was around 1973.9; for the Iraqis, about 1961.9 (see the appendix); this twelve-year lead is the largest of the sixteen wars for which data are available and exceeds the next-widest gap by more than a factor of two.

Numerical Imbalance

DESERT STORM's exact numerical balance will probably never be known, since official Iraqi strength figures are unavailable and possibly nonexistent. Nevertheless, the Coalition clearly outnumbered the Iraqis, and the Iraqi force-to-space ratio was probably quite low.

FORCE-TO-FORCE RATIOS

Wartime strength estimates by U.S. Central Command (CENTCOM) gave Coalition ground troop strength as 620,000 and credited Iraq with 540,000 troops on February 24.[20] Whereas the Coalition strength was accurate, the Iraqi estimate assumed that all units in the KTO were fully manned. Postwar prisoner interviews, however, established that most units were substantially under-strength when deployed; desertions before and during the air war further reduced Iraqi manpower. Probably the best current estimate for remaining Iraqi forces is no more than 340,000 on January 17, and probably no more than 220,000 on the eve of the ground offensive.[21] Of these figures, about 100,000 of the Coalition troops and fewer than 60,000 of the Iraqis were direct-fire combat maneuver soldiers.[22] In the new model's terms, the theaterwide FFR thus probably approached or exceeded 2:1 in combat maneuver strength and probably approached 3:1 in total personnel.

This is well beyond common standards for successful attack. The usual rule of thumb is 1.5:1 at the theater level; the DESERT STORM figure is at least one-third higher.[23] The DESERT STORM theater FFR exceeded the Israelis' for the 1967 Sinai offensive by perhaps a factor of two and was nearly three times that of Britain's reconquest of the Falklands in 1982.[24] The Coalition clearly enjoyed a major numerical advantage in the KTO by the eve of the ground invasion.[25]

FORCE-TO-SPACE RATIOS

Theaterwide, Iraqi forces were spread very thin.[26] The KTO spanned about 500 km of the Saudi border with Iraq and Kuwait, with a further 250 km of Kuwaiti coastline to be defended against possible amphibious invasion.[27] Taken together, this implied a theaterwide FSR of only about 260–290 troops per linear km, and 5–6 forward troops per square km. By contrast, standard rules of thumb for late-twentieth-century FSRs usually held that at least 300–700 or more troops per linear km were needed for stable defense.[28] The Iraqi FSR in DESERT STORM was also significantly lower than a variety of unsuccessful contemporary defenses, including the Egyptian defense of the Sinai in 1967 (which deployed 825 troops per linear km), or the Syrian/PLO defenses in Lebanon in 1982 (which deployed about 410).[29] Overall, most force-to-space theorists would thus predict failure for such a defense.

Force Employment

In DESERT STORM, the Iraqis implemented the modern system moderately well at the operational level but very poorly at the tactical level. The Americans, by contrast, implemented the modern system very thoroughly at both the tactical and operational levels.[30]

DEFENSIVE OPERATIONS

Iraqi forces were disposed in moderate depth. Prepared positions for forward infantry divisions were about 15 km deep, with two of the divisions' three maneuver brigades in a first belt of defenses and the third occupying a second belt to their rear.[31] These dispositions were deeper than some other contemporary examples: Egyptian defenses against Israeli counterattacks in the Sinai in 1973, for instance, spanned a total depth of under 6 km.[32] Iraqi dispositions were far shallower, however, than the Americans' during the defensive DESERT SHIELD phase of the Gulf War. The U.S. 1st Marine Division, for example, defended a zone more than 75 km deep.[33] The 24th Mechanized Division to its left defended in up to 120-km depth.[34] Moreover, these divisions were dug in to the rear of a mixed Arab division deployed at the border itself; the total depth of the Coalition's prepared defenses extended to more than 150 km, or about ten times the Iraqi figure.[35]

Much of Iraq's total combat power was held in mobile reserve. Seventeen of Iraq's forty-two divisions in the theater, or about 40 percent, were withheld from forward positions.[36] This understates the real proportion, however, because the forward divisions each held many fewer troops than the reserve divisions. Even before the air war, manning levels in the forward infantry divisions were far lower than the heavy army and Guard units in the mobile reserve—and during the air war, desertion rates were far higher for the forward infantry. By the time of the ground war, probably 70 percent or more of the Iraqis' theater troop strength was in reserve.[37] This was very high by historical standards: U.S. forces in DESERT SHIELD, by contrast, held just two of five divisions in reserve, with about 40 percent of U.S. ground combat manpower in the theater.[38]

DEFENSIVE TACTICS

Iraqi defenses provided neither the concealment, cover, independent small-unit maneuver, nor combined arms integration demanded by modern-system tactics. Iraqi fighting positions, for example, left their occupants radically exposed to U.S. observation and fire. Iraqi infantry was deployed in poorly camouflaged, easily visible trenches laid out in formulaic, standardized patterns.[39] Since at least 1917, Western militaries have realized that such exposed entrenchments give away defenders' locations—sacrificing concealment for cover, yet providing too little cover to protect their occupants against modern firepower. Smaller, irregularly distributed, carefully camouflaged positions combining ballistic protection with real concealment are needed to withstand offensive fire.[40] Iraqi infantry, moreover, failed to exploit even the limited potential of formulaically interconnected trenches: overhead cover was rarely provided for firing positions, which were systematically too shallow, too wide, and devoid of even rudimentary camouflage. Protective minefields and wire entanglements were haphazard, with mines mostly just scattered on the desert surface where they could be observed and avoided, and with minimal use of antitank ditches or other obstructions to offensive movement.[41]

Armored vehicle positions were even worse. Western armies dig vehicle fighting positions into the earth below grade and hide the soil removed in excavation. The Iraqis, by contrast, simply piled sand into loose berms, or mounds, on the surface around their armored vehicles.[42] This not only gave away their locations—and from literally thousands of meters away, as the berms were the only distinctive feature of an otherwise nearly flat landscape—but did so without providing any real protection against the fire it would certainly draw.[43] Loose piles of sand cannot stop modern, high-velocity tank rounds. In fact, they barely slow them down. U.S. crews at 73 Easting, for example, reported seeing 120-mm tank rounds pass through Iraqi berms, through the armored vehicle behind the berm, and off into the distance.[44] No U.S. tank crew would leave itself so exposed.

The Iraqi command system was rigid and centralized, with a nearly complete absence of initiative among junior officers and little ability to operate independently in small units.[45] This left them unable to make anything of their depth and reserves: deep, reserve-oriented, modern-system defenses require soldiers and junior leaders to operate autonomously. The Iraqis proved systematically incapable of this in 1991.

Perhaps the most glaring illustration was their inability to provide tactical warning of attack. The observation posts and covering forces at the forward edge of a deep defense are necessarily small, exposed detachments operating far from the main defenses; since at least 1917, all Western armies have relied upon them to provide the main positions to their rear with warning of attack. Ideally, these covering forces serve other functions as well (such as stripping away hostile reconnaissance elements, slowing attackers' movement, or canalizing the assault), but the minimum task they must perform is to notify the main defense of an attacker's approach. While straightforward in principle,[46] this requires a combination of discipline and independence: small, dispersed teams not under direct observation by higher command must carry out orders in the face of greatly superior enemy forces and often must maneuver to break contact and fall back before being overrun. The Iraqis in 1991 regularly failed to accomplish this. At 73 Easting, for example, observation posts were deployed well forward of the main defenses, yet they provided no warning whatsoever of the 2d ACR's approach. In fact, a captured lieutenant from the main defenses later reported that his first clue of American attack was when "the turret of the tank next to him blew off."[47]

As a result, Iraqi defenders were often unready to meet Coalition attacks. At a minimum, this slowed their reaction time. But it may also have provided some U.S. attackers an opportunity to engage empty targets for the crucial opening minutes of battle. Combat vehicles are rarely fully manned unless standing watch or otherwise on alert—which the Tawakalna, for example, was not on the afternoon of the 24th. Thus at most, a few on-watch vehicles would have been fully manned, with others empty or occupied by skeleton crews. But in fact, many Iraqis interpreted 73 Easting's opening explosions as an air attack (they had received no warning of a ground advance), hence even some skeleton crews bailed out to take cover in nearby air-raid shelters at the very moment the ground attack began. As the attack's nature became clear, many tried to remount, but by then dozens of Iraqi tanks and BMPs had already been destroyed—and by the time the remounting crews could get their weapons into action, still more had been lost.[48]

The Iraqis also systematically failed to coordinate the different arms at their disposal. In particular, artillery was very poorly integrated with direct fires, whether in defense against American assaults, or in support of their own coun- terattacks. The Iraqis tried to direct artillery against the advancing Americans but proved unable either to adjust fire against moving targets (a difficult task) or even to deliver fire in mass against fixed points as Americans moved past them (an easier job).[49] Iraqi counterattacks at 73 Easting were executed with only rudi- mentary attempts to suppress U.S. fire with Iraqi artillery, or to screen Iraqi ad- vances with artillery-delivered smoke.[50] Nor was any attempt made to scout the ACR's positions before the assault; to use engineers to create smoke or other ob- scuration; or to coordinate assault forces' movement with stationary overwatch elements to provide covering fire.[51] Overall, the Iraqis thus systematically failed to implement the modern system at the tactical level.

OFFENSIVE OPERATIONS

DESERT STORM offensive operations closely followed modern-system precepts. Four aspects warrant noting here.

First, the plan called for an orthodox breakthrough of a continuous defensive front. The Coalition is sometimes described as having waged "nonlinear" or "maneuver" warfare, or as outflanking the Iraqi defenses rather than con- fronting them directly.[52] The operation began, however, with a conventional in- terior penetration of a prepared defensive line. While five divisions were in fact directed around the Iraqis' dangling right flank, this circuitous movement cov- ered too great a distance for the forces involved to be resupplied over the same route. It was thus necessary to open a resupply corridor farther to the east, and this required a direct, frontal penetration of the Saddam Line by the U.S. 1st In- fantry Division on the opening day of the VII Corps offensive.[53] The British 1st Armoured Division was then committed through the resulting breach, exploit- ing the breakthrough by advancing rapidly to the east-northeast and joining the divisions of the flanking effort as the right wing of the VII Corps advance into the rear of the Iraqi position in the KTO. Without this orthodox breakthrough battle, VII Corps would have outrun its logistical support before engaging the Republican Guard, and the DESERT STORM concept of operation would have been unfeasible.[54]

Second, the breakthrough frontage was as narrow as logistical constraints per- mitted. The 1st Infantry Division breached Iraqi forward defenses on a 6-km front, committing 341 armored vehicles to clear eight lanes through the Iraqi ob- stacle belt.[55] These forces then turned outward, widening the gap by taking Iraqi forward defenses in flank; eventually, the Saddam Line's entire right flank was collapsed this way, affording a broad, clear resupply route for the exploita- tion forces' advance against the Republican Guard. The initial assault frontage, however, comprised less than 1 percent of the theater frontier, enabling the Coalition to concentrate a crushing local numerical advantage against the 1st Infantry's penetration corridor but without congestion at the point of attack.[56]

Third, DESERT STORM supported its breakthrough effort with an extensive deep battle program. Iraqi command posts, communications systems, transportation arteries, logistical nodes, and reserve troop concentrations were struck almost simultaneously across the theater in an effort to paralyze Iraqi command and interdict Iraqi counterconcentration.[57] This effort was only partly successful: some Iraqi movements were prevented, other Iraqi units were destroyed on the move, but many completed major movements in spite of Coalition deep strikes. In particular, the Iraqis identified and responded to the VII Corps threat by redeploying roughly six divisions across its axis of advance after the ground offensive began.[58] This blocking force fought the war's principal ground engagements as VII Corps overran it in place between February 26 and 27. Though incompletely successful, the DESERT STORM deep battle program did clearly hinder Iraqi counterconcentration and represents the twentieth century's most extensive implementation of modern-system deep attack.

Fourth, and atypically, the operation's hardest fighting took place during exploitation, not in the breakthrough per se. The battles between VII Corps and the Republican Guard occurred well to the rear of the Saddam Line at the Saudi border and involved Iraqi reserves who had maneuvered into these positions to prevent the Coalition exploitation force from closing Iraq's escape route through Basra. It is thus important to distinguish the Coalition tactics employed against the Guard from those used in the breakthrough effort: the former—as will normally be the case for modern-system attackers in the exploitation phase—were far less deliberate than the latter.[59]

OFFENSIVE TACTICS

U.S. tactics made extensive use of modern-system combined arms, independent small-unit maneuver, dispersion, cover, and concealment. The 1st Infantry Division breaching effort, for example, was led by combat engineers operating under the cover of accompanying tanks, with infantry support immediately available in armored Bradley Infantry Fighting Vehicles (IFVs) advancing directly behind the lead echelon. Three full field artillery brigades, two divisional artillery groups and ten MLRS rocket artillery batteries destroyed Iraqi artillery and suppressed forward defensive positions until assault elements closed to within just 200–300 meters, whereupon mortars and direct fires from the assault battalions took over. Fixed and rotary wing aircraft provided air cover and longer-range overwatching antitank fires; electronic warfare units jammed Iraqi communications and used Iraqi electronic emissions to provide targeting data for fire support.[60] Facilitated by extensive rehearsals, this complex combination of diverse arms focused their efforts simultaneously on the objective area, exploiting the strengths of each to cover for the shortcomings of others and presenting the Iraqis with few opportunities to engage isolated elements on favorable terms.[61]

The Coalition breakthrough effort made extensive use of terrain for cover and concealment. This was especially pronounced in the Marine Corps offensive near the coastal highway, where dismounted infantry was infiltrated into the Iraqi defensive belt under cover of darkness the evening prior to the main assault.[62]

U.S. junior officers and even enlisted soldiers were trained to operate independently in small units, using their own tactical judgment to solve problems and keep attacks moving forward. Units without orders from higher command did not simply halt awaiting direction; leaders on the scene made their own decisions, seizing fleeting opportunities and exploiting idiosyncratic local conditions. This was especially germane during the exploitation phase. At 73 Easting, for example, the commander of the 2d ACR's lead cavalry troop, a twenty-nine-year-old captain, crested a low rise, spotted dozens of Iraqi tanks, reached a snap judgment that the Iraqis had been surprised, and ordered an immediate hasty assault to exploit the opportunity without waiting for explicit orders.[63] Throughout the theater, junior leaders were expected to understand their superiors' intentions and concepts of operations and to use their own judgment and knowledge of local conditions to find the best way forward.

During the exploitation, U.S. small units typically held formation in spite of approach marches that could exceed 10–20 km over trackless desert.[64] By avoiding the common tendency to bunch up or string out, they thus exploited the potential of dispersion to reduce their vulnerability to Iraqi fire while retaining the capacity to mass their own fires once contact was gained.

Finally, much of the war's heaviest close combat was fought under the natural concealment of night and foul weather. Sandstorms through much of the theater on February 26–27, for example, reduced visibility to as little as 200 meters for many of the critical battles against the Republican Guard.[65] Some of these actions, such as the 1st Infantry Division's assault at Objective Norfolk or the 1st and 3d Armored Divisions' actions along the Wadi Al Batin, were fought in darkness.[66] Exploitation of such conditions significantly reduced U.S. exposure.

Taken together, these methods substantially reduced U.S. vulnerability to Iraqi firepower. They did so, however, at a price in velocity. While U.S. forces accelerated once the breakthrough was complete (and especially while conducting movements to contact behind Iraqi lines), deliberate assaults against prepared defenses were conducted at a much more measured pace. In the new theory's terms, the 1st Infantry Division's breakthrough effort, for example, was conducted at a net velocity of about 3 km/day.[67]

OUTCOME AND SIGNIFICANCE: TESTING BY PROCESS TRACING

Given these characterizations, how does the outcome correspond with the theories' predictions? As noted above, both the new and the orthodox theories predict the same gross outcome here: breakthrough. Moreover, each theory could in principle explain a historically low loss rate. The Coalition technology edge, for example, may have been unprecedented for major mechanized warfare. The Coalition's numerical advantage was clearly large; while probably not unprecedented, this cannot be absolutely excluded. The new theory holds that technology magnifies the effects of force employment, which could certainly explain an unprecedented result given DESERT STORM's combination of new technology and a major force employment mismatch. More formally, the model presented in the appendix predicts that against a defense with a depth of 15 km, a reserve withhold of 0.7, a reserve velocity of 50 km/day, and an exposure fraction of 0.9, an offensive with an assault velocity of 3 km/day and a frontage of 6 km will break through with the loss of fewer than 1,200 Coalition killed and wounded (in comparison to the actual figure of 1,116, of whom 148 were American fatalities), an all-time low for twentieth-century mechanized warfare.[68]

But while the gross predictions are similar, the reasons for these predictions are very different, and these contrasting reasons offer an opportunity for testing via process tracing. That is, which of the theories' accounts of *why* the Coalition broke through—and especially, of why the Coalition's losses were an all-time low—is most consistent with the observed conduct of the campaign? To answer this question, I consider each major explanation in turn, treating technology in two parts to reflect the two main subarguments in the historiography (one focusing on air technology, the other on ground weapons).

Superior Coalition Air Technology

Perhaps the most common single explanation is Coalition air technology. Many argue that new defense suppression and stealth capabilities gave Coalition aircraft near-instantaneous command of the skies, while new target acquisition and precision guidance systems radically increased their lethality. Such technologies, it is held, rendered the Iraqis incapable of meaningful resistance—either by breaking their will to fight, or by destroying their means of doing so.[69]

For Coalition air technology to explain historically unprecedented low Coalition losses, however, requires that the number of willing, surviving Iraqi shooters must have been historically low by the time of the ground invasion.[70] Yet that surviving Iraqi armor force was still very large by historical standards, and many of them fought back when attacked.

HOW MUCH IRAQI EQUIPMENT SURVIVED THE AIR WAR?

It is now known that about 2,000 Iraqi tanks and 2,100 other armored vehicles survived the air campaign and were potentially available to resist the Coalition ground attack on the 24th. Equipment attrition during the air campaign had been highly variable. While some units suffered nearly 100 percent tank losses, others were virtually untouched. Overall, Iraqi tank attrition averaged about 48 percent, armored troop carrier losses about 30 percent, and artillery losses were just under 60 percent. These were not uniformly distributed, however.

In particular, the Republican Guard was significantly less hard-hit than the infantry and army heavy divisions nearer the border—Guard tank losses, for example, came to less than 24 percent of their prewar KTO strength.[71]

DID THEY FIGHT BACK?

Of course, some of the surviving vehicles' crews surrendered without fighting, or after only token resistance—but others fought back. While the conscript infantry at the border lacked the will to fight, the Republican Guard and at least some army heavy divisions tried to resist the Coalition ground attack.

At 73 Easting, for example, 2d ACR crews reported large volumes of small arms fire rattling off their vehicles during the assault, which means that Iraqi troops stayed at their weapons, returning fire, even as U.S. tanks passed within a few hundred meters of their positions (i.e., within small arms range).[72] In fact, some Republican Guard infantry are known to have remained at their posts until U.S. attackers had actually driven through their positions, firing short-range antitank rockets at the vehicles from behind.[73] Heavy weapons fire was also received. Though large-caliber hits were rare, multiple Iraqi tank gun rounds were observed falling near U.S. targets.[74]

Perhaps most important, the Tawakalna Division not only defended itself when attacked but also counterattacked the 2d ACR after being driven from its positions. After nightfall the Iraqis struck the northernmost of the three U.S. cavalry troops engaged, attacking in multiple, reinforced company-strength waves, and supported by dismounted infantry.[75] Of course, this assault was broken up long before it posed a serious threat. Moreover, even in the Tawakalna there is little evidence to suggest fanatical combat motivation—more than 200 prisoners surrendered after the battle.[76]

Nevertheless, there is no evidence to suggest that the Iraqis gave up without fighting in 73 Easting. On the contrary, Republican Guard counterattackers' readiness to advance at all under such withering fire is difficult to square with a conclusion that the Guard had lost the will to fight. The Tawakalna had ample opportunity to surrender or escape if it wished. Iraqi conscripts at the border had given up in the midst of U.S. assaults without suffering harm; if the Tawakalna had wanted, it too could surely have surrendered without fighting. Alternatively, when the 2d ACR halted to consolidate, at least one further Iraqi battalion located within earshot of the battle had not yet been engaged; the halt offered them an ideal opportunity to escape or surrender. Yet they stayed, fought, and were destroyed when the advance resumed after midnight. In fact, few prisoners on any part of the field were taken while their equipment was still operable—the great majority of those who surrendered did so only after the battle was over and the Iraqis' armor had been destroyed (and some 600 casualties had been suffered).[77]

Nor had these vehicles' crews deserted prior to the battle. The Tawakalna had moved on February 24 from its pre-invasion locations to occupy the blocking position from which it fought on the 26th.[78] Vehicles lacking crews would not have been able to move and thus would not have been present on the 73 Easting battlefield. In fact, the entire Iraqi blocking force that opposed the VII Corps advance had redeployed into its battle positions only a few days before its destruction.[79] Though the Iraqi forces in the KTO as a whole were surely well understrength by the time of the ground attack, the Guard and army mechanized units that fought the VII Corps on the 26th to the 28th had ample crews to man the equipment the VII Corps destroyed.

And while we know more of the details for 73 Easting than for many of the war's battles, what we do know suggests that Iraqi behavior there was broadly representative of Guard and army heavy divisions elsewhere as well. Reports of small arms fire striking Coalition armor, for example, are widely distributed among accounts of the fighting on the 26th, 27th, and 28th, as are reports of Iraqi counterattacks, significant tank gun fire, and artillery action.[80] All suggest that at least a 73 Easting-style will to fight was generally representative of the Iraqi blocking force, and possibly of other Iraqi units as well.

THE ACTIVELY RESISTING IRAQI ARMOR FORCE'S SIZE IN HISTORICAL CONTEXT

We will never know exactly how many of the Iraqis' surviving tanks fought back. We do know, however, that the great majority of Iraq's armor was concentrated in the higher-quality units where Iraqi will to fight was greatest—the conscript infantry that gave up most readily was systematically underequipped in heavy weapons and especially in armored vehicles.[81]

As a conservative lower bound on the number of actively resisting Iraqi tanks, one might count only those weapons in the remnants of five divisions from the Iraqi blocking force that are known to have resisted the VII Corps advance. These alone likely disposed of at least 600 surviving tanks and an additional 600 other armored vehicles on the 24th.[82] A plausible range of active survivors might thus be 600 to 2,000 Iraqi tanks, and 600 to 2,100 other armored vehicles.

By contrast with these 1,200 to 4,100 Iraqi armored vehicles, the entire German Army in Normandy had fewer than 500 tanks in July 1944. The Iraqi lower bound still had more tanks than the entire Israeli Army in 1967. The upper bound had about as many as the entire Egyptian Army in 1973.[83] If the Iraqis had inflicted only as many casualties per capita as the Arabs in 1967, the result would still have been radically higher Coalition losses.[84] Their inability to do so is thus hard to explain by pre-invasion losses of materiel or willpower as a result of the air campaign.[85]

Superior Coalition Ground Technology

Alternatively, some have argued that a combination of thermal sights, new armor, stabilized 120-mm guns, and depleted uranium (DU) ammunition enabled U.S. ground forces to strike Iraqi armor from distances and directions that all but precluded effective return fire.[86] But for such technologies to explain radically low losses is to imply that friendly forces in close combat without these technologies ought to have fared significantly worse.

This was not so. Coalition ground force technology varied widely, but losses did not. The two U.S. Marine divisions, for example, were equipped mainly with 1960s-era M60A1 tanks with neither the thermal sights, 120-mm guns, DU ammunition, or composite armor of the Army's M1A1s, yet the Marines suffered fewer tank losses than the Army against opposition that included Iraqi heavy divisions that fought back when attacked.[87] In fact, some of the Marines' heaviest fighting was conducted not even by M60s but by wheeled, thin-skinned, light armored vehicles such as those that defended against the Iraqi counterattack at the Burqan oil field.[88] Alternatively, the army itself deployed thousands of lightly armored M2 and M3 Bradleys, while the British committed hundreds of similarly light Warrior troop carriers, all of which engaged in extensive close combat yet suffered very few losses.[89]

Second, a ground technology explanation implies that other battles between similarly equipped opponents should produce roughly similar results. Yet at the Army's National Training Center in the Mohave Desert, literally hundreds of battles have been fought between M1A1-equipped U.S. Army units and (simulated) T72-equipped OPFOR (or "opposition force") opponents—and the T72-equipped OPFOR almost always *wins*.[90]

Coalition Theater Numerical Preponderance

To explain a historically low loss rate via a radically high theater FFR or radically low theater FSR is to imply that *local* actions fought with less attacker-advantageous numerical odds should have produced higher attacker losses. Yet they did not.

At Medina Ridge, for example, a Republican Guard brigade conducted a prepared positional defense on a frontage of under 10 kilometers against an attack of roughly equal size.[91] Standard Western defensive frontages for brigade-size units are about 10–20 kilometers (or up to *twice* the Medina's), while parity is normally considered a very disadvantageous force-to-force ratio for an attack.[92] Yet the Medina Brigade was annihilated by frontal assault without inflicting a single Coalition fatality. On February 26 the 29th Brigade of the Tawakalna Division, with more than 150 dug-in armored vehicles, was struck by a force only one-fourth its size yet was wiped out, penetrating only four of forty-one U.S. tanks and killing no American soldiers.[93] At 73 Easting, the Tawakalna's 18th Brigade conducted a prepared positional defense on a 15-kilometer front and was attacked frontally by a smaller force, yet the defenders killed only one of the attackers' sixty-eight armored vehicles before losing essentially all of their own.[94] While the *theater* force-to-force and force-to-space ratios may have been very disadvantageous for the Iraqis, the *local* imbalances in many of the key battles were much less problematic—yet none produced higher Coalition casualties.[95] If preponderance were a powerful cause here, this could not be true.

The New Theory

By contrast, the new theory is consistent with large numbers of actively resisting Iraqi armored vehicles surviving the air campaign. It is consistent with poorly equipped Marine ground forces fighting with no higher losses than the better-equipped VII Corps. And it is consistent with locally outnumbered Coalition attackers overcoming dense Iraqi defenses by frontal assault. This is because the new theory affords a central role to *force employment* in explaining combat outcomes. The Iraqis employed their forces in ways that left them exposed to the full, proving-ground lethality of U.S. weapons, whereas U.S. forces were employed in ways that limited the Iraqis' ability to exploit their own firepower. In such cases, the specific nature of the weapons matters less than the exposure of their targets, and numerical imbalance matters less than either side's ability to protect its soldiers long enough for them to make their numbers tell.

But while technology and preponderance are thus less causally powerful in the new theory, neither is irrelevant. For the new theory as well as the old, advanced U.S. technology is necessary to explain a historically unprecedented low U.S. loss rate.[96] But the role technology plays is very different in the new theory, and much more consistent with the details of the way the fighting was actually conducted in 1991. For the orthodox view, advanced technology either eliminated Iraqi resistance by air attack before the ground war began or so overmatched the opposition on the ground that the Iraqis were unable to kill even when trying. Large numbers of surviving Iraqis resisting Coalition ground attack contradicts the former; the radical success of lightly equipped Coalition ground forces contradicts the latter.

In the new theory, by contrast, technology *magnifies the effects of force employment*: where non–modern-system force employment leaves targets exposed, advanced technology comes into its own and punishes exposure with increasing severity. Exposure, moreover, can be exploited in any number of ways. Lack of cover and concealment, for example, can leave T72s vulnerable to M1A1s firing from far beyond their opponents' effective range. Or the interaction of technology and force employment can be more complex. The inability of small Iraqi observation post detachments to function independently, for example, can leave T72s on the main line of resistance without tactical warning; this would be damaging at any level of technology, but against aircraft capable of sustained, unanswerable precision strike it takes on new meaning. The Iraqis knew that their vehicles were the targets for such attacks, hence they rationally reduced vehicle manning levels, leaving fewer on-watch vehicles manned, and relying more heavily on tactical warning to give units time to reoccupy tanks and BMPs in the event of ground attack. When that warning failed to appear, the result was thus a higher fraction of unmanned defending vehicles at the time of attack than would have been the case against an earlier generation of less-sophisticated air technology. This in turn assisted even lightly armed Marine ground units in wiping out dug-in Iraqi armor by frontal assault. The Iraqis' failure to operate effectively in independent small units thus left them vulnerable to a combination of Coalition air and ground technology in which the air attacks served an essentially *suppressive* purpose—that is, they induced the Iraqis to take protective postures that reduced their ability to return fire, thereby reducing their effectiveness even without killing them directly. The Iraqis' failure to implement the modern system thus exposed them to a new variation on modern-system combined arms warfare by the Coalition, in which new U.S. air technology magnified the effects of the asymmetry in the two sides' ground force employment.

ALTERNATIVE EXPLANATIONS OF THE COALITION LOSS RATE

The analysis of preponderance and technology above contradicts several of the most common explanations of the Coalition's radically low loss rate. Three further candidates warrant brief discussion, however.

"Maneuver Warfare" and the Left Hook

Some have argued that the Coalition's left-hook strategy created the low loss rate by outflanking the Iraqis, forcing them to fight a war of maneuver for which they were ill prepared.[97] But in fact, the key battles against the Republican Guard took the form of a corps-level frontal assault on a prepared positional defense from precisely the direction the Iraqis had anticipated when they established their blocking positions.[98] The U.S. 1st Infantry Division conducted a deliberate, frontal breach of the Iraqis' prepared defenses at the Saudi border.[99] Moreover, the entire Marine offensive was a direct, frontal penetration of the Saddam Line and the primary battle positions of the Iraqi heavy divisions to its rear.[100] Yet none of these attackers suffered heavily as a result, as one would expect if a flanking maneuver were the critical factor in explaining historically low losses.

Iraqi Incompetence

Others attribute the outcome to the Iraqis' weak skills and poor morale.[101] Iraqi morale was clearly far weaker than the Coalition's, and the Iraqis made many important errors in handling their forces. But Iraqi mistakes are only a part of the story and cannot explain a historically low Coalition loss rate by themselves.

To explain a historically unprecedented outcome this way is to imply that no prior war could have seen a skill imbalance as great. The Coalition loss rate was lower by at least a factor of ten than Israel's in the Six-Day War, or Britain's against the Italians in North Africa in 1941, or the Royal Marines' against Argentine Army conscripts in 1982.[102] It is far from obvious that the difference between Coalition and Iraqi skills in 1991 dwarfs the imbalance between any of these armies.[103] In each case the attacker enjoyed a major advantage in personnel quality and motivation, yet in no case were the attacker's losses anywhere near as low as 1991's. Given this, it seems more likely that skill and motivation comprise only a part of a much larger picture.

Linear Combinations of Causes

The new theory offers one account of how that larger picture fits together in the form of an interaction effect between force employment and technology. But is an interaction effect really necessary? What about a simple, noninteractive linear combination of the causes adduced in the existing historiography? In fact, much of the literature provides, implicitly, just this: it cites multiple causes but treats their effects via a series of univariate arguments about single causes and single effects, which are then concatenated into what amounts to a multivariate linear explanation.

Can this provide a satisfactory account? Maybe, but it faces a number of difficult logical and empirical hurdles. Linear accounts by definition give no reason to expect the combination of causes to yield more than just the sum of the parts taken individually. To explain DESERT STORM, however, the sum of the parts must be large indeed. The Coalition loss rate was far lower than for previous victors in even very one-sided historical battles. To explain an order-of-magnitude difference in loss rates between 1991 and 1967 or 1982, for example, by a linear combination of contributing causes thus requires either a long list of contributors, or that at least some be very powerful. Yet each existing explanation poses serious inconsistencies with the historical record. To explain, for example, the difference in attacker loss rate between the 1991 and 1967 wars by reference to the linear combination of

- 1991 air-induced attrition (or nonresistance)
- 1991 ground technology
- skill or combat motivation
- Coalition numerical superiority

is to imply that the latter three effects account for more than a factor of four in Iraqi combat performance relative to the Arabs' in 1967[104]—in spite of the facts that

- Coalition ground technology varied widely across the theater of war
- the Arab-Israeli skill/motivation imbalance in 1967 was arguably as large as that of 1991 or nearly so

- many of the key engagements in 1991 were fought without meaningful local numerical advantages.

It is thus far from obvious that the effects cited offer the necessary explanatory power. By contrast, the new theory offers a sufficient account, requires fewer independent causal factors to explain the evidence, and is at least as consistent with what is now known of the war's conduct. While a multivariate linear explanation cannot be ruled out, it thus offers a weaker account than the new theory.

CONCLUSIONS AND IMPLICATIONS

DESERT STORM thus offers important confirmatory evidence for the new theory and disconfirmatory evidence for the orthodox views. Unlike MICHAEL and GOODWOOD, DESERT STORM is not a critical case in Eckstein's terms; it is, however, a particularly important case for the contemporary defense debate, and one where process tracing yields clear and divergent implications for the respective theories' validity. The air technology explanation implies that Iraqi resistance had been eliminated before the ground war began, yet 600 to 2,000 surviving Iraqi tanks and 600 to 2,100 other armored vehicles actively fought back when the VII Corps and 1st and 2d Marine divisions struck the Republican Guard and Iraqi Army heavy divisions beginning on February 26. The ground technology argument attributes a historically low Coalition loss rate to the superiority of U.S. thermal sights, compound armor, 120-mm guns, and depleted uranium ammunition, yet Marine attackers without these advantages suffered no greater losses for their absence. The preponderance argument credits Coalition numerical superiority, yet local engagements fought at much less favorable numerical odds produced results little different from those fought with much more preponderant numbers.

By contrast, the new theory attributes DESERT STORM's extremity to an interaction between force employment and new technology: the combination of modern-system offensive methods, non–modern-system defensive methods, and advanced, late-twentieth-century Coalition technology yielded an unprecedentedly low Coalition loss rate in spite of attempted resistance by sizeable Iraqi forces dug in astride the Coalition's primary attack axes. This new explanation thus accounts for more of the details of the war's conduct than its orthodox competitors; though each theory predicts breakthrough, the case still provides determinate evidence in support of the new theory.

The result, however, is also a chance to use theory to shed light on an important case. The Gulf War's standard interpretation has proven powerfully influential for U.S. defense policy and the direction of Western military thought. The new theory presented here suggests that this conventional wisdom is dangerously unsound—and this in turn suggests very different implications for defense policy and the future of warfare, a subject to which I return in chapter 10.

CHAPTER EIGHT

Statistical Tests

I TURN NOW from small-n case method to large-n statistical analysis. Statistical methods enjoy a number of advantages, including a stronger claim to external validity and a more systematic treatment of chance and happenstance than case method can provide. Statistical analysis also suffers from some important drawbacks, however. For my purposes, the most important is data availability. The new theory turns on force employment, yet political science has systematically overlooked its role in warfare—hence none of the standard datasets treats it.[1] Moreover, even the standard data are of uneven quality and coverage. Taken alone, large-n testing would thus fall short of an adequate test.

This is not to say that meaningful statistical tests are impossible, or cannot offer important insight. But for the time being, large-n tests must necessarily be indirect, and the results are best viewed in context with those of other tests using other approaches.

Indirect tests are based not on direct observation of the key variables, but on their deduced effects on other variables whose values *are* directly observed. In astronomy, extrasolar planets were discovered indirectly: too small and dim to be seen by contemporary telescopes, their presence was deduced from their gravitational effects on stars whose movements could be observed.[2] For my purposes, standard datasets contain no observations of force employment, but the new theory predicts that force employment will have specific consequences for the variables that are observed in those datasets. These predictions conflict with orthodox theories'. This makes it possible to test the competing theories even without explicit data on force employment per se. Direct tests would be preferable—in particular, it would be easier to isolate force employment as the unique cause of observed outcome variance—but indirect testing can still shed useful light.

In fact, I argue below that indirect tests using the available data are much more consistent with the new theory than its orthodox competitors. I substantiate this claim in five steps. First, I discuss the datasets, their strengths and weaknesses, and my strategy for exploiting the former while minimizing the latter. Second, I deduce testable hypotheses from the respective theories for the available data. Third, I discuss the particular statistical techniques I use to test these hypotheses. Fourth, I present and evaluate the results. I conclude by assessing the implications for the respective theories' relative validity.

DATASETS

Two standard datasets are best suited to my purposes, though neither is ideal. The University of Michigan's Correlates of War (COW) data cover all interstate wars between 1815 and 1992 and provide information on military expenditures, troops under arms, economic output, population, casualties, war duration, and victory-defeat characterizations for all states on both sides of each war.[3] The U.S. Army's CDB90 dataset treats 660 battles fought between 1600 and 1982, providing a variety of information on troop strength, weapon counts, frontages, battle duration, penetration distances, and casualties, together with subjective assessments of variables such as "surprise," "morale," and "logistics."[4] As the theory presented here is limited to the twentieth and early twenty-first centuries, I use only the post-1900 portion of either dataset, with 46 wars for the COW dataset and 382 battles for the CDB90 data.[5]

In addition to these two preexisting datasets, I have compiled a limited database on the technological sophistication of the combatants in sixteen postwar conflicts between 1956 and 1992. These MILTECH data are derived from weapon counts in the International Institute for Strategic Studies *Military Balance* series and provide weighted mean introduction dates for the attacker's and defender's main battle tanks and fighter/ground attack aircraft for each side (i.e., τ_R and τ_B scores as defined in the appendix).[6]

Strengths and Weaknesses: COW

The COW dataset has the advantage of being exhaustive, covering all wars fought in the relevant interval. It is also among the most widely used databases in international politics, exposing it to more extensive scholarly review of its accuracy and structure. Source documentation is not readily available, however, so assessment of individual data entries can be problematic. COW also lacks explicit data on military technology or weapon holdings, making it less useful for testing dyadic technological theories of capability.[7]

For my purposes, however, COW's most important shortcoming is its unit of analysis. The new theory is specified in terms of operations; COW is structured by wars. This creates important ambiguities for tests of military capability at the theater-operational level. Loss-exchange ratios, for example, are defined as attacker casualties per defender casualty; in a long war, each side is the attacker in some actions and the defender in others. The ratio of the war initiator's overall losses to its opponent's in the COW data thus amalgamates the losses of local attackers and local defenders in both the numerator and the denominator, making it difficult to attribute the results to the properties of attack and defense per se at the operational level or below.[8] Similar difficulties face any COW outcome measure that distinguishes attacker from defender (such as attacker loss rates or defender loss inflicting rates).[9]

Strengths and Weaknesses: CDB90

CDB90, by contrast, has the advantage of treating battles rather than wars. Its identification of attacker and defender thus more closely matches the new theory's terms.[10] It also provides some coverage of weapon holdings and attack frontages and offers a wider range of military outcome measures (especially, measures of ground taken and lost). Its much larger n (382 as opposed to 46 for COW, and 16 for MILTECH) provides greater statistical power for resolving subtle effects.

CDB90 also faces some important drawbacks, however. Even with an n of 382, it still contains only a fraction of the battles fought in the relevant time period. In fact, whole wars are unrepresented: only 18 of the 46 twentieth-century wars in COW appear at all in CDB90. This sample, moreover, was neither random nor selected using any explicit or systematic rule. The result is a substantial overrepresentation of American, German, and Israeli experience: 146 of the 382 cases involve the United States as either attacker or defender; 217 involve Germany; 70 involve Israel. Fully 85 percent of the battles surveyed involve at least one of these three parties.

The dataset also lacks a consistent unit of analysis: entries range from minor tactical actions at the company and battalion level to theater offensives by multiple army groups. This poses several potential hazards. First, many military outcome measures vary with the size of the units involved regardless of technology, preponderance, or force employment. Consider casualty rates. Companies and battalions consist almost entirely of combat soldiers and are often exposed to fire in their entirety in the course of a single action; if caught in the open, they can be annihilated to the last soldier. Army groups, by contrast, contain large numbers of support personnel not normally exposed to hostile fire. Moreover, few of their component battalions are typically in intense combat at the same time; many are either in reserve or located away from the critical point at any given moment. Daily casualty rates as a fraction of total troops thus rarely exceed a few percent a day for large formations even in major battles, whereas they can easily exceed 50 percent for small subunits, due to nothing more profound than the size of the unit and its relative proportion of active shooters to other soldiers.[11] Analyses using CDB90 casualty rates as dependent variables must thus either control for the level of analysis or rely on loss-exchange ratios (which provide such control by their nature). Second, the dataset's heterogeneity creates a risk of double-counting. A review of the data by the Institute for Defense Analyses in 1997, for example, found that in 12 percent of the twentieth-century entries, single battles were recorded once for the largest formations engaged, then again for each of the component subunits, with the result that the same combat experience appeared multiple times in the same dataset.[12]

Finally, the quality of the individual data entries per se is less reliable than for COW. The initial version of CDB90 was reviewed in 1984 by the U.S. Army War College Military History Institute, the U.S. Army Center for Military History, the

U.S. Army Combat Studies Institute, and the U.S. Military Academy's Department of History; 8 randomly selected battles with 159 codings were checked. Of these 159 values, 67 percent were found to be in error and 18 percent were judged "questionable." The army subsequently revised the dataset in 1986 and again in 1987 to correct known errors, but the extent of remaining mistakes cannot be known with certainty.[13] By way of a further test, I have compared the final 1990 version of the dataset with the archivally derived values for variables covered in the case studies of Operations MICHAEL and GOODWOOD above, and with 9 values for other battles extracted from official U.S. and British histories.[14] The results were uneven. For MICHAEL and the 9 data points derived from official histories, the CDB90 values were highly accurate: 19 of 20 CDB90 codings (i.e., 95 percent) were within 20 percent of the official figures; 13 were within 10 percent. For GOODWOOD, on the other hand, the CDB90 codings were far less reliable: only 5 of 13 were within 20 percent of the official figures; 5 others were off by more than 50 percent; 2 were off by more than a factor of two. It is unreasonable to expect that any dataset's codings will agree perfectly with any other secondary source's—rarely do two secondary histories agree on any single value due to unacknowledged counting rule differences and other unstated variations in assumptions. But the differences in the GOODWOOD data are more suggestive of error than counting rule variations. Real errors thus doubtless remain in the CDB90 data, in frequency that is difficult to assess but could well be significant.

Strengths and Weaknesses: MILTECH

The new dataset's key advantage is that it provides the only available source of systematic data on the technological sophistication of the particular weapons used in twentieth-century wars. CDB90, by contrast, provides counts of weapons by type (e.g., tanks, artillery, or aircraft) but offers no information on the make, model, or sophistication of those tanks, guns, or planes. COW provides no explicit information of any kind on weapons or equipment.

MILTECH's drawbacks are its limited scope, its restriction to wars rather than battles, and the highly approximate nature of the indicators used. Secondary histories rarely provide weapon holdings by make and model for individual operations. National-level data sometimes offer more detail, but only postwar cases are covered systematically in reliable secondary compendia. Barring major cross-national archival research, this limits the new dataset to national-level holdings at the outset of wars fought since about 1956 (the beginning of the IISS *Military Balance* series' coverage), restricting both n and the unit of analysis accordingly. And as noted in chapter 2, τ_R and τ_B as used here are at best crude indicators of technological sophistication. They are, however, the best currently available—and if dyadic technological sophistication has the kind of powerful effects that many attribute to it, then even fairly crude measures like these should still show some measurable explanatory power—but they are clearly far from ideal.

Mitigating Weaknesses and Exploiting Strengths

None of these datasets can thus offer a definitive test, but each offers some degree of insight. To get the most insight with the least risk of distortion, I have adopted a four-part strategy.

First, wherever possible I use multiple datasets to address the same hypotheses. While the shortcomings in any given dataset create a danger of spurious findings from bad data, the odds that multiple datasets with different shortcomings and different sources would duplicate a spurious finding are much smaller. Multiple datasets, like multiple methods, thus provide a degree of insulation from the shortcomings of individual datasets taken alone.

Second, I control for CDB90's overrepresentation of U.S., German, and Israeli experience by including dummy variables for the nationality of attackers and defenders.[15]

Third, I have removed all double counts from the CDB90 dataset and corrected the values for MICHAEL and GOODWOOD where these were in error.[16] All analyses are performed using these modified data.[17]

Fourth, I emphasize relative strength of statistical findings, rather than absolute significance per se. Measurement error tends to bias OLS regression coefficients toward zero and to increase estimated standard errors.[18] If substantial measurement error remains in either COW or CDB90, this will thus tend to reduce the likelihood of finding strong statistical relationships of any kind—whether in support of the new theory or its orthodox alternatives. This in turn reduces the evidentiary value of null findings: if the statistical analysis shows no relationship, it may be because there really is none, or it may be because the noise in the data makes a real relationship imperceptibly dim.[19] Relative differences in the strength of findings, however, retain evidentiary value.[20] If one theory is supported much more strongly than another, this difference in strength against the same background noise is an important indicator of validity, even where noisy data make it impossible to reject alternatives outright on grounds of statistical insignificance. And findings that do attain statistical significance against a background of noisy data warrant special attention. Measurement error per se does not invalidate significant findings; on the contrary, a relationship strong enough to shine through the noise is a particularly noteworthy observation.

HYPOTHESES

The hypotheses for test are summarized in table 8.1 and derive from the respective theories' divergent implications for Loss-Exchange Ratios (LERs, or attacker casualties per defender casualty), territorial gain, and combat duration, as a function of changing force-to-force ratios, force-to-space ratios, systemic technological sophistication, and dyadic technological imbalance. In the absence of direct

TABLE 8.1.
Hypotheses

	Casualties (COW, CDB90, Miltech)	Territorial Gain (CDB90)	Duration (CDB90)
Preponderance (FFR)	*Orthodox* 1a. LER falls nonlinearly with respect to FFR 2a. Effect is stronger than national variation	*Orthodox* 3a. Gains rise with respect to FFR 4a. Effect is stronger than national variation	*Orthodox* 5a. Duration falls with respect to FFR for attacker wins 6a. Effect is stronger than national variation
	New Theory 1b. LER rises with respect to FFR 2b. Effect is weaker than national variation	*New Theory* 4b. Gains rise with respect to FFR, but effect is weaker than national variation	*New Theory* 5b. Duration increases with respect to FFR 6b. Effect is weaker than national variation
Preponderance (FSR)	*Orthodox* 7a. LER rises nonlinearly with respect to FSR 8a. Effect is stronger than national variation	*Orthodox* 9a. Gains fall with respect to FSR 10a. Effect is stronger than national variation	*Orthodox* 11a. Duration rises nonlinearly with respect to FSR 12a. Effect is stronger than national variation
	New Theory 8b. LER rises with respect to FSR, but effect is weaker than national variation	*New Theory* 10b. Gains fall with respect to FSR, but effect is weaker than national variation	*New Theory* 11b. Duration falls with respect to FSR 12b. Effect is weaker than national variation
Technology (systemic)	*Orthodox* (O-D Theory) 13a. LER falls with respect to tank prevalence 14a. LER falls with respect to ground attack air prevalence 15a. LER rises with respect to artillery prevalence 16a. LER periodic with respect to time 17a. Constant variance in LER with respect to time 18a. Across-period variation > within-period	*Orthodox* (O-D Theory) 19a. Gains rise with respect to tank prevalence 20a. Gains rise with respect to ground attack air prevalence 21a. Gains fall with respect to artillery prevalence 22a. Constant variance in gains with respect to time	*Orthodox* (O-D Theory) 23a. Duration falls with respect to tank prevalence 24a. Duration falls with respect to ground attack air prevalence 25a. Duration rises with respect to artillery prevalence 26a. Constant variance in duration with respect to time

continued

TABLE 8.1. (*cont.*)

	Casualties (COW, CDB90, Miltech)	Territorial Gain (CDB90)	Duration (CDB90)
Technology (systemic) (*cont.*)	*New Theory* 13b. LER constant with respect to tank prevalence 14b. LER constant with respect to ground attack air prevalence 15b. LER constant with respect to artillery prevalence 16b. No periodicity with respect to time 17b. Increasing variance in LER with respect to time 18b. Across-period variation < within-period	*New Theory* 19b. Gains constant with respect to tank prevalence 20b. Gains constant with respect to ground attack air prevalence 21b. Gains constant with respect to artillery prevalence 22b. Increasing variance in gains with respect to time	*New Theory* 23b. Duration constant with respect to tank prevalence 24b. Duration constant with respect to ground attack air prevalence 25b. Duration constant with respect to artillery prevalence 26b. Increasing variance in duration with respect to time
Technology (dyadic)	*Orthodox* 27a. LER falls with respect to attacker-defender tech gap *New Theory* 27b. LER falls with respect to attacker-defender tech gap, but variance > slope	[cannot be tested using CDB90 data]	[cannot be tested using CDB90 data]

measurements of key variables, I make three enabling assumptions in the hypotheses and associated tests. First, I assume that the relative incidence of shallow as opposed to deep defenses, or high-exposure as opposed to low-exposure attacks, has not changed systematically over time: at any given time, some defenses are shallow, others deep; some attacks are exposed, others not—and thus, that the distribution of force employment choices across states has constant variance with respect to time.[21] Second, where specific data on weapon types or models are unavailable, I assume that time can be used as a proxy for systemic technological sophistication: the more recent the conflict, the more sophisticated the technology. Third, I assume that force employment is weakly correlated with preponderance. Taken together, these enabling assumptions hold that force employment is not merely an epiphenomenal consequence of materiel—as I argue at length in chapter 3, states' force employment decisions are driven by a variety of political, social, and organizational factors and often do not reflect materially determined optima.[22] Although I cannot observe these force employment choices directly, I will thus assume for the purposes of the large-*n* analysis that they are poorly correlated with technology or preponderance.

Preponderance vs. the New Theory

Given these assumptions, preponderance theory implies twelve major observable divergences from the new theory. First, the most complete articulation of preponderance theory, Lanchester's Square Law, holds that the LER and the FFR should be inversely proportional (hypothesis 1a).[23] The new theory, by contrast, implies that the LER should increase with the FFR, not decrease (hypothesis 1b).[24]

The second major divergence concerns the LER's relative sensitivity to the FFR and to cross-sectional differences between states. Preponderance theory holds that the numerical balance of forces is the central determinant of capability; this in turn implies that the LER will be more sensitive to variation in the numerical balance (the FFR) than to differences in the identities of states fighting at the same FFR (hypothesis 2a). The new theory, by contrast, implies that the LER should vary widely across states (hypothesis 2b), since it sees the LER as very sensitive to force employment and treats force employment as a unit-level property of individual militaries.[25]

The third and fourth divergences concern territorial gain. Preponderance theory implies that territorial gain should increase with the FFR (hypothesis 3a), and that territorial gain will be significantly more sensitive to variation in the FFR than to differences in the identities of states fighting at the same FFR (hypothesis 4a).[26] The new theory, by contrast, agrees that, ceteris paribus, territorial gain will increase with the FFR, but it holds that force employment is a stronger effect and should be largely uncorrelated with the FFR empirically.[27] This in turn implies that for the new theory, territorial gain should be more sensitive to differences in the identities of the combatants than to variation in the FFR per se (hypothesis 4b).

The fifth and sixth divergences concern duration. Preponderance theory implies that for attacker victories, duration will decrease steeply and nonlinearly with increasing FFR (hypothesis 5a) and will be significantly more sensitive to the FFR than to differences in the identities of states fighting at the same FFR (hypothesis 6a).[28] By contrast, in the new theory duration increases with the FFR (i.e., with R/B) for all R/B (hypothesis 5b)[29] and is more sensitive to differences in the identities of states than to the FFR (hypothesis 6b).[30]

The seventh and eighth observable divergences involve the relationship between the FSR and the LER. Some preponderance theorists posit a threshold FSR, or "defensive minimum" troop density for successful defense—above this threshold, the defender enjoys major advantages; below it, defense is extremely difficult.[31] Hence LERs should increase nonlinearly with increasing FSRs (hypothesis 7a). And as before, preponderance theorists would expect LER to be more sensitive to preponderance (here, the FSR) than to force employment (hypothesis 8a). The new theory, by contrast, agrees that, ceteris paribus, LERs will increase with increasing FSRs, but it holds that force employment is a stronger effect and should be largely uncorrelated with the FSR empirically. This in turn implies that for the new theory, LER should be more sensitive to differences in the identities of the combatants than to variation in the FSR per se (hypothesis 8b).[32]

The ninth and tenth divergences concern territorial gain. If defense is undermined by low FSRs and facilitated by high ones, then it follows that territorial gain should decrease with increasing FSRs (hypothesis 9a) and should be more sensitive to variation in the FSR than to differences in the identities of states fighting at the same FSR (hypothesis 10a). The new theory, by contrast, agrees that, ceteris paribus, territorial gain will decrease with increasing FSRs, but it holds that outcomes should be more sensitive to differences in the combatants' identities than to variation in the FSR per se (hypothesis 10b).

The eleventh and twelfth divergences involve duration. Orthodox views on force-to-space ratios hold that FSRs above the defensive minimum give rise to extended battles of attrition (indeed, it is this trait that predisposes high-FSR defenses to success, as this denies attackers an opportunity for quick breakthrough).[33] Hence duration should rise nonlinearly with increasing FSRs (hypothesis 11a), and if preponderance is capability's central determinant, then duration should be more sensitive to variation in the FSR than to differences in the identities of states fighting at the same FSR (hypothesis 12a). The new theory, on the other hand, implies that duration should fall with increasing FSRs (hypothesis 11b),[34] and that duration, like casualties and territorial gain, should be more sensitive to differences in the identities of the combatants than to variation in the FSR per se (hypothesis 12b).

Systemic Technology (Offense-Defense Theory) vs. the New Theory

Offense-defense theory diverges from the new theory in fourteen observable ways.

The first six involve casualties. Offense-defense theory holds that the greater the prevalence of offense-favoring weapons like tanks and ground attack aircraft, the fewer attackers should be lost per defender lost and thus the lower the attacker:defender LER should be (hypotheses 13a and 14a). The greater the prevalence of defense-favoring weapons like artillery, the higher the LER should be (hypothesis 15a).[35]

Offense-defense theory also makes claims for the distribution of these weapons across historical periods. Weapon types are seen as arriving via successive waves of technological innovation, hence just as relatively tank-prevalent conflicts within a wave should induce lower LERs, so across waves there should be periodic upward and downward shifts in systemwide LER as eras of offense-favoring technology replace defensive and vice versa. In particular, rifled muskets, machine guns, and quick-firing artillery are held to have caused generally defense-favorable conditions in the late nineteenth and early twentieth centuries. The maturation of the tank and the ground attack airplane are said to have brought offense-favorable conditions in the mid-twentieth century. Nuclear weapons and precision-guided antitank weaponry then canceled this offensive advantage in the late twentieth century. More specifically, Van Evera's 1999 periodization implies that LERs should be [36]

- higher for 1872–1918 than for 1919–1945 (hypothesis 16.1a)
- higher for 1919–1945 than for 1946–1972 (hypothesis 16.2a)
- lower for 1946–1972 than for 1973–1992 (hypothesis 16.3a).

But whereas mean LER for wars fought in a given period should shift up and down by period, *variance* in LER should hold roughly constant across periods. For offense-defense theory, a significant increase in variance across periods would suggest specification error in the form of an important but absent time-correlated variable. Hence variance in LER should be constant with respect to time (hypothesis 17a).

Finally, offense-defense theory treats the relative ease of attack and defense chiefly as a systemic variable: though states' weapon holdings do differ at the margin,[37] significant differences are rare, and the bigger issue is the level of general technical knowledge available to all states at the time.[38] This in turn implies that variance in outcomes *across* technological eras should outweigh variance across states *within* any given era (hypothesis 18a).

By contrast, the new theory holds that the main effect of systemic technological change is a progressive increase in lethality having little to do with any given weapon type's prevalence. Hence LER should be unrelated to the incidence of tanks, aircraft, or artillery per se (hypotheses 13b, 14b, and 15b).[39] This in turn implies that there should be no meaningful periodicity in LER; any differences in mean outcomes between eras should be due merely to chance (hypothesis 16b). On the other hand, the new theory expects a systematic change in the *variance* of combat outcomes over time. I hold that progressive advances in technology increase the extremity of both offensive success and failure, but not their relative frequency (which is determined by force employment). This in turn implies a systematic increase in the variance of LER over time (hypothesis 17b).[40] And since the new theory sees force employment, a unit-level trait, as critical, I would expect variance in the relative ease of attack and defense across states *within* any given technological era to exceed variance *across* eras (hypothesis 18b).

The next four observable differences concern territorial gain, and largely parallel those described above for loss exchange ratios.[41] Orthodox offense-defense theory implies that the more offense-conducive the weapon mix, the more ground attackers should be able to take and hold in battle. Hence territorial gains should increase with increasing prevalence of tanks (hypothesis 19a) and ground attack aircraft (hypothesis 20a), and decrease with increasing prevalence of artillery (hypothesis 21a).[42] As with LER, variance in ground gain should be constant over time (hypothesis 22a). The new theory, by contrast, implies that ground gain, like LER, should be unrelated to the incidence of tanks, aircraft, or artillery per se (hypotheses 19b, 20b, and 21b)[43] but should display increasing variance over time (hypothesis 22b).[44]

The other four observable differences for systemic technology vs. the new theory involve duration and address much the same issues. For offense-defense theory, the more offense-conducive the weapons, the more quickly attackers can vanquish defenders—indeed, orthodox theory's identification of offense-conducive weaponry owes much to platform speed and the ability to reach objectives sooner.[45] Hence duration should fall with increasing prevalence of tanks (hypothesis 23a) and ground attack aircraft (hypothesis 24a) and rise with increasing prevalence of artillery (hypothesis 25a).[46] Variance in duration, like LER or territorial gain, should be constant over time (hypothesis 26a). The new theory, by contrast, implies that duration should be unrelated to the prevalence of tanks, aircraft, or artillery (hypotheses 23b, 24b, and 25b).[47] Duration should, however, display increasing variance over time (hypothesis 26b).[48]

Dyadic Technology vs. the New Theory

Dyadic technology theory implies a number of divergences from the new theory, but only one of these is observable given the structure of the available data. By combining the COW dataset with the new database on technological sophistication, it is possible to observe how LER varies with the attacker's relative technological edge.[49] Dyadic technology theory sees this relationship as central, hence LER should fall as the attacker's edge grows (hypothesis 27a). The new theory, while agreeing that, ceteris paribus, LER should fall with an increasing attacker technological edge, sees this as a second-order effect by comparison with exogenous variation between states in the way their forces are employed. For the new theory, any decline in LER should thus be small relative to the variance in the data (hypothesis 27b).[50]

STATISTICAL METHODOLOGY

The nature of the data and the claims here require a variety of statistical techniques, ranging from OLS regression with logarithmic transformations, to hazard analysis, analysis of variance (ANOVA), and Goldfeldt-Quandt tests for nonstationary variance.

Many of the hypotheses concern the sign and significance of relationships between continuous variables: does LER rise or fall with numerical preponderance; is LER constant with respect to tank prevalence; and so on. For these hypotheses, regression analysis is the most powerful tool. Ordinary least squares (OLS) is the simplest and most transparent regression technique but requires normally distributed variables. Neither loss exchange ratios, territorial gain, nor duration are normally distributed, however: LERs and duration cannot take on negative values; territorial gain can be negative, but fully 373 of the 382 values in the CDB90 dataset are zero or positive, skewing the data from normality.

For LER and territorial gain, simple logarithmic transformations can correct for these problems and provide normally distributed data. LER is a strictly positive ratio with a roughly 1.0 median, log(LER) is normal with a roughly zero mean. For territorial gain, the skew in the distribution can be eliminated by shifting the distribution upward by the magnitude of the smallest datum (creating a strictly positive variable) and taking the logarithm of the result. In particular, for LER I estimate the following model for the CDB90 dataset:[51]

$$\log(\text{LER}) = \beta_0 + \beta_1 \log(\text{FFR}) + \beta_2 \log(\text{FSR}) + \beta_3 tkscap + \beta_4 sortscap$$
$$+ \beta_5 artycap + \beta_6 natID_1 + \beta_7 natID_2 + \dots + \beta_{62} natID_{57} + \varepsilon \qquad [8.1]$$

where:

FFR is the ratio of attacker to defender troop strength;[52]
FSR is the defender's force-to-space ratio (in troops per linear km);
tkscap is the number of tanks per capita;[53]
sortscap is the number of ground attack air sorties per capita;
artycap is the number of artillery tubes per capita; and
natID$_i$ is a set of 57 dummy variables identifying unique attacker-defender nationality pairs in the CDB90 dataset.[54]

For territorial gain, I estimate the analogous model:

$$\log(G + 28.3) = \beta_0 + \beta_1 \log(\text{FFR}) + \beta_2 \log(\text{FSR}) + \beta_3 tkscap + \beta_4 sortscap$$
$$+ \beta_5 artycap + \beta_6 bnbelow + \beta_7 rgtbde + \beta_8 div + \beta_9 corps$$
$$+ \beta_{10} army + \beta_{11} natID_1 + \beta_{12} natID_2 + \dots + \beta_{67} natID_{57} + \varepsilon \qquad [8.2]$$

where:

G is the attacker's territorial gain (km);[55]
bnbelow is a dummy variable identifying actions fought at battalion level or below;
rgtbde is a dummy variable identifying actions fought at regimental or brigade level;
div is a dummy variable identifying actions fought at division level;
corps is a dummy variable identifying actions fought at corps level; and
army is a dummy variable identifying actions fought at army level.[56]

Note that whereas LER provides a natural control for the unit of analysis, territorial gain (and duration) do not; hence explicit controls are necessary in the form of dummy variables (*bnbelow* to *army*) for analyses performed on the CDB90 data for these dependent variables.

The COW data's different structure requires a different model for LER:

$$\log(\text{LER}) = \beta_0 + \beta_1 \log(\text{FFR}) + \beta_2 1872\_1918 + \beta_3 1919\_1945$$
$$+ \beta_4 1946\_1972 + \beta_5 techedge + \varepsilon \qquad [8.3]$$

where:

> *1872_1918* is a dummy variable identifying wars fought between 1872 and 1918;
> *1919_1945* is a dummy variable identifying wars fought between 1919 and 1945;
> *1946_1972* is a dummy variable identifying wars fought between 1946 and 1972;[57]
> *techedge* is the attacker's margin of techological advantage over the defender (in years).[58]

Duration, by contrast, is inherently nonnormal. It cannot be negative and is not structured as a ratio with a median at unity. OLS is thus inappropriate. Instead, duration data are properly modeled using hazard analysis.[59] Intuitively, hazard models estimate the likelihood that an ongoing event will terminate at time t as a function of some set of independent variables. More specifically, the hazard rate $h(t)$ is the probability that an event will terminate in an interval $t + \Delta t$ as Δt goes to zero, given that the event has not terminated prior to t. A variety of functional forms can be used to estimate $h(t)$; for the data used here, a Weibull specification provided the best fit. I thus estimate the following model for duration:

$$h(t) = \lambda p (\lambda t)^{p-1} \qquad [8.4]$$

where:

$$\lambda = e^{-\left[\begin{array}{l} \beta_0 + \beta_1 \log(\text{FFR}) + \beta_2\, win + \beta_3 \log(\text{FFR}) \cdot win + \beta_4 \log(\text{FSR}) + \beta_5 tkscap + \beta_6 sortscap + \beta_7 artycap \\ + \beta_8 bnbelow + \beta_9 rgtbde + \beta_{10} div + \beta_{11} corps + \beta_{12} army + \beta_{13} natID_1 + \ldots + \beta_{69} natID_{57} \end{array} \right]}$$

and where:

> t is combat duration (days);
> p is an estimated parameter determining the shape of the hazard function; and
> *win* is a dummy variable identifying attacker victories.[60]

For this model, expected duration is given by:

$$E(t) = \left(\frac{1}{\lambda} \right) \Gamma \left[\left(\frac{1}{p} \right) + 1 \right] \qquad [8.5]$$

Finally, to assess hypotheses 17, 22, and 26 on the stability of variance with respect to time I use the Goldfeldt-Quandt test for heteroskedasticity.[61] Since the hypotheses concern heteroskedasticity in the raw data rather than the error terms of a regression equation, the F statistic in the test is thus the ratio of the sum of squared deviations from the mean of the low and high groups of data, rather than the ratio of the error sum of squares for the two groups.

RESULTS

The results of these tests are summarized in tables 8.2–8.7.

Casualty Predictions

Table 8.2 presents a series of OLS regression analyses for LER using the CDB90 data. In addition to the basic model given by equation 8.1, I provide two variations in which subsets of the full independent variable set are considered: one in which only materiel variables and a constant are included, and one in which only national identity dummies and a constant are included. The results are much more supportive of the new theory than the orthodox alternatives.

In the full model, for example, neither log(FFR) nor log(FSR) are significant at any customary level, and the sign on log(FFR) is positive, as the new theory expects, rather than negative as preponderance theory predicts.[62] The log(FFR) coefficient is thus more consistent with the new than the orthodox theory, though its failure to achieve statistical significance corresponds fully with neither. Similarly, neither tank nor ground attack aircraft prevalence are significant, and both show the opposite of the sign predicted by systemic technology theory—offering contradictory evidence for the latter and corroborative evidence for the new theory. Of the five materiel variables, only artillery prevalence behaves as orthodox theory predicts.

By contrast, the national identity variables that act as proxies for unit-level variance in force employment show substantially stronger performance. The dummies are admittedly imperfect proxies; not only do they incorporate unit-level factors other than force employment (such as culture or morale), but they do not represent unique points on the force employment spectrum: Egyptian and Syrian military doctrines, for example, both drew heavily on Soviet Cold War methods and are likely to have been quite similar. Thus not all dummies represent different force employment from all others, making it unlikely that all would display statistically significant influence on log(LER), even if force employment were a powerful causal agent. Moreover, many dummies represent very few datapoints: CDB90 contains only three cases of German attacks on the French in World War II, for example; only two instances of German attacks on the U.S. in World War I; two cases of Russian attacks on Japan in the Russo-Japanese War; two cases of Bulgarian attacks on Turkey in the First Balkan War; and only one case of Jordanian attacks on Israel in 1967. The corresponding dummies would thus be unlikely to show statistical significance even if their nominal influence were large. Even if the new theory is right, it would thus be

TABLE 8.2.
OLS Regression Results for Casualty Predictions—Log (LER)—Using CDB90 Data

Dependent Variable: Log (LER) Independent Variables	Full Model	Materiel Only	No Materiel
Constant	−0.5773 (0.439)	0.3623 (0.484)	−0.010 (0.090)
Log(FFR)	0.2188 (0.174)	−0.0430 (0.159)	
Log(FSR)	0.1562 (0.123)	−0.1227 (0.137)	
Tanks per Capita	2.9655 (6.777)	−7.4998 (7.564)	
GA Air Sorties per Capita	4.7780 (5.297)	−4.1834 (6.544)	
Artillery per Capita	11.2232 (5.464)**	3.4223 (6.705)	
US v Ger WW1	(dropped)		0.122 (0.107)
US v Jpn WW2	−0.9707 (0.122)***		−0.690 (0.119)***
US v N. Korea	(dropped)		−1.124 (0.174)***
Ger v US WW1	−0.2783 (0.458)		0.062 (0.312)
Ger v US WW2	−0.2450 (0.116)**		−0.082 (0.125)
Ger v France WW1	(dropped)		0.119 (0.161)
Ger v France WW2	−0.9527 (0.469)**		−0.786 (0.432)*
Ger v UK WWl	0.4842 (0.456)		0.028 (0.183)
Ger v UK WW2	−0.1970 (0.164)		−0.015 (0.161)
Ger v Russ WW1	−0.4444 (0.334)		−0.402 (0.195)**
Ger v Russ WW2	−0.8716 (0.325)***		−0.754 (0.195)***
Ger v Ital WW1	(dropped)		−1.173 (0.432)***
France v Ger WW1	(dropped)		0.198 (0.152)
UK v Ger WW1	−0.2077 (0.461)		0.001 (0.156)
UK v Ger WW2	0.3863 (0.119)***		0.448 (0.127)***
UK v Turk WW1	0.3273 (0.326)		0.065 (0.161)
Russ v Jpn Russo-Jp War	0.4016 (0.456)		0.297 (0.312)
Russ v Jpn Manchuria	0.6529 (0.329)**		0.506 (0.260)*
Russ v Jpn WW2	−0.7872 (0.458)*		−0.546 (0.432)
Russ v Ger WW1	0.2880 (0.459)		0.481 (0.312)

continued

TABLE 8.2. (*cont.*)

Dependent Variable: Log (LER) Independent Variables	Full Model	Materiel Only	No Materiel
Russ v Ger WW2	0.4171 (0.327)		0.157 (0.129)
Russ v Austria WW1	0.3173 (0.459)		0.290 (0.432)
Russ v Turk WW1	(dropped)		−0.485 (0.432)
Israel v Egypt 1948	(dropped)		−0.112 (0.230)
Israel v Egypt 1956	(dropped)		−1.172 (0.230)***
Israel v Egypt 1967	−0.7793 (0.180)***		−0.754 (0.174)***
Israel v Egypt 1973	−0.5826 (0.180)***		−0.561 (0.161)***
Israel v Syria 1948	(dropped)		−0.499 (0.432)
Israel v Syria 1967	−0.4377 (0.275)		−0.672 (0.195)***
Israel v Syria 1973	−0.4470 (0.191)**		−0.345 (0.183)*
Israel v Syria 1982	(dropped)		−0.574 (0.432)***
Israel v Jordan 1948	(dropped)		−0.163 (0.312)
Israel v Jordan 1967	−0.0943 (0.200)		−0.026 (0.195)
Israel v Iraq 1973	−0.2755 (0.465)		−0.291 (0.432)
Israel v PLA 1967	−1.0597 (0.459)**		−1.046 (0.432)**
Egypt v Israel 1967	0.7561 (0.330)**		0.841 (0.312)***
Egypt v Israel 1973	0.2225 (0.218)		0.384 (0.195)**
Jpn v Russ Russo-Jp War	−0.3291 (0.243)		−0.290 (0.230)
Jpn v Russ Manchuria	−0.2864 (0.462)		−0.114 (0.312)
Jpn v US WW2	0.7563 (0.480)		0.890 (0.312)***
Jpn v UK WW2	−0.2638 (0.465)		−0.291 (0.432)
Serbia v Turk Balkan War	(dropped)		−0.391 (0.260)
Serbia v Austria WW1	(dropped)		−0.300 (0.432)
Bulg v Turk Balkan War	−0.2581 (0.455)		−0.182 (0.312)
Pol v Russ Russo-Pol War	(dropped)		−0.427 (0.312)
Ital v Austria WW1	(dropped)		0.223 (0.167)
Ital v Sp Rep, Sp Civ War	(dropped)		−0.003 (0.432)

continued

TABLE 8.2. (cont.)

Dependent Variable: Log (LER) Independent Variables	Full Model	Materiel Only	No Materiel
Finland v Russ WW2	(dropped)		−0.856 (0.432)**
Austria v Serbia WW	(dropped)		0.286 (0.432)
Austria v Ital WW1	(dropped)		0.049 (0.312)
Austria v Russ WW1	0.0729 (0.249)		0.092 (0.230)
Syria v Israel 1948	(dropped)		−0.507 (0.312)
Syria v Israel 1973	0.2886 (0.189)		0.392 (0.183)**
Iraq v Israel 1973	0.9611 (0.467)**		0.964 (0.432)**
Jordan v Israel 1967	0.6116 (0.463)		0.663 (0.432)
N. Korea v US	(dropped)		0.504 (0.260)*
N. Vietnam v S. Vietnam	(dropped)		(dropped)
Adj. r^2	.45	−.01	.45
N	215	215	376
F	5.39***	0.48	6.56***

Note: Entries are OLS regression coefficients, standard errors in parenthesis.
*$p < .1$, **$p < .05$, ***$p < .01$; 2 tailed tests

unlikely for all the dummies to achieve statistical significance; if none did, however, this would be an important blow to the theory. In fact, thirteen of the thirty-five dummies for which all variables in the full model could be characterized proved significant, and of those which did not, many represented very few datapoints: 80 percent of the insignificant dummies represented seven datapoints or fewer.[63]

The magnitude of the national identity dummies' effects also swamps that of the materiel variables of orthodox theory. Given the values in table 8.2, the difference between predicted log(LER) for U.S. attackers against German defenders in World War II (the dropped dummy, hence the reference benchmark) and Israeli attackers against Egyptian defenders in 1967, holding other variables at their mean values, is more than a factor of four (1.4 as opposed to −4.1); this far exceeds the effect of eliminating all artillery altogether, or decreasing the FSR by more than 2000 percent. In fact, *no* empirically relevant variation in materiel is capable of equaling the effect of even the lowest valued of the statistically significant dummies here.[64]

To sharpen the point, two variations on the basic log(LER) model were considered: one in which all national identity variables were dropped, leaving only the materiel variables of orthodox theory; and one in which the materiel variables were dropped, leaving only the dummies. Predictive performance drops radically when the dummies are excluded: whereas the full model's adjusted r^2 is 0.45 with an F statistic of 5.39, the no-dummies model has an adjusted r^2 of only -0.01 and an F statistic of only 0.48; none of the variables in the latter model are significant at any customary level. Dropping the materiel variables, on the other hand, induces no meaningful reduction in performance; in fact, the increase in n that results from including battles for which one or another materiel variable is absent from the dataset actually improves the F statistic and increases the number of significant dummies from thirteen of thirty-five in the full model to twenty-two of fifty-six in the no-materiel model.

Taken together, the results in table 8.2 thus contradict orthodox theory's predictions for the effects on log(LER) of FFR (hypotheses 1a and 2a), tanks (13a), ground attack aircraft (14a), and the relative importance of FSR and national variation (8a). They support it outright only for artillery (hypothesis 15a). For the effect of FSR per se (7a), the results are weakly contradictory, since the estimated coefficient's sign is as predicted and its failure to reach significance could be attributable to noisy data. By contrast, the results support the new theory's predictions outright for the effects of tanks (13b), ground attack aircraft (14b), and the relative strength of national variation and FFR (hypothesis 2b). The results are also supportive of the new theory on the relative importance of FSR and national variation; the associated prediction for the marginal effect of FSR per se produces the correct sign but failure to achieve statistical significance (hypothesis 8b). The results contradict the new theory but only weakly for FFR's effect on LER (hypothesis 1b), since the estimated coefficient's sign is as predicted though the coefficient falls short of customary significance levels. Only for artillery (hypothesis 15b) is the new theory contradicted outright.

Table 8.3 presents an analogous series of OLS regression analyses using the COW and MILTECH datasets. Three variations on the model in equation 8.3 are provided: one in which the COW data alone are used to assess the effects of FFR and offense-defense periodization on log(LER), one in which the merged COW/MILTECH data are used to assess the effects of FFR, offense-defense periodization, and dyadic technological asymmetry; and one in which the FFR and offense-defense variables are dropped and only dyadic technology is retained.[65]

The results offer little support for orthodox theories. None of the variables in any of the three models are significant at any customary level. The sign for log(FFR) is the opposite of the orthodox expectation (but consistent with the new theory's prediction) in each of the two models in which it is included. Attacker technological edge has the correct sign only when considered without control variables; when FFR and offense-defense periodization are included, the sign switches to the opposite of that predicted by dyadic technology theory.

TABLE 8.3.
OLS Regression Results for Casualty Predictions—Log (LER)—Using COW Data

Dependent Variable: Log (LER) Independent Variables	Model 1	Model 2	Model 3
Constant	0.057 (0.151)	0.063 (0.200)	−0.164 (0.165)
Log(FFR)	0.095 (0.085)	0.321 (0.231)	
1872–1918	−0.270 (0.188)		
1919–45	−0.315 (0.193)		
1946–72	−0.326 (0.204)	−0.698 (0.313)	
Attacker technology edge		0.001 (0.050)	−0.023 (0.050)
Adj. r^2	.02	.20	−.06
N	52	15	15
F	1.22	2.18	0.21

Note: Entries are OLS regression coefficients, standard errors in parenthesis.
$*p < .1, **p < .05, ***p < .01$; 2 tailed tests

Though insignificant, the three offense-defense period dummies do display the predicted relative rankings: 1919–1945 is more offensive (i.e., induces lower LER) than 1872–1918; 1946–1972 is more offensive than 1919–1945. All are more offensive, however, than 1973–1992 (the excluded dummy); while this is consistent with offense-defense theory for 1919–1945 and 1946–1972, most orthodox theorists see 1872–1918 as the defining example of defense dominance and would presumably expect LER to have been higher, not lower, for that period relative to 1973–1992. Adjusted r^2, moreover, is extremely low for the first and third models, and the F statistic is insignificant for all three. Orthodox theory's performance thus offers no grounds for confidence here, its predictions being contradicted for the casualty effects of FFR (hypotheses 1a and 2a), offense-defense periodicity (hypotheses 16.1a, 16.2a, and 16.3a), and dyadic technology (hypothesis 31a). This in turn suggests support for the converse predictions of the new theory (hypotheses 1b, 2b, 16b, and 31b). For FFR, the coefficient's sign is as the new theory predicts, though it fails to reach significance, implying weak contradiction but still a stronger performance than the orthodox views.[66]

Table 8.4 assesses systemic technology theory's claims for the periodic nature of combat outcomes via a one-way analysis of variance for the COW LER data. If combat outcomes are driven by epochal systemic shifts in prevailing technology, then variance across epochs should outweigh unit-level variance within epochs. On the other hand, if unit-level variance in force employment is the more important determinant, then the reverse should obtain. The results show

TABLE 8.4.
Analysis of Variance, Hypothesis 18 (F_{crit} for alpha $= 0.1$),
Correlates of War Dataset, 1872–1992

Source of Variation	SS	df	MS	F	P-value	F_{crit}
Between Groups	0.11	3	0.04	0.14	0.94	2.20
Within Groups	13.43	49	0.27			
Total	13.54	52				

that variance within technological epochs far outweighs variance across them: the within-group sum of squares exceeds the between-group sum by more than a factor of 100.[67] This suggests that properties unique to dyads are exerting a powerful influence on casualties, and a more powerful influence than the systemic technological effects captured by the period grouping embodied in hypotheses 16.1a to 16.3a.[68] The results thus contradict hypothesis 18a (the orthodox view) and support hypothesis 18b (the new theory).

Territorial Gain Predictions

Table 8.5 presents a series of OLS regression analyses for territorial gain using the CDB90 data. In addition to the basic model from equation 8.2, I again provide two variations in which subsets of the full variable set are considered: one in which only materiel variables, level-of-analysis controls, and a constant are included, and one in which only national identity dummies, level-of-analysis controls, and a constant are included. The results are again more supportive of the new theory than the orthodox alternatives.

In the full model, for example, neither log(FFR) nor any of the offense-defense variables are significant (though all take the predicted signs). Of the materiel variables, only log(FSR) is significant, at the 0.05 level. The national identity dummies again offer important explanatory power. Eleven of thirty-five dummies for which all variables in the full model could be characterized proved significant, and of those that did not, many again represented very few data points: 80 percent of the insignificant dummies represented seven data points or fewer. The magnitude of the national identity dummies' effects again swamps that of the materiel variables considered in orthodox theory. Given the values in table 8.5, the difference between the predicted territorial gain for U.S. attackers against German defenders in World War II and German attackers against Russian defenders in World War II, holding other variables at their means and assuming corps-level actions, is more than a factor of four (35.3 km versus 7.8); this effect far exceeds even a tenfold increase in FFR, tanks/capita, or sorties/capita, or a tenfold decrease in FSR or artillery/capita, relative to their means. Even the lowest-valued of the statistically significant dummies here has a stronger effect on territorial

TABLE 8.5.
OLS Regression Results for Territorial Gain Predictions Using CDB90 Data

Dependent Variable: Log (Territorial Gain + 28.3) *Independent Variables*	*Full Model*[†]	*Materiel Only*[†]	*No Materiel*[†]
Constant	1.9569 (0.131)***	1.6566 (0.121)***	1.9023 (0.065)***
Log(FFR)	0.0016 (0.035)	−0.0635 (0.037)*	
Log(FSR)	−0.0592 (0.024)**	−0.0113 (0.031)	
Tanks per Capita	1.3021 (1.889)	2.6359 (2.228)	
GA Air Sorties per Capita	0.8779 (1.092)	0.4389 (1.484)	
Artillery per Capita	−0.7849 (1.121)	−1.6957 (1.563)	
Battalion and Below	−0.4515 (0.163)***	−0.3273 (0.192)*	−0.2590 (0.150)*
Rgt – Bde Level	−0.2738 (0.098)***	−0.1097 (0.065)*	−0.3990 (0.072)***
Division Level	−0.2658 (0.094)***	−0.0896 (0.060)	−0.3772 (0.061)***
Corps Level	−0.2058 (0.097)**	−0.0354 (0.064)	−0.3419 (0.062)***
Army Level	−0.1446 (0.067)**	0.0156 (0.065)	−0.1374 (0.046)***
US v Ger WW1	(dropped)		−0.0335 (0.057)
US v Jpn WW2	−0.0377 (0.025)		−0.0493 (0.046)
US v N. Korea	(dropped)		0.1892 (0.076)**
Ger v US WW1	−0.0224 (0.091)		−0.0515 (0.148)
Ger v US WW2	−0.0292 (0.023)		−0.0393 (0.050)
Ger v France WW1	(dropped)		−0.2526 (0.088)***
Ger v France WW2	0.0342 (0.093)		0.1901 (0.144)
Ger v UK WW1	−0.0933 (0.111)		−0.1889 (0.095)**
Ger v UK WW2	−0.0237 (0.033)		−0.0621 (0.069)
Ger v Russ WW1	−0.0348 (0.094)		0.1112 (0.100)
Ger v Russ WW2	0.2458 (0.091)***		0.1705 (0.092)*
Ger v Ital WW1	(dropped)		0.2977 (0.209)
France v Ger WW1	(dropped)		−0.3691 (0.079)***
UK v Ger WW1	0.0349 (0.131)		−0.1850 (0.084)**
UK v Ger WW2	−0.0110 (0.024)		−0.0363 (0.051)

continued

TABLE 8.5. (cont.)

Dependent Variable: Log (Territorial Gain + 28.3) Independent Variables	Full Model[†]	Materiel Only[†]	No Materiel[†]
UK v Turk WW1	0.1909 (0.066)***		−0.0845 (0.076)
Russ v Jpn Russo-Jp War	−1.1020 (0.130)***		−0.7811 (0.152)***
Russ v Jpn Manchuria	−0.1264 (0.070)*		−0.1918 (0.123)
Russ v Jpn WW2	0.6863 (0.110)***		0.5100 (0.208)**
Russ v Ger WW1	−0.3331 (0.091)***		−0.3203 (0.147)**
Russ v Ger WW2	−0.0362 (0.071)***		0.1806 (0.061)***
Russ v Austria WW1	0.1807 (0.130)		0.0495 (0.209)
Russ v Turk WW1	(dropped)		0.2576 (0.208)
Israel v Egypt 1948	(dropped)		(dropped)
Israel v Egypt 1956	(dropped)		0.2360 (0.144)
Israel v Egypt 1967	0.1082 (0.036)***		0.1117 (0.076)***
Israel v Egypt 1973	0.1723 (0.036)***		0.1644 (0.069)**
Israel v Syria 1948	(dropped)		(dropped)
Israel v Syria 1967	0.0384 (0.057)		0.0709 (0.088)
Israel v Syria 1973	0.0112 (0.038)		−0.0015 (0.081)
Israel v Syria 1982	(dropped)		0.2478 (0.204)
Israel v Jordan 1948	(dropped)		(dropped)
Israel v Jordan 1967	0.0793 (0.040)**		0.0619 (0.087)
Israel v Iraq 1973	−0.0296 (0.092)		−0.0027 (0.201)
Israel v PLA 1967	0.1433 (0.089)		0.1213 (0.201)
Egypt v Israel 1967	−0.0540 (0.066)		−0.0624 (0.144)
Egypt v Israel 1973	−0.1875 (0.080)**		−0.2749 (0.101)***
Jpn v Russ Russo-Jp War	0.0083 (0.089)		−0.1507 (0.115)
Jpn v Russ Manchuria	−0.0645 (0.091)		0.0027 (0.148)
Jpn v US WW2	−0.0182 (0.095)		−0.0733 (0.144)
Jpn v UK WW2	0.0887 (0.091)		0.0693 (0.201)
Serbia v Turk Balkan War	(dropped)		−0.3670 (0.209)*

continued

TABLE 8.5. (*cont.*)

Dependent Variable: Log (Territorial Gain + 28.3) Independent Variables	Full Model[†]	Materiel Only[†]	No Materiel[†]
Serbia v Austria WW1	(dropped)		0.1991 (0.209)
Bulg v Turk Balkan War	−0.0289 (0.111)		−0.1828 (0.208)
Pol v Russ Russo-Pol War	(dropped)		0.4778 (0.155)***
Ital v Austria WW1	(dropped)		−0.3919 (0.091)***
Ital v Sp Rep, Sp Civ War	(dropped)		−0.1405 (0.204)
Finland v Russ WW2	(dropped)		−0.0733 (0.201)
Austria v Serbia WW1	(dropped)		−1.2688 (0.209)***
Austria v Ital WW1	(dropped)		−0.3395 (0.155)**
Austria v Russ WW1	−0.0602 (0.089)		−0.2279 (0.129)*
Syria v Israel 1948	(dropped)		(dropped)
Syria v Israel 1973	−0.0597 (0.038)		−0.0370 (0.081)
Iraq v Israel 1973	−0.1314 (0.093)		−0.1052 (0.201)
Jordan v Israel 1967	−0.0771 (0.094)		−0.0515 (0.204)
N. Korea v US	(dropped)		−0.0846 (0.124)
N. Vietnam v S. Vietnam	(dropped)		(dropped)
Adj. r^2	.62	.06	.40
N	214	214	363
F	8.62***	2.45***	5.18***

Note: Entries are OLS regression coefficients, standard errors in parenthesis.
*$p < .1$, **$p < .05$, ***$p < .01$; 2 tailed tests
[†]All models include level of analysis dummies.

gain than a simultaneous 500 percent increase in FFR, tanks/capita, or sorties/capita and 75 percent decrease in FSR and artillery/capita.[69]

To reinforce the point, the second model drops the national identity dummies, retaining only the orthodox materiel variables, the level-of-analysis controls and the constant. Predictive performance again drops radically: whereas the full model's adjusted r^2 is 0.62 with an F statistic of 8.62, the no-dummies model has an adjusted r^2 of only 0.06 and an F statistic of 2.45; of the substantive variables, only log(FFR) is significant at even the 0.1 level, and its sign is the opposite of the orthodox prediction. Dropping the materiel variables in the third model, by contrast, has a much smaller effect on predictive performance: adjusted r^2 falls, but only to 0.40; the F statistic falls, but only to 5.18; and nineteen of the fifty-two dummies estimated are significant at the 0.1 level or better.

Taken together, the results in table 8.5 thus contradict orthodox theory's predictions for the effects on territorial gain of tanks (hypothesis 19a), ground attack aircraft (20a), and artillery (21a).[70] Orthodox theory is also contradicted on the relative effects of FFR and national variation (hypothesis 4a), and weakly contradicted on the marginal effect of FFR per se (3a). For FSR, the results support orthodox theory on the marginal effects of FSR per se (hypothesis 9a) but contradict it on the relative importance of FSR and national variation (10a). By contrast, the results support the new theory's predictions for the effects of tanks (hypothesis 19b), ground attack aircraft (20b), and artillery (21b); they support the new theory on the marginal effects of FSR and the relative importance of national variation and FSR (hypothesis 10b); and they are mostly supportive of the new theory's predictions for FFR (hypothesis 4b), sustaining it on the relative importance of FFR and national variation, and only weakly contradicting it on the marginal effects of FFR per se (inasmuch as the sign is correct but the coefficient falls short of customary significance levels).

Duration Predictions

Table 8.6 presents a series of hazard analyses for battle duration using CDB90 data. As before, I provide two variations to the basic model from equation 8.4: one where only materiel variables, level-of-analysis controls, and a constant are included, and one in which only national identity dummies, level-of-analysis controls, and a constant are included. The results are again more supportive of the new theory than the orthodox alternatives.

In the full model, only one of the seven materiel variables is significant (tanks per capita), and its sign is opposite of that predicted by orthodox offense-defense theory. Log(FSR) and artillery per capita likewise take the wrong sign (though neither is significant). The results also suggest the opposite of the Lanchestrian prediction for the effects of FFR on duration. As noted above, Lanchester's Square Law implies that duration should increase with increasing FFR for attacker defeats, but decrease with increasing FFR for attacker victories. In the jackknife specification used here to represent this nonmonotonic relationship, the Lanchester behavior requires that: (1) the coefficient on the interaction term (Log(FFR)* Attacker win) be negative; (2) the absolute value of that coefficient must exceed that of the coefficient on Log(FFR); and (3) the coefficient on the Attacker win dummy must be positive. Though none are significant, the results are consistently the opposite of the prediction.

By contrast, the national identity dummies again offer important explanatory power. Twenty-one dummies proved significant, out of the twenty-eight for which all variables in the full model could be characterized. The magnitude of

TABLE 8.6.
Hazard Analysis Results for Duration Predictions Using CDB90 Data

Hazard Model Coefficient Estimates, Effect on Duration (Days)

Independent Variables	Full Model[†]	Materiel Only[†]	No Materiel[†]
Constant	−11.4634 (2.182)***	−1.7452 (1.172)	−4.5798 (0.385)***
Log(FFR)	−1.3689 (1.121)	−1.8839 (1.078)*	
Attacker Win	−0.5407 (0.528)	−0.4126 (0.483)	
Log(FFR)* Attacker Win	1.0907 (1.151)	0.8910 (1.125)	
Log(FSR)	−0.1602 (0.373)	−0.6998 (0.275)**	
Tanks per Capita	86.4650 (38.485)**	101.6294 (26.502)***	
GA Air Sorties per Capita	−20.4998 (18.053)	−43.7745 (13.687)***	
Artillery per Capita	−0.3386 (14.000)	−12.9484 (11.821)	
Battalion and Below	(dropped)		5.3173 (0.827)***
Rgt – Bde Level	9.3449 (1.603)***	3.7159 (0.659)***	3.6178 (0.368)***
Division Level	9.6539 (1.532)***	3.1592 (0.604)***	2.8152 (0.324)***
Corps Level	8.6203 (1.561)***	2.1849 (0.634)***	2.5286 (0.332)***
Army Level	6.6325 (1.105)***	2.8867 (0.598)***	1.0597 (0.254)***
US v Ger WW1	(dropped)		1.8320 (0.272)***
US v Jpn WW2	−0.2505 (0.404)		−0.1630 (0.231)
US v N. Korea	(dropped)		−0.2272 (0.384)
Ger v US WW1	9.1592 (1.303)***		4.4616 (0.763)***
Ger v US WW2	0.5946 (0.369)		0.3367 (0.252)
Ger v France WW1	(dropped)		2.3457 (0.449)***
Ger v France WW2	2.1280 (1.212)*		0.1356 (0.596)
Ger v UK WW1	7.3119 (1.499)***		−0.0202 (0.477)
Ger v UK WW2	0.5327 (0.618)		0.5102 (0.351)
Ger v Russ WW1	3.3498 (1.248)***		0.8765 (0.503)*
Ger v Russ WW2	2.4554 (1.200)**		−0.3303 (0.475)
Ger v Ital WW1	(dropped)		−0.5035 (1.051)
France v Ger WW1	(dropped)		−0.0492 (0.423)
UK v Ger WW1	9.4401 (1.910)***		−0.9377 (0.433)**
UK v Ger WW2	0.6092 (0.347)*		0.4653 (0.254)*

continued

TABLE 8.6. (*cont.*)

| *Hazard Model Coefficient Estimates, Effect on Duration (Days)* | | | |
Independent Variables	Full Model[†]	Materiel Only[†]	No Materiel[†]
UK v Turk WW1	2.4242 (1.092)**		1.0787 (0.357)***
Russ v Jpn Russo-Jp War	(dropped)		1.3091 (0.777)*
Russ v Jpn Manchuria	(dropped)		1.3272 (0.642)**
Russ v Jpn WW2	0.9779 (1.391)		0.4419 (1.047)
Russ v Ger WW1	(dropped)		0.9221 (0.769)
Russ v Ger WW2	1.3299 (0.865)		0.2189 (0.308)
Russ v Austria WW1	4.3313 (1.760)**		−0.6402 (1.051)
Russ v Turk WW1	(dropped)		0.6396 (1.047)
Israel v Egypt 1948	(dropped)		−1.0342 (0.522)**
Israel v Egypt 1956	(dropped)		0.6401 (0.523)
Israel v Egypt 1967	4.0620 (0.630)***		3.3421 (0.414)***
Israel v Egypt 1973	1.9407 (0.675)***		1.7670 (0.361)***
Israel v Syria 1948	(dropped)		0.1384 (1.012)
Israel v Syria 1967	4.8133 (0.876)***		1.8127 (0.448)***
Israel v Syria 1973	0.3852 (0.682)		1.0448 (0.408)***
Israel v Syria 1982	(dropped)		0.4249 (1.024)
Israel v Jordan 1948	(dropped)		−3.8259 (0.750)***
Israel v Jordan 1967	3.2608 (0.634)***		1.7983 (0.454)***
Israel v Iraq 1973	5.8533 (1.282)***		4.8428 (1.036)***
Israel v PLA 1967	1.7654 (1.097)		1.4973 (1.015)
Egypt v Israel 1967	(dropped)		3.3819 (0.739)***
Egypt v Israel 1973	5.9943 (1.238)***		4.2790 (0.547)***
Jpn v Russ Russo-Jp War	6.3323 (1.293)***		1.2940 (0.595)**
Jpn v Russ Manchuria	5.7074 (1.200)***		0.5840 (0.736)
Jpn v US WW2	(dropped)		1.2673 (0.726)*
Jpn v UK WW2	3.8135 (1.160)***		2.4603 (1.019)**
Serbia v Turk Balkan War	(dropped)		3.2137 (0.668)***

continued

TABLE 8.6. (*cont.*)

Hazard Model Coefficient Estimates, Effect on Duration (Days)

Independent Variables	Full Model[†]	Materiel Only[†]	No Materiel[†]
Serbia v Austria WW1	(dropped)		1.6993 (1.055)
Bulg v Turk Balkan War	3.4455 (1.428)**		2.0341 (0.772)***
Pol v Russ Russo-Pol War	(dropped)		1.2883 (0.781)*
Ital v Austria WW1	(dropped)		−0.0579 (0.445)
Ital v Sp Rep, Sp Civ War	(dropped)		−0.3312 (1.023)
Finland v Russ WW2	(dropped)		−3.2199 (1.016)***
Austria v Serbia WW1	(dropped)		1.5016 (1.054)
Austria v Ital WW1	(dropped)		0.2413 (0.778)
Austria v Russ WW1	2.6537 (1.244)**		1.3720 (0.585)**
Syria v Israel 1948	(dropped)		−1.5645 (0.736)**
Syria v Israel 1973	1.5846 (0.864)*		1.5204 (0.414)***
Iraq v Israel 1973	(dropped)		7.4951 (1.064)***
Jordan v Israel 1967	(dropped)		3.4399 (1.033)***
N. Korea v US	(dropped)		1.7212 (0.638)***
N. Vietnam v S. Vietnam	(dropped)		−2.9836 (1.028)***
P (duration parameter)	2.32	1.55	1.48
Log-likelihood	−106.5	−166.7	−448.2
Chi-Square	231.2***	110.9***	478.8***
N	150	150	382

Note: Entries are hazard model coefficients, standard errors in parenthesis.
*p < .1, **p < .05, ***p < .01; 2 tailed tests
[†]All models include level of analysis dummies.

their effects again swamps that of orthodox materiel variables. Given the values in table 8.6, the difference between the predicted duration for U.S. attacks against German defenders in World War II and Israeli attacks against Egyptian defenders in 1967, holding other variables at their means and assuming division-level actions, is more than a factor of ten; this effect exceeds that of a tenfold decrease in FFR, FSR, sorties per capita, or artillery per capita, or a fivefold increase in tanks/capita, relative to their mean values.[71]

Interpreting the partial models' performance in hazard analysis is harder than for OLS given the absence of a hazard equivalent to adjusted r^2. Nevertheless, the partial model of materiel effects clearly does not perform as orthodox theory would predict. Although more of the materiel variables are significant, their signs do not change—hence FFR, FSR, tanks per capita, and artillery per capita all show the opposite of the predicted effects. Only sorties per capita produces the predicted effect with statistical significance. The partial model that excludes materiel variables again shows a substantial proportion of significant national-identity dummies (33 of 57). On the other hand, the log-likelihood value for the materiel-excluded model is substantially less favorable than for the materiel-only model (-448.2 as opposed to -166.7); both are less favorable than the full model (-106.5). The chi square statistic, by contrast, is actually stronger for the materiel-excluded model than for the full model (478.8 as opposed to 231.2, the difference being attributable in large part to the former's larger n as a result of being able to include data points for which one or another materiel variable was absent from the dataset). Regardless of the quality of fit, though, the materiel-only model's failure to produce coefficients with the predicted signs is a serious problem for orthodox theory.

As a whole, table 8.6's results thus contradict orthodox predictions for the effects on duration of FFR (hypotheses 5a and 6a), FSR (hypotheses 11a and 12a), tanks (23a), and artillery (25a); the findings for ground attack aircraft (hypothesis 24a) are somewhat less clear-cut but tend toward contradiction given the variable's insignificance when controlling for national identity. By contrast, the results support the new theory's predictions for the effects of ground attack aircraft (hypothesis 24b) and artillery (25b); though they are ambiguous with respect to FFR and FSR, supporting the new theory in its prediction that national variation should show stronger effects than preponderance (hypotheses 6b and 12b), but contradicting its prediction that duration should increase with FFR (hypothesis 5b) and weakly contradicting its prediction that duration should decrease with FSR (11b). The results also contradict the new theory's predictions that duration should be invariant with respect to tank prevalence (hypothesis 23b)—though the results are no more supportive of orthodox theory on this point.

Predictions for Change in Variance

Finally, table 8.7 presents the Goldfeldt-Quandt tests for stationary variance in casualties, territorial gain, and duration. The results are broken down by dataset and dependent variable; whereas the CDB90 data permit all three dependent variables to be assessed, only log(LER) can be evaluated using COW.

The results are generally supportive of the new theory, which predicts a significant increase over time for variance in log(LER), territorial gain, and duration. Of the ten tests performed, seven reject the null hypothesis of no

TABLE 8.7.
Goldfeldt-Quandt Tests for Stationary Variance

	COW Data	CDB90 Data
Log(LER)	0.1376	.0007***
Territorial Gain (Km):		
Brigade/Below		<.0001***
Division Level		<.0001***
Corps Level		0.8484
Army/Above		<.0001***
Duration (Days):		
Brigade/Below		<.0001***
Division Level		0.9999
Corps Level		<.0001***
Army/Above		.0002***

Note: Entries are significance levels for rejecting null hypothesis of no change in variance.
$*p < .1, **p < .05, ***p < .01$

change in variance at significance levels exceeding 0.001; in fact, five reject at levels exceeding 0.0001. The COW test is suggestive of an increase in variance but does not quite achieve significance at the 0.1 level. This is attributable to the COW data's small n (46 as opposed to CDB90's 376)—the ratio of high:low group sum of squared deviations is actually higher for the COW log(LER) data than for the CDB90 values.

Moreover, the two apparent contradictions of the new theory (corps-level territorial gain and division-level duration) are driven strongly by a handful of extreme outliers. For the former, removal of a single data point (the battle of Megiddo in September 1918) from the thirty-eight cases available switches the result from contradiction to corroboration at the 0.053 level. For the latter, removal of just two of the 168 data points (the battles of Suomussalmi from the Finnish Campaign of 1939 and Sedjanne-Bizerte from the North African campaign of 1943) switches the result from contradiction to corroboration at the 0.011 level.[72]

Overall, the results thus generally support the new theory's predictions for increased variance over time in LER (hypothesis 17b), territorial gain (22b), and duration (26b). By contrast, they generally contradict orthodox theory's predictions of constant variance (hypotheses 17a, 22a, and 26a).

TABLE 8.8.
Summary of Findings

	Casualties (COW, CDB90, Miltech)	Territorial Gain (CDB90)	Duration (CDB90)
Preponderance (FFR)	*Orthodox* 1a. Contradicted 2a. Contradicted	*Orthodox* 3a. Weakly contradicted 4a. Contradicted	*Orthodox* 5a. Contradicted 6a. Contradicted
	New Theory 1b. Weakly contradicted 2b. **Supported**	*New Theory* 4b. Mostly **Supported**	*New Theory* 5b. Contradicted 6b. **Supported**
Preponderance (FSR)	*Orthodox* 7a. Weakly contradicted 8a. Contradicted	*Orthodox* 9a. **Supported** 10a. Contradicted	*Orthodox* 11a. Contradicted 12a. Contradicted
	New Theory 8b. Mostly **Supported**	*New Theory* 10b. **Supported**	*New Theory* 11b. Weakly contradicted 12b. **Supported**
Technology (systemic)	*Orthodox* (O-D Theory) 13a. Contradicted 14a. Contradicted 15a. **Supported** 16a. Contradicted 17a. Contradicted 18a. Contradicted	*Orthodox* (O-D Theory) 19a. Contradicted 20a. Contradicted 21a. Contradicted 22a. Contradicted	*Orthodox* (O-D Theory) 23a. Contradicted 24a. Contradicted 25a. Contradicted 26a. Contradicted
	New Theory 13b. **Supported** 14b. **Supported** 15b. Contradicted 16b. **Supported** 17b. Generally **Supported** 18b. **Supported**	*New Theory* 19b. **Supported** 20b. **Supported** 21b. **Supported** 22b. Generally **Supported**	*New Theory* 23b. Contradicted 24b. **Supported** 25b. **Supported** 26b. Generally **Supported**
Technology (dyadic)	*Orthodox* 27a. Contradicted *New Theory* 27b. Ambiguous	[cannot be tested using CDB90 data]	[cannot be tested using CDB90 data]

IMPLICATIONS

What, then, do these tests imply for the respective theories' validity? Though imperfect, the results display a preponderance of evidence in favor of the new theory across measures and across databases.

Table 8.8 summarizes these results in terms of the hypotheses presented above. Overall, the findings tend to contradict orthodox theories outright for twenty-three of the twenty-seven hypotheses deduced from them, and to contradict them weakly in another two; in only two cases (the effects of FSR on territorial gain, and the effects of artillery on LER) were orthodox views sustained.[73] By contrast, the new theory was supported or mostly supported for eighteen of the twenty-four hypothesis deduced from it. In only three cases (the effect of FFR on duration, the effect of artillery on LER, and the effect of tanks on duration) was it contradicted outright. For one hypothesis (technological superiority's effect on LER), the results were ambiguous, offering a split decision on different aspects of the predicted outcome; in two cases (the effect of FFR on casualties, and the effect of FSR on duration), the results were weakly contradictory, with signs as predicted but with coefficients that fell short of customary significance levels.

None of the theories conforms perfectly to the data; of course this is inherent in the nature of theory and the messiness of real world phenomena—not to mention the imperfections of available datasets. Against the same background noise, however, the new theory explained substantially more of the variance, and it did so for a variety of outcome measures in several different datasets. While this difference might still be an artifact of poor data, the diversity of hypotheses and data sources makes this significantly less likely. Overall, the results are thus broadly supportive of the new theory.

CHAPTER NINE

Experimental Tests

I NOW TURN to the final approach for testing the new theory: computer simulation experimentation. Alone among the methods used in this book, experimentation allows conditions of theoretical importance but historical rarity to be examined. This provides a degree of insulation against the problem of selection on wars; it also allows a direct look at an important prediction of the new theory for which no historical cases are yet available: what if advanced, late-twentieth-century weapons were directed at a fully modern-system opponent?

Like all methods, experimentation has drawbacks. Most important, it requires simulation rather than observation of real warfare. This is true of experimental science in many fields. Medical researchers, for example, do not begin drug testing with human subjects; they start with in vitro experiments using tissue cultures and petrie dishes—effectively, simulations of human physiology. Aircraft designers use wind tunnels to test wing configurations in simulated flight before risking pilots' lives in real airplanes. Physicists use elaborate simulations to design nuclear weapons and predict their effects before—or in lieu of—field testing.

In any of these fields, validity rests on the simulation's fidelity; for this reason I use the most rigorously validated combat simulation available in the defense analytical community, Lawrence Livermore National Laboratory's Janus system. I draw the scenario and data from the joint U.S. Army / Defense Advanced Research Projects Agency / Institute for Defense Analyses 73 Easting Project, an unprecedentedly detailed data collection effort on a representative battle from the 1991 Gulf War. While no simulation offers the verisimilitude of ex post facto observation of real warfare, the Janus 73 Easting pairing offers the closest approximation available.

The results reinforce the small and large-*n* ex post findings above: the new theory outperforms its orthodox competitors in a series of tests designed to isolate the theories' key differences experimentally. I present these findings in four steps. First, I describe the Janus simulation and the 73 Easting Project in greater detail. Second, I present the experimental design. I then discuss the results. I conclude by assessing their theoretical implications.

THE SIMULATION

The experimental apparatus consists of two main elements: the Janus computer simulation and the 73 Easting database. Janus is a highly disaggregate, stochastic, interactive, two-sided simulation of brigade-level combat with resolution to individual weapon systems. Input data include weapon descriptions (e.g., reload rates, vehicle speeds, hit and kill probabilities by range, posture, and shooter-target pair); numbers and types of weapons deployed by each side; and digitized terrain descriptions (e.g., topographic elevation; locations of forests, towns, roads, and rivers). Force employment is determined by the user—not the model—via input unit deployments, movement tracks, and firing orders, any of which the user can change in real time during a simulated battle. Outputs include casualties by target and shooter type, final unit locations, and real-time visual displays of unit positions and firing activity. Engineering algorithms used to determine physical interactions have been validated by field and lab experimentation; validity of the model overall has been established by comparing simulation output and the results of battalion and brigade-level maneuvers at the U.S. Army's National Training Center at Fort Irwin, California. Originally created to assist battlefield nuclear weapon designers in understanding target behavior, Janus is now used primarily in training U.S. Army, Marine Corps, and National Guard officers for war; it is also widely used for systems analyses by military and civilian analytical agencies and has been adopted for training purposes by several NATO allies.[1]

Note that Janus is neither a theory of combat nor a closed-form mathematical model like that presented in the appendix. Just as a wind tunnel is not a theory of lift, so Janus is not a theory of war: both are radically underspecified experimentation tools for obtaining information about the behavior of complex systems by repeated trial and error. Janus embodies no explicit assumptions about what will happen when groups of individually and exogenously maneuvered weapons interact, or about how forces will (or should) be employed; only the physics of individual-weapon interactions and performance are endogenous. The complexity of predicting from their engineering characteristics how dozens to hundreds of such independently maneuvering elements will interact on a three-dimensional terrain surface is Janus's raison d'etre; rather than trying to theorize such interactions, the modelers instead simulate them in a maximally disaggregate manner, allowing the user to observe their complex interactions as they unfold. Janus is thus a powerful tool for testing theories of aggregate combat interactions developed externally to the model, but it is radically underspecified as a theory of combat in itself. Note also that Janus neither was designed to test capability theory nor is typically used for this purpose; while it is coincidentally well suited to my purposes, the kind of experiments described here could not have been anticipated by its designers, and the model thus does not reflect any conscious bias with respect to the issues under study here.

The 73 Easting Project was a collaborative study conducted jointly by the independent Institute for Defense Analyses (IDA), the Defense Advanced Research Projects Agency (DARPA), and the U.S. Army. Its purpose was to develop a database of unprecedented detail on the conduct of a single battle (the Battle of 73 Easting), then to use modern computer simulation technology to represent that data in a "virtual re-creation" of the minute-to-minute activities of each participating tank, armored vehicle, truck, or infantry team.[2] Data were collected using traditional documentary historical techniques, extensive engineering surveys of the battlefield immediately after the fighting, and exhaustive participant interviews, integrated using the simulation itself. That is, apparent discrepancies and data gaps were identified by representing all available information in the simulation and observing the results; these results were then shown to the participants in a three-dimensional, real-time visual display of the battle that can be zoomed to follow individual combatants or replayed as needed to review events in detail. Resolutions of discrepant or missing data were then worked out by the battle participants and the analytic team in light of all known information, entered into the database, and the process repeated.[3] The resulting dataset offers probably the most complete and reliable depiction of any combat action in history.

EXPERIMENTAL DESIGN

I use this simulation to address two counterfactuals:

1. What if the Iraqis had fully implemented the modern system?
2. What if the United States had not had such advanced technology?

The new theory and the orthodox views imply very different answers to these what-ifs. The new theory requires a combination of non–modern-system Iraqi tactics and new technology to produce DESERT STORM's loss rates. Either condition without the other would be insufficient. If the new theory is correct, each counterfactual should produce results radically different from the historical battle's.

Orthodox theory's view of the Gulf War, by contrast, focuses on technology: the Iraqis were simply overmatched by radically superior U.S. weapons. If so, then neither side's tactics should matter centrally; the first counterfactual should thus differ little from the historical outcome. Only if the U.S. technology edge is reduced should outcomes change decisively.

To consider these questions, I compare a "base case" corresponding to the actual historical battle with a series of excursions in which Iraqi force employment is brought into alignment with the modern system, and U.S. technological advantages are reduced.[4] These scenarios are summarized in table 9.1, and involve:

- two of the Iraqi divergences from modern-system tactics described in chapter 7: poor defensive preparations (with armored vehicles perched on the surface behind exposed sand berms), and failure of the covering forces to provide warning; and
- two of the U.S. technological advantages described in chapter 7: the M1A1's thermal sights, and the air technology that permitted unchallenged precision engagement of Iraqi armor over a six-week air campaign.

Note that the base case reflects the real battle's technology, dispositions, movements, and U.S. combat skills but credits the Iraqis with much better skills

TABLE 9.1.
Simulation Experiment Results[†]

Scenario	Key Features	US AFV Losses			Iraqi AFV Losses			LER (Iraqi:U.S.)
		Mean	Std. Err.	Frac.	Mean	Std. Err.	Frac.	
Base		2.00	0.94	0.03	85.80	3.46	0.77	42.90
A	Modern-system Iraqi tactics: both errors corrected	48.30	4.30	0.71	31.20	5.98	0.28	0.65
B	Partial Iraqi improvement: positions properly prepared	5.30	1.83	0.08	57.20	4.24	0.51	10.79
C	Partial Iraqi improvement: tactical warning provided	1.80	0.92	0.03	86.10	3.70	0.77	47.83
D	No U.S. thermal sights; Iraqi warning error corrected	39.10	2.18	0.58	38.30	3.23	0.34	0.98
E	No U.S. thermal sights; neither Iraqi error corrected	15.90	5.13	0.23	59.80	5.35	0.53	3.76
F	No U.S. thermal sights, no U.S. air; neither Iraqi error corrected	40.00	2.10	0.59	38.00	3.30	0.34	0.95

[†]"AFV" means "armored fighting vehicle"; "LER" means "loss exchange ratio" (mean Iraqi AFV losses divided by mean U.S. AFV losses); "Frac." is the mean loss expressed as a fraction of that side's pre-battle total.

and much closer correspondence to modern-system practice than they actually displayed—even though it accounts for the two mistakes of poor position preparation and poor covering force performance. This is because Janus assumes U.S.-quality soldier performance unless told otherwise; errors must be deliberately introduced to be considered. By introducing two, the base case thus considers some, but far from all, the Iraqis' actual mistakes (excluding, for example, their poor tank gunnery, fire coordination, and vehicle maintenance). When the two introduced mistakes are removed, the result is thus a nearly complete, error-free Iraqi implementation of modern-system tactics. The results are therefore treated as properties of error-free modern-system performance, but this does not imply that the Iraqis need only have fixed their position engineering or covering force discipline to reap the benefits described. For the Republican Guard (much less Iraqi conscript infantry) to approach the performance credited them in the "modern-system" case would require much more sweeping reforms.

The 73 Easting scenario also requires careful interpretation of U.S. force employment. 73 Easting was a hasty attack during DESERT STORM's exploitation phase. Unlike the deliberate attacks in the breakthrough effort, 2d ACR's assault here thus did not attempt the full panoply of modern-system exposure reduction techniques. This is typical of exploitation (see chapter 3), and even here, U.S. troops implemented important elements of the modern system (especially the concealment afforded by operations during a raging sandstorm, and the fire

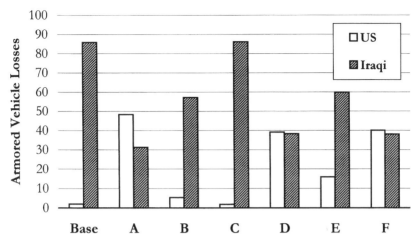

Figure 9.1. Simulation Experimentation Results, Battle of 73 Easting

coordination afforded by maintaining formation over an extended approach march). Yet there was neither the elaborate preliminary reconnaissance, nor the preparatory artillery program, methodical fire-and-movement, or dismounted infantry action of modern-system breakthrough tactics. Nor was there the local numerical advantage typical of modern system differential concentration: as a scouting element, the Americans were outnumbered by their opponents at 73 Easting. The Janus/73 Easting combination enables powerful counterfactual analysis while surmounting some of the usual verisimilitude challenges of simulation, but it imposes some constraints in exchange: while important elements of the modern system can be observed in U.S. tactics, to turn the battle from a hasty assault in exploitation to a deliberate attack in breakthrough would change the context too completely to sustain the ceteris paribus assumptions inherent in counterfactual analysis.[5]

Each scenario was run ten times.[6] Mean vehicle losses for the two sides and associated standard errors are reported in table 9.1 and illustrated graphically in figure 9.1.

RESULTS

The results are strongly consistent with the new theory, and inconsistent with the orthodox view. In particular, they suggest three key observations.

1. *Against a modern-system defense, 2d ACR's technology overmatch did not provide victory at very low losses.*

Excursion scenario A assumes that both of the Iraqi errors considered here are corrected, and thus that Iraqi defensive tactics are brought fully into alignment with the modern system (that is, the above-ground revetments of the historical battle are entirely replaced with below-ground, turret-down positions from which the occupants move up to a hull-down posture upon acquiring a target; and functioning observation posts provide tactical warning of the attackers' approach).[7] Coalition technology, Coalition force employment, and all other aspects of the base case are held constant. As a consequence, simulated U.S. vehicle losses rise from only two in the base case to almost fifty (more than 70 percent of total U.S. strength) in the excursion scenario results, while Iraqi losses fall from eighty-six to about thirty, even given the technological advantages of the M1A1, the effects of Coalition air supremacy, and the skilled handling of the U.S. attack.[8]

Why does force employment have such a large effect on attacker casualties here? The answer has to do with the way the Iraqi failure to implement the modern system played into the strengths of U.S. technology.

Many have argued, for example, that thermal sights gave the United States an enormous target acquisition advantage in 73 Easting, where a raging sandstorm blocked the Iraqis' simple optics but not the Americans' advanced sights.[9] For superior target acquisition range to be useful, however, there must be exposed targets to acquire. In the base case, the Iraqis' poorly constructed above-ground revetments guarantee this. In fact, the berms advertise the defenders' locations to attackers with advanced sights. In excursion scenario A, on the other hand, modern-system position preparation causes the Iraqis' vehicles to be concealed in turret-down positions unless their own crews see targets. At long range, where thermal sights enable the attackers to see in spite of the sandstorm but where the defenders' simple optics are blinded, the defenders (who see no targets) now remain concealed and the attackers have nothing to shoot at. Only when the attackers close the range and are seen do the defenders move into hull-down firing positions and become exposed. The net result is that the firefight takes place at much shorter range, and the thermal sight's long potential acquisition range is negated.

Similarly, the lack of meaningful depth resulting from the Iraqi covering force's failure to provide warning plays into the strengths of Coalition air technology. Advanced air technology afforded the Coalition air supremacy over the KTO. While this did not produce extensive direct air attrition to the Iraqi units that fought at 73 Easting, it did indirectly reduce their average manning levels (see chapter 7). This potentially reduced their return fire in the critical opening minutes of the battle and potentially enabled the attackers to kill undermanned Iraqi vehicles before they could be fully ready to fight. But to realize this potential required that the defenders be taken by surprise. Defense in depth normally prevents this by providing warning to the main line of resistance; if the Iraqis' main defenses had been warned in time, they could have regained full readiness before meeting the attack, thus negating the indirect effects of Coalition air supremacy. In the historical battle (and the simulated base case), however, the Iraqi covering force's failure to send an alert resulted in their main defenses being taken by surprise. In excursion scenario A, by contrast, adequate warning is provided, enabling all the defenders' vehicles to be manned and ready when the attacker appears. As a result, the indirect effects of air supremacy cannot be exploited, and the outcome is a far less one-sided firefight in spite of the U.S. technological advantage.

2. Against advanced technology, partial modern-system implementation is not enough.

Excursion scenarios B and C assume partial, but incomplete, modern-system implementation by the Iraqis.[10] In excursion B, position preparation is remedied, but the covering force still fails to alert the defenses; in excursion C, the covering force performs properly, but the defenses are still poorly prepared. In both excursion scenarios, the attacker annihilates the defender at losses little higher than those of the historical base case (in excursion B, five simulated U.S. vehicle losses rather than the two of the base case; and in excursion C, only about two).

This is because advanced weapons are potentially so lethal that a chance to use even a part of the U.S. arsenal at full capacity can be decisive in itself. The M1A1's thermal sight offered a potential range advantage of more than 1,600 meters in the sandstorm of the historical battle. If poor Iraqi position preparation allows the Americans to exploit this advantage, then it does not matter whether the victims are also surprised or not; the range advantage alone is more than enough to annihilate the defense even if the defenders are ready to fight from the outset. U.S. air supremacy induced many Iraqis to leave their vehicles unoccupied. If the Iraqis allow themselves to be surprised in this state, then the resulting chance to engage empty or unready targets through the attack's critical early minutes is decisive in itself—whether the unready defenders are destroyed from 2,000 meters away as they sit on the surface behind loose sand piles, or whether the shooting is done from point blank range against (unready) tanks sitting idly in better-dug, below-grade positions.

3. Less sophisticated or less diverse offensive technology reduces the consequences of a defender's failure to implement the modern system.

The simulation results suggest that the less advanced the attacker's technology, the less complete the defender's implementation of the modern system can be without inducing disaster. Conversely, the more advanced the technology, the more completely the defender must implement the modern system. If the simulated U.S. attacker enjoys the full technology advantage of the actual battle, virtually complete modern-system implementation is required for the Iraqis to avert disaster, as can be seen by comparing the base case with excursion scenarios A, B, and C. But if the attacker's technology advantage is reduced, the Iraqis can accept some degree of imperfection and still impose heavy losses on the attacker. In excursion D, for example, the attacker lacks thermal sights and benefits only from the indirect effects of air supremacy, while the Iraqis commit only one of the two base case errors: they are assumed to obtain adequate warning, but they retain their problematic revetted vehicle positions. The resulting attacker casualties increase substantially relative to the historical base case (thirty-nine rather than two).

But while the simulated Iraqis can tolerate somewhat more error against this lower-technology attack, they cannot tolerate much more. In excursion E, the attacker is again denied thermal sights, while the Iraqis commit both of the two base case errors; the resulting attacker losses are less than half the results that obtain when the Iraqis commit only one of the two errors (sixteen rather than thirty-nine).

If the Coalition technology advantage is reduced enough, however, then even a defense committing both base case errors can still impose severe costs on the attacker. In excursion F, the attacker lacks both the thermal sight and air supremacy, while the Iraqis commit both errors assumed in the base case. The resulting casualties are substantially higher than in the historical base case (forty rather than two).

IMPLICATIONS

Taken together, the counterfactuals suggest two broad implications. First, the results are consistent with the new theory's posited nonlinear interaction between technology and force employment but are inconsistent with orthodox dyadic technology theory. Where non–modern-system defenses provided openings for offensive technology to exploit, the result was offensive victory by an outnumbered attacker at very low losses. But against a modern-system defense, the same offensive weapons were far less lethal, and even advanced technology could not prevent many attacker casualties.[11] Moreover, the more advanced the attacker's technology, the graver were the consequences of a given defender mistake, and the fewer mistakes the defender could afford to make without courting disaster. In these simulations, technology thus magnified the effects of force employment—punishing non–modern-system force employment with increasing severity as technology advanced, but with much less effect on a low-exposure, modern-system defender. Technology thus increased the premium on the skilled performance the modern system demands and raised the standards for acceptable levels of skill on the part of armies faced with an advanced technology opponent.

Second, the simulation results are inconsistent with standard explanations of the Gulf War's outcome in particular. As noted in chapter 7, the DESERT STORM literature implies something like a linear multivariate explanation of the Coalition's radically low losses: a variety of contributing causes are identified, but the causal mechanisms are almost strictly univariate, offering no reason to expect the combination to yield more than just the sum of the parts. A linear relationship between casualties, technology, and force employment would imply that the marginal effect of any one contributing cause would be about the same regardless of the presence or absence of the others, and that the marginal effects of each would be roughly independent of its level (i.e., there should be no diminishing or increasing marginal returns: given two technologies with roughly equal independent effects on casualties, the results of introducing or removing one should be about the same whether the other is present or not). Yet the value of the attackers' weapon technology varied radically with the presence or absence of modern-system tactics. The effects of either defensive force employment error varied radically as a function of whether the other was also present. With two defensive errors, either thermal sights or air supremacy produced about the same attacker losses, whereas with only one defensive error, the two technologies produced very different results. In these simulations, the effects of the respective contributing causes thus do not simply cumulate linearly—they interact in a powerful, nonlinear way.

On balance, and together with the results of the case studies and statistical analyses presented above, the results thus warrant at least provisional confidence in the new theory's validity. And this in turn warrants careful consideration of the theory's broader implications for policy and scholarship, to which I turn in the book's concluding chapter.

CHAPTER TEN

Conclusion

THE MOST INFLUENTIAL IDEAS about capability heretofore have centered on material factors: which side has more troops or weapons? Whose weapons are superior? How sophisticated is their technology? Does that technology favor attack or defense? These issues frame the public discussion of defense policy and the use of force. They dominate the formal models that inform decision making throughout the U.S. Defense Department and in many other Western governments. And they underpin the treatment of force and power in international relations theory.

I have argued, however, that material factors alone cannot explain capability as we have observed it over the past century. To do better requires a systematic theory of how material and nonmaterial variables interact.

In particular, I have argued that a remarkably stable and essentially transnational body of doctrinal ideas emerged from the crucible of the First World War. These ideas turn on reducing exposure to the radical firepower of the modern battlefield and enabling friendly movement while slowing the enemy's. Taken together, these methods broke the trench stalemate in 1918 and defined the standard for successful military operations throughout the post-1918 era. The resulting modern system of force employment, however, is extremely difficult to implement in its entirety; some states have mastered it, but others have not. States that master it have largely insulated themselves from the effects of changing technology: their ability to reduce their exposure has kept their loss rates low even as weapons' nominal lethality has grown. States that fail to implement the modern system, on the other hand, have been fully exposed to the increasing lethality, speed, and reach of their opponents' weapons. Their loss rates have thus climbed with advancing technology. Over time, this has produced an ever-widening capability gap between states that can and those that cannot implement the modern system, but little change in combat outcomes between mutually modern-system opponents.

In this view, technology's effects are thus secondary to force employment's and cannot be properly understood except in interaction with force employment: technology alone is a poor predictor of capability. The effects of numerical preponderance, like those of technology, are determined largely by force employment. Gross resource advantages matter only if they can be exploited via modern-system force employment, and many states cannot do so. Materiel is hardly irrelevant—both advanced technology and superior numbers are valuable, and one must know both to predict outcomes accurately—but the role of materiel is very different from that assumed in current theories. Moreover, it is the nonmaterial component that is most influential in itself: modern-system force employment can compensate for substantial disadvantages in materiel, but neither technical nor numerical superiority per se can typically enable a non–modern-system military to defeat a modern-system opponent.

These claims survive a number of challenging tests using a variety of different methods. In detailed case studies of operations MICHAEL and GOODWOOD, the new theory outperforms materialist views under conditions that should have offered easy predictive successes for materialist theories if true. For Operation DESERT STORM, both the new theory and materialist orthodoxy predict Coalition victory, but the *way* the Coalition won is much more consistent with the new theory. In a series of large-*n* statistical analyses, the data contradict orthodox preponderance and technology theories for twenty-five of twenty-seven testable hypotheses; in only two of twenty-seven were they supported. By contrast, the new theory was corroborated for eighteen of twenty-four hypotheses; in three of the twenty-four the results were ambiguous or weakly contradictory; in only three of the twenty-four were the results unambiguously inconsistent with the new theory's predictions. In a series of simulation experiments using the U.S. Army, Defense Advanced Research Projects Agency, and Institute for Defense Analyses' computer reconstruction of the Battle of 73 Easting from the 1991 Gulf War, systematic, controlled variations from the conditions of the historical battle yield outcomes much more consistent with the new theory than with orthodox views.

Of course, no testing methodology is perfect, nor does the new theory fit the evidence in every detail. Perfect corroboration, however, is an unrealistic goal in a messy world of imperfect data, stochastic variation, and human actors with free will. The proper aspiration is to capture broad trends in ways that account for more of the data than competing theories. And by this standard the new theory both outperforms orthodox views and shows significant consistency with the observed record of modern warfare across three different modes of observation. This is not a proof of validity, but it demonstrates sufficient potential to warrant considering the new theory's implications for policy and scholarship.

IMPLICATIONS FOR SCHOLARSHIP

The new theory poses important implications for our understanding of international politics. Capability is a central explanatory variable in international relations theory. The realist tradition views it as the single most important determinant of state behavior; for the liberal tradition, its centrality is the chief foil against which theories of cooperation are drawn. Among the broader themes of the last generation of international relations scholarship has been the asserted weakening of its relative causal importance in the face of new theories of audience costs, sig-naling, bargaining dynamics, domestic politics, collective action problems, risk perception, norms, culture, and identity construction. While few would find it ir-relevant, much of the literature has argued that military power plays a less central role than earlier theorists like Morgenthau or Waltz had supposed.

All of this, however, is built on a fundamentally unsound conception of capa-bility itself. Both realists and liberals view capability as a product of material wherewithal; some (mainly offense-defense theorists) see the materiel's nature as key, but for most it is the relative mass of troops, population, military expendi-ture, or economic potential that creates capability. This is fundamentally mis-taken. Capability is not primarily a matter of materiel. It is chiefly a product of how states *use* their material resources—and this varies widely in ways that are not mere epiphenomenal reflections of materiel constraints. Empirical patterns in the balance of materiel are thus unlikely to reveal much about the real dis-tribution of capability among states, and the enormous body of analyses using such material indicators as measures of capability are thus misspecified. To base larger theoretical claims on such a mistaken conception of the sources of mili-tary power is to risk gross error in the analyses of international politics that emerge.

In fact, the very concept of capability in this literature is problematic regard-less of its assumed causes. IR theory treats capability as a simple, unitary entity: it can be added across alliance members, balanced against an opponent, or counted to determine a state's great power status and the polarity of the inter-national system. Having more of it conveys general-purpose military capacity that is highly fungible across specific tasks and geopolitical contexts: there is a single "balance of power," which pertains whether a given state is the aggressor or the defender, whether it values casualty minimization or territorial control, and whether it would rather bomb for a year to keep losses low or must finish the war in weeks.

This whole notion of a simple, unitary "capability" fundamentally misrepre-sents military potential, which is inherently multidimensional. Different military tasks are very dissimilar—the ability to do one (or several) well does not imply the ability to master others. There is thus no single, underlying quality of generic "capability" to which all specific mission capacities are epiphenomenal. Forces that can attack successfully may be ineffective in defense; forces that are powerful in a long campaign may be all but worthless if results are needed quickly; forces that can conquer an opponent quickly if heavy losses are accept-able may be unable to take any ground at all if losses are intolerable. The Israeli military, for example, is highly capable in short offensive wars but cannot sustain long campaigns, cannot tolerate heavy losses, and is less suited to theater de-fense than offense. Its real fighting ability is thus different in different missions—the "balance of power" between Israel and its neighbors has no single meaning independent of this context. Military mission capacity is not fungible in any simple way across missions or contexts. This is why the theory of capability advanced here does so in terms of three different, irreducible capacities: the ability to control territory, to limit (and inflict) losses, and to prevail quickly. The simple, unitary concept of capability in the IR literature, by contrast, is logically problematic; theories that aspire to generality cannot meaningfully explain political outcomes in such terms.

Of course, political decision making is based on perception rather than objective reality. Above I examined only the objective determinants of capability; how can this speak to political outcomes that rest on perceptions rather than realities? In fact, most of the literature—especially empirical studies in international politics—relies on objective measures as proxies for decision makers' actual perceptions. Given the complexity and opacity of perception, large-n analysis will probably always require such proxies. This approach has been criticized before: detailed studies of actual perceptions have typically reported a more discriminating process by which real leaders evaluate their own and others' capabilities.[1] Most IR theorists, however, continue to use unitary measures of gross material wherewithal as a proxy for leaders' actual perceptions on the argument that such measures closely approximate real military potential and that states whose perceptions fail to accord with this reality will be removed by natural selection.[2] The findings above undermine both of these claims: material wherewithal is a very poor indicator of real military outcomes, and materially inferior states are thus not unusually likely to die off via military defeat. Selection thus would not drive states to behave "as if" they believed gross material preponderance to be central, even if one otherwise accepted selection as a meaningful causal mechanism. This finding, however, rests centrally on the analysis of real military outcomes and their determinants. Only by examining objective military reality is it thus possible to address the claims underpinning the orthodox treatment of capability in the IR theoretic literature more broadly.

The enormous IR literature built on notions of military capability thus faces serious empirical and logical problems. Challenges to the causal importance of military power, for example, are on thin empirical ice without a stronger measure of capability. Yet the realist literature against which such arguments are aimed is also problematic: one can neither challenge nor demonstrate the real effects of capability on the basis of a flawed metric.

More narrowly, a variety of the particular claims in realist theory are inconsistent with the analysis above. For example, many realists argue that severe competitive pressures compel states to converge on optimal practices. This in turn implies that states can be treated as interchangeable in all respects other than their position in the hierarchy of power; given the same power position, different states would all behave the same way.[3] Yet the results above challenge this claim. Even in the use of military force—the single most important function for state survival in realist theory—critical differences persist. The modern system offers something approaching an optimal military doctrine for most states. As late as 1991, however, a major regional power in an unusually dangerous region fought two major wars without fully implementing the modern system: Iraq fell radically short of modern-system precepts in both the Iran-Iraq War of 1980–88 and the Gulf War of 1991.[4] Britain failed to implement modern-system offensive methods in Operation GOODWOOD in 1944, and even Germany sometimes fell short: whereas their methods at GOODWOOD were consistent with the modern system, at COBRA a week later their defense was radically shallower with a much smaller fraction of forces withheld in reserve.[5] The importance of national identity variables in the statistical analysis of chapter 8 is strongly suggestive of serious variance in force employment across states throughout the twentieth century. While state practices sometimes converge—the birth of the modern system itself is an especially striking example—often they do not, and the failure of convergence even in the realm of military affairs is particularly problematic given the importance of military incentives in the realist causal mechanism.[6] More broadly, the results here thus provide another way in which unit-level variables matter for international politics, contra the central claims of modern realism.[7]

The findings above also pose a major challenge to orthodox offense-defense theory's predictions for political outcomes. Offense-defense theorists hold that systemic shifts in the offense-defense balance give rise to a host of profound consequences, ranging from war causation to arms racing, alliance formation, trade policy, and international system structure. Yet systemic technological change is a weak determinant of the relative ease of attack and defense, the causal driver at the heart of offense-defense theory. Offense-defense theorists are right to distinguish attack from defense and to insist that IR theory incorporate such a distinction: the results above suggest that offensive capability is not necessarily the same as defensive, and if military capability matters for international politics, then the two cannot be conflated.[8] But it is a mistake to see the source of this difference in systemic technology, and a logic train beginning in technology and ending in war causation, arms racing, or alliance formation is thus fundamentally flawed. Given the importance of the distinction between attack and defense, it makes sense to retain it as a central feature of sound IR theory, but to do this will require a new offense-defense theory built not on technology but on the interaction between technology and force employment.[9]

But how is such a body of new theory to be built? More broadly, how can IR theory in general come to reflect a more robust conception of military capability? To the extent that theorists use objective military reality as a proxy for leaders' perceptions, three requirements suggest themselves.[10]

First, analyses must disaggregate "capability" into separate dimensions of ability to control territory, ability to inflict casualties, and ability to control duration, and specify causal effects with respect to these dimensions directly rather than conflating them. Alternatively, analyses could preserve a single-valued index of capability by specifying states' preferences over its three conflicting dimensions (defining, effectively, a state's utility over military outcomes), or by restricting causal claims to the effects of one dimension alone (though this would require some rationale to justify excluding important state concerns to focus on others). Either way, fully specified theories of the role of military power must avoid conflating mutually contradictory ends, and this requires a more disaggregate treatment of this inherently heterogeneous concept.[11]

Second, analyses must distinguish offensive from defensive capability. Both orthodox offense-defense theory and the new formulation above imply that states are sometimes able to defend their own territory but not conquer their neighbors', they are sometimes able to conquer but not defend, sometimes able both to conquer and defend, and sometimes able to do neither.[12] Given this, it is meaningless to say that a state is highly "capable" even with respect to any one dimension of casualties, territorial gain, or time; to do so implies that the ability to attack and the ability to defend are the same when they are not. Analyses that posit a unidimensional "capability" as a variable thus arbitrarily exclude politically important military possibilities.

Third, empirical analyses must reflect force employment in their measures of capability.[13] This need not take the form of explicit measurements of depth, reserve fractions, reserve or assault velocities, or exposure fractions, though of course it could. An alternative approach would be to develop auxiliary theories to predict such force employment choices as a function of broader characteristics of states that may be more convenient to observe empirically, to address at other levels of analysis, or to characterize for times of peace as well as times of war.[14] But however it is done, explicit consideration of how forces would be used is essential to any representation of capability in empirical research—without it, statistical results reflect neither actual perceptions nor objective approximations.

For historians, the findings above suggest two main implications beyond those outlined in chapter 1. First, the findings here offer further support for the view that the world wars' outcomes were more contingent and less predetermined than usually thought. For much of the postwar era, the prevailing view held that the great industrial superiority of the Western Allies made German victory in either conflict impossible.[15] Recently, Richard Overy has argued that the Second World War in particular was a much closer call, and that plausibly different decisions by either side could have produced a very different outcome.[16] The analysis above suggests that in general, the importance of material preponderance has been exaggerated, and the role of variations in the use of that materiel has been underappreciated. This in turn implies that plausible differences in doctrines and tactics could have induced major differences in military outcomes—quite possibly, differences large enough to have altered victor and vanquished in either war, which would in turn pose profound consequences for the political and social world we inhabit today.

Second, the analysis above suggests that the emerging historical reinterpretation of the First World War has broader applicability. Recent historiography has revealed more—and more effective—doctrinal adaptation in all of the great power militaries than previously recognized. This doctrinal adaptation is increasingly credited with hastening the end of the war by restoring maneuver to the battlefield in 1918; conversely, the absence of 1918-type methods in 1915–17 is increasingly seen as a central contributor to the great stalemate on the western front.[17] Doctrine—force employment—is thus receiving greater explanatory weight relative to the material factors that have dominated earlier accounts of the war. Yet the paramount importance of force employment goes far beyond the western front or even the world wars collectively. The pattern of force employment forged in response to the trench stalemate is central to understanding much of the subsequent course of twentieth-century military history as a whole and is likely to remain crucial in at least the early decades of the twenty-first. The problems of firepower, exposure, movement, and concealment have not lessened with changing technology, and the solution to those problems that arose from the mud of the western front has continued to define the key issues for military capability in an era of precision guided weapons, networked information, and stealth aircraft. The consequences of First World War doctrinal adaptation have thus been sweeping for the subsequent military history of the twentieth century, and probably beyond.

IMPLICATIONS FOR POLICY

There are also important implications for policy. I focus on six here, involving the future of warfare, defense budget priorities, force structure, weapon development and acquisition, joint campaign assessment, and military doctrine. I conclude with some final observations on directions for further inquiry.

The Future of Warfare and the RMA Thesis

Perhaps the most sweeping of these implications concerns the revolution in military affairs thesis. Many now argue that technology is creating a new form of warfare in which long-range precision air and missile strikes will dominate the fighting, ground forces will be reduced mostly to scouts, and the struggle for information supremacy will replace the breakthrough battle as the decisive issue for success. Such radically new forms of warfare, it is argued, could offer enormous military power to states that master them. U.S. leads in key technologies give it a head start in the race to do so, but no more than a head start. Ultimate success, it is argued, will require sweeping organizational and doctrinal changes to realize the new technology's potential—yet the complacency that often accompanies leadership, combined with the military's inherent conservatism, could easily block such radical change. Other powers who see the opportunity and accept radical change sooner or more completely could thus leapfrog the United States, leaving it to follow nineteenth-century France and Imperial Britain into military decline.[18]

This view has proven highly influential and is now received wisdom in much of the U.S. defense planning community.[19] If correct, its implications are sweeping. If we are indeed in the midst of a military revolution, then U.S. defense policy requires fundamental overhaul. Today's defense establishment is designed to cope with warfare of the kind seen in pre–Gulf War experience; if the future will be radically different, then a complete rethinking is needed.

The analysis above, however, suggests a very different future. Rather than a revolutionary break from the past in which only radical change can avert military decline, the findings here imply no looming discontinuity in the nature of war. The events that RMA advocates see as radical changes in fact display as much continuity as change—and these underlying continuities suggest a very different set of prescriptions for future U.S. military policies.

The technological changes most often cited as revolutionary—the increased lethality of precision guided weapons, the increased range of deep strike air and missile systems, and the increased ability to gather and process information—are all extensions of very longstanding trends. Militaries have been forced to cope with steadily increasing lethality, range, and surveillance capabilities for fully a century now; these are hardly sudden developments posing fundamentally new problems. In fact, much of the history of post-1900 tactics and doctrine has been precisely about the need to respond to these changes and how best to do so. The response that ensued—the modern system of force employment—has been tested extensively by multiple militaries under diverse conditions over more than eighty years of actual warfare. In this extended trial by fire it has proven remarkably robust over a sweeping span of historical change in weapons, platforms, and sensors. Over this period, most of the really important variance in combat outcomes has stemmed not from technological change but from the failure of particular states to implement the (very difficult) methods called for by the modern system. If militaries make the most of the modern system's ability to reduce exposure, then eighty years of increasing lethality need yield only modest increases in vulnerability; if militaries cannot exploit the modern system, on the other hand, exposure to such lethal weaponry can yield extremely—and increasingly—painful results.

This analysis implies a different policy program from the RMA view. I take up many of the specifics below, but in the aggregate, the theory of capability presented here implies that traditional approaches to warfare are in fact essential for survival on the emerging battlefield—*because the emerging battlefield is a further extension of the one for which traditional approaches were designed.* This is not to say that defense policy should freeze in time or that the military of the future should be identical to today's; below I outline some of the changes needed. But the central themes of the analysis above are that the need for continuity is much stronger than generally recognized; that wholesale change is not warranted by ongoing changes in technology; and that future warfare is best understood as a continuation of trends and relationships that have been evident for at least one hundred years, rather than as a radical departure from historical precedent.

But why, then, do RMA advocates see the future as such an extraordinary break from the past?[20] Is there nothing unique or different about new lethality, range, or information at the dawn of the twenty-first century? The *pace* of technological change, for example, seems to have accelerated dramatically in recent years; although lethality has grown continuously since 1900, has the rate of growth not exploded in the last decade or so in ways that imply a need for radical change in response? How can one exclude the possibility that this acceleration might yet bring a revolution?

Of course, one can never exclude the possibility that the future might be surprising, and it is certainly conceivable that lethality could eventually exceed the modern system's limits of adaptation (more on this in the discussion of research and development below). Yet it is important to view today's pace of change in perspective. There is always a temptation to view one's own era as a critical fork in the road, or as a period of unusual change relative to what has come before. Some of this is inherent in the need to draw attention to one's claims; some is an understandable if fallacious response to exponential growth as a phenomenon. The increases in lethality and range described in chapter 4, for example, display an exponential growth pattern.[21] A mathematical property of exponential growth is that it always displays a rapidly growing rate of change with a sharp upturn at the end of the period, whatever period one considers. If one plots lethality from 1900 to 2000, one sees rapid increase at the end of the century, but if one looked at the same data from the perspective of an observer in, say, 1950, the result would also look like a rapidly growing rate of change with a sharp upturn at the end of the *half*-century. There would be a difference in scale, but the shape of the relationship would be the same, and both would seem to imply explosive growth in the observer's own time. To the extent that one is watching exponential growth, this will always be true for any observer at any time—it tells us nothing unique about the world of 2004.

In fact, predictions of revolutionary change lying just around the next bend are commonplace in military history. Alfred Nobel thought dynamite was such a radical change from the past that it would render armed conflict impossibly costly and lead to the end of war.[22] Ivan Bloch thought the same for the machine gun.[23] The *jeune école* navalists in France thought the development of torpedo-wielding light surface vessels would sweep the capital ship from the waves in the 1880s and lead to a whole new era of naval warfare.[24] Prior to World War I, air-power visionaries looked at the new technology of the airplane and reasoned that this changed everything: land warfare would become impossible in the face of bomber fleets attacking cities directly from the air.[25] Strategic bombing advocates then made the same mistake on the basis of the improved air technology of the interwar years and judged that the new bombers would prevail with a "knockout blow" against enemy cities in the opening weeks of a second world war.[26] After the war, the U.S. Army and Air Force concluded that the atom bomb would revolutionize warfare and make traditional continental operations impossible; both organizations abandoned their conventional methods and restructured to fight the atomic wars of the future. For the Air Force, this cost lives in subsequent nonnuclear land wars in Korea and Vietnam; for the Army, it resulted in the ignominious abandonment of the atomic-optimized Pentomic Division structure by 1961.[27]

All of these cases show forward-looking thinkers who saw the technological change of their own day as so explosive as to imply military revolution; all were wrong. The better-known counterexamples of reactionary battleship admirals, cavalry generals, or business executives who thought radio or computers were just a flash in the pan can easily lead to an assumption that the real danger is to underestimate the effects of technological change. Yet this fails to consider the many instances of forecasters *overestimating* the effects of change in the face of apparently exponential growth in key enabling technologies, and it fails to account for the real costs of those overestimates. Technological change that looks very rapid has been a constant throughout modern history. It has often failed to bring the revolutionary military changes that many have expected in the past, and it is not in itself a sufficient reason to expect an RMA now either.[28]

What about the recent fighting in Afghanistan? Many now see the Taliban's collapse under American air strikes as corroborating the RMA thesis. If precision bombing annihilated Taliban positions from standoff range, enabling a ragtag militia to walk forward in the bombing's wake and conquer the country with no more than a handful of American commandos on the ground, then this would certainly seem to imply a revolutionary change in war.[29]

Yet this is not what actually happened. The Afghan campaign was not fought exclusively at long range, nor was precision strike sufficient to defeat the Taliban. There was actually plenty of close combat in Afghanistan. The course of this close combat, moreover, was shaped by variations in force employment on the ground, and its outcome was central to the campaign. The war was thus surprisingly orthodox in many important respects.

The Taliban were not a modern-system military (and their inability to master the modern system contributed decisively to their rapid defeat once America joined the war). But their foreign elements—especially al Qaeda—did adopt enough of the modern system's components to survive precision bombing in meaningful numbers. The bombing, though it hurt the Taliban badly, thus could not defeat them in itself. Partial modern-system implementation cannot defeat a diverse panoply of modern weapon technologies (see chapter 9), but it can thwart particular technologies employed singly.[30] To defeat even a partially modern-system opponent in Afghanistan required a combination of modern precision strike technology and ground action, at close quarters, by troops whose grasp of modern system principles was at least comparable to their opponents'. The contending armies in Afghanistan were not uniformly bumblers; they were actually diverse mixtures of more- and less-motivated, better- and worse-skilled units. On balance, America's Afghan allies implemented enough of the modern system to enable them to exploit the lethality of American air power and thus prevail, but the diversity of either army provides some instructive examples of variance in force employment and its impact on modern, high-technology warfare. The results suggest that even in the twenty-first century, technology alone does not predetermine outcomes—the presence or absence of modern-system force employment remains critical.

Early in the campaign, for example, indigenous Afghan Taliban made little attempt to cover, conceal, or disperse their forces. Once American special operations forces (SOF) arrived to direct precision airstrikes against such targets, the result was slaughter in actions such as Bishqab on October 21, 2001, Cobaki on October 22, and Ac'capruk on November 4.[31]

The Taliban, however—and especially its foreign and al Qaeda components—quickly realized that such exposed dispositions were suicidal and began to disperse, seek cover and concealment, limit their radio transmissions, and enforce rigid camouflage discipline. That is, they adopted some key elements of the modern system. Within days of the first SOF-directed air strikes, for example, American commandos reported that the Taliban were smearing their vehicles with mud to reduce their infrared signatures.[32] By the time of Bai Beche on November 5, Sayed Slim Kalay on December 2–4, the fighting along Highway 4 through December 6, and Operation ANACONDA in March 2002, the now mostly foreign Taliban and al Qaeda fighters had reduced their exposure to the point where they could survive multiday Western bombing efforts in meaningful numbers. At Bai Beche, for example, a mostly al Qaeda force occupying a deliberate defensive system built by the Soviets in the 1980s was bombed for over two days by Western aircraft. Yet enough defenders survived as to thwart the initial assault by Gen. Abdul Rashid Dostum's American-allied Afghans.[33] Along Highway 4, al Qaeda defenders hidden among culverts and in burned-out vehicles along the roadway remained undetected by any Allied surveillance system and unengaged by Western aircraft until they fired upon and threw back an advance by Allied infantry; an al Qaeda counterattack using a system of wadis for cover and concealment closed to within a few hundred meters of Allied positions before being detected, much less fired upon.[34] At Sayed Slim Kalay, al Qaeda counterattacks again closed to within small arms range of Allied forces before being detected.[35] At ANACONDA, fewer than half the al Qaeda defensive positions ultimately discovered were known to American intelligence prior to direct ground contact with Allied infantry.[36]

This is not to say that al Qaeda had mastered the modern system: through at least March 2002 they fell far short of its precepts in important respects.[37] But by mid-November 2001 they had realized enough of it to render standoff warfare alone insufficient to dislodge them.

This in turn meant that sizeable friendly ground forces capable of executing something like modern-system offensive methods were necessary to dislodge surviving, actively resisting Taliban defenses. Where American or Allied ground troops were capable of limiting their own exposure and coordinating their movement with American airstrikes, the result was rapid success against enemies whose grasp of modern-system principles was sufficient to shield them from aerial annihilation per se, but insufficient to sustain a defense against a combined air-ground offensive with modern weapons.[38] At Bai Beche, Highway 4, Operation ANACONDA, and elsewhere, this combination of precision firepower and limited-exposure ground attack ultimately defeated stiff Taliban resistance and enabled the country's rapid conquest.[39]

By contrast, where Allied ground forces faced surviving defenders but could not limit their own exposure or coordinate their maneuver with American airstrikes, the result was often failure—even with the support of twenty-first-century precision firepower. At Arghestan bridge on December 5, for example, an American-allied but untrained Pashtun militia failed to take an al Qaeda defensive position in spite of a day of trying, and in spite of American precision air support.[40] On the first day of Operation ANACONDA, an allied Afghan force with limited tactical skills encountered concealed, dug-in al Qaeda defenses and proved unable to advance. Pinned down under heavy fire, the allied Afghans ultimately withdrew; the al Qaeda positions were later taken by better-trained Western infantry.[41]

There are thus important elements of continuity linking the Afghan campaign and the preceding century of military experience.[42] But what about the 2003 campaign in Iraq? If Operation ENDURING FREEDOM in Afghanistan was not a revolutionary departure, was Operation IRAQI FREEDOM in Iraq?

Here, too, the evidence suggests not. As this book goes to press, publicly released information does not yet enable a detailed assessment of the war in Iraq to compare with that possible for the fighting in Afghanistan. I am now in the process of conducting a study to provide such an account of Operation IRAQI FREEDOM on the basis of primary source evidence collected in Iraq, Kuwait, and the United States, but this research cannot be completed in time for full discussion here. In the meantime, however, the gross contours of the war's conduct and outcomes seem consistent with a hypothesis that the war was a further continuation of the trends discussed above.

The theory presented above explained the 1991 Gulf War outcome as the product of an interaction effect between non–modern-system Iraqi force employment, modern-system Coalition force employment, and advanced Coalition technology. What would the theory predict for a 2003 encounter between an Iraqi military whose skills and weaponry had probably not improved markedly since 1991, and a Coalition military whose skills were comparable to those of 1991 but whose technology was even more advanced? The answer is a dramatically one-sided Coalition victory—which is, of course, what obtained in the high-intensity phase of the 2003 campaign.

The Coalition loss rate of about one fatality per 2,500 military personnel in 2003 was slightly higher than 1991's one per 3,700, but the mission in 2003 was much more demanding, requiring the Coalition to destroy the entire Iraqi national military and occupy an entire country of twenty-four million people covering 437,000 square kilometers. By contrast, the mission in 1991 required only that a subset of the Iraqi military be removed from a country with one-twenty-fourth the land area and only one-twelfth the population.[43] To accomplish this more-demanding mission with a loss rate not significantly higher than that of 1991 is suggestive of a continued increase in the lethality of modern technology against non–modern-system opposition—precisely as the theory presented here would predict. While this is far from a definitive test of the theory (or a definitive assessment of Operation IRAQI FREEDOM), it does at least suggest that the evidence available to date on the 2003 campaign does not appear to undermine the argument presented here.

Even today, then, military experience suggests that the lessons of 1918 remain critical to success in battle. Armies, like Iraq's, who cannot exploit modern-system exposure reduction are fatally exposed to modern weapons. And conversely, even very superior weapon technology cannot in itself defeat armies who do exploit modern-system methods to reduce their exposure, as al Qaeda did to a meaningful degree in Afghanistan. Of course technology does matter—the Taliban suffered heavily under Allied air attack, and the introduction of precision air power is what turned a stalemated civil war into a decisive Taliban defeat. But technology does not predetermine outcomes, and its role is both different and more limited than often supposed. In Afghanistan and IRAQI FREEDOM, as in DESERT SRORM before them, advanced technology magnified the consequences of failure to implement the modern system in its entirety. But Western technology could not compensate for allied Afghan troops' occasional failure to reduce their own exposure, and it could not defeat even partially modern-system opponents in Afghanistan without significant close combat by friendly ground forces whose tactics were at least as close to modern-system precepts as their enemies'. Either campaign's outcome was indeed different from what one might have observed if it had been waged in 1918, 1944, or even 1991—but it was different in degree, not in kind. New technology reinforced the lessons learned in 1918 and increased the penalty for those who learned them incompletely. But it did not overturn them. And it thus does not signal a revolutionary discontinuity in the relationship between technology and force employment.

The strength of any prediction is its ability to account for what has been observed and to project demonstrable trends into the future; the RMA prediction rests on a misreading of the key observable trends and is thus deeply problematic. Nor does safety lie in erring on the side of overanticipating the scale of future change. Others before us have made similar overpredictions and sometimes suffered gravely for their error; moreover, the specific policy implications of an overprediction of future change are problematic for U.S. defense policy in the early twenty-first century in particular. I thus turn to several of the key particulars.

Defense Budget Priorities

After the September 11 attacks, a sustained increase in American defense spending is likely. No foreseeable spending increase, however, can free decision makers from painful choices: even budgets in excess of $300 billion a year cannot simultaneously modernize traditional "legacy" systems like howitzers and manned fighter aircraft; accelerate "transformational" purchases such as information infrastructure, pilotless aircraft, and precision weapons; increase the size of the military; increase spending for training and readiness; and underwrite ongoing operations, potentially in multiple theaters of war. Even after September 11, powerful incentives thus remain to cut back on at least one of the budget's three major components (readiness, force structure, and modernization) in order to preserve the others. RMA advocates have long argued that modernization must take higher priority in the future—which necessarily implies opportunity costs against spending for readiness and force structure.[44]

One should be wary, however, of proposals to protect modernization at the expense of readiness. This is not to say that modernization should be halted: weapons, like any other capital stock, wear out and must be replaced. The issue is the relative pace of modernization, and the analysis above suggests that trading slower modernization for lesser cutbacks in training, schools, and quality-of-life accounts (i.e., those parts of the budget that help create and retain skilled personnel capable of implementing demanding modern-system force employment) would be a better choice than the reverse. At the margin, a less-skilled military is more dangerous than less-advanced technology. U.S. weapons are already so lethal that any non–modern-system opponent can be annihilated at minor risk to the United States; rapid modernization guilds the lily against such enemies but cannot bring dramatic change against modern-system opponents. By contrast, readiness cutbacks that allowed today's combat skills to decay would not only forfeit the ability to exploit current technical advantages against less skilled opponents, but would also enable future challengers to turn the tables by acquiring better technology themselves and using it to its full potential against inadequately skilled Americans. Neither is a risk worth taking.

Force Structure

Many RMA advocates call for a radical restructuring of the U.S. military away from direct-fire ground forces and toward heavier reliance on air and deep strike missile systems.[45] The analysis here, on the other hand, suggests that such a restructuring could be very risky. Sometimes it would be highly effective: against non–modern-system enemies, a mostly air and deep strike–oriented U.S. military would in fact be the ideal solution. Against an opponent better able to limit its exposure, however, such an imbalanced U.S. force would be at a grave disadvantage. By giving up direct fire ground capability in exchange for more deep strike systems, such a force would be much weaker than today's against opponents able to escape destruction at extreme range and close with American ground forces (as al Qaeda, for example, proved able to do in Afghanistan). Such a restructuring would thus strengthen U.S. capability mostly where it is already so strong as to be nearly beyond challenge (that is, against exposed, non–modern-system opponents) by creating weaknesses elsewhere. Unless it is certain America will never again face skilled opposition, this could be a dangerous approach.

The findings above thus augur against a major restructuring away from close combat capability and toward deep strike, but this does not mean that today's close combat forces should simply be retained, unchanged. As massed armor in the open becomes ever more vulnerable, potential opponents are likely to move more of their activities into covered terrain. Many will prove unable to exploit such terrain completely or to articulate complex maneuvers without exposure, but all face growing incentives to shift as much of their activities as possible into forests, mountains, urban areas, refugee camps, or other settings offering cover, intermingling with civilians, or both. As they do so, American incentives shift at the margin away from the heavy armor typically thought best suited to relatively open terrain, and toward the lighter, more infantry-intensive forces typically thought best for warfare in close terrain and built-up areas.[46] Regardless of terrain, combined arms will remain essential, but the optimal balance of arms within any given formation may well shift. And as technological change drives opponents out of the open (or allows exposed opponents to be destroyed with smaller and smaller deep strike forces), this in turn provides a strong incentive to lighten American close combat forces and to increase the availability of dismounted infantry.

Of course, lighter-weight ground forces have other advantages as well—especially their superior strategic mobility. As post–Cold War geopolitics make strategic mobility more important for U.S. forces, this provides strong logistical incentives to move toward lighter, "medium-weight" units.[47] Some argue, however, that such forces would be too vulnerable against heavier opponents, and thus that the United States should retain its current force structure, accepting slower deployment in exchange for more capability once deployed.[48] The analysis above suggests this is a false dichotomy. Regardless of geopolitics, technological change creates incentives for lighter forces better suited to operating in the kinds of close terrain and dispersed postures that all armies will increasingly need to seek out to survive against twenty-first-century firepower. Those who insist on massed operations in the open will be too vulnerable to deep precision strike systems to threaten friendly ground forces; a balanced U.S. force structure will provide increasingly ample air and missile capability against such targets as technology advances. The real mission for close combat forces is to deal with opponents who implement enough of the modern system to counteract long-range firepower. And the best choice against such opponents is a lighter-weight force with more dismounted infantry strength and less orientation toward weight of steel per se for survivability.[49]

Research, Development, and System Acquisition

The analysis above also implies some different directions for system acquisition, research, and development. In particular, it suggests that pilot programs to explore remote surveillance against targets in wooded and built-up areas merit higher priority and accelerated development relative to other ongoing surveillance initiatives. Similarly, new precision munitions effective against dispersed targets in such terrain also warrant greater relative attention.

If they could be made effective at reasonable cost, such developments could have sweeping consequences. The only technical development in the foreseeable future that could cause a truly revolutionary change in warfare—that is, one that would overturn the dominance of force employment and break the twentieth-century pattern of slow change in outcomes between modern-system opponents—would be one that could make terrain, dispersion, and combined arms irrelevant. If deep strike systems really could destroy any target anywhere regardless of its apparent exposure or concentration, this would overturn skilled armies' ability to limit their vulnerability to hostile firepower and bring about a truly new situation. It is far from clear that such developments are attainable, but the attempt warrants the highest priority.

Joint Campaign Assessment

Many defense planners now feel that traditional force planning and joint campaign assessment methodologies are too focused on individual weapons per se and not enough on the role of the supporting information infrastructure and highly integrated cross-service and cross-branch "systems of systems" that are held to be such important elements of the RMA.[50] The Defense Department has thus recently embarked on a major program to update current methods and overcome these perceived shortcomings.[51]

Yet while current methods are problematic, the main difficulty lies elsewhere. Even if new models treat information technology and joint precision strike in great detail, they will still risk serious error if they overlook the key relationship between technology and force employment.[52] In fact, by focusing on the new-technology components of the RMA thesis and overlooking the ways in which real militaries differ in their vulnerability to such systems, the new methods could actually leave the Defense Department worse off. To capture the dynamics of actual warfare, new methods must account for the crucial interaction between new technology and variations in the ways different enemies will actually use their forces; this is not an impossible task, but it cannot be accomplished without sustained, systematic analytical effort.

Military Doctrine

Finally, much of the RMA literature advocates radical doctrinal change and argues that the chief obstacle to exploiting the RMA is the inherent conservatism of military organizations.[53] This case, however, has not been made. If the new theory above is correct, then radical doctrinal change would be neither necessary nor desirable. It would be unnecessary because warfare would not be on the verge of revolution. It would be undesirable because many of the proposed innovations would rest on technologies that would be effective enough only against non–modern-system opponents; against tougher opposition, doctrines dependent on such technologies could be highly problematic.

In fact it is not the case that the only real risk is to underinnovate in the face of technological progress, or that the main challenge is simply to induce unwilling organizations to change. While there are historical examples of militaries that adapted too slowly, there are also examples of ones that changed too fast or too much. The interwar RAF, the U.S. Army in the Pentomic era, the U.S. Air Force in the late 1940s, and the French *jeune école* navalists of the 1880s have already been mentioned; one could add the British Army in the late 1930s, whose radically tank-heavy armored division organization was a much more sweeping departure from precedent than the Germans' combined arms Panzer Division, yet the British innovation was hardly more effective for its being more radical.[54] All of these examples represent large, professional military bureaucracies adapting too quickly for their own, or their nation's, good.

This is not to argue that doctrine should stand still. U.S. military doctrine has changed regularly since World War II and will surely continue to do so.[55] Ensuring that this continuing evolution is sound and sufficient is an important, challenging job for the defense planning community, both military and civilian. Rather, my point is that this normal process of incremental adaptation to changing technology is entirely appropriate to the times. To retain methods that have worked well in prior conflicts is not a sign of hopeless shortsightedness, nor is novelty per se a sign of vision or foresight. The measure of an analysis is its deductive rigor and its support in the evidence—not its nonconformity or the scale of its apparent departure from current practice.

Directions for Further Inquiry

Finally, an important implication for both scholars and policy planners concerns the importance of further research on the causes and consequences of variance in force employment. For scholars, this issue bears on virtually the entire gamut of international political questions involving the use of force; for policy practitioners, it is central for accurate assessment of foreign militaries, prudent development of military doctrine and U.S. national strategy, and sound decision making on a host of issues ranging from the use of force to weapon development and acquisition, force structure, or service roles and missions. I have tried to (1) provide a clear statement of this subject's importance, (2) show that current policy and scholarship have treated it inadequately, and (3) articulate a particular body of claims and evidence toward a better understanding. Much remains to be done, however. It is one thing to argue that unit-level factors give rise to important variation in force employment, but another to construct a systematic theory to predict force employment as a function of observable variations in states and institutions. A proper database on historical patterns of actual force employment is essential. Forms of conflict other than mid to high intensity continental warfare need to be considered. Additional non-material variables—such as organization, morale, or combat motivation—need systematic theoretical attention. IR theory and joint campaign assessment modeling need to be adapted to reflect a logically sound conception of capability and the empirical importance of force employment.

Perhaps most broadly of all, war's conduct and outcomes need to receive the same kind of sustained, explicit, rigorous theoretical analysis that other social phenomena have come to receive—not just because war affects politics or society, but because victory and defeat is an objectively important subject in its own right. War's causes have received intensive study in the hope of finding means of prevention; preventing war is crucial, but not all wars can be prevented. And where they cannot be prevented, winning rather than losing has tremendous importance. The difference between victory and defeat can mean the difference between freedom and oppression, or between life and death itself. America is now engaged in a potentially global war on whose outcome thousands to millions of lives may rest. Explaining success and failure in such struggles is a matter of paramount national importance—it deserves the most penetrating research that modern scholarship can provide simply on the basis of its intrinsic significance alone.

Yet for at least a generation, the study of war's conduct has fallen between the stools of the institutional structure of modern academia and government. Political scientists often treat war itself as outside their subject matter; while its causes are seen as political and hence legitimate subjects of study, its conduct and outcomes are more often excluded. Since the 1970s, historians have turned away from the conduct of operations to focus on war's effects on social, economic, and political structures. Military officers have deep subject matter knowledge but are rarely trained as theoreticians and have pressing operational demands on their professional attention. Policy analysts and operations researchers focus so tightly on short-deadline decision analysis (should the government buy the F22 or cancel it? Should the Army have 10 divisions or 8?) that underlying issues of cause and effect are often overlooked—even when the decisions under analysis turn on embedded assumptions about the causes of military outcomes. Operations research has also gradually lost much of its original empirical focus; modeling is now a chiefly deductive undertaking, with little systematic effort to test deductive claims against real world evidence.[56] Over forty years ago, Thomas Schelling and Bernard Brodie argued that without an academic discipline of military science, the study of the conduct of war had languished;[57] the passage of time has done little to overturn their assessment. Yet the subject is simply too important to treat by proxy and assumption on the margins of other questions. In the absence of an institutional home for the study of warfare, it is all the more essential that analysts in existing disciplines recognize its importance and take up the business of investigating capability and its causes directly and rigorously.[58] Few subjects are more important—or less studied by theoretical social scientists. With so much at stake, we surely must do better.

A Formal Model of Capability

IN THIS APPENDIX I formalize the presentation of the theory described qualitatively in chapters 3 and 4. I do so in ten steps. First, I present the variables and notation used. Second, I describe a notional theater geometry and outline the dynamics of a typical continental military operation in its terms. Third, I establish the initial conditions for such an operation in terms of the variables defined in step 1. Fourth, I develop the dynamics of the operation, or how these initial conditions change over time; from these dynamics I derive expressions for the end-state values of the dependent variables of territorial gain, casualties, and campaign duration. Fifth, I present a simple auxiliary model of ground force attrition in an air-only campaign (which I use as a preprocessor to the main model for analyzing cases of extensive pre-invasion air bombardment). Sixth, I discuss the calculation of ground-gain-maximizing and ground-gain-minimizing force employment choices. Seventh, I present in tabular form the specific variable values used to compute the model's comparative statics. Eighth, I present the comparative statics results. The model and these results treat force employment choices as exogenous variables—that is, they assume that states choose tactics and doctrines according to some logic that I do not seek to explain here; those choices are thus taken as givens for any one run of the model, and I depict their consequences without any claims about which states will make which choices. The results, however, imply strong military incentives for states to employ their forces in particular ways—specifically, to follow modern-system guidelines. The ninth section systematizes this finding in game theoretic terms by structuring a simple two-player, zero-sum game where the game strategies are the two sides' force employment choices and the game payoffs are the model's computed capability findings for those choices. The results show that the modern system constitutes a saddle point solution to this game—that is, that modern-system force employment really is in both sides' best *military* interest. The final section provides a sensitivity analysis on some of the model's key constants.

NOTATION

Let:

$R \equiv$ invader troop strength (total direct-fire combat arms personnel in theater)[1]
$B \equiv$ defender troop strength (total direct-fire combat arms personnel in theater)

$\tau_R \equiv$ weighted mean introduction date for invader's major weapon systems (years)[2]
$\tau_B \equiv$ weighted mean introduction date for defender's major weapon systems (years)
$d \equiv$ depth of the defender's forward positions (km)
$f_r \equiv$ fraction of the defender's troops withheld in mobile reserve
$f_e \equiv$ fraction of the defender's forward garrison exposed
$V_r \equiv$ velocity of the defender's rear-area reserve movements (km/day)[3]
$V_a \equiv$ velocity of the invader's assault at the point of attack (km/day)[4]
$w_a \equiv$ invader's assault frontage (km)
$w_{th} \equiv$ theater frontage overall (km)
$k_1 \equiv$ constant: number of invaders one defender can halt when fully reinforced and fully concealed (personnel)
$k_2 \equiv$ constant: fit parameter in equation (A.5) below (dimensionless)
$k_3 \equiv$ constant: number of invaders needed to pin one defender in position away from point of attack (personnel)
$k_4 \equiv$ constant: fit parameter in equation (A.7) below (dimensionless)
$k_5 \equiv$ constant: invader off-axis casualties (personnel killed and wounded in action)
$k_6 \equiv$ constant: defender off-axis casualties (personnel killed and wounded in action)
$k_7 \equiv$ constant: fit parameter in equation (A.11) below (dimensionless)
$k_8 \equiv$ constant: invader casualties per defender per day at zero assault velocity (personnel killed and wounded in action)
$k_9 \equiv$ constant: invader flank defenders required per kilometer of flank per defensive reserve soldier (invader personnel/[defender personnel*km])

THEATER GEOMETRY

I assume a notional theater of war described by the length of its assailable frontier (w_{th}) between the invading and defending combatant. The invader chooses a point of attack and concentrates a disproportionate fraction of its overall troop strength on a chosen frontage (w_a) at that point. Initially, the location of this assault frontage is unknown to the defender. Prior to its discovery, the defender is thus distributed more uniformly along the theater frontier than is the invader.

Once the defender locates this point of attack, it attempts to counterconcentrate by moving reserves to the threatened sector. This process takes time, however. Prior to the reserves' arrival, the invader enjoys a high local numerical preponderance on the assault frontage. The invader seeks to exploit this local advantage by overwhelming the initially outnumbered local defenders and breaking through the prepared defenses before the defender can amass reserves sufficient to halt the advance.

As the invader advances, its forces at the point of attack are progressively weakened by a combination of casualties suffered in overcoming the prepared defenses and the diversion of forces into flank defense. Meanwhile, the defenses in front of the advance are progressively strengthened by the arrival of incoming

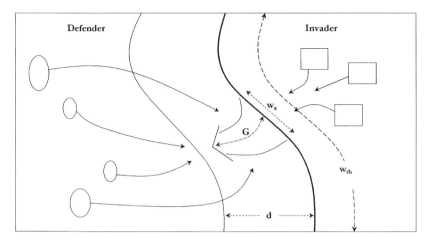

Figure A.1. Notional Theater Geometry

reserves.[5] If at any point the combination of a weakening invader and a strengthening defender produces an attacker too weak to overcome the defenses in front of it on the given assault frontage, the offensive halts there and the operation terminates as a contained offensive. If, however, the advance breaches the defender's rearmost prepared positions before being halted, breakthrough occurs. The purpose of the formal model is to distinguish those combinations of conditions that yield breakthrough from those that yield containment, and to compute net penetration depth, casualties, and campaign duration for conditions that yield contained attacks.[6]

INITIAL CONDITIONS

I now develop characterizations of several important initial conditions that will be needed to describe the dynamics of such a campaign. First, it will be useful to transform the weighted mean introduction dates of the two sides' weapons (τ_R and τ_B) into indices showing greater proportional variance for the time period of interest (1900–2020):

$$T_R = \frac{\tau_R - 1900}{10} \qquad\qquad [A.1]$$

$$T_B = \frac{\tau_B - 1900}{10} \qquad\qquad [A.2]$$

Next, I define two expressions for the dyadic technological balance in an engagement, one, T_C, for actual engagements at the point of attack (where the invader is on the tactical offensive), and one, T_ρ, for putative engagements on the invasion's flanks (where the invader is on the tactical defensive):

$$T_C = \frac{T_B^2}{T_R} \qquad\qquad\qquad [A.3]$$

$$T_\rho = \frac{T_R^2}{T_B} \qquad\qquad\qquad [A.4]$$

Note that where the two sides' technology is equal, T_C and T_ρ both reduce to the shared level of technical sophistication. When the tactical defender's technology is inferior, the expression for dyadic technological imbalance yields a value lower than the defender's; the greater the imbalance, the lower the value. When the tactical defender's technology is superior, the expression for dyadic technological imbalance yields a value greater than the defender's; the greater the imbalance, the higher the value. For example, where the invader (R) and defender (B) each deploy technology with a mean introduction date of 1950, T_C and T_ρ both equal 5. Where R's technology is ca. 1950 and B's technology is superior at ca. 1970, $T_B = 7$, $T_R = 5$, and T_C (where B is on the tactical defensive) $= 9.8$; T_ρ (where R is on the tactical offense) $= 3.6.$[7]

Next I define an expression for the fraction of moving reserves that survive to reach their destination, P_s. This expression must meet several requirements. It must decrease monotonically with increasing hostile technological sophistication and with increasing reserve velocity. It must also remain nonnegative for all possible levels of technology and all possible reserve velocities. A simple formulation that meets these requirements is:

$$P_S = T_R^{(-k_2 V_r)} \qquad\qquad\qquad [A.5]$$

I now describe the maximum number of attacking troops a single dug-in defensive soldier can halt when fully reinforced, H. This number must decrease as the defender's exposure increases and remain nonnegative for all values of defensive exposure. A simple formulation that meets these requirements is:

$$H = k_1(1 - f_e) \qquad\qquad\qquad [A.6]$$

Next I define two required troop densities. The first, ρ_1, describes the linear density (personnel per km) of flank defenders the invader requires to prevent a defensive counterattack from breaking through and cutting off the offensive spearhead. This density must increase with the size of the potential counterattack force, decrease with the dyadic invader-defender technological imbalance, and remain nonnegative for all possible values of these variables. A simple formulation that meets these requirements is:

$$\rho_1 = \frac{k_9 \, Bf_r \, P_S}{T_\rho^{k_4}} \qquad\qquad\qquad [A.7]$$

The second, ρ_2, describes the linear density (personnel per km) of invader forces needed to pin down the defender's forward garrisons along the international border away from the point of attack. This density must increase with the strength of the defensive garrisons to be pinned and remain nonnegative for all possible defensive strengths. A simple formulation that meets these requirements is:

$$\rho_2 = \frac{k_3 B(1 - f_r)}{w_{th}} \tag{A.8}$$

It is now possible to define the invader's initial troop strength at the point of attack, r_0, as the surplus of total strength above the requirement for pinning the defender's forces in place away from the point of attack:

$$r_0 = R - \rho_2(w_{th} - w_a) \tag{A.9}$$

The defender's initial troop strength opposite this assault force at the point of attack, b_0, can be defined as:

$$b_0 = \frac{B(1 - f_r)w_a}{w_{th}d} \tag{A.10}$$

The invader's casualties (killed and wounded in action) per kilometer gained, C_a, must increase monotonically with assault velocity and defensive troop strength;[8] it must decrease monotonically with the defender's exposure rate and the dyadic invader-defender technological imbalance; and it must remain nonnegative for all possible values of these variables. A simple formulation that meets these requirements is:

$$C_a = k_7(1 - f_e)T_c b_0(V_a + k_8) \tag{A.11}$$

DYNAMICS

The key dynamic changes determining the offensive's ultimate progress and cost involve the invader's loss of strength over time at the point of attack, and the defender's gain of strength over time at that point. I model these dynamics by developing expressions for the change in each sides' strength as a function of time, then solving for the time at which the two strengths become so close that the invader can no longer advance (i.e., the campaign's duration barring breakthrough). I then deduce losses and territorial gain from campaign duration.

Specifically, the change in invader strength at the point of attack, Δ_r (in troops removed from offensive duty per day), is a function both of casualties and of diversion into flank defense:

$$\Delta_r = C_a V_a + 2\rho_1 V_a \tag{A.12}$$

The invader's actual strength at the point of attack at any given time t (in days), r_t, is thus the initial strength less the daily loss times the number of days in combat:

$$r_t = r_0 - \Delta_r t \qquad\qquad [A.13]$$

For the defender, change in strength at the point of attack, Δ_b (in troops added per day), is:

$$\Delta_b = \begin{cases} \dfrac{Bf_r V_r P_s}{w_{th}} & for\ 0 < t < \dfrac{w_{th}}{V_r} \\ 0, & otherwise \end{cases} \qquad\qquad [A.14]$$

Note that the defender's strength at the point of attack ceases to increase beyond the time at which the entire reserve has arrived (i.e., $t > [w_{th}/V_r]$).

The defender's actual strength at the point of attack at any given time t (in days), b_t, is thus the initial strength plus the daily gain times the number of days in combat (t) for times t prior to the exhaustion of the reserve; or the initial strength plus the entire surviving reserve for all times t thereafter:

$$b_t = \begin{cases} b_0 + \Delta_b t & for\ 0 < t < \dfrac{w_{th}}{V_r} \\ b_0 + Bf_r P_s & for\ t \geq \dfrac{w_{th}}{V_r} \end{cases} \qquad\qquad [A.15]$$

Let $t^\star$ be defined as the time t at which the attacker's strength has declined to within the critical ratio, H, of the defender's strength (and thus the offensive has been halted):

$$t^\star \equiv t,\ s.t.:$$

$$r_t = Hb_t \qquad\qquad [A.16]$$

which implies, substituting for r_t and b_t, and solving for t:

$$t^* = \begin{cases} \dfrac{r_0 - Hb_0}{\Delta_r + H\Delta_b} & for\ \dfrac{r_0 - Hb_0}{\Delta_r + H\Delta_b} < \dfrac{w_{th}}{V_r} \\ \dfrac{r_0 - Hb_0 - HBf_r P_S}{\Delta_r} & for\ \dfrac{r_0 - Hb_0}{\Delta_r + H\Delta_b} \geq \dfrac{w_{th}}{V_r} \end{cases} \qquad\qquad [A.17]$$

This in turn implies that the net penetration depth for the offensive before it is halted, G, will be given by:

$$G = t^\star V_a \qquad\qquad [A.18]$$

and that breakthrough will occur if and only if:

$$t^\star V_a > d \qquad\qquad [A.19]$$

Casualties (killed and wounded in action) to the invader, C_R, and to the defender, C_B, are closely related to G and $t^\star$. I estimate casualties explicitly only for offensives that fail to break through; where breakthrough and successful exploitation occur, capability is assumed to be high for invaders and low for defenders across all three dependent variables (with the magnitudes increasing for invaders and declining for defenders with advancing technology). For contained offensives, invader casualties are the sum of casualties at the point of attack and those suffered in the secondary pinning attacks elsewhere:

$$C_R = C_a G + k_5 \qquad\qquad\qquad [A.20]$$

Defender casualties are the sum of casualties at the point of attack, those suffered by reserves in movement to the point of attack, and those suffered against the invader's pinning attacks elsewhere:

$$C_B = b_0 G + (1 - P_s)\Delta_b t^\star + k_6 \qquad\qquad\qquad [A.21]$$

completing the analysis. Together, equations A.17–A.21 thus explain the dependent variables of campaign duration ($t^\star$), territorial gain (G), and casualties (C_R and C_B), as a function of the independent variables of preponderance (R/B, B/w_{th}), technology (τ_R and τ_B) and force employment ($d, f_r, f_e, V_r, V_a, w_a$).

AN AUXILIARY MODEL OF GROUND FORCE ATTRITION IN AIR-ONLY CAMPAIGNS

The campaign dynamics described above assume that hostilities begin with the initiation of offensive action at the point of attack. Where invaders enjoy air supremacy, however (and are relatively secure from the threat of spoiling attacks on the ground by defenders), hostilities sometimes begin with an extended preliminary air campaign designed to wear down the defender across the theater of war before exposing offensive ground forces to combat. Once the ground invasion begins, the logic above pertains, but the result of the preliminary air campaign will be to reduce the defender's theaterwide troop strength, B. I thus present here a simple auxiliary model to compute this reduction as a function of the size of the invader's air force, its sortie rate, its net effectiveness (i.e., the real lethality of its weapons in light of the defender's ability to exploit cover), the area over which the defender is deployed (and over which the invader's air force must thus search for targets), and the duration of the air campaign.

Specifically, I use an exponential form to compute the expected kills of defensive ground forces by offensive air power prior to the commencement of the assault:[9]

$$EK = 1 - (1 - P_k)^n \qquad\qquad\qquad [A.22]$$

where:

$$n = \frac{N_a S_d \alpha_s N_d}{\alpha}$$

and where:

> $n \equiv$ number of times each defending ground force target is overflown
>
> $P_k \equiv$ probability that a target is killed given an overflight
>
> $N_a \equiv$ number of invader ground attack aircraft
>
> $S_d \equiv$ sorties per day per aircraft
>
> $\alpha_S \equiv$ area searched per sortie (square km)
>
> $N_d \equiv$ preliminary air campaign duration (days)
>
> $\alpha \equiv$ area to be searched (square km)
>
> $EK \equiv$ expected fractional kill of defensive ground targets for the preliminary air campaign

Ground-Gain-Maximizing and Minimizing Force Employment

Several of the comparative statics analyses below assume ground-gain-maximizing offensive force employment and/or ground-gain-minimizing defensive force employment. These values are identified as the solutions to a simple two-person zero-sum game in which the strategies for the two sides are the possible combinations of depth, reserve withhold, and reserve velocity for the defender, and assault velocity for the invader; and in which the payoffs are the computed territorial gains for the given strategies as implied by equations A.18 and A.19 above.[10] I assume that the defender seeks to minimize invader territorial gain and the invader seeks to maximize it. I further assume that since the invader chooses the time and place of the attack, the defender must deploy its forces before the invader decides upon a choice of assault velocity, and that the invader is able to observe the depth of the defender's prepared positions and the fraction of overall defensive strength deployed forward in them. The invader is thus able to use the initiative to make its choice with advance knowledge of the defender's choices, whereas the defender cannot observe the invader's actual choices before disposing its forces. A rational, conservative defender under such conditions will thus adopt a minimax approach, choosing the force employment for which the invader's best possible velocity choice yields the smallest territorial loss. The invader, on the other hand, adopts the velocity choice that maximizes territorial gain given the defender's prior choices.[11]

Defender minimax solutions were approximated by considering a finite set of discrete alternatives obtained by uniform-step increments over the relevant parameter range.[12] Invader velocity optima were computed for the given defender choices by classical optimization—that is, by obtaining the partial derivative of equation A.18 with respect to V_a, setting this expression equal to zero, and solving for the G-maximizing assault velocity, $\hat{V}_a$:

$$\hat{V}_a = \sqrt{\frac{H\Delta_b}{k_7(1 - f_e)T_C b_0}} \quad for \quad \frac{r_0 - Hb_0}{\Delta_r + H\Delta_b} < \frac{w_{th}}{V_r} \qquad [\text{A.23}]$$

Note that where:

$$\frac{r_0 - Hb_0}{\Delta_r + H\Delta_b} \geq \frac{w_{th}}{V_r} \qquad\qquad [A.24]$$

the invader has no incentive to move at greater than minimum velocity, since the defender has already exhausted its reserves (hence haste on the invader's part averts no defensive reserve arrivals but does incur greater casualties). Defensive force employment choices satisfying A.24 above were thus evaluated against an arbitrarily low V_a of 0.000001 km/day as an approximation of the optimum invader assault velocity; no defensive choices meeting this criterion emerged as minimax solutions.

PARAMETER VALUES FOR COMPARATIVE STATICS

The specific values used in the comparative statics analysis are summarized in tables A.1 and A.2.

COMPARATIVE STATICS

Chapters 3 and 4 summarize qualitatively some of the model's more important implications; with the formal version above I can now present a more complete analysis. I focus particularly on several questions of degree and interaction, for which quantitative treatment is especially helpful: what if only parts of the modern system are implemented, or if any given part is implemented incompletely? The qualitative discussion tends to treat the modern system as indivisible, yet it consists of multiple elements. What if militaries implement some elements well but others badly, or attain only intermediate degrees of implementation for some or all? How complete must modern-system implementation be in order to forestall (or permit) breakthrough, and how does this change as technology or preponderance vary? The qualitative discussion holds that force employment and materiel are poor substitutes, yet surely there are tradeoffs. To what degree can superior numbers or technology substitute for imperfect force employment, and to what extent can modern-system force employment compensate for inferiority in numbers or technology? How do material quantity and quality (i.e., preponderance and technology) trade off, and how is their interaction affected by force employment?

I answer these questions in three steps. First, I vary offensive and defensive force employment, holding technology and preponderance constant. Second, I vary technology and preponderance, holding force employment constant. Finally, I consider simultaneous variations in force employment, technology, and preponderance together.

TABLE A.1.
Parameter Values Used for Figures A.2–A.9

	Figure							
	A.2	A.3	A.4	A.5	A.6	A.7	A.8	A.9
R	1250000	=	=	=	=	=	=	Param.[†]
B	1000000	=	=	=	=	=	=	=
τ_R	1910	=	=	=	=	=	=	=
τ_B	1910	=	=	=	=	=	=	=
d	Param.	=	=	=	Gminimax[††]	=	10	Gminimax
f_r	Param.	=	0.45	Gminimax	Param.	Gminimax	0.5	Gminimax
f_e	0	0, 0.25	0	=	=	Param.	0	=
V_r	100	=	=	=	=	=	=	=
V_a	Gmax[†††]	=	Param.	Gmax	=	=	Param.	Gmax
w_a	25	=	=	=	=	=	=	=
w_{th}	500	=	=	=	=	=	=	=
k_1	2.5	=	=	=	=	=	=	=
k_2	0.01	=	=	=	=	=	=	=
k_3	0.4	=	=	=	=	=	=	=
k_4	0.5	=	=	=	=	=	=	=
k_5	200000	=	=	=	=	=	=	=
k_6	200000	=	=	=	=	=	=	=
k_7	5	=	=	=	=	=	=	=
k_8	0.1	=	=	=	=	=	=	=
k_9	0.01	=	=	=	=	=	=	=

[†]"Param." denotes parametrically varied values.
[††]"Gminimax" denotes G-minimizing values.
[†††]"Gmax" denotes G-maximizing values.

The Effects of Variance in Force Employment

Figures A.2 to A.4 plot the combinations of invader and defender force employment that yield breakthrough as opposed to a contained offensive, holding technology and theater numerical preponderance constant. Figure A.2 distinguishes the combinations of defender reserves and depth that permit breakthrough from those that yield containment assuming modern-system offensive tactics by the

TABLE A.2.
Parameter Values Used for Figures A.10–A.17

	Figure							
	A.10	A.11	A.12[†]	A.13	A.14	A.15	A.16	A.17
R	1250000	=	=	=	=	Param.	1250000	=
B	1000000	=	Variable[††]	1000000	=	=	=	=
τ_R	Param.	=	2000	Param.	1910, 2000	1910	Param.	1910
τ_B	Param.	1970	=	Param.	1910, 2000	1910	Param.	1910
d	Gminimax	=	=	Gminimax	8, 15	Gminimax	=	=
f_r	Gminimax	=	=	Gminimax	0.45, 0.7	Gminimax	=	=
f_e	0	=	=	=	=	=	=	=
V_r	Gminimax	=	=	Param.	100, 20	Gminimax	=	=
V_a	Gmax	=	$C_R\text{min}$[†††]	Gmax	Param.	Gmax	=	Param.
w_a	25	=	=	=	=	=	=	=
w_{th}	500	=	=	=	=	=	=	=
k_1	2.5	=	=	=	=	1.25, 2.5, 5	=	=
k_2	0.01	=	=	=	=	0.005, 0.01, 0.02	=	=
k_3	0.4	=	=	=	=	0.2, 0.4, 0.8	=	=
k_4	0.5	=	=	=	=	0.25, 0.5, 1	=	=
k_5	200000	=	=	=	=	1E5, 2E5, 4E5	=	=
k_6	200000	=	=	=	=	1E5, 2E5, 4E5	=	=
k_7	5	=	=	=	=	2.5, 5, 10	=	=
k_8	0.1	=	=	=	=	0.05, 0.1, 0.2	=	=
k_9	0.01	=	=	=	=	0.005, 0.01, 0.02	=	=

[†]Figure A.12 was prepared using the air-only auxiliary model presented above as a preprocessor to compute B as a function of the duration of a preliminary air campaign. The auxiliary model parameter values used were: $P_k = 0.005$, $N_a = 100$, $S_d = 2$, $\alpha = 10000$, $\alpha_s = 50$, with N_d parameterized. These values were chosen to provide a crude fit to actual Serbian ground weapon losses in the 78-day NATO air campaign in Kosovo: Clark and Corley, "Press Conference on the Kosovo Strike Assessment."

[††]B values were computed as outputs of the air-only auxilliary model, with $B = 1000000$ as the $N_d = 0$ baseline value.

[†††]For the given G presented in figure A.12: V_a was selected to minimize casualties subject to the constraint that the attacker penetrate at least to the specified distance.

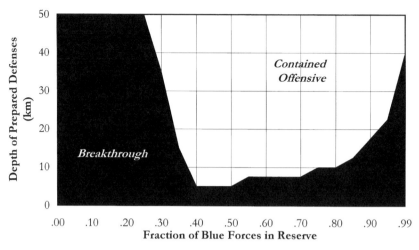

Figure A.2. Depth, Reserves, and Breakthrough

invader.[13] In general, poor modern-system implementation by the defender in the form of low reserve allocations and shallow defenses yields breakthrough against the modern-system attacks assumed here; more complete modern-system implementation via higher reserve allocations and deeper defenses yields contained offensives in spite of modern-system offensive methods. To some extent, the defender can compensate for smaller reserves with greater depth and vice versa, but depth and reserves are weak substitutes. For the conditions assumed here, for example, a combination of 15 kilometers depth and a reserve allocation of 0.4 yields a contained offensive, but to contain an offensive with a reserve withhold of 0.3 requires more than twice the depth (over 35 kilometers). Alternatively, to contain a modern-system offensive with less than 5 kilometers of defensive depth is impossible regardless of how large a reserve the defender withholds.

Although deep defenses and large reserves generally preclude breakthrough, there are exceptions. If depth is held constant and only the defender's reserve fraction is increased, for example (or if both increase, but reserve fraction increases more rapidly), breakthrough can in principle replace containment. A defense with a depth of 10 kilometers and a reserve fraction of 0.45 yields a contained offensive, but a reserve fraction of 0.75 for the same depth yields breakthrough; similarly, a deeper defense of 20 kilometers depth and a higher reserve fraction of 0.95 yields breakthrough. These exceptions require very high reserve fractions, however: for depths above 10 kilometers, reserve fractions must exceed 0.75 to produce breakthrough; for depths above 15 kilometers, they must exceed 0.90. Moreover, an increase in depth alone never moves a contained offensive into breakthrough. Logically, these exceptions clearly must obtain: a defense with its entire strength in reserve, for example, would have no troops to garrison its prepared positions, which could then be taken by attackers without loss at very high velocity.[14] For the limit behavior of the model to make sense, it thus must be the case that extreme reserve allocations can yield attacker advances exceeding the depth of all but the deepest prepared positions. In practical terms, however, these exceptions are of little empirical consequence. Even very reserve-heavy defenses such as the German elastic defense system of 1917–18 rarely exceeded a reserve fraction of 0.60; more common values lay between 0.30 and 0.45.[15] The Soviet defense at Kursk is considered one of the most reserve-heavy of the Second World War yet withheld less than 50 percent of its total forces from forward positions.[16] NATO's Central Region defense plans in the late 1980s called for reserve fractions of about 0.45.[17] The political and organizational pressures discussed in chapter 3 all drive militaries toward lower, not higher, reserve fractions; while in theory extreme versions of modern-system reserve withholds can yield breakthrough, the odds of observing this empirically are low.

Figure A.3 considers how variations in defensive *tactics* affect the likelihood of breakthrough. Figure A.2 assumed modern-system defensive tactics with minimal exposure; here, that condition is juxtaposed with a non–modern-system alternative in which one-third of the defender's forward positions are exposed to long-range observation and fire.[18] The results suggest that the less completely the defender implements the modern system at the tactical level, the more completely it must be implemented at the operational level to avert breakthrough. With minimum tactical exposure, a defensive depth of 10 kilometers and a reserve

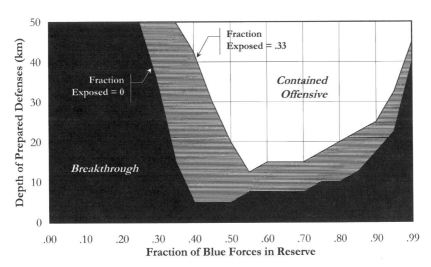

Figure A.3. Defensive Exposure and Breakthrough

fraction of 0.45 yields a contained offensive; with 33 percent tactical exposure, at least 15 kilometers of depth and 0.55 of total forces in reserve are required to prevent breakthrough. For defenders, modern-system operations can thus compensate to a degree for exposed tactical dispositions, but the levels of depth and reserves needed can be prohibitive. This in turn suggests that it is hard to adopt only parts of the modern system and still succeed—while possible, the extremity of the compensations needed will often be beyond states' political or organizational limits. It is thus hard to keep a modern system attacker from breaking through without implementing modern system defense in its entirety.

Figure A.4 holds the defender's reserve allocation constant and varies defensive depth and *offensive* tactics.[19] The latter are represented via the invader's net closure velocity, where high velocity implies limited opportunity to employ modern-system exposure reduction methods, and low velocity implies greater opportunity; thus the higher the velocity, the lower the degree of possible modern system implementation. The results indicate that breakthrough requires a combination of modern-system offensive tactics and shallow defensive depth. For depths under three kilometers, for example, closure velocities of under 6 kilometers per day generally yield breakthrough. Velocities in excess of 7 kilometers per day produce contained offensives regardless of defensive depth; depths in excess of 8 kilometers preclude breakthrough regardless of the attacker's velocity. Shallow defenses thus create an opportunity for breakthrough, but only if the invader uses modern-system offensive tactics. Against a deep, modern-system defense, even modern-system offensive methods cannot break through.

As in figure A.2, however, there are exceptions. In particular, very low closure velocities preclude breakthrough regardless of depth—and as depth increases, the range of low-velocity choices that preclude breakthrough grows, from 0–0.5 kilometers per day at a depth of 3 kilometers, to 0–2.5 at 7 kilometers

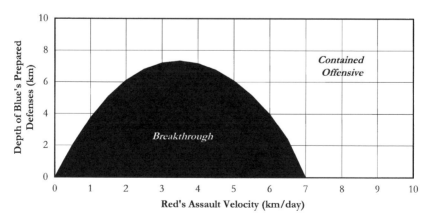

Figure A.4. Assault Velocity, Depth, and Breakthrough

depth. Logically, these exceptions must obtain: a closure rate of zero would preclude the attacker from advancing at all, thus obviously precluding breakthrough; at the opposite extreme, a closure rate of 100 kilometers per day would require attackers to drive down roads fully exposed in administrative march formation with no fire preparation and no reconnaissance. Neither extreme could possibly yield breakthrough, which must therefore require intermediate values. Again, however, the empirical frequency of post-1918 cases in which breakthrough is precluded by insufficient velocity is likely to be small. Prior to 1918, the ponderous pace of the Allies' artillery offensives (0.001–0.0001 km/day) was a major contributor to stalemate;[20] since 1918, however, such extrema have rarely been seen. And only for a narrow range of depth choices can insufficient velocity per se preclude breakthrough: in figure A.4, only defensive depths between 3 and 7 kilometers yield containment for assault velocities that are low enough to be consistent with the modern system but not so radically low as to be implausible.

Preventing breakthrough is necessary for high defensive capability but insufficient in itself. Contained offensives that nevertheless yield major territorial gains, favorable casualty ratios, or quick attacker advances can still imply low defensive or fairly high offensive capability. The remaining figures thus turn from identifying breakthrough conditions to assessing contained offensives in terms of their resulting territorial gains, casualties, and campaign duration.

Figure A.5 considers the effects of defensive depth for contained offensives.[21] Attacker casualties are plotted using the values on the right-hand vertical axis;

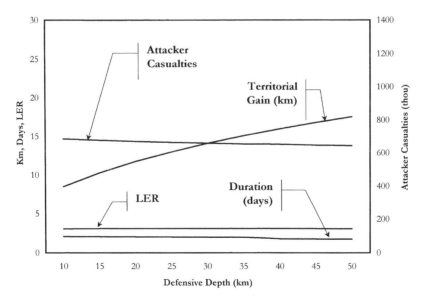

Figure A.5. Depth in Contained Offensives

territorial gain, campaign duration, and the attacker:defender loss-exchange ratio are plotted using the values on the left-hand vertical axis.[22] Only values yielding contained offensives are shown (depths below about 10 km yield breakthrough and are thus excluded here). The results indicate that deeper defenses permit attackers greater territorial gains, modestly lower casualties, and modestly shorter campaigns: for the conditions assumed here, a 40-kilometer increase in defensive depth increases attacker penetration by about a factor of two, reduces attacker casualties by about 5 percent, and reduces campaign duration by about 15 percent (defender casualties fall as well, hence the LER holds almost constant).[23]

On the margin, increasing defensive depth beyond the minimum needed to prevent breakthrough thus tends to *decrease* defender capability, not increase it. Modern-system depth thus presents a tradeoff: deeper defenses ensure against breakthrough (recall figures A.2–A.4), but only at the cost of allowing modern-system attackers to gain more ground at lower cost in contained limited-aims offensives. This in turn means that the modern system cannot enable defenders to hold every inch of national territory against a modern-system attack—the depth needed to prevent breakthrough necessarily sacrifices territory. A defender's only chance to hold its entire territory is to concentrate forward, but this risks catastrophic rupture and the loss of the entire national landmass should the attacker exploit breakthrough successfully. Modern-system force employment is thus not simply a trivial synonym for "good practice"—while on balance it offers better outcomes than its alternatives, it is nevertheless a choice with important costs as well as benefits.[24]

Figure A.6 considers the effects of defensive reserves.[25] The results indicate that attacker territorial gains fall dramatically as reserve fractions rise from 0.1 to about 0.3, then hold roughly constant from 0.3 to 0.6 before rising moderately for values above 0.6. Attacker casualties and LER hold roughly constant, while campaign duration falls rapidly as reserve fractions increase.[26] For the empirically meaningful range of reserve fractions (i.e., 0.1 to perhaps 0.7), high modern-system reserve allocations thus generally reduce the territorial gains achievable by limited aims attacks, and shorten the resulting campaigns. Shorter campaigns conduce to higher offensive capability when the campaign is otherwise successful; when, as here, attacks are halted quickly with little ground gain, the result is more favorable to defenders than attackers.

Figure A.7 considers the effects of defensive tactics.[27] The results suggest that capability is highly sensitive to the defender's tactics, and that non–modern-system exposure strongly reduces defensive and increases offensive capability. An increase in defensive tactical exposure from 0.0 to 0.3, for example, nearly doubles attacker territorial gain for roughly constant attacker casualties, LER, and campaign duration. A defensive exposure fraction of 0.6 increases territorial gain by almost a factor of four relative to the zero-exposure benchmark, while reducing attacker casualties by 20 percent and LER by 15 percent; an exposure fraction

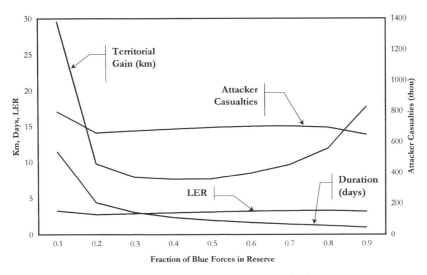

Figure A.6. Defensive Reserves in Contained Offensives

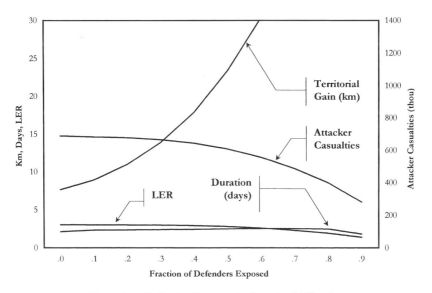

Figure A.7. Defensive Exposure in Contained Offensives

of 0.9 increases territorial gain by about a factor of eight relative to the zero-exposure benchmark, reduces attacker casualties by 60 percent, LER by 55 percent, and campaign duration by 15 percent. Only radical increases in depth and reserve withholds enable defenders to prevent breakthrough for such high levels of tactical exposure: for an exposure fraction of 0.3, for example, depth must be increased from the zero-exposure benchmark of 8 km to 14 km, and the reserve withhold must be increased from 0.45 to 0.55; for an exposure fraction of 0.6, depth must be increased to 31 km and reserve withhold to 0.7; for an exposure fraction of 0.9, depth must reach 59 km, and reserve withhold must reach 0.9. The ability of any real-world defense to achieve such radical depth and, especially, reserve withholds is far from clear.

This in turn reinforces the earlier observation that defenders cannot readily compensate for tactical shortcomings with operational-level virtuosity. To offset non–modern-system tactics requires such complete modern-system implementation at the operational level that most real-world armies will be unable to do so given real-world political and organizational constraints. And even if such extreme depth and reserve fractions were attainable, they would still be insufficient to prevent major territorial losses to a limited-aims modern-system attacker.

Figure A.8 considers the effects of *attacker* tactics in the form of the attacker's choice of assault velocity.[28] The results show no territorial gain when velocity is minimized at 0.01 km/day; ground gain rises rapidly to a maximum of 8.5 km at a velocity of 4–5 km/day, then falls progressively for all higher velocities, declining to 6.5 km at 10 km/day, and 3.8 km at 20 km/day.[29] Attacker casualties and LER rise steeply and monotonically with increasing velocity: each increases by a factor of about five when velocity rises from 1 to 20 km/day. Conversely, campaign duration falls rapidly as velocity increases: when velocity reaches 20 km/day, campaign duration falls to only about 5 percent of its 1 km/day value.

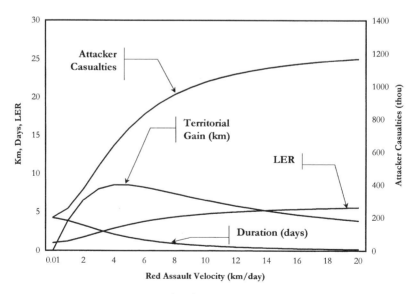

Figure A.8. Assault Velocity in Contained Offensives

Offensive tactics thus pose complex implications for capability in limited-aims attacks. Lower velocity (and thus, more complete modern-system implementation) always reduces the attacker's casualties, which conduces to higher offensive capability ceteris paribus. Lower velocity generally increases territorial gain, which also conduces to higher capability, but not for very low velocities (below 3–4 km/day), which reduce it. Lower velocity always increases campaign duration, which conduces to lower capability ceteris paribus. High velocity is clearly inconsistent with high offensive capability, since a short campaign is only beneficial when otherwise successful, which it cannot be when territorial gains are low and casualties high. High-velocity, non–modern-system tactics are thus always problematic. Low-velocity, modern-system tactics, however, are unambiguously beneficial only to a point: if velocity is reduced below 3 km/day, attackers must begin to trade reduced mission accomplishment (i.e., reduced ability to take and hold ground) for further casualty reduction. As with defensive depth, modern-system offensive tactics are thus not simply a trivial synonym for "good practice"—while attackers who ignore exposure reduction and attempt high-velocity assaults will generally fail, low-velocity, modern-system tactics nevertheless impose costs as well as benefits.

The Effects of Variance in Numerical Preponderance and Technology

Figures A.9 to A.12 vary materiel, given modern-system force employment on both sides. Figure A.9 considers theater attacker:defender numerical imbalances ranging from a minimum of 0.75:1 to a maximum of 3:1. Superior numbers permit greater territorial gains, even against a modern-system defense: a 50 percent

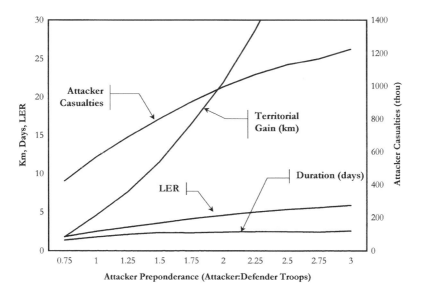

Figure A.9. Effects of Preponderance

increase in attacker:defender troop strength from 1:1 to 1.5:1 more than doubles penetration depth; an increase in preponderance from 1:1 to 2.5:1 increases penetration depth by a factor of eight.[30] Preponderance alone, however, does not induce breakthrough against a modern-system defense: even at 3:1, the offensive is contained (though not without yielding significant depth of advance). This increased territorial gain, moreover, comes at a price. Attacker casualties also rise, increasing 41 percent when preponderance grows from 1:1 to 1.5:1, and 100 percent when preponderance grows from 1:1 to 2.5:1. Likewise, LER increases by 43 percent and 113 percent, respectively (campaign duration holds relatively constant).[31] Attackers can reduce the price by terminating operations early (or by adopting more cautious tactics), but only by reducing territorial gain relative to the maxima shown here: for a 1.5:1 numerical preponderance, for example, an attacker who opts to hold casualties down to their nominal 1:1 level could do so by halting the offensive about a day early, reducing territorial gain by 3.4 kilometers relative to the maximum shown in figure A.9 (though still yielding about 3.6 kilometers more ground than the 1:1 maximum).[32]

When both attacker and defender use modern-system methods, preponderance thus tips the scales—a very preponderant modern-system attacker can simply push a smaller modern-system defender out of the theater in successive operations—but this cannot be done cheaply or quickly.[33] On balance, preponderance conduces to capability, but preponderance alone cannot provide for quick, one-sided victories against modern-system defenders regardless of the attacker's force employment.

Figure A.10 considers systemic technological change given modern-system force employment on both sides. The results show little change in any dimension of

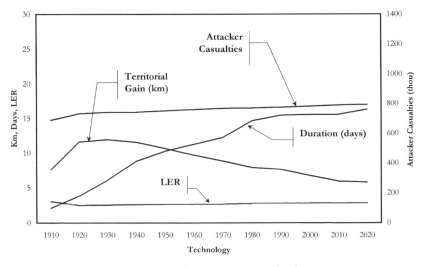

Figure A.10. Effects of Systemic Technology

capability save campaign duration as technology becomes more sophisticated: territorial gain varies within a narrow band of only 5 kilometers width over roughly a century of technological change; attacker casualties vary by less than 20 percent; and LER varies by only 7 percent. Campaign duration, however, increases by more than 670 percent from 1900 to 2020.

This is because modern-system force employment shields both sides' forces from the increasing lethality of more sophisticated weapons, but the increasingly aggressive implementation of modern-system methods that this requires slows both sides' movement dramatically. The attacker's ground-gain-maximizing velocity choice, for example, falls 90 percent from 1900 to 2020; the defender's ground-gain-minimizing choice of reserve velocity falls 85 percent over the same interval. The net result of a much-slower attack and a much-slower defensive response is a much longer campaign. Were the attacker to forgo such aggressive exposure reduction in an effort to maintain higher movement rates, campaign duration would fall, but territorial gains would fall even faster in the face of the large increase in attacker losses this would produce against advanced weapons. For 2020, an attacker velocity choice of 3.5 km/day (roughly equal to the ground-gain-maximizing choice for 1910 technology, but an order of magnitude higher than that for 2020) would result in a 99 percent shorter campaign, but a territorial gain of less than one-tenth of one kilometer. Defenders who try to maintain high reserve velocities in the face of twenty-first-century technology suffer comparably grim fates. For 2020 technology, a defender reserve velocity of 100 km/day results in the virtual annihilation of the defender's reserves long before they can reach the threatened point, enabling the attacker to break through regardless of the defender's choice of depth or reserve withhold. Systemic technological change thus has little net effect on capability when both sides implement the modern system fully, but if either side *fails* to do so, outcomes become increasingly one-sided as time passes and technology improves.

Figure A.11 assesses the effects of dyadic technological imbalance given modern-system force employment on both sides; whereas figure A.10 assumes that both sides deploy the same technology, figure A.11 assumes that the attacker leads the defender technologically by the number of years given on the horizontal axis.[34] The results show that superior technology helps, but that its effects are far less decisive than often assumed. To put the results in context, note that a thirty-year average technological lead is more than twice the largest gap on record (i.e., the 1991 Gulf War, where the Coalition enjoyed about a twelve-year average lead over the Iraqis).[35] Unsurprisingly, such an edge conduces to greater offensive capability. Yet the magnitude of the capability increase is hardly revolutionary: territorial gain increases by about 75 percent relative to an assumption of technological parity; attacker losses fall by less than 5 percent; LER falls by about 4 percent. Campaign duration, however, actually increases by 20 percent, and even with a thirty-year edge the attacker still fails to break through the defense.[36]

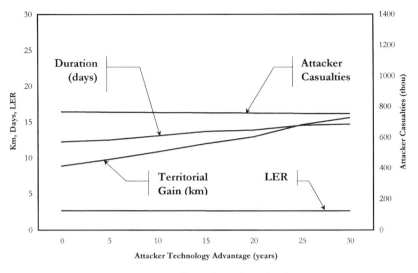

Figure A.11. Effects of Dyadic Technology

The reason such large imbalances do not produce bigger results is the defender's use of modern-system methods.[37] Aggressive exposure reduction shields the defender from the worst effects of more-lethal offensive weapons: while thirty-year-superior deep strike weapons can nominally inflict 90 percent losses on defensive reserve movements in the open, for example, defenders who exploit modern-system exposure reduction can cut those losses by two-thirds or more. Of course, this exposure reduction comes at the price of slower reserve movement, but deeper defenses can buy defenders time for slower-moving reserves to arrive. Defenders are still hurt by the combination of slower counterconcentration, reduced effectiveness for dug-in defenses at the point of attack, and more spread-out dispositions, but not enough to allow an attacker to break through—and without breakthrough, an attacker's ability to take ground cheaply or rapidly is limited.

Given this, the most important effects of technological imbalance may be to increase the degree of modern-system implementation needed to prevent disaster. To prevent breakthrough under technological parity at roughly the 1970 state of the art, for example, defenders need to deploy in at least 9 kilometers depth and to reduce exposure aggressively enough to cap reserve speed at about 20 kilometers per day; for a 1970s-era defender to contain an attack by a 2000-era attacker demands more than a 70 percent increase in depth and a more thoroughgoing exposure-reduction that would limit reserve speeds to a level at least 15 percent lower than that needed under technological parity.[38] Thus the greater one's technological inferiority, the more completely the modern system must be implemented to prevent a radical loss of capability.

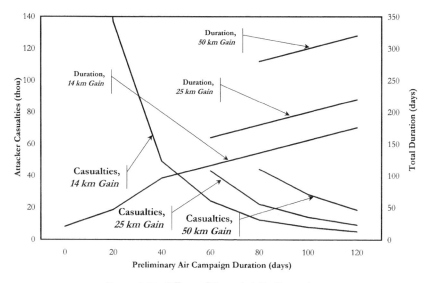

Figure A.12. Effects of Extended Air Campaigns

Figure A.12 considers an increasingly important special case: technologically advanced attackers with air supremacy and a strong preference for casualty minimization. In particular, the figure assumes an attacker with 2000-era technology engaging a defender with 1970s-era weapons; it further assumes that the attacker is willing to postpone offensive action on the ground to permit an extended preliminary air campaign designed to weaken the defenses and thereby reduce offensive ground-force losses once the invasion begins. Of course, it is always possible that a defender will concede before the attacker would choose to invade; in such cases, the attacker's aims can be secured without actual invasion. The odds of such a settlement will vary with the issues at stake and other features of the confrontation and the contestants; for my immediate purposes, however, the key issue is how quickly and how cheaply the attacker can prevail militarily in such a campaign—and how the presence or absence of modern-system methods by the defender can affect this.

The answer is that if the defender uses modern-system methods, it can take a very long time for such attacks to succeed. An unopposed air force with modern weapons can progressively wear down any defense; if attackers are willing to wait long enough, any defense can eventually be crippled by such bombing. In fact, this is not new: in 1944, the United States enjoyed air supremacy and could, if it chose, have delayed offensive ground operations in northwest Europe until the Wehrmacht had been effectively destroyed from the air. The problem in such approaches is always *time*—to cripple a defense through air action alone has always required more time than political leaders are willing to allow. The growing interest in this approach today stems from the implicit assumption that the time needed to do this has shrunk drastically with new technology.[39] Against a modern-system defender able to limit its exposure, however, it is far from clear that this is yet the case—or that it will be any time soon. Figure A.12 assumes a per-sortie air-to-ground kill rate roughly equal to NATO's in the recent Kosovo campaign, and an air force roughly as large relative to the area being searched as that of NATO's air force in Kosovo.[40] The results suggest that modern-system defenses can continue to inflict significant losses on even modern-system attackers after absorbing extended punishment from the air. Even after withstanding a 120-day air campaign, for example (fully 50 percent longer than NATO's 78 days of bombing in Kosovo), a modern-system defense can still inflict almost 20,000 casualties on a 2.5-million-soldier attacker in a 50-kilometer advance (or a loss rate about an order of magnitude higher than U.S. forces' in the Persian Gulf in 1991).[41] To bring losses down to their 1991 level against a skilled modern-system defender would thus require air campaigns lasting years (followed by cautious ground offensives adding months of additional time in themselves). If the time is available, such methods can bring about the intended results, but the time needed is likely to be far longer than typically expected, *if* the defender is able to implement modern-system methods.[42]

Interactions between Force Employment and Technology

The discussion of figures A.9–A.12 above has already touched on some important interactions between force employment and materiel—especially, the findings that (1) modern-system defenses can prevent breakthrough against even very preponderant or very technologically superior attackers, and (2) as material conditions become less favorable, more-extensive modern-system implementation is necessary (and sufficient) to prevent disaster. Figures A.13 and A.14 explore several aspects of these interactions more systematically.

Figure A.13 considers the interaction between territorial gain, systemic technology, and the net velocity of the defender's reserves. Recall that the greater their velocity, the greater the reserves' exposure to deep attack—but the sooner the survivors will arrive at their destination. Early in the century, where deep attack capabilities were very limited, exposure brought little risk and rapid movement in the open was the defender's best choice: for the 1910s, the greater the reserve velocity, the lower the attacker's net territorial gain, and thus the defender's best choice was to move as quickly as possible. As technology advanced, however, deep attack became more lethal, and the defender's best choice of reserve velocity switched from the corner solution of the 1910s to an internal optimum at progressively lower values thereafter: in the 1930s, for example, the defender minimized the attacker's ground gain by voluntarily restricting reserve velocity to about 30–40 km/day (with the reduction used to permit time-consuming exposure reduction via movement halts during daylight hours, use of circuitous but covered routes, and so on). Although faster movement was

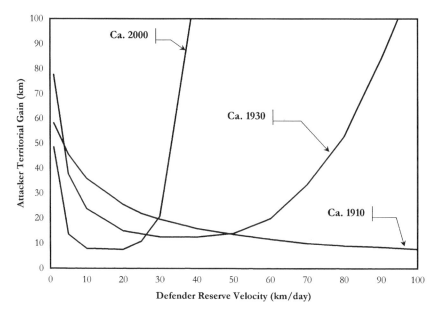

Figure A.13. Interaction of Defender Velocity and Systemic Technology

certainly possible, any reduction in transit time was more than offset by increased losses en route: an increase in defensive reserve velocity from 40 to 80 km/day, for example, increased the attacker's territorial gain from 12 to more than 50 km. Under such conditions, it made sense for defenders to deliberately hold back from full exploitation of their vehicles' speed in order to reduce their vulnerability. By the same token, though, *minimum* velocity is also a poor choice: if the reserves *never* arrive, they never reinforce the forward defenders at the key point, and thus attacker ground gain again rises (for example, from 12 to almost 40 km as defender reserve velocity falls from 40 to 5 km/day). The defender's best choice must thus balance the conflicting demands of survival and speed, and the nature of the best balance between these conflicting goals is strongly influenced by prevailing technology: the more lethal the weapons, the lower the defender's best choice of reserve velocity. (By the 2000s, for example, the continuation of this trend produces a best choice of only 20 km/day, in spite of having vehicles nominally capable of moving radically faster than this). Here, too, increasingly sophisticated technology thus demands a more complete implementation of modern-system methods—in this case, more complete use of modern-system techniques for reducing the exposure of rear-area reserve movements.

The figure also suggests a second important interaction: the higher the technology, the more painful the consequences of failing to adopt the modern system. For example, if a 1930-era defender insists on an excessively exposed 80 km/day reserve velocity, this increases the attacker's net territorial gain by 41 km (from

12 to 53) relative to the lower-exposure modern-system choice of 40 km/day. If a 2000s-era defender makes the same mistake, however, the penalty is radically more severe: attacker territorial gain skyrockets to more than 800 km, or over 100 times that yielded by a lower-exposure choice of 20 km/day. Even for 1930-era technology, non–modern-system exposure is damaging, but for 2000-era technology the damage is far worse—*technology thus magnifies the consequences of force employment*.

Figure A.14 looks at the flip side of this interaction between velocity choice and systemic technology by considering how the *attacker's* ground-gain-maximizing velocity choice changes as technology advances.[43] For attackers, too, survivability trades off against speed: the faster the penetration, the more exposed the penetrators, ceteris paribus. As technology has become more lethal—and thus, as exposure's consequences have grown—the best choice between these conflicting goals has shifted downward, in the direction of slower penetration but lesser exposure. In the 1910s, for example, the attacker's best velocity choice was around 3–5 km/day against a modern-system defense; by the 2000s, it had shrunk to only about 1 km/day. This in turn reduces the consequences of the *defender's* reduction in reserve velocity as noted in figure A.13: more lethal weapons compel *both* sides to slow down and take cover in order to survive. Once again, higher technology thus demands more aggressive implementation of modern-system exposure reduction. Similarly, advancing technology again

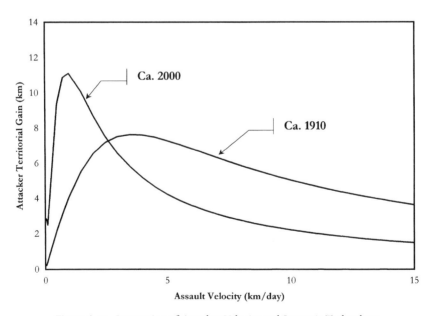

Figure A.14. Interaction of Attacker Velocity and Systemic Technology

magnifies the consequences of force employment: for 1910-era technology, an excessively exposed, 15 km/day assault velocity reduces attacker territorial gain by about 50 percent (from about 8 to 4 km); for 2000-era technology, however, the same choice reduces territorial gain by more than 85 percent (from about 11 to 1.5 km).

MILITARY INCENTIVES FOR FORCE EMPLOYMENT CHOICE

The modern system thus has important advantages, but it also has drawbacks. Chapter 3 presented a variety of political, organizational, and social shortcomings, but even in strictly military terms the modern system has important downsides. Defensive depth precludes breakthrough but yields ground to limited aims attacks. Defensive reserves facilitate counterconcentration but weaken forward defenses. Reduced velocity limits exposure but slows movement. On balance, how do these pros and cons net out? Are the military interests of the state better served by the modern system or by a non–modern-system alternative?

There will clearly be many cases where nonmilitary constraints rule out the modern system. But where it can be implemented, it offers the militarily optimal choice for any state waging mid- to high-intensity continental warfare against a rational opponent with the potential to do the same. More formally, the modern system constitutes a saddle point solution to a two-person zero sum game in which either side can either implement the modern system or not. Table A.3 presents this game in matrix form, with strategies described as "M" (modern system) or "N" (not), and where the cell payoffs are the invader's net territorial gains (in kilometers) for the given strategies, as computed by the model presented above.[44]

If each side assumes the other is capable of modern-system methods, if the invader is assumed to seek maximum territorial gain and the defender to seek minimum territorial loss, and if each side adopts a rationally conservative strategy in light of these assumptions, the defender will play the minimax choice of M, and the invader will play the maximin choice of M, yielding an equilibrium territorial gain of 11.6 kilometers. Neither side has a rational military incentive

TABLE A.3.
Force Employment Incentives Approached Game Theoretically

		Defender	
		M	N
Invader	M	11.6	200.9
	N	3.2	0.1

to deviate from this equilibrium, even though, from the defender's standpoint, 11.6 kilometers is not the minimum territorial gain possible. Modern-system defenses inevitably yield some ground; this is an inherent byproduct of defensive depth and reserves. To have any hope of stopping an attack cold at the border, defenders must concentrate their forces in prepared positions well forward. Only if the invader obliges by adopting exposed, non–modern-system methods can this approach succeed, however. If the invader instead implements a modern-system attack, the best a defender can hope for is a major loss of territory; more likely is a clean breakthrough and the danger of a systemic collapse of the theater defense as a whole.[45]

No system of force employment is without tradeoffs or drawbacks, but the modern system's drawbacks are counterbalanced by critical advantages. In a world in which either side could implement it, the modern system would thus be the militarily optimal solution for both attackers and defenders, yielding the most capability possible against a rational, adaptive opponent.

SENSITIVITY ANALYSIS

The values of the constants $(k_1–k_9)$ represent assumptions rather than observed values. Are the findings presented above sensitive to the particular values assumed? A complete sensitivity analysis would be unwieldy given the number of variables involved, but to provide an initial assessment I have recomputed invader territorial gain as a function of preponderance, systemic technology, and invader assault velocity (the latter as a representative dimension of force employment) for two sets of alternative values for k_1 through k_9. In the first set, the values of all constants are doubled relative to the values reported in tables A.1 and A.2; in the second set, they are halved. The results are presented in figures A.15 through A.17.[46]

In general, changes in the constants' values affect the curves' heights but not their shapes. In figure A.15, for example, doubling all constants drops territorial gain at a preponderance of 2:1 from about 22 to about 4 km; halving all constants raises territorial gain from 22 to about 100 km. In each case, however, the curve increases monotonically with increasing preponderance, as does its slope. In figure A.16, doubling all constants drops territorial gain for symmetric 1950s-era technology from about 11 to about 0.4 km; halving all constants raises territorial gain from 11 to about 64 km. In each case, technological progress is relatively invader-favorable early in the century but becomes more defender favorable after about 1930, and in each case, technological change per se brings only small differences in penetration depth (when the constants are halved, a century of technological change increases territorial gain from 37 to 64 km; when the constants are doubled, 100 years of technological variance decreases territorial gains from 0.7 to 0.2 km).

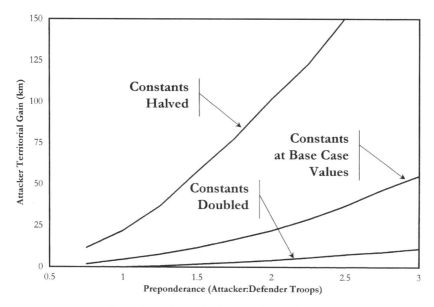

Figure A.15. Sensitivity Analysis: Preponderance

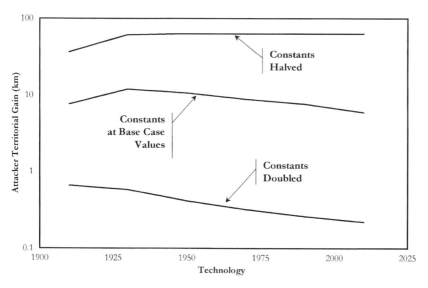

Figure A.16. Sensitivity Analysis: Systemic Technology

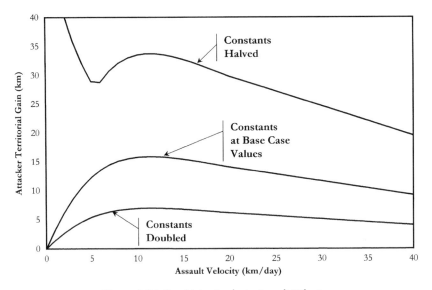

Figure A.17. Sensitivity Analysis: Assault Velocity

Figure A.17 presents an exception, as the shape of the curve changes when the constants are halved, albeit only for part of the relevant domain. As in figures A.15 and A.16, the heights of the curves vary with changes in the constants (for example, from 14- to 6-km penetration at a velocity of 20 km/day when the constants are halved, and from 14- to 30-km penetration when the constants are doubled). Here, however, halving the constants produces an internal local minimum to territorial gain in the vicinity of 6 km/day, whereas the baseline and doubled values both lack internal minima. The reason for the change in the shape of the curve is that halving the constants satisfies the inequality in equation A.24 above for velocities below about 6 km/day—that is, halved constants enable the invader to continue to advance even after the defender has completely counterconcentrated, which in turn enables the invader to increase ground gain by reducing velocity below 6 km/day (since doing so reduces casualties without allowing any additional defender reserves to arrive). Hence territorial gain becomes asymptotic at the origin. Of the six constants that play some role in A.24, k_1, k_2, k_4, k_7, k_8, and k_9, the shape of the curve in figure A.17 is far more sensitive to k_1 than the others: if k_1 alone is returned to its baseline value then the curve regains its baseline shape, even if all other constants are halved; if k_1 is halved, returning all other constants to their baseline values will not return the curve to its baseline shape. More specifically, solving A.24 for k_1 and evaluating the resulting expression indicates that values of k_1 below 1.81 (i.e., below 73 percent of its baseline value) induce a change in the shape of the curve in figure A.17 when all other constants are halved. (With all other constants at their baseline levels, only values of k_1 below 1.72, or 69 percent of its baseline value, change the shape of the curve.) Arbitrarily large values of k_1 above these critical cutoffs do not affect the shape of the curve. The nature of the relationship between assault velocity and territorial gain is thus sensitive to some possible values of the constants and in particular to the value of k_1, but a significant reduction in the assumed value of k_1 is required to induce a change in the shape of the curve, and this for only part of the relevant domain.

Similar results obtain for casualties and campaign duration.[47] In general, the heights, but not the shapes, of these curves are sensitive to the particular values assumed. The nature of the key relationships among technology, preponderance, force employment, and capability is thus substantially robust, though particular values for particular outcomes vary with the assumptions made for k_1 through k_9.

Notes

1. *Crisis in the Persian Gulf: Sanctions, Diplomacy and War, Hearings Before the Committee on Armed Services, House of Representatives* (Washington, DC: USGPO, 1991), HASC no. 101–57, pp. 448, 462, 463, 485, 917; John Mearsheimer, "Liberation in Less than a Week," *New York Times*, February 8, 1991, p. A31; "Defense Analysts: Limited War to Free Kuwait Could Cut Casualties by Over Half," *Inside the Army*, December 10, 1990, p. 11; "Air Strike on Iraq, the Favored Strategy, Means Big Risks for Both Sides," *New York Times*, October 23, 1990, p. A10. For reported prewar Defense Department estimates, see, e.g., Lawrence Freedman and Efraim Karsh, *The Gulf Conflict, 1990–1991: Diplomacy and War in the New World Order* (Princeton: Princeton University Press, 1993), p. 391; Michael Gordon and Bernard Trainor, *The Generals' War* (Boston: Little, Brown, 1995), pp. 132–33, 174; U.S. News and World Report, *Triumph without Victory* (New York: Random House, 1992), pp. 129, 141; Bob Woodward, *The Commanders* (New York: Simon and Schuster, 1991), p. 349; Tom Matthews, "The Secret History of the War," *Newsweek*, March 18, 1991, pp. 28ff.

2. Stephen Van Evera, "The Cult of the Offensive and the Origins of the First World War," *International Security* 9, 1 (Summer 1984), pp. 58–107; Jack Snyder, *The Ideology of the Offensive: Military Decision Making and the Disasters of 1914* (Ithaca: Cornell University Press, 1984); Geoffrey Blainey, *The Causes of War*, 3rd ed. (New York: Macmillan, 1988), pp. 108–24.

3. See, e.g., Gerhard Weinberg, *A World at Arms* (New York: Cambridge University Press, 1994), pp. 67–68, 109–12; John Mearsheimer, *Conventional Deterrence* (Ithaca: Cornell University Press, 1983), pp. 67–133.

4. For an overview of this debate, see James Jay Carafano, "Myth of the Silver Bullet: Contrasting Air Force-Army Perspectives on 'Smart Weapons' after the 1973 Arab-Israeli War and the 1991 Gulf War," *National Security Studies Quarterly* 4, 1 (Winter 1998), pp. 1–20.

5. After Orr Kelley, *King of the Killing Zone* (New York: W. W. Norton, 1989).

6. For an overview, see Brian Gibbs and J. David Singer, *Empirical Knowledge on World Politics* (Westport, CT: Greenwood, 1993).

7. See the analysis in table 2.1 and accompanying text in chapter 2.

8. By "rigorous" I mean only explicit, precise specification of variables and interactions; few combat models are fully rigorous in the sense of formal axiomatic derivation. See, e.g., Edmund DuBois, Wayne Hughes, and Lawrence Low, *A Concise Theory of Combat* (Monterey, CA: U.S. Naval Postgraduate School, 1998), chap. 1.

9. Many associate World War I with the dawn of "modern" warfare, but interpretations of modernity and its properties differ. See, e.g., Timothy Travers, *The Killing Ground: The British Army, the Western Front and the Emergence of Modern Warfare, 1900–1918* (London: Allen and Unwin, 1987); Jonathan Bailey, *The First World War and the Birth of the*

Modern Style of Warfare (Camberley: British Army Strategic and Combat Studies Institute, 1996), SCSI Occasional Paper No. 22; John Terraine, *White Heat: The New Warfare, 1914–18* (London: Sidgwick and Jackson, 1982); Colin McInnes, *Men, Machines and the Emergence of Modern Warfare 1914–1945* (Camberley: British Army Strategic and Combat Studies Institute, 1992), SCSI Occasional Paper No. 2; G. D. Sheffield, "Blitzkrieg and Attrition," in G. D. Sheffield and Colin McInnes, *Warfare in the Twentieth Century* (London: Unwin Hyman, 1988), pp. 51–79; Sheffield, *Forgotten Victory* (London: Headline, 2001), pp. 140–46. My usage of "modern system" comes closest to Bailey's but corresponds exactly to no one use of the phrase in extant historiography. Bailey, for example, focuses on the use of artillery, especially in deep fires—he sees efforts to maximize deep fires' effectiveness as the central theme of post-1914 warfare (pp. 3–7, 17–21). By contrast, I frame the "modern system" in terms of a wider range of arms and methods, I focus on efforts to *survive* artillery and other firepower, and I conclude that these were ultimately successful, permitting meaningful maneuver in spite of even twenty-first-century fires. Modernity has many traits; while my usage is informed by the historical literature and owes much both to Bailey's analysis and to the broader ongoing historical reinterpretation of World War I (see below), the theory presented here is different in its particulars, specified and tested quite differently, and distinct in its implications for both post-1918 warfare and current policy.

10. See, e.g., Basil Liddell Hart, *The Real War, 1914–1918* (1930; reprint Boston: Little, Brown, 1964); Liddell Hart, *History of the Second World War* (New York: G. P. Putnam's Sons, 1970); J.F.C. Fuller, *A Military History of the Western World*, 3 vols. (New York: Funk and Wagnalls, 1954–56); Fuller, *Armament and History* (New York: Charles Scribner's Sons, 1945); Theodore Ropp, *War in the Modern World* (New York: Macmillan, 1962), pp. 267–70; Bernard and Fawn Brodie, *From Crossbow to H-Bomb* (Bloomington: Indiana University Press, 1973), pp. 124–308; Charles Messenger, *The Art of Blitzkrieg* (London: Ian Allen, 1976); Bryan Perret, *The History of Blitzkrieg* (London: Robert Hale, 1983).

11. See, e.g., John Ellis, *Brute Force: Allied Strategy and Tactics in the Second World War* (New York: Viking, 1990); R.A.C. Parker, *Struggle for Survival: The History of the Second World War* (Oxford: Oxford University Press, 1989), pp. 86, 131–50; Clive Pointing, *Armageddon* (New York: Random House, 1995), p. 163.

12. See especially Joseph Nye, *The Paradox of American Power* (New York: Oxford University Press, 2002).

13. The U.S. Army, for example, has argued that peacekeeping and taking or holding territory demand skills different enough to require retraining before troops can change missions: Gen. Henry Shelton, "Peace Operations: The Forces Required," *National Security Studies Quarterly* 6, 3 (Summer 2000). Offense-defense theory holds that the capacity to attack and the capacity to defend are not inherently the same; many offense-defense theorists hold that forces can be designed to accomplish the latter but not the former. See, e.g., Charles Glaser and Chaim Kaufmann, "What Is the Offense-Defense Balance and How Can We Measure It?" *International Security* 22, 4 (Spring 1998), pp. 44–82.

14. In 1940 France surrendered most of the country to German occupation to forgo further losses in continued resistance; Britain, by contrast, fought on and urged the French to do likewise from France's surviving bases in North Africa: Weinberg, *A World at Arms*, pp. 138–46. In 1945 the United States was prepared to invade Japan in spite of heavy expected losses; less than ten years later, it would forgo conquering North Korea to limit casualties following China's entry into the war.

15. In 1999, for example, Russian forces in Chechnya exchanged reduced casualties for a prolonged campaign by besieging Grozny rather than assaulting it. In 1996, by contrast, they chose the opposite to seek a quicker conclusion: International Institute for Strategic Studies, *Strategic Survey 1999/2000* (London: Oxford University Press, 2000), pp. 125–27. In 1991 America waited through a six-week air campaign but ultimately risked a more costly ground invasion to end the war in Kuwait before centrifugal political forces could divide the coalition: Gordon and Trainor, *The Generals' War*, p. 307; Department of Defense, *Conduct of the Persian Gulf War* (Washington, DC: USGPO, April 1992), p. xv. In 1999 NATO persisted in a much longer seventy-eight-day air war but was apparently exhausting its patience when Milosevic finally conceded—preparations for a land invasion had begun in the war's final weeks: Ivo Daalder and Michael O'Hanlon, *Winning Ugly* (Washington, DC: Brookings, 2000), pp. 155–64.

16. On the distinctions among combat outcomes, see DuBois, Hughes, and Low, *Concise Theory of Combat*, chap 4.

17. A series of one or more interconnected operations in a single theater constitute a *campaign*, as in the Normandy breakout campaign of 1944, which consisted, inter alia, of Operations EPSOM, GOODWOOD, and COBRA; wars sometimes encompass multiple campaigns in multiple theaters. This choice for a unit of analysis follows from the empirical argument in chapter 2: see the discussion under "Implications."

18. See *National Military Strategy of the United States* (Washington, DC: The White House, 2002).

19. For a more complete account, see Stephen Biddle, *Afghanistan and the Future of Warfare: Implications for Army and Defense Policy* (Carlisle, PA: U.S. Army War College Strategic Studies Institute, 2002); Biddle, "Afghanistan and the Future of Warfare," *Foreign Affairs* 82, 2 (March/April 2003).

20. See Operation Enduring Freedom Strategic Studies Institute Research Collection, U.S. Army Military History Institute, hereafter MHI: Tape 032802a, MAJ D. int.; Tape 032802p, MAJ C. int.; Tape 032602a, CPT H. et al. int.; Tape 032602p, CPT M. int.; Tape 041902p, LTC Briley int.; Tape 042002p, LTC Gray int.; Tape 041802p, LTC Lundy int.; Tape 041802p, LTC Preysler int.; Tape 041902a, MAJ Busko int.; Tape 041902a, CPT Murphy int.; Tape 041902a, CPT Lecklenburg int.

21. MHI, Tape 032602p, CPT M. int.

22. In Afghanistan, for example, lack of early progress in the bombing campaign led the Bush administration to prepare plans for a major U.S. ground force commitment of fifty thousand troops or more: Bob Woodward, "Doubts and Debate before Victory over Taliban," *Washington Post*, November 18, 2002, pp. A1ff.

23. Department of Defense, *Quadrennial Defense Review Report* (Washington, DC: USGPO, Sept. 30, 2001).

24. Personal communication, COL Eugene Thompson, U.S. Army War College, October 4, 2001.

25. See, e.g., Karl Vick, "Desperate Battle Defines Congo's Warlike Peace: Massive Government Attack Turns into Bloody Retreat," *Washington Post*, January 2, 2001, p. A1; Michael Dobbs, "Armenia Pins Economic Hopes on Peace," *Washington Post*, September 6, 2000, p. A13; Colum Lynch, "Ethiopia and Eritrea Sign a Peace Accord," *Washington Post*, June 19, 2000, p. A10; International Institute for Strategic Studies, *Strategic Survey 1995/96* (London: Oxford University Press, 1996), pp. 126–38; IISS, *Strategic Survey 1994/95*, pp. 207–10.

26. Some project that Western high-intensity prowess will eventually drive most enemies to low-intensity conflict (LIC), possibly eliminating high-intensity warfare

altogether: Martin Van Creveld, *The Transformation of War* (New York: Free Press, 1991); A. J. Bacevich, "Preserving the Well-Bred Horse," *The National Interest*, no. 37 (Fall 1994), pp. 43–49; Richard Betts, "The Downside of the Cutting Edge," *The National Interest* (Fall 1996), pp. 80–83 (emphasizing weapons of mass destruction rather than LIC). While some will choose LIC, this does not render high-intensity capability unimportant. For most, LIC is a second-best option; Western high-intensity capability is needed to limit opponents to LIC. Second, regional powers will retain conventional armies to fight one another even if they are ineffective against the West; if Westerners lose proficiency, regional armies will become tougher opponents. Third, as I argue below, regional armies *in skilled hands* are potentially more capable than often assumed; unless skilled opposition can be ruled out, vigilance is a crucial hedge.

27. On countervalue warfare, see, e.g., Thomas Schelling, *Arms and Influence* (New Haven: Yale University Press, 1966); Daniel Ellsberg, *The Theory and Practice of Blackmail* (Santa Monica: RAND, 1968), P-3883; Richard Betts, *Nuclear Blackmail and Nuclear Balance* (Washington, DC: Brookings, 1987); Robert Powell, *Nuclear Deterrence Theory: The Search for Credibility* (Cambridge: Cambridge University Press, 1990); Alexander George, David Hall, and William Simons, *The Limits of Coercive Diplomacy* (Boston: Little, Brown, 1971); Robert Pape, *Bombing to Win: Air Power and Coercion in War* (Ithaca: Cornell University Press, 1996); Daniel Byman and Matthew Waxman, *The Dynamics of Coercion* (New York: Cambridge University Press, 2002).

28. See, e.g., Tami Davis Biddle, *Rhetoric and Reality in Air Warfare: The Evolution of British and American Ideas about Strategic Bombing, 1917–1945* (Princeton: Princeton University Press, 2002), pp. 285–86. In the rare cases where countervalue intentions have been explicit, these proved highly controversial: Tami Davis Biddle, "Bombing by the Square Yard: Sir Arthur Harris at War, 1942–1945," *International History Review* 21, 3 (September 1999), pp. 626–64.

29. T. Biddle, *Rhetoric and Reality*, chap. 5.

30. See, e.g., Conrad Crane, *American Airpower Strategy in Korea, 1950–1953* (Lawrence: University Press of Kansas, 2000); Pape, *Bombing to Win*, pp. 137–210.

31. Eliot Cohen, et al. *Gulf War Air Power Survey* (Washington, DC: USGPO, 1993), (hereafter *GWAPS*), vol. 2, pt. 2, pp. 274–90.

32. See Daalder and O'Hanlon, *Winning Ugly*, pp. 137–81, 203–4; also Stephen Biddle, "The New Way of War? Debating the Kosovo Model," *Foreign Affairs* 81, 3 (May–June 2002), pp. 138–44.

33. Iraq, for example, could clearly have used both chemical (CW) and biological weapons (BW) in 1991 yet did neither. All major powers in World War II had CW and many had BW, yet neither were used—not even by Germany or Japan to avert unconditional surrender. Iran and Iraq both had CW throughout the nearly decade-long Iran-Iraq War yet used them only in the war's last stages, after years of indecisive conventional fighting. This is not to suggest that WMD will never be used. But mere possession does not imply use—the proliferation rate does not imply an equivalent frequency of WMD use in battle. On Iraqi CW nonuse in 1991, see Cohen, *GWAPS*, vol. 2, pt. 2, pp. 323–26. On German and Japanese nonuse of CW and BW in World War II, see Jeffrey Legro, *Cooperation under Fire* (Ithaca: Cornell University Press, 1995). On CW in the Iran-Iraq War, see Anthony Cordesman and Abraham Wagner, *The Lessons of Modern War*, vol. 2 (Boulder: Westview, 1990), pp. 506–18.

34. On North Korean nuclear inventories, see Leon Sigal, *Disarming Strangers: Nuclear Diplomacy with North Korea* (Princeton: Princeton University Press, 1998), pp. 90–95, 110. On great power preparations for CW and BW, see, e.g., Victor Utgoff, *The Challenge of*

Chemical Weapons (New York: St. Martin's, 1991). On great powers and regional WMD use, see Lawrence Freedman, "Great Powers, Vital Interests and Nuclear Weapons," *Survival* 36, 4 (Winter 1994–95), pp. 35–52; Barry Posen, "U.S. Security Policy in a Nuclear-Armed World, or What If Iraq Had Nuclear Weapons?" Stephen Rosen, "Nuclear Proliferation and Alliance Relations," and Victor Utgoff, "The Coming Crisis," each in Utgoff, *The Coming Crisis* (Cambridge: MIT Press, 2000), pp. 157–90, 125–56, and 279–302, respectively.

35. J. David Singer and Melvin Small, Correlates of War Project: International and Civil War Data, 1816–1992 [computer file] (Ann Arbor MI: Inter-University Consortium for Political and Social Research, 1994), henceforth COW database. Three were primarily maritime: the Italo-Turkish War of 1911, the Spanish-Moroccan War of 1909, and the Falklands War of 1982. Three were primarily guerilla conflicts: the Boxer Rebellion of 1900, the Russo-Hungarian War of 1956, and the Vietnam War of 1965. None was primarily aerial.

36. Donald Polkinghorne, *Methodology for the Human Sciences* (Albany: State University of New York Press, 1983), pp. 253–54. See also Colin Elman and Miriam Fendius Elman, eds., *Bridges and Boundaries: Historians, Political Scientists, and the Study of International Relations* (Cambridge: MIT Press, 2001).

37. Shelford Bidwell and Dominick Graham, *Firepower: British Army Weapons and Theories of War, 1904–1945* (London: Allen and Unwin, 1985); Robin Prior and Trevor Wilson, *Command on the Western Front* (Oxford: Blackwell, 1992); David Herrmann, *The Arming of Europe and the Making of the First World War* (Princeton: Princeton University Press, 1996); Paddy Griffith, *Battle Tactics of the Western Front* (New Haven: Yale University Press, 1994); Griffith, *Forward into Battle* (Sussex: Antony Bird, 1981); Timothy Lupfer, *The Dynamics of Doctrine: Changes in German Tactical Doctrine During the First World War* (Ft. Leavenworth, KS: U.S. Army Combat Studies Institute, 1981); Antulio Echevarria II, *After Clausewitz: German Military Thinkers before the Great War* (Lawrence: University Press of Kansas, 2000); McInnes, *Men, Machines*; Bailey, *First World War*; Sheffield, *Forgotten Victory*; Sheffield, "Blitzkrieg and Attrition"; J. P. Harris, "The Myth of Blitzkrieg," *War in History* 2, 3 (November 1995), pp. 335–52; Robert Doughty, *The Breaking Point: Sedan and the Fall of France, 1940* (Hamden, CT: Archon Books, 1990); Eugenia Kiesling, *Arming against Hitler: France and the Limits of Military Planning* (Lawrence: University Press of Kansas, 1996); Peter Mansoor, *The GI Offensive in Europe: The Triumph of American Infantry Divisions, 1941–1945* (Lawrence: University Press of Kansas, 1999); Michael Doubler, *Closing with the Enemy: How GIs Fought the War in Europe* (Lawrence: University Press of Kansas, 1994).

38. On the distinction between capability and its observable realization (what they term "combat potential" as opposed to "combat power"), see DuBois, Hughes, and Low, *Concise Theory of Combat*, chap. 7.

39. James Fearon, "Rationalist Explanations for War," *International Organization* 49, 3 (1995), pp. 379–414; Bruce Bueno de Mesquita and David Lalman, *War and Reason* (New Haven: Yale University Press, 1992).

CHAPTER TWO

A LITERATURE BUILT ON WEAK FOUNDATIONS

1. John Bartlett, *Familiar Quotations*, 10th ed. (Boston: Little, Brown, 1919), no. 9707.

2. See, e.g., Basil Liddell Hart, *Strategy* (1954; reprint New York: Penguin, 1991), pp. 321–22, 353–60; Michael Howard, "The Forgotten Dimensions of Strategy," in

Howard, *The Causes of Wars* (Cambridge: Harvard University Press, 1983), pp. 101–9; Paul Kennedy, *The Rise and Fall of the Great Powers* (New York: Random House, 1987), esp. pp. xv–xxv, 536–40; Kennedy, "Grand Strategy in War and Peace: Toward a Broader Definition," in Kennedy, ed., *Grand Strategies in War and Peace* (New Haven: Yale University Press, 1991), pp. 1–7; Robert Gilpin, *War and Change in World Politics* (New York: Cambridge University Press, 1981), esp. pp. 65–66, 123–24, who limits this to modern warfare; Joseph Grieco, *Cooperation among Nations* (Ithaca: Cornell University Press, 1990), pp. 36–50.

3. For reviews, see William Wohlforth, *The Elusive Balance: Power and Perceptions during the Cold War* (Ithaca: Cornell University Press, 1993), pp. 1–10; Richard L. Merritt and Dina Zinnes, "Alternative Indexes of National Power," in Richard Stoll and Michael Ward, eds., *Power in World Politics* (Boulder: Lynne Rienner, 1989), pp. 11–28.

4. See, e.g., Jacob Viner, "Power vs. Plenty as Objectives of Foreign Policy in the Seventeenth and Eighteenth Centuries," *World Politics* 1 (1948) pp. 1–29; Albert O. Hirschman, *National Power and the Structure of Foreign Trade*, 2d ed, (Berkeley: University of California Press, 1980), pp. v–xx, 3–81; Gilpin, *War and Change*; Grieco, *Cooperation among Nations*.

5. See especially Basil Liddell Hart, "The Ratio of Troops to Space," *Military Review* 40 (April 1960); also Mearsheimer, *Conventional Deterrence*, pp. 47–48, 181–83; James Thompson and Nanette Gantz, *Conventional Arms Control Revisited* (Santa Monica, CA: RAND, 1987), N-2697-AF; Paul Davis et al., *Variables Affecting Central Region Stability: The "Operational Minimum" and Other Issues at Low Force Levels* (Santa Monica, CA: RAND, 1989); John Galvin, "Some Thoughts on Conventional Arms Control," *Survival* 31, 2 (March/April), pp. 99–107; Jack Snyder, "Limiting Offensive Conventional Forces: Soviet Proposals and Western Options," *International Security* 12, 4 (Spring 1988), pp. 66–67.

6. See, e.g., Basil Liddell Hart, *The Defense of Britain* (London: Faber and Faber, 1939), pp. 54–55; John Mearsheimer, "Assessing the Conventional Balance: The 3:1 Rule and Its Critics," *International Security* 13, 4 (Spring 1989), pp. 54–89; Congressional Budget Office, *Strengthening NATO* (Washington, DC: USGPO, 1979), pp. 11–13, app. C; Congressional Budget Office, *Army Ground Force Modernization for the 1980s* (Washington, DC: USGPO, 1982), pp. 30–31.

7. See, e.g., Liddell Hart, *Defense of Britain*, pp. 54–55; Mearsheimer, "Assessing the Conventional Balance," pp. 63–64.

8. Some offense-defense theorists consider other variables, especially geography, but technology is the heart of the theory: Sean Lynn Jones, "Offense-Defense Theory and Its Critics," *Security Studies* 4, 4 (Summer 1995), pp. 660–91; Stephen Biddle, "Rebuilding the Foundations of Offense Defense Theory," *Journal of Politics* 63, 3 (August 2001). On offense-defense theory generally, see, e.g., Robert Jervis, "Cooperation under the Security Dilemma," *World Politics* 30, 2 (January 1978), pp. 167–214; George Quester, *Offense and Defense in the International System* (New York: Wiley, 1977); Stephen Van Evera, *Causes of War* (Ithaca: Cornell University Press, 1999); Snyder, *The Ideology of the Offensive*, pp. 9–22; Glaser and Kaufmann, "Offense-Defense Balance," pp. 44–82.

9. See, e.g., Jervis, "Cooperation"; Quester, *Offense and Defense*; Van Evera, *Causes of War*; Ted Hopf, "Polarity, the Offense-Defense Balance, and War," *American Political Science Review* 85, 2 (June 1991), pp. 475–94; Thomas Christensen and Jack Snyder, "Chain Gangs and Passed Bucks: Predicting Alliance Patterns in Multipolarity," *International Organization* 44 (Spring 1990), pp. 137–68; Stephen Walt, *The Origins of Alliances* (Ithaca: Cornell University Press, 1987), pp. 1–49, 147–217; Jack Levy, "Alliance Formation and War Behavior," *Journal of Conflict Resolution* 25, 4 (December 1981), pp. 605ff; George

Downs, David Rocke, and Randolph Siverson, "Arms Races and Cooperation," *World Politics* 38, 1 (October 1985), pp. 118–46; Stanislav Andreski, *Military Organization and Society* (Berkeley: University of California Press, 1968), pp. 75–78; Gilpin, *War and Change*, pp. 59–63.

10. Stephen Van Evera, "The Cult of the Offensive," pp. 58–107; Snyder, *Ideology of the Offensive*, pp. 9–22; Barry Posen, "The Security Dilemma and Ethnic Conflict," *Survival* 35 (Spring 1993), pp. 27–47.

11. Robert Powell, *The Shadow of Power* (Princeton: Princeton University Press, 1999), chap. 2; Helen Milner, "International Theories of Cooperation among Nations: Strengths and Weaknesses," *World Politics* 44, 3 (April 1992), pp. 466–96 at 483–84; Charles Glaser, "Realists as Optimists: Cooperation as Self-Help," *International Security* 19, 3 (Winter 1994/5), p. 79.

12. Glaser, "Realists as Optimists"; Van Evera, *Causes of War*.

13. Basil Liddell Hart, "Aggression and the Problem of Weapons," *English Review* (July 1932), pp. 71–78; J. F .C. Fuller, "What Is an Aggressive Weapon?" *English Review* (June 1932), pp. 601–5; Marion William Boggs, *Attempts to Define and Limit "Aggressive" Armament in Diplomacy and Strategy*, University of Missouri Studies, vol. 16, no. 1 (Columbia: University of Missouri, 1941); Dorn Crawford, *Conventional Armed Forces in Europe (CFE): An Overview of Key Treaty Elements* (Bethesda, MD: U.S. Army CAA, May 1991); Alvin Z. Rubinstein, "New World Order or Hollow Victory?" *Foreign Affairs* 70, 4 (Fall 1991), pp. 53–65.

14. M. O'Connor, "US Is Supplying Army in Sarajevo with 116 Big Guns," *New York Times*, 10 May 1997; Thomas Schelling and Morton Halperin, *Strategy and Arms Control* (New York: Twentieth Century Fund, 1961); John Newhouse, *Cold Dawn: The Story of SALT* (New York: Holt, Rinehart and Winston, 1973).

15. Alvin and Heidi Toffler, *War and Anti-War* (Boston: Little, Brown, 1993); Paul Bracken, "The Military after Next," *The Washington Quarterly* 16, 4 (Autumn 1993), pp. 157–74; Gordon Sullivan and Anthony Coroalles, *The Army in the Information Age* (Carlisle: U.S. Army War College, March 1995); also references in chapter 10, note 18.

16. Harold Brown, *Thinking about National Security* (Boulder: Westview, 1983), pp. 225–33; William Perry, "Defense Technology," in Asa Clark and John Lilley, eds., *Defense Technology* (New York: Praeger, 1989), pp. 28–29; Jacques Gansler, "Managing Defense Technology," in ibid., p. 207.

17. Stuart Johnson and James Blaker, "The FY 1997–2001 Defense Budget," *Strategic Forum*, no. 80 (July 1996), pp. 3–4; also Richard J. Newman, "Warfare 2020," *U.S. News and World Report*, August 5, 1996, pp. 34–41; Jim Hoagland, "Ready for What?" *Washington Post*, March 28, 1996, p. A27.

18. See, e.g., U. Candan et al., *Present NATO Practice in Land Wargaming* (The Hague: SHAPE Technical Center, 1987), STC-PP-252; Jerome Bracken et al., eds., *Warfare Modeling* (Alexandria, VA: Military Operations Research Society, 1995); Wayne Hughes, ed., *Military Modeling* (Alexandria, VA: Military Operations Research Society, 1984); John Battilega and Judith Grange, eds., *The Military Applications of Modeling* (Wright-Patterson AFB: Air Force Institute of Technology Press, 1984). In addition to Lanchester theory, which underpins most dynamic models, there are also a variety of static measures that compute indices of "effectiveness" (often denominated in units of "armored division equivalents," or ADEs) without advancing explicit claims for their relationship to combat outcomes. These, too, focus on materiel. For reviews, see Stephen Biddle, "The European Conventional Balance," *Survival* 30, 2 (March/April 1988), pp. 99–121; John Bode, *Indices of Effectiveness in General Purpose Force Analysis* (Washington, DC: BDM, 1974), BDM-74-070-TR.

19. Frederick William Lanchester, *Aircraft in Warfare: The Dawn of the Fourth Arm* (London: Constable, 1916), reprinted at article length as "Mathematics in Warfare," in James R. Newman, *The World of Mathematics*, vol. 4 (New York: Simon and Schuster, 1956), pp. 2139–57.

20. Nor does Lanchester theory distinguish "attackers" from "defenders": it simply posits two sides in contact and exchanging fire. Users sometimes hypothesize higher per-weapon attrition coefficients for "defending" weapons, but Lanchester theory itself provides no basis for this, and no method for computing any such bonus.

21. For reviews, see James Taylor, *Lanchester Models of Warfare*, 2 vols. (Arlington, VA: Operations Research Society of America, 1983); Alan F. Karr, "Lanchester Attrition Processes and Theater-Level Combat Models," in Martin Shubik, ed., *Mathematics of Conflict* (Amsterdam: Elsevier, 1983), pp. 89–126; Battilega and Grange, *Military Applications of Modeling*, pp. 88–103.

22. Jack Levy, "The Offensive/Defensive Balance of Military Technology: A Theoretical and Historical Analysis," *International Studies Quarterly* 28, 2 (June 1984), pp. 219–38. For exceptions, see Biddle, "Rebuilding the Foundations"; Hopf, "Polarity"; James Fearon, "The Offense-Defense Balance and War since 1648," presented to the annual meeting of the International Studies Association, Chicago, 1995. For other critiques, see Mearsheimer, *Conventional Deterrence*, pp. 24–27; Colin Gray, *Weapons Don't Make War* (Lawrence: University Press of Kansas, 1993); Dan Reiter, "Exploding the Powder Keg Myth: Preemptive Wars Almost Never Happen," *International Security* 20, 2 (Fall 1995), pp. 5–34; Jonathan Shimshoni, "Technology, Military Advantage, and World War I," *International Security* 15, 3 (Winter 1990/91), pp. 187–215; Kier Lieber, "Grasping the Technological Peace," *International Security* 25, 1 (Summer 2000), pp. 71–104.

23. Institute for Defense Analyses/OJCS(J-8) TACWAR model, vers. 47.0, file tacdata.dat [computer file]. For a description, see Francis P. Hoeber, *Military Applications of Modeling: Selected Case Studies* (New York: Gordon and Breach Science Publishers, 1981), pp. 132–53. For two attempts to test large-scale theater combat models against historical data, see Seth Bonder, "Summary of a Verification Study of VECTOR-2 with the Arab-Israeli War," in Reiner K. Huber, ed., *Systems Analysis and Modeling in Defense* (New York: Plenum, 1984), pp. 155–70; Walter J. Bauman, "Ardennes Campaign Simulation (ARCAS)," *Military Operations Research* 2, 4 (1996), pp. 21–38. Each reconstructed a single historical battle using, respectively, the VECTOR-2 and STOCEM models. The former claims the model performed well; the latter is less sanguine. Neither, however, advances any case selection logic to establish the cases' external validity or theoretical significance, and neither provides sufficient documentation to evaluate the test fully. For both, inherent problems of data reliability for such enormous arrays of variables, combined with the subjective nature of many of the required values, counsel caution in assessing validation claims.

24. Robert Helmbold, *Personnel Attrition Rates in Historical Land Combat Operations* (Washington, DC: U.S. Army Concepts Analysis Agency, 1995), CAA-RP-95-1; Jerome Bracken, "Lanchester Models of the Ardennes Campaign," *Naval Research Logistics* 42, 4 (June 1995), pp. 559–77, which finds a linear form of Lanchester's equations is better supported than the more commonly used square law; Dean Hartley and Robert Helmbold, "Validating Lanchester's Square Law and Other Attrition Models," *Naval Research Logistics* 42, 4 (June 1995), pp. 609–33; Dean Hartley, *Can the Square Law Be Validated?* (Oak Ridge: Martin Marietta, 1989), K/DSRD-57; Hartley, *Confirming the Lanchester Linear-Logarithmic*

Model of Attrition (Oak Ridge: Martin Marietta, 1991), K/DSRD-263/R1, which finds evidence for a linear-logarithmic form, but not the square law; D.L.I. Kirkpatrick, "Do Lanchester's Equations Adequately Model Real Battles?" *Journal of the Royal United Services Institute* 130, 2 (June 1985), pp. 25–27; Janice Fain, "The Lanchester Equations and Historical Warfare," *History, Numbers, and War* 1, 1 (Spring 1977), pp. 34–52; James Busse, "An Attempt to Verify Lanchester's Equations," in Benjamin Avi-Itzhak, ed., *Developments in Operations Research*, vol. 2 (New York: Gordon and Breach, 1971), pp. 587–97; William Fain et al., *Validation of Combat Models Against Historical Data* (Arlington, VA: Center for Naval Analyses, 1970), CNA Professional Paper No. 27; William Schmiemann, "The Use of Lanchester-Type Equations in the Analysis of Past Military Engagements" (Ph.D. Diss., Georgia Institute of Technology, 1967); Herbert Weiss, "Combat Models and Historical Data: The U.S. Civil War," *Operations Research* 14, 5 (September–October 1966), pp. 759–90; Robert Helmbold, "Some Observations on the Use of Lanchester's Theory for Prediction," *Operations Research* 12, 5 (September–October 1964), pp. 778–81; Daniel Willard, *Lanchester as a Force in History* (Bethesda, MD: Research Analysis Corporation, 1962), RAC-TP-74; Robert Helmbold, *Historical Data and Lanchester's Theory of Combat* (Ft. Belvoir, VA: Combat Operations Research Group, 1961), part 1: CORG-SP-128, part 2 (1964): CORG-SP-190. For partial validations, see J. H. Engel, "A Verification of Lanchester's Law," *Operations Research* 2, 2 (May 1954), pp. 163–71; Robert Samz, "Some Comments on Engel's 'A Verification of Lanchester's Law,'" *Operations Research* 20, 1 (January–February 1972), pp. 49–52. On the community's response to these tests, see Battilega and Grange, *Military Applications of Modeling*, p. 92. For a sharply critical (and highly controversial) assessment, see Paul Davis and Donald Blumenthal, *The Base of Sand Problem: A White Paper on the State of Military Combat Modeling* (Santa Monica: RAND, 1991), N-3148-OSD/DARPA.

25. Basil Liddell Hart, *The Real War*, pp. 49–50.

26. Weinberg, *A World at Arms*, pp. 67–68, 109–12; Mearsheimer, *Conventional Deterrence*, pp. 67–133.

27. See, e.g., *Crisis in the Persian Gulf: Sanctions, Diplomacy and War, Hearings Before the Committee on Armed Services, House of Representatives* (Washington, DC: USGPO, 1991), HASC No. 101-57, pp. 448, 462, 463, 485; Mearsheimer, "Liberation in Less than a Week"; Joshua Epstein, *War with Iraq: What Price Victory?* (Washington, DC: Brookings, January 10, 1991), p. 25; Barry Posen, "Political Objectives and Military Options in the Persian Gulf," Defense and Arms Control Studies Working Paper, November 5, 1990, p. 24.

28. Liddell Hart, *The Real War*, pp. 49–50; Weinberg, *A World at Arms*, pp. 67–68, 109–12; Mearsheimer, "Liberation in Less than a Week;" Les Aspin, "The Military Option," reprinted in Les Aspin, *The Aspin Papers* (Washington, DC: CSIS, 1991), p. 86; U.S. News and World Report, *Triumph without Victory*, pp. 129, 141.

29. See, e.g., Lowell Bruce Anderson, *Decision Modeling in Large Scale Conflict Simulations* (Alexandria, VA: Institute for Defense Analyses, 1978), IDA P-1355; Paul Davis and James Winnefield, *The RAND Strategic Assessment Center* (Santa Monica: RAND, 1983), R-2945-DNA; James G. Taylor, "Attrition Modeling," in Reiner K. Huber et al., eds., *Operational Research Games for Defense* (Munich: R. Oldenbourg, 1979), pp. 139–89; J. A. Dewar et al., "Non-Monotonicity, Chaos and Combat Models," *Military Operations Research* 2, 2 (1996); Candan et al., *Present NATO Practice* (The Hague: Supreme Headquarters Allied Powers Europe Technical Center, 1987), Professional Paper STC-PP-252; Bracken et al., *Warfare Modeling*; Battilega and Grange, *Military Applications of Modeling*.

30. See, e.g., Eliot Cohen, "Guessing Game: A Reappraisal of Systems Analysis," in Samuel Huntington, ed., *The Strategic Imperative* (Cambridge, MA: Ballenger, 1982), pp. 163–92; Cohen, "Toward Better Net Assessment: Rethinking the European Conventional Balance," *International Security* 13, 1 (Summer 1988), pp. 50–89; Stephen Rosen, "Net Assessment as an Analytical Concept," in Andrew W. Marshall et al., eds., *On Not Confusing Ourselves: Essays in Honor of Albert and Roberta Wohlstetter* (Boulder: Westview, 1991), pp. 284–85, 297–99; Aaron Friedberg, "The Assessment of Military Power: A Review Essay," *International Security* 12, 3 (Winter 1987/88), pp. 190–202. Much of the official interest in less materially focused approaches centers in the Defense Department's Office of Net Assessment; for a review of its efforts, see George Pickett, James Roche, and Barry Watts, "Net Assessment: A Historical Review," in Marshall et al., eds., *On Not Confusing Ourselves*, pp. 158–85; also Thomas Mahnken and Barry Watts, "What the Gulf War Can (and Cannot) Tell Us about the Future of Warfare," *International Security* 21, 2 (Fall 1997), pp. 151, 154.

31. See, e.g., Charles Marshall and Randy Garrett, "Simulation for C4ISR: Command, Control, Communications, Intelligence, Surveillance, and Reconnaissance," *Phalanx* 29, 1 (March 1996), pp. 1ff.; Terry Prosser, "JWARS Role in Joint Analysis," briefing presented to the 64th Military Operations Research Society Symposium, Ft. Leavenworth, KS, June 18, 1996; Stephen Biddle, Wade Hinkle, and Michael Fischerkeller, "Skill and Technology in Modern Warfare," *Joint Force Quarterly*, 22 (Summer 1999), pp. 18–27.

32. See, e.g., Glaser and Kaufmann, "Offense-Defense Balance," pp. 55–57. More broadly, all structural IR theory posits that states make optimizing choices guided chiefly by material constraints; for a critique, see Timothy McKeown, "The Limitations of 'Structural' Theories of Commercial Policy," *International Organization* 40 (Winter 1986), pp. 43–64.

33. Hans Morgenthau, *Politics among Nations*, 6th ed. (New York: McGraw Hill, 1985), pp. 141–42; Klaus Knorr, *Military Power and Potential* (Lexington: D. C. Heath, 1970), pp. 119–36. Other classical realists ignore military doctrine altogether: see, e.g., Martin Wight, *Power Politics* (Leicester: Leicester University Press, 1978), pp. 26–27, which notes the importance of nonmaterial "intangibles" but sees these as matters of commitment and national will rather than force employment, as treated here.

34. Neither the Correlates of War nor the Militarized Interstate Disputes data, for example, contain any information on force employment, though both treat capability via a variety of material indices.

35. Mearsheimer, *Conventional Deterrence*; Allan Stam, *Win, Lose or Draw* (Ann Arbor: University of Michigan Press, 1996); D. Scott Bennett and Allan Stam, "The Duration of Interstate Wars, 1816–1985," *American Political Science Review* 90, 2 (1996), pp. 239–57; Dan Reiter and Allan Stam, "Democracy and Battlefield Military Effectiveness," *Journal of Conflict Resolution* 42, 3 (June 1998), pp. 259–77. The determinants of military doctrine literature also treats force employment, though only as a dependent variable. Moreover, the range of force employment distinctions considered is often quite narrow, with a particular focus on "offensive" versus "defensive" orientations: e.g., Barry Posen, *The Sources of Military Doctrine* (Ithaca: Cornell University Press, 1984); Snyder, *Ideology of the Offensive*.

36. See, e.g., Richard Betts, "Dubious Reform: Strategism versus Managerialism," in Asa Clark et al., eds., *The Defense Reform Debate* (Baltimore: Johns Hopkins University Press, 1984), pp. 74–77.

37. Without addressing "force employment" per se, a few other IR theorists consider nonmaterial contributors to capability. Among the most important are Stephen Rosen,

David Lake, Alastair Johnson, Eliot Cohen, and John Gooch, who focus on social structure, regime type, culture, and organization, respectively: Rosen, *Societies and Military Power* (Ithaca: Cornell University Press, 1996); Johnson, "Thinking about Strategic Culture," *International Security* 19, 4 (Spring 1995); Lake, "Powerful Pacifists: Democratic States and War," *American Political Science Review* 86, 1 (1992), pp. 24–38; Cohen and Gooch, *Military Misfortunes: The Anatomy of Failure in War* (New York: Free Press, 1990). None is inconsistent with the theory below, which can be thought of as elaborating a causal mechanism by which such broader characteristics affect military outcomes. See also Ivan Arreguin-Toft, "How the Weak Win Wars: A Theory of Asymmetrical Conflict," *International Security* 26, 1 (Summer 2001), pp. 93–128, which addresses nonmaterial issues for materially mismatched opponents.

38. The *security dilemma* is the inability to defend oneself without simultaneously threatening one's neighbors. The related *spiral model* sees war arising from states interpreting neighboring military preparations as hostile (even when meant for self-defense), yielding reciprocal buildups and rising tensions even without aggressive intent. By contrast, the *deterrence model* sees war arising from an insufficiency of power on one side, enabling opportunistic neighbors to strike the weaker state. On the security dilemma, see especially Jervis, "Cooperation"; on the spiral and deterrence models, see Robert Jervis, *Perception and Misperception in International Politics* (Princeton: Princeton University Press, 1976), chap. 3.

39. COW database. COW covers all interstate wars involving at least one thousand battle deaths between 1816 and 1992; since the theory advanced here is limited to the twentieth century, however, only twentieth-century data are considered in table 2.1.

40. Replacing LER with either the victorious or defeated side's loss rate (deaths per thousand combatants per month), attackers' loss infliction rate (defenders killed per attacker), or defenders' loss infliction rate (attackers killed per defender), for example, yields no improvement. An exception is the *fractional loss-exchange ratio* (FLER), or the attacker's loss rate (attackers killed per thousand attacker personnel) divided by the defender's loss rate (defenders killed per thousand defender personnel). For OLS regression with log(FLER) as the dependent variable, the logarithms of the attacker:defender balance for all independent variables in table 2.1 save population yield significant coefficients at the 0.05 level, with r^2 between 0.2 and 0.5. This result, however, is an artifact of the COW data structure. COW's military personnel data count a state's entire military rather than just the part committed to a given war. This artificially depresses FLERs for large states that do not commit their entire military to the conflict (since the denominator includes personnel not actually exposed to combat), but not for smaller states whose militaries are wholly engaged. This artificial reduction of large states' apparent loss rates exaggerates preponderance's real benefits, since very preponderant states receive artificially low FLERs but smaller states do not.

41. For complete statistical results, see chapter 8.

42. In 1815 rates of advance for lightly engaged infantry averaged 19.5 kilometers per day; by the mid-1960s, rates of advance for lightly engaged mechanized forces averaged 21.2 kilometers per day. The difference was somewhat more pronounced for heavily engaged forces, but even here some 150 years of technological change induced an increase of only about a factor of two in average rate of advance: in 1815, heavily engaged infantry averaged 1.7 kilometers per day; by the mid-1960s, heavily engaged mechanized forces still averaged under 3.7: Robert Helmbold, *Rates of Advance in Historical Land Combat Operations*, CAA-RP-90-1 (Bethesda: U.S. Army CAA, 1990), pp. 4-9 to 4-10. This

relative stasis in spite of major increases in platform speed has produced a yawning gap between modern weapons' nominal mobility and their average battlefield performance: in the late twentieth century, weapons' nominal speeds typically differed from realized rates of advance by factors of 30 to 100. Tanks from the 1970s able to drive 30–40 kilometers per *hour* on the proving ground, for example, averaged less than 4 kilometers per *day* in combat against significant opposition. Ibid.

43. Stephen Biddle, "Past as Prologue: Assessing Theories of Future Warfare," *Security Studies* 8, 1 (Fall 1998), pp. 13–14.

44. Values obtained from OLS regression on COW data.

45. Most see the first quarter-century as dominated by the machine gun, barbed wire, and long-range artillery; the second and third by the tank, the airplane, and the radio, which appeared in the second but matured in the third; and the fourth by precision-guided antitank and anti-aircraft missiles, which were widely held to counterbalance the tank and the ground-attack airplane. See, e.g., Ropp, *War in the Modern World*, pp. 267–70, 393; Brodie, *Crossbow to H-Bomb*, pp. 124–232, 281–89; Charles Messenger, *Blitzkrieg* (London: Ian Allen, 1976); Perret, *History of Blitzkrieg*. Some see the post-1945 period as uniformly defense-dominant by virtue of nuclear weapons: e.g., Van Evera, *Causes of War*. Others who focus on nonnuclear conflict see the postwar period as outlined above: e.g., Quester, *Offense and Defense*, pp. 163–70; David Gates, "Area Defense Concepts: The West German Debate," *Survival* 29, 4 (July/August 1987), pp. 301–17; Bjorn Moller, *Common Security and Nonoffensive Defense* (Boulder: Lynn Reiner, 1992). Given nuclear-nuclear dyads' empirical infrequency, I focus on conventional conflict here.

46. More formally, the null hypothesis of no change in mean frequency of attacker victory cannot be rejected for the transition from the first to the second, or the second to the third, quarter-century, at any customary level of significance. The null hypothesis of no change between the third and fourth quarter-century, however, can be rejected at the 0.05 level.

47. Logarithms of neither LER nor attacker loss rate nor attacker loss infliction rate show statistically significant differences between any two quarter-centuries at the standard 0.05 level. (Logarithms are needed to accord equal weight to attacker-favorable and defender-favorable shifts: whereas a defender-favorable LER of 10:1 and an attacker-favorable value of 1:10 ought to receive the same weight relative to a neutral value of 1:1, the difference in raw LER between the former and 1:1 is 9.0, but the latter only 0.9. The log of LER ascribes both the same value of 1.0.)

48. See Biddle, "Rebuilding the Foundations."

49. For complete statistical results, see chapter 8.

50. Among the few attempts is Pierre Sprey's "The Case for Better and Cheaper Weapons," in Clark et al., *The Defense Reform Debate*, pp. 193–210, although the evidence adduced is anecdotal rather than systematic. Sprey's conclusions are broadly consistent with the analysis below. While some empirical studies include "technology" or "weapon quality" (e.g., Stam, *Win, Lose or Draw*), these are typically measured by computing defense expenditure per soldier. This conflates technology with training, pay, and quality-of-life accounts. It also biases the measure in favor of air and naval powers (whose militaries are more capital-intensive regardless of their relative technological sophistication), and against land powers (whose militaries are more labor intensive). While not necessarily problematic for the studies' original purposes, for mine this renders the findings inapplicable.

51. As above, data on operations rather than wars would be preferable, but are unavailable: weapon counts by make and model for prewar national inventories are provided in

the International Institute for Strategic Studies *Military Balance* series (London: IISS, various years), but no such counts are available for specific battles or operations (one sometimes sees counts of "tanks" or "aircraft," but I require counts for specific models).

52. Or, more formally, the measure of dyadic technological advantage ΔT for a given war is defined as:

$$\Delta T = \left| T_1 - T_2 \right|$$

where:

$$T_i = \frac{1}{2} \left(\frac{\sum_a y_{a_i} n_{a_i}}{\sum_a n_{a_i}} + \frac{\sum_t y_{t_i} n_{t_i}}{\sum_t n_{t_i}} \right)$$

y_{a_i} = year of introduction for aircraft type a for side i
n_{a_i} = number of aircraft of type a on side i
y_{t_i} = year of introduction for tank type t for side i
n_{t_i} = number of tanks of type t on side i

Data are drawn from IISS, *The Military Balance; Jane's All the World's Aircraft* (London: Jane's, various years); Norman Polmar, ed., *World Combat Aircraft Directory* (Garden City, NY: Doubleday, 1976); Nikolaus Krivinyi, *Warplanes of the World 1983/84* (Annapolis: Nautical and Aviation Publishing Co. of America, 1983); Christopher Foss, ed., *Jane's Armour and Artillery*, 4th ed. (London: Jane's, 1983); John Milsom, *Russian Tanks: 1900–1970* (New York: Galahad, 1970); F. M. Von Senger und Etterlin, *German Tanks of World War II*, trans. J. Lucas (Munich: J. F. Lehmans Verlag, 1968). Identification of wars and participants is from COW; of the 1956–92 interval for which COW and IISS overlap, sixteen of nineteen wars are represented, with the 1969 Football War, the 1975 Turko-Cypriot, war and 1979 Vietnamese-Cambodian War excluded for lack of IISS data.

53. OLS regression using log(LER) as the dependent variable and the difference between the attacker's and defender's technology index as the independent variable yields a coefficient of −0.07 with a standard error of 0.04, which is not significant at the 0.05 level. Without the Gulf War outlier, the coefficient falls to −0.02, the standard error grows to 0.05, and r^2 falls from 0.19 to under 0.02. As I argue in detail in chapter 7, there is strong reason to doubt that technology explains the Gulf LER. Note that COW radically overestimates Iraqi losses in 1991; I thus use the Gulf War Air Power Survey figure of 22,000 throughout: *Summary Report* (Washington, DC: USGPO, 1993), p. 249n. For a more complete statistical analysis, see chapter 8.

54. Yet the results seem robust for at least some, first-order sensitivity tests. For example, an assumption that weapons of non-Western origin are ten years behind Western-built systems' performance makes little difference in the predictor's success. While crude, the measure is not obviously biased.

55. Official models, by contrast, are complex and multivariate but effectively untested empirically and seriously at odds with the one historical case (the Gulf War) in which they produced ex ante predictions.

56. Gary King, Robert Keohane, and Sidney Verba, *Designing Social Inquiry* (Princeton: Princeton University Press, 1994), pp. 168–82.

57. Theories of war often distinguish grand strategic, military strategic, operational, and tactical levels of analysis. *Grand strategy* defines the state's ultimate ends and employs

both military and nonmilitary (e.g., economic, diplomatic, social, and political) means to secure those ends. *Military strategy* governs the use of military means per se and focuses on using campaigns to win wars. *Operational art* uses battles to win operations and campaigns. *Tactics* concerns the conduct of battles. See, e.g., Liddell Hart, *Strategy*, pp. 319–37; Kennedy, "Grand Strategy"; Michael Howard, "Forgotten Dimensions," pp. 101–9; John Alger, *Definitions and Doctrine of the Military Art* (Wayne, NJ: Avery, 1985), p. 5.

58. See, e.g., Liddell Hart, *Strategy*, pp. 321–22; Kennedy, "Grand Strategy," pp. 1–11; Allan R. Millett, Williamson Murray, and Kenneth H. Watman, "The Effectiveness of Military Organizations," in Millett and Murray, eds., *Military Effectiveness*, vol. 1 (Boston: Allen and Unwin, 1988), pp. 4–6.

59. Similarly, organizational adaptability, administrative skill, or politicomilitary integration can be viewed as deeper causes of preponderance, technology, and force employment. Institutions that translate national wealth into military forces with less waste, or balance logistical and combat elements more efficiently, make their effects felt via greater realized material preponderance. Organizations that promote creativity and innovation make their effects felt via a higher rate of new weapon introduction or faster operational and tactical adaptation. Organizations that learn more effectively make their effects felt via more appropriate force employment in the field. All are important, but their effects can be understood by considering their fruits in the more proximate factors of preponderance, technology, operations, and tactics.

60. Put differently, grand strategy is not really left out here: it is largely embodied in the included variables of preponderance and technology. If left-out-variable bias is contaminating preponderance and technology's effects, it will do the same for grand strategy. To make empirical sense of grand strategy's role, it is thus necessary to introduce a variable whose effects have been truly left out—as force employment's at the operational and tactical levels have.

61. The *military-strategic* level could in principle offer similar opportunities, yet most twentieth-century interstate wars have fallen within a comparatively narrow range of basic military strategies. Of the forty-six twentieth-century interstate wars in the COW dataset, for example, thirty-nine involved chiefly continental counterforce strategies: COW dataset. By contrast, implementation of continental counterforce at the operational and tactical levels has varied widely: see, e.g., Millet and Murray, *Military Effectiveness* (Boston: Allen and Unwin, 1988) vols. 1–3; Jonathan House, *Toward Combined Arms Warfare* (Ft. Leavenworth, KS: U.S. Army Combat Studies Institute, 1984); John Gooch, ed., *The Origins of Contemporary Doctrine* (Camberley, UK: Strategic and Combat Studies Institute, 1997), SCSI Occasional Paper No. 30; John English, *A Perspective on Infantry* (New York: Praeger, 1981); Robert Doughty, *The Evolution of U.S. Army Tactical Doctrine, 1946–76* (Ft. Leavenworth, KS: U.S. Army Combat Studies Institute), Leavenworth Paper No. 1. The operational and tactical levels thus provide ample variance to explain differences in observed capability; the military-strategic level may not.

CHAPTER THREE
THE MODERN SYSTEM

1. For reviews of key developments, see, e.g., Hew Strachan, *European Armies and the Conduct of War* (London: Allen and Unwin, 1983), pp. 41, 108–50; William McNeill, *The Pursuit of Power* (Chicago: University of Chicago Press, 1982), pp. 185, 223–306; McNeill,

Plagues and Peoples (New York: Doubleday, 1976), pp. 240–56; Dennis Showalter, *Railroads and Rifles: Soldiers, Technology, and the Unification of Germany* (Hamden, CT: Shoestring Press, 1975); Echevarria, *After Clausewitz*, pp. 13–31; Richard Preston, Alex Roland, and Sydney Wise, *Men in Arms: A History of Warfare and Its Interrelationships with Western Society* (New York: Harcourt Brace, 1991), pp. 215–16.

2. Larry H. Addington, *The Patterns of War since the Eighteenth Century* (Bloomington: Indiana University Press, 1994), pp. 38, 103

3. Strachan, *European Armies and the Conduct of War*, p. 117; Addington, *Patterns of War*, p. 104; B. P. Hughes, *Firepower: Weapons Effectiveness on the Battlefield, 1630–1850* (New York: Chas. Scribners' Sons, 1974).

4. Addington, *Patterns of War*, p. 3, assuming a closing speed of 6 km per hour.

5. Ibid., p. 103; Robin Prior and Trevor Wilson, *Command on the Western Front* (Oxford: Blackwell, 1992), p. 311.

6. COW dataset; Steven Ross, *From Flintlock to Rifle: Infantry Tactics, 1740–1866* (Madison, NJ: Fairleigh Dickinson University Press, 1979), p. 89; J.B.A. Bailey, *Field Artillery and Firepower* (Oxford: Military Press, 1989), p. 127, and conservatively assuming a ratio of at least one crew-served machine gun per artillery piece.

7. Ernst Junger, *The Storm of Steel*, trans. Basil Creighton (London: Chatto and Windus, 1929).

8. Brodie, *Crossbow to H-Bomb*, pp. 151–52.

9. On the eve of the battle, British General Hubert Plumer is said to have observed to his staff: "Gentlemen, we may not make history tomorrow, but we shall certainly change the geography." Ian Hogg, *The Guns, 1914–1918* (New York: Ballantine, 1971), p. 131. On the artillery program at Messines, see John Terraine, "Indirect Fire as a Battle Winner/Loser," in Corelli Barnett et al., *Old Battles and New Defenses: Can We Learn from Military History?* (London: Brassey's, 1986), p. 11; explosive weight per shell is computed from John Keegan, *The Face of Battle* (New York: Random House, 1977), p. 235, and Prior and Wilson, *Command on the Western Front*, p. 363. For W48 yield, see Thomas Cochran et al., *Nuclear Weapons Databook*, vol. 1: *U.S. Nuclear Forces and Capabilities* (Cambridge: Ballinger, 1984), p. 54.

10. Hogg, *The Guns, 1914–18*; David Isby, *Weapons and Tactics of the Soviet Army* (New York: Jane's, 1988); Ian Hogg and John Weeks, *Military Small Arms of the 20th Century* (New York: Hippocrene, 1977); Gordon Swanborough and Peter Bowers, *United States Military Aircraft since 1909* (London: Putnam, 1989), pp. 241, 248, 420–21; Von Senger und Etterlin, *German Tanks of World War II*; Ellis, *Brute Force*, table 62; T. Nicholas and R. Rossi, *U.S. Missile Data Book, 1996* (Fountain Valley, CA: Data Search Assocs., 1995); R. M. Ogorkiewicz, *Technology of Tanks*, vol. 1 (Coulsden, Surrey: Jane's, 1991), p. 111.

11. Representative opposing tanks are the German PzKw IVh for 1945, and the Soviet T72 for 2000. Penetration ranges for U.S. weapons against the PzKw IVh are taken from Ellis, *Brute Force*, table 62; Von Senger und Etterlin, *German Tanks*, pp. 21–28, 34–74, 194–210. Penetration ranges for U.S. weapons vs. the T72 are inferred from Gulf War experience: e.g., Rick Atkinson, *Crusade: The Untold Story of the Persian Gulf War* (Boston: Houghton-Mifflin, 1993), pp. 447, 466; Robert Scales et al., *Certain Victory: The U.S. Army in the Gulf War* (Washington, DC: Office of the Chief of Staff, 1993), p. 293; and missile ranges per Nicholas and Rossi, *U.S. Missile Data Book*.

12. Bidwell and Graham, *Firepower*, pp. 7–60; Herrmann, *Arming of Europe*, pp. 59–112; Griffith, *Battle Tactics*, pp. 48–52; Hew Strachan, *The First World War*, vol. 1: *To Arms*

(Oxford: Oxford University Press, 2001), pp. 187–88; Echevarria, *After Clausewitz*, pp. 121–81; Paul Kennedy, "Britain in the First World War," in Allan R. Millett and Williamson Murray, eds., *Military Effectiveness*, vol. 1 (Boston: Allen and Unwin, 1988), p. 50; House, *Combined Arms Warfare*, pp. 7–18; John English, *Infantry*, pp. 1–11.

13. Bidwell and Graham, *Firepower*, p. 31; Herrmann, *Arming of Europe*, pp. 81–83, 96; Echevarria, *After Clausewitz*, pp. 218–20.

14. Bidwell and Graham, *Firepower*, pp. 7–11, 22–30; Bailey, *Field Artillery and Firepower*, pp. 116–25; Prior and Wilson, *Command on the Western Front*, pp. 36–43.

15. See, e.g., Herrmann, *Arming of Europe*, pp. 199–224; Echevarria, *After Clausewitz* pp. 213–28; Bailey, *Field Artillery and Firepower*, pp. 127–30; Bidwell and Graham, *Firepower*, pp. 7–37.

16. Keegan, *Face of Battle*, p. 215.

17. Ibid., pp. 227–31; Bailey, *Field Artillery and Firepower*, pp. 130–41; Prior and Wilson, *Command on the Western Front*, pp. 154–70; Robin Prior and Trevor Wilson, *Passchendaele* (New Haven: Yale University Press, 1996), pp. 11–13.

18. Kennedy, "Britain," p. 55.

19. At Passchendaele, for example, Gough's XIV Corps captured two German defensive lines on the first day's fighting, advancing 3,000 yards at a cost of only 5,000 casualties. In the Battles of the Scarpe, various units took sections of the German forward trenches, and British attackers north of the Scarpe River advanced 1,000–1,500 yards on the opening day. Vimy Ridge and Messines produced even greater initial gains: Prior and Wilson, *Passchendaele*, pp. 55–66, 89–90; G. C. Wynne, *If Germany Attacks: The Battle in Depth in the West* (London: Faber and Faber, 1940; reprint Greenwood Press, 1976), pp. 168–88, 226–57.

20. The Germans termed this the *An-sich-herankommen-lassen*, or "invitation-to-walk-right-in," system: Wynne, *If Germany Attacks*, p. 149. Elsewhere it is typically termed the *elastic defense*. On its conduct and evolution, see, e.g., ibid., pp. 191–318; Timothy Lupfer, *Dynamics of Doctrine*, pp. 1–36; Griffith, *Forward into Battle*, pp. 75–85; Wilhelm Balck, *Development of Tactics, World War*, trans. Harry Bell (1920; reprint Ft. Leavenworth, KS: General Service Schools Press, 1922), pp. 151–68; Ritter von Leeb, *Defense*, trans. Stefan Possony and Daniel Vilfroy (1938; reprint Harrisburg, PA: Military Service Pub. Co., 1943), pp. 77–99.

21. See Bailey, *Field Artillery and Firepower*, pp. 141–52; Bidwell and Graham, *Firepower*, pp. 94–130, 139–46; Prior and Wilson, *Passchendaele*, pp. 311–15, 362–66; Wynne, *If Germany Attacks*, p. 327; Lupfer, *Dynamics of Doctrine*, pp. 43–46; Griffith, *Battle Tactics*, pp. 93–100, 120–58; Bruce Gudmundsson, *Stormtroop Tactics: Innovation in the German Army, 1914–1918* (New York: Praeger, 1989); English, *Infantry*, pp. 17–26; Sheffield, *Forgotten Victory*, pp. 221–63.

22. Bidwell and Graham, *Firepower*, pp. 61–148; Echevarria, *After Clausewitz*, pp. 1–12, 213–28; Sheffield, *Forgotten Victory*, pp. 112–13, 236–37.

23. The elite *stosstruppen* instructor units remained substantially more capable of modern system methods through the end of the war. On German implementation of the modern system, see Wynne, *If Germany Attacks*; Lupfer, *Dynamics of Doctrine*; Gudmundsson, *Stormtroop Tactics*; Holger Herwig, "The Dynamics of Necessity: German Military Policy during the First World War," in Allan R. Millett and Williamson Murray, eds., *Military Effectiveness*, vol. 1 (Boston: Allen and Unwin, 1988), p. 101.

24. See, e.g., Kennedy, "Britain," pp. 51, 69–70; Griffith, *Battle Tactics*, pp. 84–191; Niall Barr, "The Elusive Victory: The BEF and the Operational Level of War, September 1918,"

in Geoffrey Jensen and Andrew Wiest, eds., *War in the Age of Technology* (New York: New York University Press, 2001), pp. 211–38; Ian M. Brown, "Not Glamorous, but Effective: The Canadian Corps and the Set-piece Attack, 1917–1918," *Journal of Military History* 58 (July 1994), pp. 421–44.

25. Douglas Porch, "The French Army in the First World War," in Millett and Murray, *Military Effectiveness*, vol. 1, pp. 211–25.

26. On the German Spring Offensives, see, e.g., John Terraine, *To Win a War: 1918, The Year of Victory* (London: Sidgwick and Jackson, 1978), pp. 31–101; Barrie Pitt, *1918: The Last Act* (New York: Norton, 1962), pp. 75–192; C.R.M.F. Cruttwell, *A History of the Great War, 1914–1918* (Oxford: Clarendon Press, 1934), pp. 505–35.

27. See Terraine, *To Win a War*, pp. 102–260; Pitt, *1918*, pp. 193–267; Cruttwell, *A History of the Great War*, pp. 543–76; Griffith, *Battle Tactics*, p. 94.

28. Vincent Esposito, ed., *The West Point Atlas of American Wars*, vol. 2 (New York: Praeger, 1959), maps 62, 65, 69.

29. Terraine, *To Win a War*, p. 39; Martin Middlebrook, *The Kaiser's Battle* (London: Allen Lane, 1978), pp. 56, 322, 347.

30. As Bidwell and Graham put it: "The crews were exhausted by temperatures of well over 100 degrees Fahrenheit and the fumes and noise from engines and guns. A night on the march before a battle and another spent returning to harbour for maintenance usually meant thirty-six hours without sleep amid the strain of battle. Neither men nor machines were of much use on a second day of fighting" (*Firepower*, pp. 137–38). Or as the Royal Armoured Corps reported: "It is very often not realized what is meant by the exhaustion of the crews; this in the case of tanks does not merely mean bodily fatigue. The crews of one battalion after some hard fighting became absolutely exhausted and most of them physically ill. The pulses of one crew were taken immediately they got out of their tank; the beats averaged 130 to the minute or just twice as fast as they should have been. Two men of one crew temporarily lost their reason and had to be restrained by force, and one tank commander became delirious" (Royal Armoured Corps Papers, Bovington: "Short Report on Tank Corps Operations," as quoted in Terraine, *To Win a War*, p. 117).

31. Bidwell and Graham, *Firepower*, pp. 137–38.

32. John Terraine, *The Smoke and the Fire* (London: Sidgwick and Jackson, 1980), p. 154. As early as August 11, fully 480 of the 688 British tanks that had yet seen action in the war—70 percent of the total—had been sent to salvage as too badly damaged to be repaired at the unit level: Terraine, *To Win A War*, p. 116. On the tank's role in the 1918 offensives more generally, see esp. J. P. Harris, *Men, Tanks, and Ideas* (Manchester: Manchester University Press, 1995), pp. 59–94, 315–19; cf. Timothy Travers, *How the War Was Won* (London: Routledge, 1992), which attributes greater importance to the tank but understates contemporaneous improvement in British infantry and artillery tactics.

33. Others see German exhaustion as the main cause. Most recently, Niall Ferguson argues that Allied casualties were as heavy in the Hundred Days as previously and concludes from this that only a German loss of will enabled the Allied advance; tactical innovations were neither significant nor decisive: *The Pity of War* (New York: Basic Books, 1999 ed.), pp. 310–14. Yet the Germans, whom Ferguson sees as lacking motivation, suffered grievously to inflict those casualties; doing so required sustained resistance in the face of great personal risk. Broken armies can simply quit rather than fight at such huge cost; the Germans did not. If they had, the Allies' cost would have been vastly lower. German surrender rates were clearly higher in 1918, but this was often a consequence of battlefield

defeat, and the new Allied methods were defeating the Germans after the Second Battle of the Marne. The German surrenders followed local Allied victories, they did not precede them—they were effects, not causes. More broadly, Ferguson conflates effectiveness with casualty rates. Yet casualties are only one dimension of capability. The ability to take ground is also key—and Allied 1918 performance was dramatically different here. Whereas heavy losses yielded no meaningful ground gain before 1918, by March 1918 losses could be converted into territorial gain: armies willing to pay the price could now take and hold ground. Others who see Germany's defeat in the overextension or casualties suffered in the Spring Offensives—e.g., Travers, *How the War Was Won*, p. 175—must explain the Allies' subsequent ability to penetrate the Germans' prepared defenses of the Hindenburg Line at unremarkable local numerical odds: see, e.g., Griffith, *Battle Tactics*, pp. 84–100; Sheffield, *Forgotten Victory*, pp. 248–51.

34. See, e.g., Van Evera, "Cult of the Offensive," Snyder, *Ideology of the Offensive*, pp. 9–22; Liddell Hart, *Defence of Britain*, e.g., pp. 105, 120–21.

35. For a colorful account, see E. D. Swinton, *The Defence of Duffer's Drift* (1907; reprint Wayne, NJ: Avery, 1986), pp. 53–54.

36. L. G. Starkey et al., *Capabilities of Selected U.S. and Allied Antiarmor Weapon Systems* (Alexandria, VA: Weapon System Evaluation Group, May 1975), WSEG Report 263, declassified December 31, 1983, pp. 35–36; Warren Olson, *A Terrain Analysis of Four Tactical Situations* (Aberdeen, MD: U.S. Army Materiel Systems Analysis Agency, 1972), AMSAA Tech. Memorandum No. 158; Richard Simpkin, *Race to the Swift: Thoughts on Twenty-First Century Warfare* (New York: Brasseys, 1985), p. 69.

37. Assuming a battalion of eighteen 122 mm howitzers using airbursts given perfect accuracy and fire distribution: W. J. Schultis et al., *Comparison of Military Potential: NATO and Warsaw Pact* (Alexandria, VA: Weapon System Evaluation Group, June 1974), WSEG Report 238, declassified December 31, 1982, p. 67.

38. Assuming that the element identified is in the lead or on the flank of the formation.

39. Headquarters, Department of the Army, *FM 6–20: Fire Support in Combined Arms Operations* (Washington, DC: USGPO, 1977), pp. 3–9.

40. Terraine, "Indirect Fire," p. 11; James Edmonds, *Military Operations, France and Belgium 1918*, vol. 4 (London: His Majesty's Stationery Office, 1947), p. 23.

41. For the Allies, infantry-tank cooperation was also significant, at least for situations where operable tanks were available in quantity: Bidwell and Graham, *Firepower*, pp. 131–46; Griffith, *Battle Tactics*, pp. 165–69.

42. Bailey, *Field Artillery and Firepower*; Bidwell and Graham, *Firepower*, pp. 66–93; Shelford Bidwell, *Modern Warfare: A Survey of Men, Weapons, and Theories* (London: Allen Lane, 1973), pp. 53–59; House, *Combined Arms Warfare*, e.g., pp. 20–22; Griffith, *Battle Tactics*, pp. 135–58.

43. See, e.g., Gudmundsson, *Stormtroop Tactics*; Lupfer, *Dynamics of Doctrine*, pp. 37–54; English, *Infantry*, pp. 18–22; House, *Combined Arms Warfare*, pp. 25–27, 33–37; Griffith, *Battle Tactics*, pp. 192–200; Brown, "Not Glamorous," pp. 437–44; McInnes, *Men, Machines*; Sheffield, *Forgotten Victory*, pp. 221–63.

44. See, e.g., Bailey, *Field Artillery and Firepower*, pp. 132–34, 169–71, 184–86, Bidwell and Graham, *Firepower*, pp. 21, 253–57.

45. On the morale implications of dispersion under cover and the resulting "empty battlefield," see Richard Holmes, *Acts of War: The Behavior of Men in Battle* (New York: Free Press, 1986).

46. As in the techniques for tank-infantry intercommunication improvised in World War II: Michael D. Doubler, *Closing with the Enemy* (Lawrence: University Press of Kansas, 1994), e.g., pp. 16–17, 47–51.

47. Some armies suffer paralysis if their command and logistical infrastructure is destroyed, becoming incapable of further meaningful resistance. The French in 1940 are often cited as an example: see, e.g., Liddell Hart, *History of the Second World War*, pp. 73–74; Fuller, *Armament and History*, p. 149; Messenger, *Blitzkrieg*, p. 156. In fact, Fuller's theory of "strategic paralysis" holds that mental dislocation following mechanized breakthrough will ordinarily defeat armies without extensive destruction of their forces per se: see Fuller, e.g. *Lectures on FSR III* (London: Sifton Praed, 1932), pp. 7, 41; also Basil Liddell Hart, *Memoirs*, vol. 1 (New York: Putnam, 1965), pp. 159–68. Fuller was mistaken, however: as Operation BARBAROSSA demonstrated, encircled units fighting without higher command or logistical support can resist for extended periods if their morale and training are sufficient. See, e.g., Lester Grau, *Fighting within an Encirclement: A Comparison of National Concepts* (Ft. Leavenworth, KS: Soviet Army Studies Office, 1991); also Brian Holden Reid, *J.F.C. Fuller: Military Thinker* (New York: St. Martin's, 1987), pp. 157–58. Whether paralyzed or not, however, defenses are seriously disadvantaged by the loss of their supporting infrastructure, and this severely restricts their ability to avoid subsequent destruction should they continue to resist.

48. In fact, attackers who concentrate differentially can almost always obtain a greater advantage at the key point than the disadvantage they give away elsewhere. An invader with a theaterwide force equal to the defender's but concentrating differentially on an attack frontage of 50 kilometers out of a 600-kilometer frontier, for example, can obtain a 2:1 advantage on that frontage by accepting a 1:1.1 disadvantage elsewhere, or a 4:1 advantage by accepting a 1:1.3 disadvantage elsewhere, or a 6.5:1 advantage by accepting a 1:2 disadvantage elsewhere.

49. Breakthrough is thus an important intermediate variable for a theory of capability. To establish the ultimate dependent variable values of ground gain, duration, and casualties, one must first determine whether the offensive breaks through or is contained: see table 4.1 and the appendix.

50. See, e.g., Clausewitz's discussion of threats to the rear: *On War*, trans. Michael Howard and Peter Paret (1832; reprint Princeton: Princeton University Press, 1976), p. 233. Clausewitz's contemporary Jomini saw differential concentration as "the fundamental principle of war": Henri Jomini, *The Art of War*, trans. G. H. Mendell and W. P. Craighill (1862; reprint Westport, CT: Greenwood, 1971), pp. 70–71.

51. Effective deep battle would preserve the attacker's local numerical edge from differential concentration by preventing the defender from shifting reserves; given breakthrough, it would enhance exploitation's effects by blocking defensive counteractions. For discussions of deep battle theory, most of which focus on its later fruition in interwar and early World War II developments, see David Glantz, *Soviet Military Operational Art: In Pursuit of Deep Battle* (London: Frank Cass, 1991); Richard Simpkin, *Deep Battle* (Washington, DC: Brassey's, 1987); Shimon Naveh, *In Pursuit of Excellence: The Evolution of Operational Theory* (London: Frank Cass, 1997); Mary Ruth Habeck, "Imagining War: The Development of Armored Doctrine in Germany and the Soviet Union, 1919–1939" (Ph.D. diss., Yale University, 1996).

52. See, e.g., U.S. Air Force Historical Research Center: 512.621 v11/14, "Development of the German Ground Attack Arm and Principles Governing its Operations up to the

End of 1944," a study prepared by the German Air Historical Branch (8th Abteilung) dated 1 December 1944, pp. 1–2; also H. A. Jones, *The War in the Air* (Oxford: Clarendon, 1934), pp. 275, 363; S. F. Wise, *Canadian Airmen and the First World War*, vol. 1 (Toronto: University of Toronto Press, 1980), pp. 492–93; Lee Kennett, *The First Air War, 1914–1918* (New York: The Free Press, 1991), pp. 211–13; Jonathan Bailey, *The First World War and the Birth of the Modern Style of Warfare* (Camberley: British Army Strategic and Combat Studies Institute, 1996), SCSI Occasional Paper No. 22; Bidwell and Graham, *Firepower*, pp. 143–46; Griffith, *Battle Tactics*, pp. 156–57.

53. Plan 1919 is reprinted in J.F.C. Fuller, *Memoirs of an Unconventional Soldier* (London: Nicholson and Watson, 1936), pp. 322–36; see also Reid, *J.F.C. Fuller*, pp. 48–55.

54. RMA advocates often hold that deep strike is now, or will soon be, able to defeat armies by itself; chapter 4 presents an extended counterargument.

55. In addition to deep battle, a further twentieth-century adaptation concerns the way encirclement or isolation would be achieved: continuous fronts required an interior penetration—a breakthrough battle—first. While sometimes necessary even before 1900, it would become the norm thereafter.

56. On limited aims attacks in 1917–18, including their advantages and disadvantages, see, e.g., Prior and Wilson, *Command on the Western Front*, pp. 289–398; Prior and Wilson, *Passchendaele*, pp. 31–66, 194–200.

57. In 1977 Normandy, for example, an attack frontage of at least 4 km would typically be needed to provide even a single hard-surface east-west route transiting a notional 15-km-deep defended zone; to provide two nonintersecting routes free of hostile artillery fire over a 15-km zone would require a frontage of at least 34-km (assuming artillery of 20-km range with a 6-km setback): *Institut Geographique National Carte Serie M761, Feuille XVI-13 (Mezidon)*. For theaters with less-developed road networks than modern France, even wider frontages would be needed.

58. Narrow fronts also reduce the space available for dispersed modern system tactics, requiring attackers to echelon forces at the point of attack: Stephen Biddle et al., *Defense at Low Force Levels* (Alexandria, VA: Institute for Defense Analyses, 1991), IDA P-2380.

59. In fact, British topographic maps in 1916 and 1917 were produced with the locations of named friendly and enemy trench lines preprinted on the maps by the publishers in Britain before being shipped to the troops on the continent: see, e.g., Peter Chasseaud, *Trench Maps: A Cartobibliography* (Lewes, Sussex: Mapbooks, 1986).

60. Lupfer, *Dynamics of Doctrine*, p. 15. On the importance of defensive concealment in general, see, e.g., Headquarters, Department of the Army, *FM 5-103, Survivability* (Washington, DC: USGPO, 1985).

61. On interlocking fields of fire, see, e.g., Headquarters, Department of the Army, *FM 7-7J, Mechanized Infantry Platoon and Squad, Bradley* (Washington, DC: USGPO, 1993), pp. 2-116 to 2-122.

62. Lupfer, *Dynamics of Doctrine*, pp. 13–16; Wynne, *If Germany Attacks*, pp. 150–58; Timothy Wray, *Standing Fast: German Defensive Doctrine on the Russian Front during World War II* (Ft. Leavenworth, KS: U.S. Army Combat Studies Institute, 1986), pp. 3–5, 118–23.

63. In fact, withdrawal under pressure is among the modern battlefield's most technically challenging maneuvers. It is easy to turn a tactical setback into a rout via poorly implemented withdrawal. For a recent assessment, see Headquarters, Department of the Army, *FM 3-90, Tactics* (Washington, DC: USGPO, 2001), pp. 11-1 to 11-31.

64. While machine guns can be fired indirectly, their relatively flat trajectory limits their ability to hit targets in the lee of masking terrain; indirect machine gun fire is restricted mainly to suppressive "barrage fire" directed over the heads of attacking infantry to land in the defenders' positions on the objective. Though First World War machine gunners were intrigued with such methods, they proved of limited practical utility. See, e.g., G. S. Hutchison, *Machine Guns: Their History and Tactical Employment* (London: Macmillan, 1938); Griffith, *Battle Tactics*, pp. 123–24.

65. See, e.g., House, *Combined Arms Warfare*; Headquarters, Department of the Army, *FM 7-8, Infantry Rifle Platoon and Squad* (Washington, DC: USGPO, 2001), pp. 2–74.

66. On the complexity of using ground properly in the tactical defense, see, e.g., Swinton, *Duffer's Drift*.

67. Note that although a less-dense modern system defense allows a modern system attacker somewhat more speed for the same losses, the difference is small relative to the speed attainable in the absence of a modern system tactical defense: see appendix.

68. Lupfer, *Dynamics of Doctrine,* pp. 12, 13–16; Wynne, *If Germany Attacks,* pp. 142, 155–56; Wray, *Standing Fast*, pp. 1–21; Griffith, *Forward into Battle*, pp. 79–80.

69. This analysis echoes Clausewitz's discussion of the "culminating point of the attack": see *On War*, book 7, chaps. 2–5, pp. 524–28.

70. Light "fixing attacks" can make it costly for forward defenders away from the key sector to break contact, withdraw, and shift laterally to reinforce elsewhere. This is a consequence of the great difference in weapon effectiveness against exposed as opposed to covered targets. When dug into prepared positions, forward defenders are covered and concealed and can thus survive all but very heavy fire. To leave these positions often requires exposure, which radically increases vulnerability. Of course, just as attackers can limit exposure by careful use of terrain, suppressive fire, dispersion, and combined arms, so can defenders in retrograde movements. But just as such methods take time for attackers, so they impose delay on defenders in withdrawal. And neither attackers nor defenders can move under fire without losses. While modern-system movement techniques reduce these losses to allow locally superior attackers to take ground, they cannot eliminate losses altogether, and defenders typically do not enjoy a large numerical advantage over the attackers who seek to fix them in place. Defenders in withdrawal can thus suffer larger proportional casualties even when they move cautiously. Reserves in assembly areas behind the front, by contrast, can redeploy with neither the delays nor the losses associated with disengagement. Note that much of the controversy over the U.S. Army's "Active Defense" doctrine of the mid-1970s stemmed from skepticism over the practicality of the doctrine's provisions for lateral displacement in lieu of withheld reserves: John Romjue, *From Active Defense to AirLand Battle* (Ft. Monroe, VA: U.S. Army Training and Doctrine Command, 1984), pp. 19–21.

71. Counterattack also reduces attackers' ability to exploit differential concentration. To concentrate differentially at the point of attack is to accept risks elsewhere; the greater the concentration, the greater the risk. A large defensive reserve able to counterattack at a point of the defender's choosing makes such risks more dangerous, encouraging attackers to divert forces into flank protection and reducing the attacker's ability to create large local superiorities at the invader's point of attack. For example, an invader at theaterwide numerical parity who faces a powerful counterattack threat and can thus tolerate no worse than a 1:1.1 numerical disadvantage on its flanks can amass no more than a 2:1 local advantage in its main effort; if a weaker counterattack threat enables the invader to

get away with a 1:2 disadvantage elsewhere, the local preponderance in the main attack sector can be as great as 6.5:1.

72. See, e.g., Headquarters, Department of the Army, *FM100-5: Operations* (Washington, DC: USGPO, 1982), pp. 158–60.

73. See, e.g., COL Ted A. Cimral, "Moving the Heavy Corps," *Military Review* 68, 7 (July 1988), pp. 28–34.

74. Roger L. L. Facer, *Conventional Forces and the NATO Strategy of Flexible Response* (Santa Monica: RAND, 1985), pp. 15–17. In fact, NATO's actual plans, by contrast with its declaratory policy, quietly provided for considerable defensive depth: Biddle et al., *Defense at Low Force Levels*, pp. 39–40.

75. Ariel Levite, *Offense and Defense in Israeli Military Doctrine* (Boulder, Westview Press, 1990); Strachan, *First World War*, p. 163.

76. Facer, *Conventional Forces*, pp. 59–64.

77. Nicholas Kristof, "Bills Allow Japan to Back up U.S.," *New York Times*, April 28, 1999.

78. Stephen Biddle and Robert Zirkle, "Technology, Civil-Military Relations, and Warfare in the Developing World," *Journal of Strategic Studies* 19, 2 (June 1996), pp. 171–212; Risa Brooks, *Political-Military Relations and the Stability of Arab Regimes* (London: IISS, 1998), Adelphi Paper No. 324.

79. See, e.g., Travers, *The Killing Ground*.

80. Stephen Peter Rosen, "Military Effectiveness: Why Society Matters," *International Security* 19, 4 (Spring 1995), pp. 5–31.

81. Kiesling, *Arming against Hitler*; Elizabeth Kier, *Imagining War* (Princeton: Princeton University Press, 1997).

82. See, e.g., Samuel Huntington, *The Soldier and the State: The Theory and Politics of Civil-Military Relations* (Cambridge: Harvard University Press, 1957), p. 82; Amos Perlmutter and Valerie Plave Bennett, eds., *The Political Influence of the Military* (New Haven: Yale University Press, 1980), pp. 205–8; Eliot Cohen, "Distant Battles: Modern War in the Third World," *International Security* 10, 4 (Spring 1986), p. 168.

83. For a more detailed discussion, see Biddle and Zirkle, "Technology," pp. 171–212.

84. Kenneth M. Pollack, "The Influence of Arab Culture on Arab Military Effectiveness" (Ph.D. diss., MIT, 1996); Wade Hinkle et al., *Why Nations Differ in Military Skill* (Alexandria: Institute for Defense Analyses, 1999), IDA D-2372. On the importance of strategic culture for Chinese military behavior, see Johnson, "Strategic Culture." Michael Desch, "Culture Clash: Assessing the Importance of Ideas in Security Studies," *International Security* 23, 1 (Summer 1998), pp. 141–70, sees culture as a potentially valuable explanation of apparently suboptimal behavior—as I would characterize non–modern-system force employment.

85. George C. Wilson, *This War Really Matters: Inside the Fight for Defense Dollars* (Washington, DC: CQ Press, 2000), p. 50.

86. The Cabinet agreed in principle to rescind the Rule on March 23, 1932, but this did not become effective until February 15, 1933. Public Records Office: AIR 41/39, appendix 1.

87. James Kitfield, *Prodigal Soldiers* (New York: Simon and Schuster, 1995), pp. 299–320.

88. On the military and nonmilitary determinants of doctrine, see Posen, *Sources of Military Doctrine*; Snyder, *Ideology of the Offensive*; Stephen Peter Rosen, *Winning the Next War: Innovation and the Modern Military* (Ithaca: Cornell University Press, 1991); Kimberly Zisk, *Engaging the Enemy: Organization Theory and Soviet Military Innovations, 1955–1991* (Princeton: Princeton University Press, 1993); Deborah Avant, *Political Institutions and*

Military Change (Ithaca: Cornell University Press, 1994); Allan C. Stam III, *Win, Lose or Draw* (Ann Arbor: University of Michigan Press, 1996); Kier, *Imagining War.*

CHAPTER FOUR
THE MODERN SYSTEM, PREPONDERANCE, AND CHANGING TECHNOLOGY

1. See, e.g., William J. Perry, "Desert Storm and Deterrence," *Foreign Affairs* 70, 4 (Fall 1991), pp. 66–82; Andrew F. Krepinevich, "Cavalry to Computer: The Pattern of Military Revolutions," *The National Interest*, no. 37 (Fall 1994), pp. 30–42; Toffler, *War and Anti-War*; Eliot Cohen, "A Revolution in Warfare," *Foreign Affairs* 75, 2 (March/April 1996), pp. 37–54.

2. Headquarters, Department of the Army, *FM 5-103: Survivability* (Washington, DC: USGPO, 1985), p. 4–13.

3. See, e.g., Swinton, *Duffer's Drift*, pp. 35, 48.

4. Schultis et al., *Military Potential*, p. 65, assuming for the 8-inch howitzer, M404 ICM ammunition vs. exposed targets and M106 HE ammunition vs. targets in foxholes, and for the 105-mm, HE ammunition vs both. For range, see David Isby and Charles Kamps, *Armies of NATO's Central Front* (New York: Jane's, 1985), pp. 414–15, assuming M102/HE as a proxy for 1942 ordnance.

5. Especially through improved communications, and most recently via new techniques for reducing errors in self-location by spotters in the field: R. B. Pengelley, "HELBAT: The Way to Tomorrow's Artillery," *International Defense Review* 13, 1 (1980), pp. 83–88.

6. Artillery spotters do have two advantages over direct-fire weapons against covered targets. First, they can sometimes use higher elevation (e.g., observation posts in church steeples or hilltops) to see over low obstructions and lengthen their field of view. Second, they can tolerate greater error in target location (since artillery is an area-fire, rather than a point-fire, weapon), hence targets whose general location is known but which have hidden behind minor terrain features can still be engaged. Neither advantage is unalloyed, however. Elevation increases vulnerability: elevated points stand out, attracting hostile fire. Most observers are thus taught to avoid conspicuous elevation and must observe from surface level like the direct-fire shooters around them. Artillery observers' ability to tolerate error also has limits; even tactical nuclear weapons require reasonably accurate target locations: Victor Utgoff and W.M. Christenson, "Battlefield Nuclear Forces," in Stephen Biddle and Peter Feaver, eds., *Battlefield Nuclear Weapons: Issues and Options* (Lanham, MD: University Press of America, 1989), pp. 97–124, 128–34.

7. See, e.g. Griffith, *Battle Tactics*, pp. 153–54; Bidwell and Graham, *Firepower*, pp. 109–10.

8. See, e.g., J. Bailey, *Field Artillery and Firepower*, pp. 60–61; Headquarters, Department of the Army, *FM 6-20-1: Field Artillery Cannon Battalion* (Washington, DC: USGPO, 1983), pp. 1-19 to 1-26.

9. See, e.g., *FM 6–20*, pp. 1-44 to 1-45.

10. Swanborough and Bowers, *Military Aircraft*, pp. 241, 248, 329.

11. On January 29, 1991, for example, three Iraqi armored columns totaling over two brigades attempted an offensive against Coalition forces in the Gulf War. One brigade reached and briefly held the Saudi town of Khajfi, but the other two were caught in the open by Coalition aircraft and annihilated in a matter of hours: *GWAPS*, vol. 2, pt. I,

pp. 273–74; Scales, *Certain Victory*, pp. 189–91. In fact, massed aircraft operating with air supremacy have long been able to inflict extreme damage on exposed ground forces. In 1944, for example, German ground forces trying to escape the Falaise Pocket suffered staggering losses to Allied air attack: Ian Gooderson, *Air Power at the Battlefront* (London: Cass, 1998), pp. 117–19; Martin Blumenson, *Breakout and Pursuit* (Washington, DC: Office of the Chief of Military History, 1961), pp. 506–58. While the time and aircraft numbers needed have fallen, massed ground forces caught in the open have been vulnerable for a long time.

12. RAF night bombers encountered serious difficulties hitting even targets as large and static as cities in World War II; small mobile targets were all but immune to night attack: see, e.g., T. Biddle, *Rhetoric and Reality*, pp. 184–85, 195.

13. The only weapon routinely able to hit targets through cloud cover in the recent NATO air campaign in Kosovo, for example, was the Joint Direct Attack Munition (JDAM), delivered by U.S. B-2 bombers. JDAMs constituted a minority of all NATO ordnance delivered in the war: Benjamin Lambeth, *NATO's Air War for Kosovo* (Santa Monica: RAND, 2001), pp. 88, 91.

14. See, e.g., Headquarters, Department of the Army, *FM 7-92: The Infantry Reconnaissance Platoon and Squad* (Washington, DC: USGPO, 1992), appendix A: Limited Visibility Operations. For a more technical treatment of radar and laser attenuation, see Merrill Skolnik, *Radar Handbook*, 2d ed. (New York: McGraw Hill, 1990), pp. 1.13–1.18, 23.5–23.10.

15. *United States Strategic Bombing Survey*, Vol. 62: *Weather Factors in Combat Bombardment Operations in the European Theater*, 2d ed. (Washington, DC: USGPO, 1947), p. 8. Moreover, cloud cover of at least 50 percent, considered too great for accurate bombing in 1945, can be expected almost two-thirds of the time: ibid.

16. Department of the Army, *FM 100-5*, pp. 13-10 to 13-12.

17. William S. Cohen and Henry H. Shelton, "Joint Statement on the Kosovo after Action Review," presented to the Senate Armed Services Committee, October 14, 1999. Defense Dept. News Release No. 478–99, p. 11.

18. Alan Vick et al., *Enhancing Air Power's Contribution against Light Infantry Targets* (Santa Monica, CA: RAND, 1996), pp. 13–30; Peter Brooks and Edward Smith, "Evaluation of Airborne Surveillance Systems," *IDA Research Summaries* 3, 1 (Winter/Spring 1996), pp. 4–5; Dominick Giglio, "Overview of Foliage/Ground Penetration and Interferometric SAR Experiments," *SPIE Proceedings*, 2230 (1994), pp. 209–17.

19. Robert H. Scales, Jr., "Accuracy Defeated Range in Artillery Duel," *International Defense Review* 24, 5 (May 1991), pp. 478–79; Vick et al., *Enhancing Air Power's Contribution*, pp. 19–20. The use of COMINT and SIGINT for surveillance rather than target acquisition is discussed below.

20. On the DARPA FOLPEN (foliage penetrating radar) initiative, see Michael O'Hanlon, *Technological Change and the Future of Warfare* (Washington, DC: Brookings, 2000), p. 49; Giglio, "Foliage/Ground Penetration"; Vick et al., *Enhancing Air Power's Contribution*, pp. 17–20.

21. Victor Utgoff and Ivan Oelrich, "Confidence-building with Unmanned Sensors," in Barry Blechman, ed., *Technology and the Limitation of International Conflict* (Lanham, MD: University Press of America, 1989), pp. 13–31.

22. The low-frequency radars needed for foliage penetration require large apertures to provide the necessary resolution; for a terminal guidance system whose physical aperture is limited to the weapon's diameter, this would require synthetic aperture (SAR)

techniques. These are expensive for use in an expendable munition and would also be impractical for terminal descent, since SAR flight paths must be offset from the direction of surveillance (most current SARs use flight paths roughly perpendicular to the direction of surveillance). See John W. Sherman, III, "Aperture-antenna Analysis," in Skolnik, ed., *Radar Handbook*, 1st ed., pp. 9.1–9.40. Munition guidance might thus have to be provided by reference to an external coordinate system (such as the global positioning system, or GPS), in whose terms target locations could be described and transmitted to the munition. Since initial target location errors cannot be overcome by terminal homing, such a weapon would suffer compounding of inaccuracies arising from the surveillance device and the guidance system of the munition itself. On the relative accuracy of terminal guidance and GPS/inertial systems, see David Fulghum, "Small Smart Bomb to Raise Stealth Aircraft's Punch," *Aviation Week and Space Technology*, February 27, 1995, pp. 50ff.

23. Central Intelligence Agency, *The World Factbook, 1999*, available at www.odci.gov/cia/publications/factbook; Hans Essmann, "Land Use and Forest Policies to Enhance Biodiversity in Germany," Finnish Forest Research Institute, available at www.metla.fi/conf/iufro95abs/d6pap104.htm (both accessed January 19, 2002).

24. CIA, *World Factbook*.

25. Ibid.; *Statistical Abstract of the United States* (Washington, DC: U.S. Census Bureau, 1995), table 365.

26. media.maps.com/magellan/images/BAGHDA-W1.gif.

27. Of the 45 kilometers covered in this route (roughly Bretteville-sur-Laize to May-sur-Orne to Caen to Benouville to Ouistreham), 38.9 would be covered to overhead observation. The length of the median exposed stretch is 175 meters, with the longest single exposed stretch being 1300 meters. At a nominal cross-country speed of 6 kilometers per hour for dismounted infantry, the median exposure to overhead observation would thus last about two minutes: *Institut Geographique National Carte Serie M761, Feuilles XVI-12 (Caen)* and *XVI-13 (Mezidon)*. Of the 162 square kilometers of Northwest Durham County, North Carolina, surrounding the office where this book was written, more than 95 percent of all 1-km grid squares contain at least some cover (over 60 percent of the total area is forested, and over 15 percent is built up); many paths exist by which dismounted units could traverse the area with under 100 meters of total exposure in months where deciduous trees are in leaf: U.S. Department of the Interior Geological Survey Map, Northwest Durham, NC, SW/4 Durham North, 15' Quadrangle, 36078-A8-TF-024, rev. 1987.

28. NATO currently claims to have killed 93 tanks, 153 armored personnel carriers, 389 mortars, anti-aircraft guns, and artillery pieces, plus 339 "other military vehicles": Gen. Wesley Clark and Brig. Gen. John Corley, "Press Conference on the Kosovo Strike Assessment," NATO Headquarters Brussels, September 16, 1999, p. 9. These figures are 10–15 percent below initial claims and are not necessarily authoritative (only 26 destroyed tank hulks were ever found on the battlefield, for example; the great majority of claimed kills are based on softer data). Serb holdings in Kosovo are estimated to have been 350 tanks, 430–50 armored personnel carriers, and 750 mortars, anti-aircraft guns, and artillery pieces: ibid. Serb holdings overall were far larger: International Institute for Strategic Studies, *The Military Balance, 1998/99*, pp. 99–100.

29. MHI, Tape 032602p, CPT M. int.

30. MHI, Tape 032602a, CPT H. et al. int.

31. MHI, Tape 032802a, MAJ D. int.; Tape 032602a, CPT H. et al. int.

32. MHI: Tape 041902p, LTC Briley int.; Tape 042002p, LTC Gray int.; Tape 041802p, LTC Lundy int.; Tape 041802p, LTC Preysler int.; Tape 041902a, MAJ Busko int.; Tape 041902a, CPT Murphy int.; Tape 041902a, CPT Lecklenburg int. For a more detailed discussion of sensor performance in Afghanistan, see Biddle, *Afghanistan*, pp. 26–33.

33. On al Qaeda's tactical shortcomings, see MHI, Tape 032802a, MAJ D. int.; Tape 041902a, CPT Lecklenburg int.; Tape 041902a, CPT Murphy int.; Tape 041902a, MAJ Busko int.

34. Some now expect unmanned reconnaissance drones to provide near-continuous aerial surveillance, but as ground forces learn to shoot them down, their vulnerability will limit their ability to loiter indefinitely over battlefields. In 1999, for example, NATO lost fifteen drones over Kosovo, most to hostile ground fire, and this against air defenses that had not been specially adapted to small targets: Cohen and Shelton, "Joint Statement on the Kosovo AAR," p. 14.

35. Gordon and Trainor, *The Generals' War*, pp. 267–88, 363–69, 387; Scales, *Certain Victory*, pp. 232–36, 266.

36. MHI, Tape 041902a, CPT Lecklenburg int.; Tape 041902a, CPT Murphy int.

37. See, e.g., R. M. Ogorkiewicz, "Automating Tank Fire Controls," *International Defense Review* 24, 9 (September 1991), pp. 973–74; Stephen Biddle, "Can Conventional Forces Substitute for Battlefield Nuclear Weapons?" in Biddle and Feaver, eds., *Battlefield Nuclear Weapons*, pp. 74–81.

38. See, e.g., Defense Science Board, *Summer Study Task Force on Tactics and Technology for 21st Century Military Superiority* (Washington, DC: Department of Defense, 1996); Stuart Johnson and Martin Libicki, *Dominant Battlespace Knowledge* (Washington, DC: National Defense University, 1996).

39. The U.S. M58, for example, is an M113 armored personnel carrier modified as a dedicated obscurant smoke transporter and dispenser. Its entire payload produces only thirty minutes of continuous coverage against infrared sensors: www.uniteddefense.com/www.m113.com/m58.html (accessed January 19, 2002).

40. On synergies between modern technical countermeasures and traditional cover, concealment, and dispersion, see Gen. John Shalikashvili, *Joint Vision 2010* (Washington, DC: Joint Staff, 1996), pp. 15–16. For an overview and technical assessment of countermeasure developments, see O'Hanlon, *Technological Change*, pp. 45–52, 58–64.

41. More formally, to hold survivability constant as technology improves requires ever more complete modern-system implementation. On the relationship between technological change and modern-system implementation, see the appendix, figures A.10–A.14 and accompanying text.

42. Martin Van Creveld, *Supplying War* (New York: Cambridge University Press, 1977), p. 116; Von Senger und Etterlin, *German Tanks*, p. 194; Foss, ed., *Jane's Armour and Artillery*, p. 143. For a review of recent developments, see O'Hanlon, *Technological Change*, chap. 4.

43. See, e.g., Liddell Hart, *The Real War*, pp. 249–51; Liddell Hart, *History of the Second World War*, pp. 65–86; Ropp, *War in the Modern World*, pp. 267–70; Brodie, *Crossbow to H-Bomb*, pp. 196–99; Messenger, *Blitzkrieg*; Perret, *History of Blitzkrieg*. Cf. Harris, "Myth of Blitzkrieg," pp. 335–52.

44. See, e.g., Simpkin, *Race to the Swift*; Giulio Douhet, *The Command of the Air* (1921; reprint Washington, DC: Office of Air Force History, 1983).

45. See, e.g., the accounts in Daniel P. Bolger, *Dragons at War: 2-34 Infantry in the Mohave* (Novato, CA: Presidio Press, 1986).

46. This capacity is sometimes called "simultaneity" or "simultaneous operations." On simultaneity, see, e.g., Headquarters, Department of the Air Force, *AFM 1-1: Basic Aerospace Doctrine of the United States Air Force* (Washington, DC: US GPO, 1992), vol. 1, p. 5; Morris J. Boyd and Michael Woodgerd, "Force XXI Operations," *Military Review* 74, 11 (November 1994), pp. 22–24; Michael J. Mazarr, *The Military-Technical Revolution: A Structural Framework* (Washington, DC: Center for Strategic and International Studies, 1993), pp. 25–27; U.S. Army Training and Doctrine Command, *TRADOC Pamphlet 525–5: Force XXI Operations* (Ft. Monroe, VA: TRADOC, August 1994), pp. 2-8 to 2-11.

47. Hence even for defenders, systemic increases in platform speed have not been fully realizable in faster counterconcentration against opponents with modern-system deep attack capabilities. For a more detailed treatment of the net effect of systemic increases in platform speed for attackers and defenders, see the appendix.

48. On command post security techniques, see, e.g., Headquarters, Department of the Army, *FM 71-3: The Armored and Mechanized Infantry Brigade* (Washington, DC: USGPO, 1996), pp. 3-10 to 3-21.

49. Ground force exploitation of breakthrough, by contrast, can stop hostile movement altogether by imposing an impenetrable cordon of persistent ground troops across both open and covered terrain; it can destroy hostile supplies directly even when stockpiled in forests or towns; and it can overrun command posts whatever the enemy's success in signature suppression or local security precautions. Ground force exploitation thus offers more complete denial of hostile infrastructure than does deep strike alone.

50. On the "information revolution," see especially Tofflers, *War and Antiwar*; Joseph Nye and William Owens, "America's Information Edge," *Foreign Affairs* 75, 2 (March/April 1996), pp. 21–36. On the history of information technology, see especially, Martin Van Creveld, *Technology in War* (New York: Free Press, 1989); also Alfred Price, *Instruments of Darkness: The History of Electronic Warfare* (London: Macdonald and Jane's, 1977).

51. Note that complete knowledge by attackers would not have the same consequences. Modern-system defensive operations assume attackers will choose the defense's weakest point. Depth and reserves are intended precisely to allow the defender to recover from this by containing the offensive while counterconcentrating, and to provide enough combat power in the reserve to make counterconcentration effective. Modern-system defensive operations are thus designed to hedge against the inherent information superiority initiative affords attackers; increasing this asymmetry via attacker-favorable information improvements would only make this more important.

52. In Afghanistan, for example, al Qaeda made extensive use of dummy fighting positions; together with cover and concealment, this created significant uncertainly over their actual strength and dispositions in Operation ANACONDA. MHI, AFZS-LF-B, Memo, FOB 3/3 SSE Support Intelligence Summary, March 25–29, 2002; Tape 041902p, LTC Briley int.

53. See, e.g., Richard K. Betts, *Surprise Attack* (Washington, DC: Brookings, 1982); James Wirtz, *The Tet Offensive: Intelligence Failure in War* (Ithaca: Cornell University Press, 1991); Ephraim Kam, *Surprise Attack: The Victim's Perspective* (Cambridge: Harvard University Press, 1988); Roberta Wohlstetter, *Pearl Harbor: Warning and Decision* (Stanford: Stanford University Press, 1962); Klaus Knorr, "Threat Perception," in Knorr, ed., *Historical Dimensions of National Security Problems* (Lawrence: University Press of Kansas, 1976); Michael Handel, *Perception, Deception and Surprise: The Case of the Yom Kippur War* (Jerusalem: Hebrew University of Jerusalem, 1976); Barton Whaley, *Codeword Barbarossa* (Cambridge: MIT Press, 1973); Amos Perlmutter and John Gooch, eds., "Special Issue on

Military Deception and Strategic Surprise," *Journal of Strategic Studies* 5, 1 (1982); Klaus Knorr and Patrick Morgan, eds., *Strategic Military Surprise* (New Brunswick, NJ: Transaction, 1983). For a heterodox view, see Ariel Levite, *Intelligence and Strategic Surprises* (New York: Columbia University Press, 1987).

54. See especially Jervis, *Perception and Misperception*; also Richard Ned Lebow, *Between Peace and War: The Nature of International Crisis* (Baltimore: Johns Hopkins University Press, 1981); Lebow, "Deterrence: A Political and Psychological Critique," in Paul C. Stern et al., eds., *Perspectives on Deterrence* (New York: Oxford University Press, 1989), pp. 25–51.

55. Roy Appleman, *South to the Naktong, North to the Yalu* (Washington, DC: Office of the Chief of Military History, 1961), pp. 751–65; Billy Mossman, *Ebb and Flow: November 1950–July 1951* (Washington, DC: Center of Military History, U.S. Army, 1990), pp. 61–83.

56. Personal communication, LTC Andrew Milani, USA, Carlisle Barracks PA, November 26, 2002.

57. T. L. Cubbage, "German Misapprehensions Regarding Overlord," in Michael Handel, ed., *Strategic and Operational Deception in the Second World War* (London: Cass, 1987), pp. 114–74.

58. See, e.g., Thomas Landauer, *The Trouble with Computers* (Cambridge: MIT Press, 1996); W. Wayt Gibbs, "Taking Computers to Task," *Scientific American* 277, 1 (July 1997), pp. 82–89.

59. Patton's Third Army, for example, required forty-eight hours to plan and execute a hundred-mile movement from front-line positions near Saarbrucken to counterattack locations around Bastogne at the Battle of the Bulge; this is widely considered a remarkable achievement. See, e.g., Paul Munch, "Patton's Staff and the Battle of the Bulge," *Military Review* 7, 5 (May 1990), pp. 46–54.

60. Henry L. Mason, "War Comes to the Netherlands: September 1939–May 1940," *Political Science Quarterly* 78, 4 (December 1963), pp. 557, 562–64.

61. In 1918, for example, the Allies learned enough to conclude that the Germans were preparing a major spring offensive that would probably strike the British Third and Fifth Army's sectors, which it did. This did not prevent the Germans from achieving differential concentration: see, e.g., Travers, *How the War Was Won*, pp. 51–53; Terraine, *White Heat*, pp. 282–83.

62. Some RMA proponents argue that defenders will soon be able to defend with long-range fires alone, obviating the need to move and dig-in masses of ground forces at the point of attack. If so, this would remove the logistical constraints on response described above. But while this might suffice against attackers who mass in the open, attackers who implement modern-system exposure reduction techniques would be much less vulnerable, making defense via long-range fires alone extremely risky.

63. See chapter 2. For a review of historical efforts to provide decisive technological asymmetries, see George Raudzens, "War Winning Weapons: The Measurement of Technological Determinism in Military History," *Journal of Military History* 54, 4 (October 1990), pp. 403–34. Even in nineteenth-century colonial warfare, where technology was extraordinarily asymmetrical, indigenous armies sometimes defeated European forces with vastly superior weapons. At Isandlwana in 1879, for example, Zulus armed mainly with spears defeated a British force with modern rifles: Donald Morris, *The Washing of the Spears: The Rise and Fall of the Zulu Nation* (New York: Simon and Schuster, 1965), pp. 352–88.

64. See, e.g., *Jane's Weapon Systems, 1988–89* (Coulsden, Surrey: Jane's, 1988).

65. Vipin Gupta, "New Satellite Images for Sale," *International Security* 20, 1 (Summer 1995), pp. 94–125; Ann Florini, "The Opening Skies: Third-Party Imaging Satellites and U.S. Security," *International Security* 13, 2 (Fall 1988), pp. 91–123.

66. See, e.g., Clive Walker, ed., *Jane's C⁴I Systems, 2000–2001* (Coulsden, Surrey: Jane's, 2000).

67. Some argue that America is now so far ahead that it alone can exploit the RMA, hence its lead will only widen: see, e.g., Joseph Nye and William Owens, "America's Information Edge," *Foreign Affairs* 75, 2 (March/April 1996), pp. 21–36. Others expect the opposite—that late entrants will more readily overtake the early leader due to the particular nature of new information technology: see, e.g., Krepinevich, "Cavalry to Computer," pp. 30–42. The latter is more consistent with the historical trend; yet even the current U.S. lead is insufficient to overcome adverse force employment, as I argue below.

68. Unhindered by suppression, a single TOW missile crew can kill as many as seven targets in five minutes at ranges of up to three kilometers; if the crew is forced by suppressive fire to take cover and reposition between shots, its kill rate can be cut to one or less even if the crew is unharmed: L. G. Starkey et al., *Capabilities of Selected U.S. and Allied Antiarmor Weapon Systems* (Alexandria, VA: Weapon System Evaluation Group, May 1975), WSEG Report 263, declassified Dec. 31, 1983, p. 49, for M113/TOW combination ca. 1975. By forcing hostile artillery to "shoot and scoot," counterbattery suppression can reduce its targets' net firing rate by a factor of ten or more even if it kills none: Vick et al., *Enhancing Air Power's Contribution*, p. 49, assuming five to ten minutes to reach and occupy new firing positions, recompute firing data, and commence firing.

69. Starkey et al., *Capabilities*, pp. 35–36, implies 1–2-km difference in range of first observation for tanks attacking typical weapon sites in the North German Plain and Fulda Gap as a function of their approach route.

70. For rates of change in maximum weapon range, see Biddle, "Past as Prologue," p. 69.

71. For a formal analysis of tradeoffs between weapon quantity and quality as a function of force employment, see the appendix.

72. On the ground forces in Afghanistan, see Biddle, *Afghanistan*, pp. 38–49.

73. MHI, Tape 032602a, CPT H. et al. int.; Memorandum for the Record, CPT H. int., July 2, 2002.

74. MHI, Tape 042002p, LTC Gray int.; Memorandum for the Record, COL J. int., July 2, 2002.

75. Clark and Corley, "Press Conference on the Kosovo Strike Assessment," p. 9.

76. Ironically, perhaps the most important effect of radically one-sided technology would be if it could enable its holders to ignore parts of the modern system (and its burdens) themselves while forcing their opponents to use it. Complete command of the skies, for example, might enable its possessor to move safely in the open in friendly rear areas while denying this to the enemy. Exposed movement is much faster, hence this would be an important advantage—though not a sufficient advantage to enable breakthrough against a modern-system defense or stop a modern-system attack cold in its tracks.

77. Hogg and Weeks, *Military Small Arms*, pp. 205, 210, 220.

78. Schultis et al., *Military Potential*, p. 65.

79. Isby and Kamps, *NATO's Central Front*, pp. 50–51, assuming four shots per minute. In 1991 U.S. tank crews attained firing rates of over ten rounds per minute: Michael Krause, *The Battle of 73 Easting, 26 February 1991* (Washington, DC: U.S. Army Center for

Military History and the Defense Advanced Research Projects Agency, 27 August 1991), pp. 11–12; personal communcation, MAJ H. R. McMaster, USA, September 8, 1995.

80. Deliberate, successful, firepower-saturating "human wave" tactics are rare historically; most alleged examples reflect defenders' flawed perception rather than attackers' actual behavior. Even the Chinese in Korea relied heavily on infiltration and flank attacks rather than merely throwing exposed forces at dug-in defenses frontally: Clay Blair, *The Forgotten War* (New York: Doubleday, 1988), p. 382; Max Hastings, *The Korean War* (New York: Simon and Schuster, 1987), p. 335.

81. By contrast, the defender's manning requirements are constant with increasing penetration depth. Attackers within the prepared defenses are moving through a pregarrisoned area: defenders were deployed throughout this zone before the assault began. The deeper the defense, the less dense these deployments will be, *ceteris paribus*, but they will be in place whether the attacker reaches them or not. Thus deeper advances do not demand new defensive positions (unless the attack breaks through). Note that in the limit, if a theaterwide frontal assault (i.e., an attack with no flanks) is preponderant enough to advance at all points simultaneously to the entire depth of the theater, then counterattack threats cannot halt it and an attacker can take the entire theater without breaking through, albeit at a casualty price proportional to the amount of ground taken (see the appendix).

82. This assumes a 2:1 minimum local preponderance for a modern-system attacker to advance against a tactically modern-system defender.

83. See chapter 2.

84. For a detailed analysis, see Stephen Biddle et al., *Defense at Low Force Levels*, IDA P-2380.

85. That is, I hold the theory to be valid from 1900 to at least the first decades of the twenty-first century; this does not imply that the same values of depth, reserves, exposure, or concentration are sufficient against all technologies or numerical imbalances. The *relationship* among variables is constant, not the *values* of the variables. On the needed force employment values as a function of changing technology and preponderance, see the appendix.

86. Purely aerial and naval warfare differ profoundly from continental warfare, and a major reason is the radical simplicity of the sky or surface of the sea relative to terra firma. In aerial and naval warfare there is no place to hide, hence technology and preponderance have greater rein, and the resulting combat dynamics are very different from continental wars': see, e.g., Wayne Hughes, *Fleet Tactics* (Annapolis: Naval Institute Press, 1986). Note that where continental campaigns accompany aerial and naval ones, the latter are typically decided sooner and more completely. Preemptive aerial campaigns in 1940 and 1967, for example, crippled the Allied and Arab air forces, respectively, in just hours; subsequent ground offensives took weeks to achieve successes that still left substantial ground-force opponents in the field. The Luftwaffe was virtually driven from the skies in a roughly five-month period from February to June 1944, whereas the Allied ground campaign in Europe required almost a year to impose lesser damage on the German Wehrmacht. The U.S. Navy had essentially destroyed the Japanese fleet by the Battle of Leyte Gulf in October 1944, yet the ground war continued until August 1945. Were technology to make the Earth's surface as simple and exposed as the air or surface of the sea, continental war might well come to resemble the quasi-naval conflict many RMA advocates now anticipate.

87. William Owens, "The Emerging System of Systems," *U.S. Naval Institute Proceedings* 121, 5 (May 1995), pp. 35–39; Alan D. Zim, "Human-Centric Warfare," *U.S. Naval Institute Proceedings* 125, 5 (May 1999), pp. 28–31.

88. Stephen Biddle et al., *New Approaches to Planning for Emerging Long Term Threats* (Alexandria, VA: Institute for Defense Analyses, 1994), IDA P-2896, vol. 1, pp. 26–27, 54.

89. Specifically, non–modern-system defense assumes that 50 percent of the defender's forward garrison is exposed, and that reserve velocity equals 80 km/day (i.e., $f_e = 0.5$ and $V_r = 80$ in the formal model's terms). To prevent breakthrough in the non–modern-system defense cases, depth is set as high as necessary, yielding extreme depths of 80 km for 1900–1920, 300 km for 1921–1940, 600 km for 1941–1960, 800 km for 1961–1980, and 1,300 km for 1981–2000. Reserve withholds are set at 50 percent ($f_r = 0.5$). Non–modern-system attack assumes a 20-km/day assault velocity ($V_a = 20$). Modern-system defense assumes zero exposure, 15-km depth, and 0.5 reserve withhold throughout ($f_e = 0$, $d = 15$, $f_r = 0.5$); reserve velocity (V_r) is set at 60 km/day for 1900–1920, 30 km/day for 1921–1940, 20 km/day for 1941–1980, and 15 km/day for 1981–2000. Modern-system attack assumes a 3-km/day assault velocity (V_a) for 1900–1920, 1.5 km/day for 1921–1940, 0.8 km/day for 1941–1980, and 0.4 km/day for 1981–2000. Other parameter values are per table A.1. Note that "velocity" is not a speedometer reading in a vehicle, but rather the net rate at which forces progress toward an objective, inclusive of planning, reconnaissance, laagering, and fire preparation, inter alia: see the appendix.

90. Capping defensive depth at 5 km and reserve withhold at 0.25, for example, yields breakthrough against modern-system attackers uniformly from 1900 to 2000; non–modern-system assault velocities in excess of 30 km/day with a wide frontage of 100 km (on a 500-km theater frontier) would yield no more than 1 km of ground gain against a modern-system defense at any point between 1900 and 2000.

91. Modern-system and non–modern-system force employment are as defined for figure 4.1; defender technology is held constant at 1940 ($\tau_B = 1940$); other values are per table A-1.

92. Modern-system and non–modern system force employment are again as defined for figure 4.1; the theater force-to-force ratio (R/B) is varied parametrically from 0.5 to 3.5; other values are per table A-1.

CHAPTER FIVE
OPERATION MICHAEL

1. Critical-case method thus does not rely on "representative" cases to combat selection bias; on the contrary, it seeks out extrema but structures these to enable valid inference. It emphasizes outliers, but not misleading ones. Harry Eckstein, "Case Study and Theory in Political Science," in Fred Greenstein and Nelson Polsby, eds., *Strategies of Inquiry*, vol. 7 of *The Handbook of Political Science* (Menlo Park, CA: Addison-Wesley, 1975), pp. 79–137. On case method and case selection criteria generally, see Timothy McKcown, "Case Studies and the Statistical Worldview," *International Organization* 53, 1 (Winter 1999), pp. 161–90; Andrew Bennett, "Lost in the Translation: Big (N) Misinterpretations of Case Study Research," paper presented to the International Studies Association Annual Meeting, Toronto, 1997; Alexander George, "Case Studies and Theory Development: The Method

of Structured, Focused Comparison," in Paul G. Lauren, ed., *Diplomacy: New Approaches in History, Theory, and Policy* (New York: Free Press, 1979), pp. 43–68; Alexander George and Timothy McKeown, "Case Studies and Theories of Organizational Decision Making," *Advances in Information Processing in Organizations* 2 (1985), pp. 21–58; Arend Lijphart, "Comparative Politics and the Comparative Method," *American Political Science Review* 65, 3 (September 1971), pp. 682–93; Lijphart, "The Comparable-Cases Strategy in Comparative Research," *Comparative Political Studies* 8, 2 (July 1975), pp. 158–77.

2. Note, however, that the case is a stronger test of systemic than dyadic technology theory. For systemic theorists, MICHAEL is an extremum; in dyadic terms, MICHAEL's technological parity (see below) is less remarkable, falling short of Ecksteinian criticality. This does not make the case indeterminate for dyadic theory: *ceteris paribus*, MICHAEL's technological parity would predict a draw, with neither breakthrough nor utter offensive frustration (either of which would tend to disconfirm if observed, as breakthrough is here). Moreover, Lanchester theory's bivariate combination of dyadic technology and preponderance would predict, incorrectly, offensive failure here if one assumes attrition coefficients consistent with stalemate in the preceding forty months of warfare under comparable technology and greater preponderance (see below). An orthodox theorist willing to combine linearly all three materialist variables would presumably see technological parity's effects as overwhelmed by numerical and systemic technological defense-dominance here, predicting, again incorrectly, offensive failure (Lanchester theory is bivariate and nonlinear; no such linear trivariate synthesis has been advanced to date). It is hard to imagine a straightforward materialist theory that would predict anything other than offensive failure here. MICHAEL is thus as close to *tout azimuth* criticality as real-life cases are ever likely to be; in a world of imperfect data, no case is likely to provide simultaneous extrema for all conceivable combinations of multiple variables. Across all possible materialist foils, MICHAEL is thus most dispositive of numerical and systemic technological theories, but it is also a determinate—if less powerful—test of dyadic technology theory.

3. In fact, much of the offense-defense literature is inspired by the World War I western front as the paradigm of defense-dominance: e.g., Van Evera, "The Cult of the Offensive"; Jack Snyder, "Civil-Military Relations and the Cult of the Offensive," *International Security* 9, 1 (Summer 1984), pp. 108–46; Snyder, *Ideology of the Offensive*, pp. 9, 15–18, 20–22.

4. Middlebrook, *The Kaiser's Battle*, p. 308.

5. The others were Lys River (April 9); the Third Battle of the Aisne, sometimes called the Chemin des Dames offensive (May 27); and the Second Battle of the Marne (July 15), culminating in the Allied July 17 counteroffensive, which swung the strategic initiative to the Allies. For overviews, see Terraine, *To Win a War*, pp. 59–102; Liddell Hart, *The Real War*, pp. 387–428; Pitt, *1918*, pp. 75–192.

6. A notable exception was Falkenhayn's attrition offensive at Verdun in 1916; see, e.g., Liddell Hart, *The Real War*, pp. 214–23.

7. Terraine, *To Win a War*, p. 37.

8. Correlli Barnett, *The Swordbearers: Supreme Command in the First World War* (New York: William Morrow, 1964), p. 278. For short summaries of the strategic background, see ibid., pp. 272–82; Sir James Edmonds, *Military Operations, France and Belgium, 1918* British Official History (London: Macmillan, 1935) (hereafter "BOH"), pp. 34–37; Cruttwell, *A History of the Great War*, pp. 486–90.

9. For details, see BOH, pp. 138–52; Barnett, *The Swordbearers*, pp. 278–89; Cruttwell, *A History of the Great War*, pp. 490–92; and Pitt, *1918*, pp. 47–51.

10. BOH, pp. 98–99. For details, see Travers, *The Killing Ground*, pp. 223–28; Barnett, The *Swordbearers*, pp. 299–300; Middlebrook, *The Kaiser's Battle*, pp. 71–73; Pitt, *1918*, pp. 52–60. Note that Haig clearly neither anticipated nor intended the Germans' speed or depth of advance. John Toland, for example, quotes Haig claiming he was "only afraid that the enemy would find our front so very strong that he will hesitate to commit his Army to the attack with the almost certainty of losing very heavily." *No Man's Land: 1918, The Last Year of the Great War* (New York: Doubleday, 1980), p. 8. From his own experience, Haig expected a slow, costly German grind forward, which could be halted by methodically repositioning reserves after the Germans had spent themselves: BOH, pp. 91–94.

11. Public Record Office (hereafter PRO), W.O.95/2846, 51st Div. Gen. Staff War Diary, attachment, "Report on the Operations from March 21st–26th 1918," 51st (H) Div., No. S.G.740.; W.O.95/1607, 16th Infantry Brigade Headquarters War Diary; W.O.95/1874, 14th Div. Gen. Staff War Diary, App. D, "Report on Operations during the Period 21st March to 31st March 1918."

12. BOH, pp. 161–302; for a detailed account of the first day's fighting, see especially Middlebrook, *The Kaiser's Battle*, pp. 108–307.

13. For more personalized accounts of the retreat, see Herbert Read, *In Retreat* (London: Faber and Faber, 1925); Charles R. Benstead, *Retreat: A Story of 1918* (London: Methuen, 1930).

14. On March 25: BOH, p. 462.

15. See BOH, pp. 448–50, 538–44; also Barnett, *The Swordbearers*, pp. 319–27; Toland, *No Man's Land*, pp. 70–73, 88–93, 98–100; Pitt, *1918*, pp. 97–102; Joseph Gies, *Crisis 1918* (New York: W. W. Norton, 1974), pp. 99–104; Winston S. Churchill, *The World Crisis, 1911–1918* (London: Thornton Butterworth, 1931), pp. 763–64; Cyril Falls, *The First World War* (London: Longmans, 1960), p. 318.

16. Scattered fighting continued until April 9, albeit with little or no change in either side's lines: Erich von Ludendorff, *My War Memories, 1914–1918* (London: Hutchinson, 1920), vol. 2, p. 600.

17. Given the negligible role of tanks and ground attack aircraft here (see below), the calculations consider the artillery and small-arms technologies on which the battle actually turned. The figures average mean introduction dates for rifle, machine gun, heavy artillery, and field artillery types on each side. The most prevalent weapon of each type and calibre is scored; different calibres within a category (e.g., 150-mm and 210-mm heavy artillery) are accorded equal weight. Weapons considered for the Germans in March 1918 are the GW98 rifle of 1898; MG08 heavy machine gun of 1901; MG08/15 light machine gun of 1915; FK16 and lFH16 field guns, both of 1916; and sFH13, Mrs, and lg 21-cm Mrs heavy artillery of 1913, 1910, and 1918, respectively (the lg 21-cm Mrs howitzer, introduced in 1918, is assumed to have made up only one-third of the 210-mm inventory by March; the remainder are assumed to have been Mrs). British weapons considered for 1918 are the SM Lee Enfield Mk1 rifle of 1903; Vickers Mk1 heavy machine gun of 1912; Lewis Mk1 light machine gun of 1915; 18 pounder field gun of 1904; and 6- and 9.2-inch heavy howitzers, both of 1915. For 1916, the German FK16 and lFH16 field guns are assumed to constitute only one-third of the field artillery, with the C96n/A of 1908 and lFH98/09 of 1910 comprising the remainder; all 210-mm howitzers are assumed to have been Mrs. Other values are per 1918. Data were taken from Hogg and Weeks, *Military*

Small Arms, pp. 127, 131, 210, 222–24; D. B. Nash, *German Army Handbook* (London: Ian Allen, 1980), pp. 95–99; Leslie W.C.S. Barnes, *Canada's Guns: An Illustrated History of Artillery* (Ottawa: Canadian War Museum, 1979), pp. 69, 78. Late war developments in counterbattery targeting had been more sweeping than in the guns themselves, but the principal innovations involved methods for using pre-existing technologies (especially airborne recce) rather than new equipment per se; even flash and sound ranging devices had been used since 1915 and were relatively mature by late 1916, long before the stalemate ended: Paddy Griffith, *Battle Tactics of the Western Front* (New Haven: Yale University Press, 1994), pp. 153–54. The most important developments in artillery effectiveness thus involved force employment—improvements in the use of materiel rather than the materiel itself.

18. Maximum range for the German FK16n/A 7.7-cm. field gun, for example, was 11,264 yards, and for the 10.5-cm. field howitzer model lFHKp, 11,210 yards; while the British 18-pounder field gun (firing H.E.) had a maximum range of 9,500 yards, and the 4.5-inch field howitzer had a maximum range of 7,000 yards with H.E. The German sFH13 15-cm howitzer and lg 21 cm Mrs mortar had maximum ranges of 9,296 and 11,155 yards, respectively; the British 60-pounder gun and 6-inch howitzer had maximum ranges of 16,000 and 17,500 yards. Nash, *German Army Handbook*, pp. 95–300; Shelford Bidwell, *Gunners at War: A Tactical Study of the Royal Artillery in the Twentieth Century* (London: Arrow, 1972), p. 243.

19. Guy Hartcup, *The War of Invention: Scientific Developments, 1914–18* (New York: Brassey's, 1988), pp. 61–68; Bidwell and Graham, *Firepower*, pp. 125–26.

20. Heavy machine gun *availability*, however, was greater in late-war British infantry divisions. By 1917, British divisions commonly deployed 64 heavy Vickers machine guns, while Canadian divisions sometimes acquired as many as 96; in 1918, British divisional machine gun battalions were expanded from three to four companies. German divisions, by contrast, had between 36 and 54 guns each: Middlebrook, *The Kaiser's Battle*, p. 89; Bidwell and Graham, *Firepower*, p. 123; Gudmundsson, *Stormtroop Tactics*, pp. 95–97.

21. Gudmundsson, *Stormtroop Tactics*, pp. 98–99.

22. Although implementation was uneven, by 1918 many German platoons had two squads of riflemen and up to two squads of light machine guns (with one rifle grenadier squad at company level). British platoons had one Lewis gun squad, two rifle grenade squads, and one pure rifle squad. In many cases, British platoons thus had fewer light machine guns but more rifle grenades, than the Germans: Gudmundsson, *Stormtroop Tactics*, p. 101; Bidwell and Graham, *Firepower*, pp. 126–27.

23. BOH, pp. 114–15, 152.

24. Where "maneuver unit" refers to infantry, armor, and cavalry—as distinct from *fire support* such as artillery and naval gunfire, or *combat service support* such as supply or engineering units. For division totals by type, see BOH, p. 116n.

25. BOH, appendix 7, p. 33.

26. BOH, pp. 114–15; for trench mortars, see Middlebrook, *The Kaiser's Battle,* p. 99.

27. BOH, p. 153n.

28. On artillery's prominence in World War I, see, e.g., Terraine, *To Win a War*, pp. 87, 187–88; and *Smoke and Fire*, pp. 127–28, 119, 132, 173.

29. Terraine, *To Win a War*, p. 39; Middlebrook, *The Kaiser's Battle*, p. 56; Liddell Hart, *The Real War*, p. 391.

30. BOH, p. 118; Gies, *Crisis 1918*, p. 85.

31. For one of MICHAEL's few recorded instances of combat activity by British tanks— notable for its rarity rather than its efficacy—see Middlebrook, *The Kaiser's Battle*,

pp. 294–95. Also note the Ninth Division commanding general's postbattle assessment: "If tanks couldn't function in this show when Hun Artillery fire was negligible, of what use are they?" PRO, W.O.95/1741, Tudor to Congreve, March 30, 1918.

32. As noted in chapter 3, at Amiens, for example, only 6 of the 414 Allied tanks that opened the battle on August 8, 1918, were still operational on August 12: Bidwell and Graham, *Firepower*, pp. 137–38.

33. Terraine, *To Win a War*, p. 117.

34. Although the RFC slightly outnumbered the Germans (by 1,144—plus 111 Royal Naval Air Service aircraft—to 1,130) across the British front overall: BOH, p. 118.

35. Middlebrook, *The Kaiser's Battle*, p. 203. Moreover, the few aircraft that tried to fly in spite of the fog proved unable to function effectively: e.g., PRO, W.O.95/2017, 18th Division General Staff War Diary, attachment, "The 18th Division in the Retreat to the Oise, March 1918," appendix A, p. 25; W.O.95/3035 61st Division Diary, attachment, "Preliminary Notes on Points That Have Come to Notice during Recent Operations," G.C.40/5, April 4, 1918, p. 2; AIR 1/475/15/312/201, Salmond to Trenchard, March 22, 1918.

36. H. A. Jones, *The War in the Air* (Oxford: Clarendon, 1934), British Official History of the Air War, hereafter BOHAW, pp. 293–301; S. F. Wise, *Canadian Airmen and the First World War* (Toronto: University of Toronto Press, 1980), Canadian Official History, hereafter COHAW, vol. 1, pp. 490–94.

37. Ernest Wilhelm von Hoeppner, *Germany's War in the Air* (Leipsig: A. F. Koehler, 1921), p. 106; BOHAW, pp. 301, 364–65.

38. BOHAW, pp. 297n, 301.

39. On aircraft technology in World War I, see, e.g., Kennett, *First Air War*, pp. 93–112; Terraine, *White Heat*, pp. 190–202. On aerial tactics, see also War Department Document No. 883, "A Survey of German Tactics, 1918," prepared by Historical Subsection, General Staff, A.E.F., Monograph No. 1, December 1918, pp. 15–22, 55–59.

40. In practical effect, World War I aircraft were more a branch of the artillery than an independent form of combat power: e.g., Kennett, *First Air War*, pp. 93–112, 207–16; Bidwell and Graham, *Firepower*, pp. 101–3, 143–44; Terraine, *White Heat*, pp. 190–202.

41. Kennett, *First Air War*, pp. 41–62, 211–12. In fact, their primary mission was strategic/terror bombing of population centers and industrial targets, rather than engaging military targets on the battlefield.

42. As even Major General Trenchard, Royal Flying Corps commander in chief, put it in 1918: "The best way, therefore, in which the Flying Corps can assist at this period is by assuring a continuance in the air of artillery [spotting] machines. If this object can be attained it will be a far more effectual help to the infantry and artillery, though invisible to them, than any amount of low-flying or bombing against the enemy front-line troops." Quoted in BOHAW, p. 359n. For the official historian's own, very similar, views, see ibid., p. 358. Germany, by contrast, had introduced the concentrated use of special ground attack squadrons (*Schlachtstaffeln*) in Operation MICHAEL. See United States Air Force Historical Research Center, 512.621 v11/14, "Development of the German Ground Attack Arm and Principles Governing Its Operations Up to the End of 1944," German Air Historical Branch (8th Abteilung), December 1, 1944, pp. 1–2; BOHAW, p. 275; Kennett, *First Air War*, pp. 211–12. While a harbinger of things to come, their casualties were very high, their effectiveness was minimal, and there is no evidence that they produced significant battlefield effects in MICHAEL: COHAW, pp. 492–93; Kennett, *First Air War*, pp. 212–13; BOHAW, p. 363.

43. COHAW, pp. 492–510.

44. Hoeppner, *Germany's War in the Air*, p. 106; COHAW, pp. 492–93. While the British retreat provided comparable targets (i.e., march columns in the open), the Germans failed to exploit the opportunity: BOHAW, pp. 363–64.

45. Using division counts as a proxy for direct fire combat arms manpower (as specified in the model presented in the appendix). Continental Allied and German divisions over this interval were broadly similar in strength and composition. BOH, pp. 103, 142, 152, 116, 117. The figure above excludes American divisions (some of which were combat-ready but others not) and thus overestimates Germany's actual preponderance.

46. Treating the Allies as the primary attackers in 1915–17; data are derived from Liddell Hart, "Ratio of Troops to Space," pp. 3–14.

47. In the new theory, local balances are endogenous, not externally given independent variables.

48. BOH, pp. 114–15, 116, 152, 153n. The Germans here had the war's largest total of tubes supporting a single offensive, but by other indicators—e.g., tubes per mile, heavy artillery per mile, duration of preparatory barrage, total rounds delivered, or rounds per mile—MICHAEL'S artillery support was less intense than the Allied "artillery offensives" of 1916–17. Only in intensity (rounds per mile per hour) was the barrage here unusually heavy. The Germans assembled a large artillery park but spread it over an unusually wide fifty-mile frontage. The net result was a brief, high-intensity barrage with a low total volume of firepower by contemporary standards.

49. One can compute higher FFRs from these dispositions, but only by using intuitively unreasonable counting rules. Counting all three German attack waves but only the twenty-one British divisions initially online, for example, yields an FFR of 3.0. Counting only the roughly one-third of the online British battalions in the forwardmost trench system but including all three waves of German assault divisions can push the FFR as high as 9.0. Either approach arbitrarily excludes large numbers of British defenders while including analogous Germans.

50. Sources for these data are Girard Lindsley McEntee, *Military History of the World War* (New York: Charles Scribner's Sons, 1937), pp. 182, 186, 276–77, 291; Wynne, *If Germany Attacks*, pp. 166–67, 186, 217–18, 268, 274. For reasons of compact presentation, the figure excludes Neuve Chapelle (March 10, 1915), Wynne, pp. 21–23: engaged = 9.1; engaged plus reserve = 6.6; Aubers Ridge (May 9, 1915), Wynne, pp. 45, 48: engaged = 12.0; Festubert (May 16, 1915), Wynne, p. 60: engaged = 16.0. These latter data represent failed offensives at radically higher FFRs than MICHAEL'S (i.e., 1.5 in engaged divisions and 1.8 in engaged plus reserve); thus the conclusions above are conservative.

51. Available data do not permit as systematic a depiction for heavy artillery, but MICHAEL'S ratio of heavy calibers was no higher than at Messines in 1917 (2.6:1), and much lower than at Aubers Ridge in 1915 (3.8:1): Sir James E. Edmonds, *Military Operations, France and Belgium, 1915*, British Official History (London: Macmillan, 1928), hereafter BOH1915, p. 9n; Edmonds, *Military Operations, France and Belgium, 1917: Vol. 2*, British Official History (London: His Majesty's Stationery Office, 1948), hereafter BOH1917, pp. 41n, 49.

52. Some argue that the 3:1 rule, for example, is properly measured in net "combat power," not weapon or formation counts: Liddell Hart, *Defense of Britain*, pp. 54–57; Mearsheimer, "Assessing the Conventional Balance", and "Numbers, Strategy and the European Balance," *International Security* 12, 4 (Spring 1988), pp. 174–85. Measuring "combat power," however, has proven controversial: Joshua Epstein, "Dynamic Analysis and the Conventional Balance in Europe," *International Security* 12, 2 (Spring 1988); and

"The 3:1 Rule, the Adaptive Dynamic Model, and the Future of Security Studies," *International Security* 13, 4 (Spring 1989), pp. 90–127. The new theory treats troop strength, technology, and troop behavior as logically distinct independent variables rather than aggregating them in an opaque measure of "combat power," but even if one considers troop "quality" as a component of preponderance for use in a rule of thumb, MICHAEL offers no important quality differences that could explain the German success (see below).

53. Gudmundsson, *Stormtroop Tactics*, pp. 162–63.

54. Fewer than 32 company-size *sturmblocks* were available on March 21 (32 first-wave divisions each had a nominal attachment of one *sturmblock*, but some had none: ibid.). Scoring each *sturmblock* as equal to 10 regular infantry companies thus yields under 320 "company equivalents." Assuming 18 infantry companies per 1918 German division implies under 18 "division equivalents" of combat power in the *sturmblocks*. This in turn yields a total-divisions-at-point-of-attack "combat power" FFR of $(63 + 18)/31 = 2.6:1$, and an online-divisions-at-point-of-attack "combat power" FFR of $(32 + 18)/21 = 2.4:1$. These upper bound "combat power" ratios are very conservative—not only for the *stosstruppen*'s actual combat effectiveness (surely less than ten times their regular infantry colleagues'), but also with respect to variations in reported German 1918 division organization. Sources vary on the number of infantry companies in a standard German 1918 division. Gudmundsson, e.g., gives 18 per division (p. 96); Nash gives 36 (pp. 35, 40). Nash's estimate would score the 32 *sturmblocks* as $(32*10)/36 = 9$ division equivalents, rather than the 18 assumed above. This in turn would reduce the upper bound "combat power" FFRs to only $(63 + 9)/31 = 2.3:1$ in total-divisions-at-point-of-attack, and $(32 + 9)/21 = 2.0:1$ in online-divisions-at-point-of-attack. Finally, scoring 32 *sturmblocks* as equal to 18 regular infantry divisions credits the *sturmblocks* with organic fire support equal to a regular division's—even though *sturmblocks* had no organic heavy ordnance.

55. On training and professionalism in the German and British armies in 1918, see Middlebrook, *Kaiser's Battle*, pp. 43–44, 82–84. Morale in either army (with the exception of the highly motivated *sturmblocks*) was best described, in Middlebrook's phrase, as "steady" (pp. 105, 63). For a more detailed assessment, see G. D. Sheffield, "The Morale of the British Army on the Western Front, 1914–18," in Geoffrey Jensen and Andrew Wiest, eds., *War in the Age of Technology* (New York: New York University Press, 2001), pp. 125–28.

56. See, e.g., Mearsheimer, "Numbers, Strategy".

57. See, e.g., Congressional Budget Office, *U.S. Ground Forces and the Conventional Balance in Europe* (Washington, DC: USGPO, 1988), e.g., pp. xv, 25–26.

58. See, e.g., Liddell Hart, "Ratio of Troops to Space"; Mearsheimer, "Numbers, Strategy".

59. See, e.g., Liddell Hart, "Ratio of Troops to Space," p. 11.

60. This excludes the mountainous, thinly held, sector between the Vosges and the Swiss border, and accounts for the shortened German front following their 1917 withdrawal to the Hindenburg Line: ibid., p. 4.

61. This includes the four GHQ divisions held behind the Third and Fifth Army fronts and counts each cavalry division as one-third an infantry division's strength: BOH, pp. 116, 116n.

62. BOH, pp. 38 (sketch 2), 40 (sketch 3), 122–5; BOH, map vol., sheets for March 21, 1918.

63. This is higher than the number of tubes per mile of frontage *occupied* (versus *attacked*, as above), which was about 38 tubes per mile. Defensive artillery totals are typically given as the number of tubes firing against the attack frontage, rather than tubes deployed there; for comparability with other First World War experience, I express local artillery densities this way throughout.

64. Liddell Hart, "Ratio of Troops to Space," p. 4; Liddell Hart, *Deterrent or Defense: A Fresh Look at the West's Military Position* (New York: Praeger, 1960), pp. 97–109.

65. Sources for these data are McEntee, *Military History*, pp. 178, 276; Wynne, *If Germany Attacks*, pp. 23, 63–65, 67n, 68, 192, 218, 228, 264–66, 296, 300, 310; Balck, *Development of Tactics*, pp. 63–65, 75; Liddell Hart, *The Real War*, pp. 406–7; BOH, p. 114.

66. Sources for these data are Wynne, *If Germany Attacks*, pp. 67–68, 70, 93, 95, 102, 264–66, 285, 300; Balck, *Development of Tactics*, pp. 63–65, 75; McEntee, *Military History*, pp. 274, 276.

67. Sources for these data are Wynne, *If Germany Attacks*, pp. 20, 24, 47, 51, 106, 166–67, 176, 230, 266; John Terraine, "Indirect Fire," pp. 9–11; BOH1915, pp. 19n, 177–78; BOH1917, pp. 49, 135–36; McEntee, *Military History*, p. 277.

68. Haig assumed that any offensive would be preceded by an extended barrage and would make only slow progress, affording him ample time to reallocate forces if necessary. The actual outcome was an unwelcome surprise: BOH, pp. 91–94; Toland, *No Man's Land*, pp. 8ff.

69. By contrast, the British attack frontage at Passchendaele (July 1917) was only seventeen miles; at Arras (April 1917), twelve miles; at First Somme (July 1916), fourteen miles; and at Aubers Ridge (May 1915), less than two miles: Terraine, "Indirect Fire as a Battle Winner/Loser," pp. 20–21; Terraine, *Passchendaele* (London: Leo Cooper, 1977), p. 64; Balck, *Development of Tactics*, p. 75; Liddell Hart, *The Real War*, pp. 325, 335; Keegan, *Face of Battle* p. 240; Wynne, *If Germany Attacks*, pp. 45, 47; BOH1915, p. 9n.

70. This extremely high square area density for the British defense at MICHAEL is the result of their massing the available forces well forward; see the discussion under "Force Employment" below. Depth and density trade off—for *all* defenders—and the British in March 1918 chose density over depth.

71. BOH, pp. 38, 40, 103, 114–15, 116, 117, 122–25, 142, 152, 153n; Wynne, *If Germany Attacks*, pp. 102, 106; McEntee, *Military History*, p. 291; Liddell Hart, "Ratio of Troops to Space," pp. 3–14; Balck, *Development of Tactics*, p. 75.

72. See, e.g., Timothy Lupfer, *The Dynamics of Doctrine* (Ft. Leavenworth, KS: U.S. Army CSI, 1981), pp. 37–48; Gudmundsson, *Stormtroop Tactics*, pp. 155–70; David Zabecki, *Steel Wind* (Westport: Praeger, 1994), pp. 33–77; English, *Infantry*, pp. 18–22; Rod Paschall, *The Defeat of Imperial Germany, 1917–1918* (Chapel Hill: Algonquin Books, 1989), pp. 130–38; Pitt, *1918*, pp. 45–47, 75–78; Middlebrook, *Kaiser's Battle*, pp. 52–55, 63; Barnett, *Swordbearers*, pp. 290–91; Cruttwell, *A History of the Great War*, pp. 494–95, 505; House, *Combined Arms Warfare*, pp. 25–27, 33–37; Georg Bruchmuller, *The German Artillery in the Breakthrough Battles of the World War*, 2d ed. (Berlin, 1922), trans. J. H. Wallace and H. D. Kehrn (Ft. Sill: U.S. Army Field Artillery School, n.d.); BOH, pp. 143, 153–56, 156–60.

73. In the new theory's formal specification, closure rate is used as an index of modern-system adherence (see appendix) and is computed as the distance (in kilometers) between the assault's jump-off point (typically the attacker's forwardmost trench line) and its initial objectives (typically the defender's first trench system), divided by the elapsed time

(in hours) from the opening of the preparatory barrage to the time the first assault units would reach the objective if unhindered.

74. Wynne, *If Germany Attacks*, pp. 20–25, 45, 47.

75. Terraine, "Indirect Fire," pp. 20–21.

76. Liddell Hart, *The Real War*, p. 177; Wynne, *If Germany Attacks*, pp. 68–70; Terraine, "Indirect Fire," pp. 10–11, 20–21.

77. Liddell Hart, *The Real War*, pp. 455, 463–64; Middlebrook, *Kaiser's Battle*, p. 525.

78. Lupfer, *Dynamics of Doctrine*, p. 15; Wynne, *If Germany Attacks*, pp. 129–30

79. See, e.g., Middlebrook, *Kaiser's Battle*, pp. 170–202; Travers, *How the War Was Won*, p. 64.

80. Lupfer, *Dynamics of Doctrine*, pp. 13, 30, 34; Wynne, *If Germany Attacks*, pp. 133–64.

81. I have surveyed representative British March 1918 positions on either side of St. Quentin and verified that for these, the entire forward zone was visible from the prebattle German front line; across much of the assault frontage, significant sections of the British battle zone were exposed as well: Stephen Biddle, "Trip Memorandum: Notes on Battle-field Survey, St. Quentin, 15–19 June 1995," Institute for Defense Analyses, typescript.

82. Note that a heavy fog on the opening morning greatly reduced both sides' visibility (see below); prebattle reconnaissance, however, benefited from clear lines of sight into the fixed, permanent British positions, and this preliminary recce assisted German assault waves in maneuvering through British defenses on March 21.

83. In the terms of the formal model presented in the appendix, the fraction of the defender's forward garrison in exposed positions, f_e, was thus 0.5, as opposed to 0.0 for contemporaneous German defenses: although the British forward defenders were covered, they were not concealed inasmuch as their locations were largely known to the attackers beforehand. By contrast, German defenders in 1917–18 were both covered and concealed, implying an f_e of 0. A defense that was neither covered nor concealed would imply an f_e value of 1.0.

84. Wynne, *If Germany Attacks*, e.g., pp. 143, 185–88, 288.

85. BOH, pp. 38 (sketch 2), 40 (sketch 3), 122–25; BOH, map vol., sheets for March 21, 1918.

86. BOH, appendix 6, pp. 23–24. GHQ had recognized by late 1917 that British defensive doctrine was obsolete. As it became clearer that the spring would bring a major German offensive, the British staff thus tried to update BEF defensive doctrine by copying what they understood to be the German system of 1916–17. On British doctrine as an imitation of the German system, see, e.g., Barnett, *Swordbearers*, p. 310; Middlebrook, *Kaiser's Battle*, p. 329; Woodward, "Doubts and Debate," p. 291; Falls, *First World War*, p. 314; A.J.P. Taylor, *The First World War* (New York: G. P. Putnam's Sons, 1980), pp. 217–18. The copy, however, fell well short of the original.

87. The forward zone was to contain one "system" of three trenches; the battle zone, two such systems; and the rear zone: one: BOH, appendix 15, pp. 75–76.

88. BOH, appendix 6, p. 23, given a forward zone depth of 2,000–3,000 yards. GHQ doctrinal guidance was neither fully understood nor faithfully implemented by all divisions. Nomenclature, for example, varied from division to division (and sometimes even within divisions), including use of "blue-red-brown" color systems, retention of the old "front-support-reserve-intermediate" zone designations, and various hybrids: e.g., PRO, W.O.95/2133, 21st Division General Staff War Diary; W.O.95/1956, 16th Division Diary; W.O.95/3121, 66th Division Diary; W.O.95/2846, 51st Division Diary; W.O.95/3011, 59th

Division Diary; W.O.95/1380, 3d Division Diary; W.O.95/2205, 24th Division, 17th Infantry Brigade Headquarters War Diary; and W.O.95/2208, 24th Division, 8th Battalion Royal West Surrey Regiment (The Queen's) War Diary. Actual practice thus varied widely and in many cases failed to keep up with current GHQ guidance even at the conceptual level, much less in actual construction.

89. BOH, p. 45.

90. BOH, pp. 38 (sketch 2), 40 (sketch 3), 122–5; BOH, map vol., sheets for March 21, 1918.

91. Sources for these data are McEntee, *Military History*, p. 274; Wynne, *If Germany Attacks*, pp. 23, 45, 70, 93, 95, 102, 169, 264, 285; BOH, map vol., sheets for March 21, 1918; operations maps from PRO, W.O.95/2436, 34th Division General Staff War Diary; W.O.95/3011, 59th Division Diary; W.O.95/1874, 14th Division Diary; 58th Division Diary; W.O.95/3121, 66th Division Diary.

92. Figure 5.9 includes only local reserve fractions—i.e., division-size reserves under operational control of the army group, army, and corps commanders opposing a given offensive. In general, however, theater reserve withholds tend to parallel the practices followed at army group to corps levels: armies that value mobile reserves tend to do so consistently rather than at a single echelon. I define "mobile reserve" as a force meant to move at least a division frontage before commitment to combat, as opposed to forward forces intended to fight from positions they occupy at the outset (or their immediate vicinity). For several 1915 battles, however, I make an exception: where the entire defensive operation is conducted below division level (as were several in early 1915), and where individual divisions were split between prepared and rearward positions located behind the rear defense line, I define "mobile reserves" at the level of the largest unit that one can uniquely characterize as "forward" or "reserve": at Neuve Chapelle, for example, even battalions were split between forward companies occupying the single trench line that constituted the bulk of the prepared defense, and rearward companies in unprepared assembly areas. Since any given battalion thus cannot be characterized as "forward" or "reserve," the German defense at Neuve Chapelle is characterized company by company. Sources for these data are McEntee, *Military History*, p. 276; Wynne, *If Germany Attacks*, pp. 23, 106, 167, 180, 182, 185, 192, 218, 228, 265–67, 288, 296, 297, 310, 311; BOH, pp. 114, 116.

93. Even if one includes the British GHQ reserves, the March 1918 reserve fraction rises only to about 30 percent (i.e., Six Third and Fifth Army reserve divisions, five First and Second Army reserve divisions, and eight divisions in GHQ reserve, relative to sixty-one divisions overall)—a lower theaterwide figure than contemporary German *local* reserve fractions.

94. Given $\tau_R = 0.87$; $\tau_B = 0.89$; $R/B = 1.17$; $w_{th} = 524$ (i.e., 325 miles); and values for constants per table A-1 (save that $k_5 = k_6 = 0$, since the calculation here focuses on losses in a single offensive sector, rather than theaterwide).

95. BOH, pp. 160, 264, 307, 312; W.O.95/2846, 51st Div. Gen. Staff War Diary, attachment, "Report on the Operations from March 21st—26th 1918", 51st (H) Div., No. S.G.740; W.O.95/1607, 16th Infantry Brigade Headquarters War Diary; W.O.95/1874, 14th Div. Gen. Staff War Diary, App. D, "Report on Operations during the Period 21st March to 31st March 1918."

96. BOH, p. 326.

97. Terraine, *To Win A War*, p. 60. For similar assessments, see, e.g., Cruttwell, *A History of the Great War*, p. 508; Barnett, *Swordbearers*, p. 319. Alternatively, some argue that the

Germans never "broke through": e.g., Middlebrook, *Kaiser's Battle*, pp. 339–48; Churchill, *World Crisis*, p. 760; Falls, *First World War*, pp. 319–20. It is not clear what their criteria are, however. By the usual definition above, "breakthrough" clearly occurred here. Middlebrook, Churchill, and Falls all argue that the Germans fell short of strategic victory (certainly true; see discussion below), but this does not mean they failed to break through—only that they failed to *exploit* that breakthrough, a distinction treated in detail below.

98. Middlebrook, *Kaiser's Battle*, p. 341.

99. BOHAW, p. 297n, 301.

100. There were about 190 battalions in the twenty-one forward divisions of Third and Fifth armies. Middlebrook, p. 204.

101. Indeed, at times the German and British armies moved almost in formation with each other: "[T]here were several occasions when the British retired at a slow walk—for exhaustion was affecting them, too—and the Germans followed at a distance of a few hundred yards at the same pace." Pitt, *1918*, p. 103.

102. Middlebrook, *Kaiser's Battle*, p. 322, estimates that 10,851 of these were killed on the first day, 28,778 wounded, and 300 taken prisoner. For final German casualties see ibid., p. 347; also Sir James E. Edmonds, *A Short History of World War I* (London: Oxford University Press, 1951), p. 297; Terraine, *To Win a War*, p. 65; all of which estimate total German losses at 240,000–250,000. By comparison, Allied attackers in the First Battle of the Somme lost perhaps more than 610,000—about 60,000 on the first day; Verdun cost the German attackers some 434,000 casualties between February 21 and December 18, 1916: George Bruce, ed. *Harbottle's Dictionary of Battles* (New York: Van Nostrand Reinhold, 1979), pp. 238, 264.

103. Middlebrook (pp. 322, 347) estimates 7,512 British killed, 10,000 wounded, and 21,000 taken prisoner on the first day, and a total of 22,000 Allied killed, 63,000 wounded, and 75,000 taken prisoner for the battle as a whole. Edmonds, *Short History*, p. 297; Terraine, *To Win a War*, p. 65; Toland, *No Man's Land*, p. 121, estimate total Allied losses at between 234,000 (Toland) and 250,000 (Terraine); of this total, 70,000–80,000 were French. By comparison, German defenders in the First Battle of the Somme lost about 650,000 killed and wounded, perhaps 8,000 on the first day; French defenders at Verdun lost 542,000 men between February 21 and December 18, 1916: Bruce, *Harbottle's Dictionary*, pp. 238, 264; Middlebrook, *Kaiser's Battle*, p. 322.

104. Churchill, *World Crisis*, p. 758.

105. The causal logic of neither non-Lanchestrian preponderance theories nor dyadic technology theory is clear enough for process tracing.

106. This assumes roughly equal kill-rate coefficients, as March 1918's technological parity would imply. Some Lanchester theorists boost the defender's coefficients, often by a factor of three, to reflect a "defender's advantage" associated with cover and concealment. Even a factor-of-three increase, however, would still not outweigh the attrition effects of a 2:1 local numerical advantage for the attacker in a Lanchester Square Law engagement.

107. BOH, pp. 246–47.

108. British prepared defenses averaged 4-km depth over the 80 km of German assault frontage, yielding 320 square km of entrenchments: BOH, pp. 38, 40, 122–25; map vol., sheets for March 21, 1918. German casualties in the breakthrough per se totaled roughly 40,000; the initial assault wave of thirty-two divisions constituted about half of the million-soldier offensive, implying a loss rate of roughly 8 percent for the breakthrough

itself. Most German losses occurred after, not before, the breakthrough. Middlebrook, *Kaiser's Battle*, pp. 322, 347.

109. This assumes, first, predicted prebreakthrough attacker casualties of d^*C_a and defender casualties of $b0^*d$ (equations 20 and 21 of the appendix pertain only to contained offensives), and second, that direct fire combat maneuver personnel constitute about 30 percent of total manpower in 1918. The model is specified in terms of direct-fire combat maneuver personnel, rather than total troops (see appendix). Total troop figures are reported in the text for comparability with values reported in secondary histories, but the model calculations revolve around the direct-fire combat maneuver arms subset of these. (As long as the ratio of direct-fire combat maneuver personnel to total troops is comparable for the Allies and the Germans, the only outcome sensitive to this second assumption is the casualty total: a higher ratio yields higher predicted losses, ceteris paribus.)

110. Ibid., pp. 322, 347.

111. Barnett, *Swordbearers*, p. 285.

112. Ibid.

113. For arguments on the importance of German force employment, see Cruttwell, *A History of the Great War*, p. 505; Pitt, *1918*, pp. 43–44, 60–61; Taylor, *First World War*, p. 215; Paschall, *Defeat of Imperial Germany*, pp. 130–40; Lynn Montross, *War through the Ages* (New York: Harper and Brothers, 1946), p. 745; House, *Combined Arms Warfare*, p. 34; Gudmundsson, *Stormtroop Tactics*, pp. 155–70; Falls, *First World War*, pp. 314–19. Cf. Terraine, *To Win a War*, p. 38. Timothy Travers and Brian Bond have suggested that German doctrine, while significant, was of contributory rather than decisive importance: Travers, *Killing Fields*, pp. 228, 231; Bond, "The First World War," in C. L. Mowat, ed., *The Shifting Balance of World Forces, 1898–1945* (Cambridge: Cambridge University Press, 1968), p. 202. For arguments citing the importance of the shallowness of British defenses, see Paul Kennedy, "Britain," p. 52; Taylor, "First World War," pp. 217–18; Woodward, "Doubts and Debate," p. 291; House, *Combined Arms Warfare*, p. 27. On the quality of British entrenchments, see Pitt, *1918*, pp. 7–12; Bond, "First World War," p. 251; Stokesbury, p. 263; Woodward, p. 291. On the importance of British misunderstanding of defense in depth, see Travers, *How the War Was Won*, e.g., p. 65; Barnett, *Swordbearers*, p. 310; Middlebrook, *Kaiser's Battle*, p. 329; Taylor, pp. 217–18; Woodward, p. 291; Falls, p. 314.

114. The phrase "Mist and Masses" has been attributed to Maxwell Morrison: Travers, *The Killing Ground*, p. 231 and n. 32.

115. BOH, pp. 50, 114–15, 255–58; also Edmonds' much later *Short History*, pp. 275–80, 284.

116. See, e.g., Terraine, *To Win a War*, pp. 38, 42–49 (who emphasizes German artillery superiority); and the much earlier W. Shaw Sparrow, *The Fifth Army in March 1918* (London: John Lane, 1921), pp. 4, 9, 15–18, 33–36, 38, 39, 80, 99, 105–6, 123, 128, 246, 253, 259, 279–80, 292, 300–311; Falls, *First World War*, pp. 314–5; Bond, "First World War," p. 201. Pitt, *1918*, pp. 60–61; Travers, *The Killing Ground*, p. 231; and Montross, *War through the Ages*, p. 745, though they disagree on the relative weight of causation, all attribute at least a secondary role to German numerical superiority and British overextension. This was also Haig's own explanation for the breakthrough, as well as that of the British press in the immediate aftermath: Woodward, pp. 290–92.

117. Moreover, at the theater level (where Lloyd George's manpower decisions were most germane), the German advantage was especially small relative to earlier—unsuccessful—Allied offensives (see discussion above).

118. BOH, pp. 127, 130–31, 300–303, 324–25.

119. Ibid., pp. 114, 116.

120. Ibid., pp. 198–99, 244–47.

121. PRO, W.O.95/2846, 51st Division General Staff War Diary; W.O.95/1607, 16th Infantry Brigade Headquarters War Diary; BOH, pp. 244–45.

122. These units were the 8th and 9th battalions, the Rifle Brigade, and the 5th Oxford & Bucks Light Infantry, all of the 14th Division. PRO, W.O.95/1874, 14th Division General Staff War Diary, appendix D, "Report on Operations during the Period 21st March to 31st March 1918"; also William W. Seymour, *The History of the Rifle Brigade in the War of 1914–1918* (London: Butler and Tanner, 1936), pp. 232–34, map oppos. p. 248; BOH, pp. 148–49. On the fighting to the breach's immediate flanks, see also Richard Byron, ed., *The King's Royal Rifle Corps Chronicle* (London: Warren and Son, 1919), pp. 120–22.

123. BOH, pp. 195–99. The responsible corps commander, Gen. Butler of III Corps, had only recently been promoted and was in action at this level of command for the first time on March 21. Gough met with Butler in early afternoon and found him "despondent" (Middlebrook, *Kaiser's Battle*, p. 278); Gough's orders for the withdrawal to the Crozat Canal were issued shortly thereafter. It could be argued that Butler's inexperience contributed to a degree of pessimism that misled Gough as to the immediacy of the need for withdrawal, leading to premature abandonment of the defended zone; for accounts of the withdrawal decision, see General Sir Hubert Gough, *The Fifth Army* (London: Hodder and Stoughton, 1931), pp. 266–67; and *Soldiering On* (London: Arthur Barker, 1954), p. 155; Anthony Farrar-Hockley, *Goughie: The Life of General Sir Hubert Gough* (London: Hart-Davis, MacGibbon, 1975), pp. 277–83, which argues that Gough had made up his mind prior to the Butler meeting; Sparrow, *Fifth Army*, pp. 79–81; Middlebrook, *Kaiser's Battle*, pp. 276–79. Of course the Germans overran the surviving battle-zone positions on a broad front the following day; at issue is merely the relative fortunes of the two British armies on the battle's first day, not either's ability to hold thereafter.

124. E.g., Middlebrook, *Kaiser's Battle*, pp. 329–32; Pitt, *1918*, pp. 78–80; Liddell Hart, *The Real War*, pp. 391, 398; Churchill, *World Crisis*, p. 756. Many more see the fog playing at least a contributory (if not primary) role: Terraine, *To Win A War*, p. 60; Cruttwell, *A History of the Great War*, pp. 506–7; Taylor, *First World War*, p. 218; Paschall, *Defeat of Imperial Germany*, pp. 139, 140; Travers, *Killing Ground*, pp. 228, 231; Gies, *Crisis 1918*, p. 83; Montross, *War through the Ages*, p. 742.

125. PRO, W.O.95/3000, 173rd Infantry Brigade (58th Division) Headquarters War Diary, attachment, "Report on Operations, 21 March 1918 and Succeeding Days," p. 1; W.O.95/2017, 18th Division Diary, attachment, "The 18th Division in the Retreat to the Oise, March 1918," pp. 7, 8; W.O.95/1874, 14th Division Diary, appendix D, p. 3; W.O.95/3035, 61st Division Diary, entry for 10:50 P.M., March 21; also attachment, "Narrative of Operations," G.C.40/5, p. 1; and Report of Maxse, XVIII Corps No. G.a.155/5, p. 1; W.O.95/2492, 36th Division Diary, attachment, "Account of Operations," p. 2; W.O.95/2313, 30th Division Diary, attachment, "Narrative of Operations," n.p.; W.O.95/1741, 9th Division Diary, attachment, "Lessons Learned," p. 1, and "Report on Operations of the South African Brigade," p. 1; W.O.95/2846, 51st Division Diary, attachment, "Report on the Operations from March 21st–26th 1918," No.S.G.740, p. 4; W.O.95/2436, 34th Division Diary, attachment, "The Action of the 34th Division in the Battle of the Sensee River 21st March 1918," p. 6; W.O.95/2212, 72nd Infantry Brigade (24th Division) Headquarters War Diary, entry for 10:30 P.M., March 21.

126. See BOH, e.g., pp. 112, 163, 166, and 255–56.

127. For dissenting views, see Baldwin, p. 141; and Sparrow, *Fifth Army*, pp. 59–60. Barnett (*Swordbearers*, pp. 309–10) sees the fog mainly as a scapegoat to excuse British command failings.

128. Fog is even more common (and of longer average duration) in fall and winter than in spring. See, e.g., the statistics in Headquarters, U.S. Department of the Army, *FM 100-5*, pp. 13–10 to 13–12: "Environmental Conditions."

129. On fog at Neuve Chapelle, see Wynne, *If Germany Attacks*, pp. 25, 36, 40. For examples of mist-shrouded attacks during the Somme and Verdun campaigns, see, e.g., Terraine, *Smoke and Fire*, p. 124; and Sparrow, *Fifth Army*, p. 58. On fog in the battles of the Scarpe, see Wynne, *If Germany Attacks,* pp. 221, 230. For weather conditions during Passchendaele, see Balck, p.104; Terraine, *Passchendaele*, pp. 206, 216, 217, 255, 271, 320, and esp. 280–81, where twilight and drizzling rain on October 4 limits visibility to "about 30 yards" during the British dawn assault—or less than one-fifth that of the worst sector at MICHAEL—according to Haig's diary entry for the day. Yet this attack advanced only as far as the village of Broodseinde, again far short of breaking through the German defense.

130. See, e.g., Edmonds' discussion of the similarities between warfare at night and in fog: BOH, p. 255.

131. On Festubert, see Wynne, *If Germany Attacks,* p. 61. Arras was launched in predawn darkness, with sleet and snow blowing into the faces of the German defenders and further reducing defensive visibility: ibid., p. 175.

132. Ibid., p. 69.

133. Hartcup, *War of Invention*, pp. 66–67. On First World War smoke tactics and employment, see Balck, *Development of Tactics*, pp. 147–48.

134. On smoke at Champagne, see Wynne, *If Germany Attacks,* p. 90; in the First Somme campaign, see Balck, p. 73; at Arras, see Wynne, pp. 175, 219; at Passchendaele, see Balck, *Development of Tactics*, p. 104.

135. BOH, p. 165. Smoke was reported on at least four division fronts on March 21. PRO, W.O.95/1741, 9th Division Gen. Staff War Diary, attachment, "Narrative of Operations, 21st to 27th March, 1918," G.S.22/50, p. 4; W.O.95/1380, 3rd Division Diary, attachment, "Lessons Learned from the Recent Fighting 21st March–30th March 1918," p. 3; W.O.95/2436, 34th Division Diary, attachment, message from 9th Brigade, 11.30 A.M.; W.O.95/1615, 18th Infantry Brigade (6th Division) Headquarters War Diary, attachment, "Narrative of the Fighting on the 21st and 22nd March," p. 1. See also Middlebrook, p. 80; Sparrow, p. 152; Bond, p. 202. The British themselves used smoke to screen counterattacks during MICHAEL, and to screen trench raids beforehand: W.O.95/2205, 17th Brigade (24th Division) Headquarters War Diary, Operation Order No. 218, January 18, 1918, appendix A, artillery tables; BOH, p. 309.

136. Fog and smoke are thus special cases of the general tendency for attacks to be strongest in the early stages, but to lose efficiency over extended advances into depth. An astute attacker can exploit a foggy morning to cloak an attack's early stages, just as one can most carefully coordinate maneuver and fire support in the early going. As one advances into depth, this initially careful coordination breaks down, just as the concealment afforded by low visibility eventually disappears. If defenses are shallow, this eventual loss of offensive efficiency will be little felt, and the defense will stand or fall on its ability to withstand the full force of an optimally organized attack. If defenses are deep, they can exploit the attacker's inability to maintain ideal initial conditions throughout a longer

advance, and fight the decisive engagements under more favorable conditions deep within the defense.

137. Liddell Hart, *The Real War*, p. 415.

138. Ibid., pp. 71, 439–48.

139. For examples from MICHAEL, see PRO, W.O.95/3035, 61st Division Gen. Staff War Diary, entry for 12:05 P.M., March 21, 1918; W.O.95/2133, 21st Division Diary, attachment, "Report on Operations from March 21st to March 30, 1918," p. 2; W.O.95/3011, 59th Division Diary, attachment, "Narrative of Operations, March 21–6, 1918," p. 4.

140. See, e.g., Liddell Hart, *The Real War*; Fuller, *Armament and History*, chap. 6; Ferguson, *The Pity of War*; Travers, *How the War Was Won*.

CHAPTER SIX
OPERATION GOODWOOD

1. For a discussion of most likely and least likely case methodologies, see chapter 5.

2. As with MICHAEL, the dyadic technological balance was about even here. Hence, like MICHAEL, GOODWOOD is a stronger test of systemic than dyadic technology theory; again as in MICHAEL, the case is nevertheless determinate (and disconfirmatory) for dyadic technology theory, but this finding is less powerful as the case falls short of Ecksteinian criticality in this one dimension.

3. In fact, the offense-defense literature typically treats Second World War armored offensives as the paradigm of offense-dominance: e.g., Van Evera, "The Cult of the Offensive," and Snyder, "Civil-Military Relations"; Snyder, *Ideology of the Offensive*, pp. 9, 15–18, 20–22.

4. See, e.g., L. F. Ellis, *Victory in the West*, Vol. 1: *The Battle of Normandy*, British Official History (London: Her Majesty's Stationery Office, 1962), hereafter *BOHN*, pp. 149–326; Martin Blumenson, *Breakout and Pursuit* (Washington, DC: Office of the Chief of Military History, 1961), the American official history, hereafter *AOHN*, pp. 188–96; Carlo D'Este, *Decision in Normandy* (New York: HarperCollins, 1983), pp. 105–334; Max Hastings, *Overlord* (New York: Simon and Schuster, 1984), pp. 69–169; Alexander McKee, *Caen: Anvil of Victory* (London: Souvenir Press, 1964), pp. 246–304; Eversley Belfield and H. Essame, *The Battle for Normandy* (London: B. T. Batsford, 1965), pp. 128–46; Henry Maule, *Normandy Breakout* (New York: Quadrangle, 1977), pp. 80–111; David Belchem, *Victory in Normandy* (London: Chatto and Windus, 1981), pp. 154–57; Chester Wilmot, *The Struggle for Europe* (New York: Harper and Row, 1952), pp. 353–64; Weinberg, *A World at Arms*, pp. 689–90.

5. On fears of stalemate in Allied councils, see BOHN, p. 352; D'Este, *Decision in Normandy*, p. 321; Hastings, *Overlord*, pp. 221, 228.

6. Whether Montgomery intended GOODWOOD as a breakthrough in its own right or merely an auxiliary to COBRA is controversial. Montgomery's own statements before the battle are ambiguous. Following GOODWOOD's failure to break through, Montgomery and his defenders portrayed the battle as a limited—and successful—pinning attack, while his detractors have viewed the action as a failed breakthrough attempt and thus a major British defeat: see, e.g., D'Este, *Decision in Normandy*, pp. 391–99; BOHN, pp. 327–37, 347–61, 493–96; AOHN, pp. 194–96. Regardless of Montgomery's intentions, however, Dempsey (who commanded the assault forces) and his staff (who planned the battle) clearly intended GOODWOOD as a breakthrough attempt: e.g., D'Este, pp. 334, 337–51,

354. For my purposes, GOODWOOD is thus a (failed) breakthrough operation in its actual conduct and planning, whatever one thinks of Montgomery, his intentions, and his generalship in Normandy.

7. *BOHN*, pp. 327–40; D'Este, *Decision in Normandy*, pp. 352–69.

8. *BOHN*, pp. 332–34; *AOHN*, pp. 191–92; John J. T. Sweet, *Mounting the Threat: The Battle of Bourguebus Ridge, 18–23 July 1944* (San Rafael, CA: Presidio, 1977), pp. 61–65; A. G. Heywood, "Goodwood," *Household Brigade Magazine* (Winter 1956/7), pp. 171–77.

9. On the GOODWOOD fire preparation, see Department of the Scientific Advisor to the Army Council, *Military Operational Research Unit Report No. 23: Battle Study, Operation "Goodwood,"* October 1946, declassified January 16, 1984, pp. 13–20; *BOHN*, pp. 337–40.

10. On the conduct of the battle, see, e.g., *BOHN*, D'Este, *Decision in Normandy*, pp. 370–85; Sweet, *Mounting the Threat*, pp. 67–106; Hastings, *Overlord*, pp. 233–36.

11. British Army Tactical Doctrine Retrieval Cell, *Battlefield Tour: Operation Goodwood* (Camberly, n.d.), TDRC-7725, pp. A-4 to A-5; Sweet, *Mounting the Threat*, p. 112; *BOHN*, pp. 336, 338; and assuming 14,964 troops per British armoured division and 18,347 per infantry division, following *BOHN*, p. 535. Unlike the German defenders, the British attacking divisions were at full strength on July 18: *BOHN*, p. 332.

12. National Archives (hereafter NA) RG242, T-313-420, Kriegstagbuche der Panzer Gruppe West, Nachtrag zur Tagesmeldung (hereafter KTB PzW), 15.7.44, Anlage 135; KTB PzW 10.7.44, Anlage 105; British Army Tactical Doctrine Retrieval Cell, untitled (Camberly, n.d.), TDRC-5041, p. 6. TDRC-7725, based on postwar participant interviews, estimates 118 German tanks (p. B-1); the Panzer Gruppe West war diaries, on the other hand, show a total of 319 serviceable tanks and assault guns of all types on the eve of the battle (July 15–16) in the 21st, 1st SS, and 12th SS Panzer Divisions and the 503d Heavy Panzer, 101st SS Panzer, and 200th Assault Gun Battalions collectively. Not all, however, were initially allocated to the GOODWOOD frontage; hence the 319 figure represents an upper bound. For infantry and air strengths, see TDRC-7725, pp. A-6 to A-7; TDRC-5041, pp. 6, b-1; Wesley Craven and Frank Cate, *The Army Air Forces in World War II* (1951; reprint, Washington, DC: Office of Air Force History, 1983), p. 62n. Luftflotte 3, commanding German aircraft in France and Belgium, deployed 244 single-engine fighters in July 1944; neither these fighters nor any other German aircraft played an important role in the battle, however.

13. Eliot Cohen and Thomas Keaney, *Gulf War Air Power Survey Summary Report* (Washington, DC: USGPO, 1993), p. 7.

14. Larry Addington, *The Patterns of War since the Eighteenth Century* (Bloomington: Indiana University Press, 1994), pp. 202, 213; Bruce, ed., *Harbottle's Dictionary*, pp. 87–88; Geoffrey Jukes, *Kursk* (New York: Ballantine, 1969), pp. 53–55.

15. The Prokhorovka counterattack at Kursk pitted 850 Soviet and 700 German tanks on a battlefield of about 7-km frontage (Jukes, *Kursk*, pp. 94, 100–103), yielding a density of about 220 tanks/km, as opposed to the GOODWOOD density of about 460 (927 tanks on a 2-km front). For the GOODWOOD tank frontage, see TDRC-5041, p. 1.

16. Stephen Biddle, "Victory Misunderstood: What the Gulf War Tells Us about the Future of Conflict," *International Security* 21, 2 (Fall 1996), p. 155.

17. These figures assume 432 Sherman and 306 Cromwell tanks; 39.5 squadrons of Spitfire, 19 of Typhoon, 13 of Mosquito, 20.5 of Mustang, 3 of Tempest, 13 of Lightning, 4.5 of Black Widow, and 37.5 of Thunderbolt fighter aircraft for the Allies; and for the Germans, 110 Pzkw IV, 62 Pzkw V, and 53 Pzkw VI tanks; 44 StuG III and IV assault guns;

50 tracked 75-mm assault guns converted from obsolescent captured French tank chassis (all assault guns are counted as tanks here); and 283 Bf 109 and 229 FW 190 fighter aircraft. Weapon counts are taken from NA RG242, T-313-420, KTB PzW 15.7.44, Anlage 135; KTB PzW 10.7.44, Anlage 105; TDRC 5041, p. 6; TDRC 7725, pp. A-4 to A-7; *BOHN*, pp. 556–60; and Craven and Cate, *Army Air Forces*, p. 62n. Introduction dates are taken from Peter Chamberlain and Chris Ellis, *British and American Tanks of World War II* (New York: Arco, 1981), pp. 43, 114, 130; F. M. Von Senger und Etterlin, *German Tanks*; Swanborough and Bowers, *Military Aircraft*, pp. 359, 466, 502, 523; Bill Gunston, *Allied Fighters of World War II* (New York: Arco, 1981), pp. 32, 48, 50, 54; Bryan Philpott, *German Military Aircraft* (London: Arms and Armour Press, 1980), pp. 102, 131. These figures represent upper bounds for German tank strength, and especially, upper-bound counts for Pzkw Vs and VIs (all but five of the Pzkw Vs and many of the VIs were held in mobile reserve units not precommitted to the GOODWOOD front); this likely overestimates the prevalence of newer over older German tanks on the first-day battlefield. These figures also use July 1944 aircraft deliveries to Luftflotte 3 as an approximation of its fighter strength on July 18. This likely overestimates the prevalence of the (newer) FW 190 over the (older) Bf 109: over time, German aircraft production shifted from the Bf 109 to the FW 190, hence deliveries would be more FW 190-heavy than inventories at any given time. German fighter losses in July 1944 were so heavy, however, that deliveries and inventories were probably very similar by July 18 (notwithstanding deliveries of 512 single-engine fighter aircraft in July, Luftflotte 3's total strength at the end of the month was only 244: Craven and Cate, p. 62n). Overall, the estimations required thus uniformly credit the Germans with newer weapons than actually present on the GOODWOOD battlefield and are thus conservative with respect to my theoretical conclusions.

18. See, e.g., Hastings, *Overlord*, pp. 186–95; D'Este, *Decision in Normandy*, pp. 71–72.

19. See, e.g., Hastings, *Overlord*, pp. 190–95.

20. NA RG242, T-313-420, KTB PzW 15.7.44, Anlage 135; KTB PzW 10.7.44, Anlage 105; TDRC 5041, pp. 6, b-1.

21. The Pzkw IVh of 1944 had a road speed of 38 kph, a cross-country speed of 16 kph, a range of 200 km, a horsepower:weight ratio of 12, a bow armor basis of 82-mm RHA 90 deg. equivalent thickness, and a 75-mm gun with 92-mm RHA 30 deg. equivalent thickness penetration at 500 yds. The M4A4 of 1944 had a road speed of 40 kph, a cross-country speed of 32 kph, a range of 240 km, a horsepower:weight ratio of 12, a bow armor basis of 68-mm RHA 90 deg. equivalent thickness, and a 75-mm gun with 68-mm RHA 30 deg. equivalent thickness penetration at 500 yds; the "Firefly" variant (comprising about one-fourth of the Shermans at GOODWOOD) was armed with a 17-pounder gun with 140-mm RHA 30 deg. equivalent thickness penetration at 500 yds. The Sherman was thus more mobile but less well-protected than the Pzkw IVh. The Sherman Firefly outgunned the Pzkw IVh; the standard Sherman was outgunned by it. Perhaps the most important differences between the two tanks in the field, however, were the Sherman's advantages in mechanical reliability, rate of fire, and turret slew rate: the Sherman's all-power traverse, for example, frequently allowed it to lay its gun and engage before its German opponents could fire. Chamberlain and Ellis, *British and American Tanks*, pp. 114–30; Von Senger und Etterlin, *German Tanks*, pp. 198–99; *BOHN*, p. 549; Hastings, *Overlord*, p. 191. Armor basis calculated using formulae in I.F.B. Tytler et al., *Vehicles and Bridging* (London: Brassey's, 1985), p. 141. The Sherman's mechanical reliability advantages

were even more pronounced vis-à-vis later-model German tanks; fully 50 percent of the 9th SS Panzer Division's Panthers, for example, were reported out of service for mechanical reasons on July 4, 1944: NA RG 242 T-354-147, KTB PzW, Lagebericht für die Zeit vom 4.7.19.00–5.7.19.00 Uhr.

22. NA RG242, T-313-420, KTB PzW 15.7.44, Anlage 135; TDRC-5041, p. 6; Heywood, "Goodwood" p. 173; Von Senger und Etterlin, *German Tanks*, pls. 205, 208.

23. *BOHN*, p. 549.

24. Hastings, *Overlord*, pp. 186–95; *BOHN*, pp. 541–45.

25. Swanborough and Bowers, *Military Aircraft*, pp. 475, 528; Philpott, *German Military Aircraft*, p. 99.

26. *BOHN*, pp. 563, 570.

27. Roland Ruppenthal, *Logistical Support of the Armies*, vol 1 (Washington, DC: Office of the Chief of Military History, 1953), pp. 457n, 458.

28. *BOHN*, p. 58 and map opposite p. 120. This figure credits 130,000 German air force personnel in air defense artillery and parachute units (in addition to "Luftwaffe" ground divisions) as available to the ground forces.

29. *BOHN*, p. 323, maps opposite pp. 120, 378. Two German divisions, the 9th and 10th SS Panzer, had been transferred to France from Russia after D-Day, but two divisions originally deployed in France, the 703d and 716th, had been destroyed in combat by July 18: *BOHN*, p. 259. The division count for France and the low countries on July 18 was thus unchanged from D-Day's count of fifty-seven.

30. The new theory, by contrast, operationalizes numerical preponderance in terms of direct-fire combat maneuver personnel (see appendix), rather than total manpower (or "ration strength") as reported above; the former comprises only a small proportion of soldiers overall. For the British Army in Normandy in July 1944, this proportion was around 16 percent; for the Germans, about 27 percent. In the new theory's terms, the values for R and B in the formal model come to 208,000 and 91,800, respectively (as a theaterwide figure, R includes both British and American armies). For the Allies, these figures derive from data in *BOHN*, appendix 4, pt. 2, map, Situation Midnight 30th June 1944, and assume comparable U.S. and British divisional slices. For the Germans, these values derive from data in TDRC-7725, pp. A-6 and A-7; TDRC-5041, p. 6; and James Hodgson, "The Eve of Defeat," Office of the Chief of Military History MS R-57, October 1954, pp. 25, 37, 38; together with my own estimations for the seven divisions (of twenty-three) and three independent tank battalions not covered in these sources. My estimates assume 5,000 direct-fire combat effectives for fresh infantry divisions (per data developed from W.J.K. Davies, *German Army Handbook, 1939–1945* (New York: Arco, 1974), pp. 28, 30, 39; and *BOHN*, p. 539); 2,800 for the 2d Panzer Division; five soldiers per available tank for 101st and 102d SS Tank Battalions and 503d Heavy Tank Battalion; and scaled values for 9th and 10th SS Panzer Divisions relative to the (known) value for 1st SS Panzer using on-hand tank strength as the basis, given tank strengths in NA RG242 / T-313-420, Anlage 135 zu KTB PzW, Nachtrag zur Tagesmeldung, 15.7.44; Anlage 105 zu KTB PzW, Nachtrag zur Tagesmeldung, 10.7.44 (unchanged for 7/16): Anlage 135; and TDRC-5041, p. 6.

31. CBO, *Strengthening NATO*, pp. 11–13, appendix C; and *Army Ground Force Modernization*, pp. 30–31.

32. Liddell Hart, *Defence of Britain*, pp. 54–55; Mearsheimer, "Assessing the Conventional Balance."

33. Philip Karber et al., *Assessing the Correlation of Forces: France 1940* (McLean, VA: BDM Corp., 1979), BDM/W-79-560-TR; David Glantz and Jonathan House, *When Titans Clashed* (Lawrence: University Press of Kansas, 1995), p. 301.

34. TDRC-5041, p. 1.

35. Terrain also played a role in the narrowness of the VIII Corps front, as a narrow bridgehead over the Orne River east of Caen constricted the route by which the corps could deploy from its assembly areas north of the river to the jump off line on the other side; matters were made worse by the need to clear passage routes through an old British minefield en route: *BOHN*, pp. 334–35, 339; McKee, *Caen*, p. 255. Terrain did not predetermine a 2-km VIII Corps frontage, however. Another point of attack could have been selected without such constraints (e.g., the sector near Cheux where EPSOM had been launched), or preliminary attacks could have been used to widen the bridgehead before committing a three-division armored corps on such a narrow front (in fact, preliminary attacks were conducted just west of the VIII Corps frontage the night before the offensive). Central to Dempsey's choice was the desire to mass great striking power on a narrow frontage with a minimum of preliminary action.

36. *BOHN*, p. 343.

37. About 80 percent of the troops and 55 percent of the tanks in LXXXVI and I SS Panzer Corps were held by the two mobile reserve divisions: TDRC-7725, pp. A-6 to A-7; TDRC-5041, p. 6; NA RG242, T-313-420, KTB PzW 15.7.44, Anlage 135.

38. What about the "quality-adjusted" FFR? As noted in chapter 5, some preponderance theorists hold that numerical criteria like the 3:1 rule should be assessed in quality-adjusted "combat power" terms rather than raw numbers of combatants. While British and German weaponry at GOODWOOD were roughly equal, troop skill clearly was not. Both armies committed many of what they considered their best formations at GOODWOOD, but the elite German Waffen SS units were widely considered much more proficient than their equivalents in the British Guards Armoured, 7th Armoured, and 51st (Highland) divisions: Hastings, *Overlord*, pp. 179–86; D'Este, *Decision in Normandy*, chap. 16. SS units, moreover, comprised a significant fraction of the German forces ultimately engaged at GOODWOOD: perhaps 70 percent of the troops and 55 percent of the tanks the Germans committed by July 19 were assigned to the 1st and 12th SS Panzer divisions: TDRC-7725, pp. A-6 to A-7; TDRC-5041, p. 6; NA RG242, T-313-420, KTB PzW 15.7.44, Anlage 135. One could thus argue that raw numerical comparisons are misleading at GOODWOOD. In fact, this is precisely my point: the kinds of simple numerical comparisons that dominate capability assessment both in government and academia are very problematic without a systematic consideration of variations in the ways those forces actually fight. The 3:1 rule literature, however, offers no explicit, determinate guidance on how such "quality adjustments" are to be made, and this ambiguity has given rise to considerable controversy, as detailed in chapter 5. By contrast, the theory described above offers a systematic, determinate account of *how* the nonmaterial dimensions of "quality" affect military outcomes. I thus concur with John Mearsheimer and Basil Liddell Hart that quality matters, but I advocate addressing it explicitly and systematically rather than embedding it implicitly in an opaque adjustment to a numerical rule of thumb. The Mearsheimer/Liddell Hart view and the new theory proposed here are thus not true alternatives: the latter represents an extension and refinement of the former, rather than a mutually exclusive competitor, and thus I test the new theory here against the exclusive alternative of a strict numerical explanation of capability.

39. These data are taken from *AOHN*, pp. 224–28; Charles B. MacDonald, *The Siegfried Line Campaign* (Washington, DC: Office of the Chief of Military History, 1963), p. 409; I.S.O. Playfair, *The Mediterranean and Middle East* (London: Her Majesty's Stationery Office, 1954–60), vol. 1, pp. 282–87, 290–93; vol. 3, pp. 30, 97, 220, 260–62, 265, 274; Ward Miller, *The 9th Australian Division versus the Africa Corps* (Ft. Leavenworth, KS: U.S. Army Combat Studies Institute, 1986), pp. 11–17; Bruce, ed., *Harbottle's Dictionary*, pp. 87–88, 110, 232, 240, 253; Jukes, *Kursk*, pp. 53–54, 108, 110, 112, 151, 152; David M. Glantz, *From the Don to the Dnepr* (London: Cass, 1991), pp. 27–29, 35, 74, 87–89, 152–53, 225, 230, 381; Glantz, *Zhukov's Greatest Defeat: The Red Army's Epic Disaster in Operation Mars, 1942* (Lawrence: University Press of Kansas, 1999), p. 336; R. Ernest Dupuy and Trevor Dupuy, *The Harper Encyclopedia of Military History*, 4th ed. (New York: HarperCollins, 1993), pp. 1173–75, 1185–87, 1230, 1280–81; Glantz and House, *When Titans Clashed*, p. 301; and D'Este, *Decision in Normandy*, p. 400. (All values are ration strengths.)

40. *Military Operational Research Unit Report No. 23*, pp. 13–20; *BOHN*, pp. 337–40.

41. See, e.g., Liddell Hart, "Ratio of Troops to Space," pp. 3–14; Mearsheimer, "Numbers, Strategy," pp. 174–85.

42. Sources are TDRC-7725, p. A7; TDRC-5041, p. 6; NA RG242, T-313-420, KTB PzW 15.7.44, Anlage 135. Troop totals are ration strengths, per the standard treatment in orthodox theory, and total 28,800 for I SS and LXXXVI Corps. None of these sources report troop totals for 22d Panzer regiment, 503d Heavy Tank Battalion, 101st SS Panzer Battalion, or the 200th Assault Gun Battalion; strengths for these subunits were estimated from their tank and gun strengths, assuming that two-thirds of the troops at regimental and battalion level are weapon crews, with five-soldier crews per operational tank or gun. TDRC-7725 reports 1st SS Panzer Division's troop strength as "up to 15,000" (p. A7); a figure of 13,500 (90 percent of this value) is assumed here. TDRC-5041 reports 272d Infantry Division's strength as effectively "one regiment" (p. 6); I thus assume 1,400 troops for the division. Frontages for the two corps are derived from Hodgson, "Eve of Defeat," situation map, 15/16 July 1944, and total 26 km. Troop strength per square kilometer is computed using a depth of 16 km: TDRC-5041, p. 7.

43. These data are taken from *AOHN*, pp. 224–28; Jukes, *Kursk*, pp. 53–54, 108, 110, 112; Glantz, *Don to the Dnepr*, pp. 27–29, 35, 74, 87–89, 152–53, 225, 230, 381; Playfair, *Mediterranean*, vol. 1, pp. 282–87, 290–93; vol. 3, pp. 260–62, 265, 274; Bruce, *Harbottle's Dictionary*, p. 253; Miller, *9th Australian Division*, pp. 8, 11, 12; Dupuy, *Harper Encyclopedia*, pp. 1186–87; Esposito, ed., *West Point Atlas*, vol. 2, maps 24, 78; John Erickson, *The Road to Stalingrad* (New York: Harper and Row, 1975), p. 71; Glantz and House, *When Titans Clashed*, pp. 133–35, 301; Martin Blumenson, *Salerno to Cassino* (Washington, DC: OCMH, 1969), pp. 189–90; Ernest F. Fisher, Jr., *Cassino to the Alps* (Washington, DC: Center of Military History, U.S. Army, 1977), pp. 17–19; Martin Blumenson, *Bloody River* (Boston: Houghton Mifflin, 1970), pp. 24, 55; MacDonald, *Siegfried Line Campaign*, pp. 283–84, 330, map 6; Glantz, *Zhukov's Greatest Defeat*, pp. 336, 34–35, 51, 49, 54, 55, 62, 68. (All values are ration strengths.)

44. And by roughly equal magnitudes in either direction: the GOODWOOD value is 0.4 standard deviations above the mean value in the data for linear units of frontage, and 0.36 standard deviations below it for square units of area.

45. *AOHN*, pp. 224–28, map V; D'Este, *Decision in Normandy*, p. 400.

46. In fact, by either measure GOODWOOD presented a lower FSR than many prominent Second World War defensive failures. On July 18 the Germans in Normandy deployed

340,000 troops (as documented above) on a 130-km frontage (Esposito, *West Point Atlas*, vol. 2, map 51) for a theaterwide FSR of about 2,600 soldiers per kilometer. The Allied defenders of France in May 1940, by contrast, fielded more than 4,100 soldiers per kilometer yet failed to prevent a German breakthrough and exploitation to the Channel: Dupuy, *Harper Encyclopedia*, p. 1158; Esposito, vol. 2, map 12. At the point of attack, German defenses opposite GOODWOOD were less dense than their positions in the Orel Salient in June 1943 or Alamein in September 1942, and about equal in density to their defenses at Stalingrad in November 1942—all of which were broken through: Jukes, *Kursk*, pp. 108, 110, 112; Dupuy, pp. 1186–87, Esposito, map 78; Glantz and House, *When Titans Clashed*, pp. 133–35. What about rules of thumb? As noted in chapter 5, rules of thumb are less clearly articulated for FSRs than FFRs, and this is especially true for the period between 1918 and the mid-1980s. Liddell Hart implied that for the Second World War, defensive FSRs above 1,250 troops per km at the point of attack usually succeeded; FSRs as high as 1,200, on the other hand, could still be broken through by astute attackers: *Deterrent or Defense*, pp. 102–8. (The 1,200 troops/km figure derives from Liddell Hart's discussion of the FSR at Sedan in 1940, pp. 102–5.) I use troops/km rather than divisions/km here because many German divisions in Normandy were so far below nominal strength by July 1944. The Germans opposite GOODWOOD deployed about 1,100 troops per kilometer on July 18; given the imprecision in Liddell Hart's mostly implicit thresholds (and imperfect strength reporting in the field, which limits the precision attainable even from archival data on FSRs), this figure is best treated as too close to call in Liddell Hart's terms. (All values are ration strengths.)

47. See, e.g., *BOHN*, pp. 327–32; Alun Chalfont, *Montgomery of Alamein* (New York: Atheneum, 1976), pp. 242–44; Nigel Hamilton, *Master of the Battlefield: Monty's War Years, 1942–44* (New York: McGraw Hill, 1983), pp. 713–45. Perhaps Montgomery's single most strident defender is Sweet, *Mounting the Threat*, pp. 116–22.

48. See, e.g., *AOHN*, p. 195; Ralph Ingersoll, *Top Secret* (New York: Harcourt Brace, 1946), pp. 162–63; Martin Blumenson, "Some Reflections on the Immediate Post-Assault Strategy," in *D-Day: The Normandy Invasion in Retrospect* (Lawrence: University Press of Kansas, 1971), pp. 210–18; Russell Weigley, *Eisenhower's Lieutenants* (Bloomington: Indiana University Press, 1981), pp. 211–15.

49. D'Este, *Decision in Normandy*, chap. 19.

50. *BOHN*, map oppos. p. 350; TDRC-5041, p. 1.

51. Doughty, *Breaking Point*, pp. 34, 37; I.S.O. Playfair and C.J.C. Molony, *The Mediterranean and Middle East*, vol. 4 (London: Her Majesty's Stationery Office, 1966), map 4; *AOHN*, map 10.

52. D'Este, *Decision in Normandy*, p. 380.

53. *BOHN*, p. 335; as D'Este notes, VIII Corps' 2-km frontage was more common for a brigade than a 3-division corps: *Decision in Normandy*, p. 376.

54. D'Este, *Decision in Normandy*, p. 376.

55. Ibid., pp. 281–82, 295; NA RG 338, FMS MS B-470, Generalmajor Sylvester Stadler, 9.SS.Pz.Div (20.6.44–24.7.44), p. 10; NA RG 338, FMS MS B-630, Oberstleutnant l.G. Horst von Wangenheim, 277.I.D. (Januar bis 24. Juli 1944), p. 20; note also the exposure of British tanks at GOODWOOD as seen in plates 50 and 51 of *BOHN*, and plate 32 of Keegan, *Six Armies*.

56. NA RG 338, FMS MS B-630, Oberstleutnant l.G. Horst von Wangenheim, 277.I.D. (Januar bis 24. Juli 1944), p. 20; D'Este, *Decision in Normandy*, pp. 291–96, 490; Hastings, *Overlord*, pp. 135–36, 145–46, 218, 237.

57. D'Este, *Decision in Normandy*, p. 372.

58. Ibid., p. 376; TDRC-5041, pp. 10–11.

59. *BOHN*, pp. 340–45; TDRC-5041, pp. 10–12; Keegan, *Six Armies*, pp. 204–5; Belfield and Essame, *Battle for Normandy*, p. 145.

60. As Freiherr von Rosen, a company commander in the German 503d Heavy Tank Battalion, described his unit in the aftermath of the bombing: "Fifteen men of the company were dead, two soldiers who had not been able to stand up under the terrific nervous strain committed suicide during the bombardment, another soldier had to be sent to a lunatic asylum for observation. The psychological shock of these terrible experiences remained with all of us for a long time" (quoted in Heywood, "Goodwood," p. 174). The barrage also buried many German tanks and antitank guns (most of which had been placed in deep, steep-walled entrenchments); while often intact, they had to be dug out before they could be used: see, e.g., NA RG 242 T-313-420, Anlage 156 zu KTB PzW, Tagesmeldung 18.7.44. Many of the gunlaying optics had also been jarred out of alignment and needed to be zeroed before the weapons could be used effectively. In the 503d Heavy Tank Battalion, for example, it took until noon for the unit's Tiger tanks to be made useable: D'Este, *Decision in Normandy*, p. 371; Hans von Luck, *Panzer Commander* (Westport: Praeger, 1989), pp. 154, 158; Heywood, "Goodwood," pp. 174, 176; Hodgson, "Eve of Defeat," p. 10.

61. Von Luck, *Panzer Commander*, pp. 154, 158; Heywood, "Goodwood," pp. 174, 176.

62. *BOHN*, p. 340; D'Este, *Decision in Normandy*, p. 360; Keegan, *Six Armies*, p. 205.

63. D'Este, *Decision in Normandy*, pp. 378–79.

64. Ibid., pp. 283–84, 286; Tim Harrison Place, "Lionel Wigram, Battle Drill, and the British Army in the Second World War," *War in History* 7, 1 (November 2000), pp. 442–62.

65. D'Este, *Decision in Normandy*, pp. 279–80, 287; Hastings, *Overlord*, pp. 48, 149, 210.

66. D'Este, *Decision in Normandy*, p. 283; see also pp. 280–81, 284, 286–87, 356; Hastings, *Overlord* pp. 145–50; NA RG 338, FMS MS B-470, Generalmajor Sylvester Stadler, 9.SS.Pz.Div (20.6.44–24.7.44), p. 10.

67. Montgomery's operations order for GOODWOOD established VIII Corps' first-day objective as "to dominate the area Bourguebus-Vimont-Bretteville" (para. 5, reprinted in *BOHN*, pp. 330–31). These points demark a triangular objective area whose nearest edge (the line Bourguebus-Vimont) was 10 km from the initial British front lines, and whose furthest point (Bretteville-sur-Laize) was 19 km away. In the new theory's terms, British tactics thus imply an intended net assault velocity of 10–19 km/day. By contrast, American first-day objectives in COBRA, the villages of St. Gilles and Marigny, were less than 3.5 and 6.5 km, respectively, from the U.S. departure line: *BOHN*, pp. 380–81; *AOHN*, pp. 216, 219.

68. These data are taken from from Jukes, *Kursk*, pp. 53–54; Glantz, *Don to Dnepr*, pp. 27–29, 35, 74, 225, 230, 381; Glantz, *Zhukov's Greatest Defeat*, pp. 336, 34–35, 51, 49, 54, 55, 62, 68; *AOHN*, pp. 224–28, map V; Doughty, *Breaking Point*, pp. 103–4, 123; Miller, *9th Australian Division*, p. 11; Playfair, *Mediterranean*, vol. 1, pp. 282–7, vol. 3, pp. 260–62, 265, 274, 383–84, 391, map 39; Erickson, *Road to Stalingrad*, p. 71; Keegan, *Six Armies*, pp. 171–73; Blumenson, *Salerno to Cassino*, pp. 207–8, map 8; Fisher, *Cassino to the Alps*, pp. 17–19; Blumenson, *Bloody River*, pp. 24, 55. One outlier, Kursk, with a depth of 160 km in July 1943, is excluded from the figure for reasons of compact graphical presentation but included in the median value calculation in the text.

69. NA RG 338, FMS MS P-157 (unfinished), Generalmajor a.D. Hellmuth Reinhardt, Das LXXXVI Armeekorps in der Zeit von Juni bis Nov. 1944, Anlage B, Zeittafel für

Antransport und Einsatz der 16.Lw.F.Div. in der Normandie beiderseits der Ornemün-dung von Mitte Juni 1944 bis 22.Juli 1944, pp. 2–3.

70. TDRC-5041, pp. 9–10.

71. TDRC-7725, p. A-7; TDRC-5041, p. 6; Hodgson, "Eve of Defeat," p. 25, situation map for 15/16 July 1944, and assuming that forward:reserve allocations in 271st, 276th, 277th, and 711th infantry and 9th SS, 10th SS and 2d Panzer divisions mirrored those for the other sixteen divisions in the theater on July 18.

72. These data are taken from from Jukes, *Kursk*, pp. 53–54; Glantz, *Don to the Dnepr*, pp. 27–29, 35, 74, 225, 230, 381; AOHN, pp. 224–28, map V; Doughty, *Breaking Point*, pp. 103–4, 123; Miller, *9th Australian Division*, pp. 13–17; Playfair, *Mediterranean*, vol. 3, pp. 383–84, 391, map 39; Fisher, *Cassino to the Alps*, pp. 17–19; Blumenson, *Bloody River*, pp. 24, 55; MacDonald, *Siegfried Line Campaign*, map 6, p. 330; Glantz, *Zhukov's Greatest Defeat*, pp. 336, 34–35, 51, 49, 54, 55, 62, 68, 11. (All values are ration strengths.)

73. D'Este, *Decision in Normandy*, pp. 98–99, 101–3. On German cover and conceal-ment, see also Paul Carrell, *Invasion—They're Coming* (London: Harrap, 1962), pp. 142–47; Keegan, *Six Armies*, p. 177; Hastings, *Overlord*, p. 212.

74. Ralph Bennett, *Ultra in the West* (New York: Charles Scribner's Sons, 1979), p. 106; Von Luck, *Panzer Commander*, p. 151.

75. *BOHN*, p. 306.

76. In fact, the great majority of German troops who fought in Normandy were moved there from elsewhere after the invasion; only nine divisions were deployed be-tween Cabourg and Avranches prior to June 6, 1944, as opposed to the twenty-one that moved into the theater between June 6 and July 24: *BOHN*, situation maps for June 6, 17, 30 and July 24.

77. Gooderson, *Air Power*, pp. 213–14.

78. NARA RG 338 FMS MS P-162, Walter Harzer, Oberst a.D., Der Einsatz der 9.SS-Pz.Div. "Hohenstaufen" im Westen vom 20. Juni 1944 bis 31. Oktober 1944, p. 23; RG 338, FMS MS B-470, Generalmajor Sylvester Stadler, 9.SS.Pz.Div (20.6.44–24.7.44), p. 16; RG 242 T-354-623, SS-Panzer-Grenadier-Regiment 2, Leibstandarte SS Adolf Hitler, Kriegstagebuch Nr. 157/44, 15.7.1944 02.00 Uhr, paragraph 6; Ralf Tiemann, *Chronicle of the 7. Panzer-Kompanie 1.SS-Panzer Division "Liebstandarte,"* trans. Allen Brandt (Atglen, PA: Schiffer, 1998), pp. 92–93, 95; Von Luck, *Panzer Commander*, p. 152; Carell, *Invasion*, p. 221.

79. NARA RG 338, FMS MS B-470, Generalmajor Sylvester Stadler, 9.SS.Pz.Div (20.6.44–24.7.44), p. 1; Keegan, *Six Armics*, pp. 179, 177–78.

80. 9th SS Panzer, for example, covered 340 km in 8 days, for a net V_r of 42.5 km/day; 1st SS Panzer covered 350 km in 11 days for a net V_r of 31.8; 2nd SS Panzergrenadier cov-ered 720 km in 22 days for a net V_r of 32.6: NARA RG 338, FMS MS B-470, Generalmajor Sylvester Stadler, 9.SS.Pz.Div (20.6.44–24.7.44), p. 1; Tiemann, *Chronicle*, pp. 91–92; Max Hastings, *Das Reich* (New York: Holt, Reinhart and Winston, 1981), pp. 1, 211. The nomi-nal no-interdiction baseline V_r of 100 km/day assumed in the appendix subsumes both movement time and delays associated with digging in and preparing fighting positions in the new location.

81. On the Falaise Pocket, see, e.g., D'Este, *Decision in Normandy*, pp. 418–34; AOHN, pp. 479–558. For German division count, see Keegan, *Six Armies*, p. 250.

82. Gooderson, *Air Power*, pp. 117–19. Vehicle and gun losses are taken from battlefield inspections conducted immediately after the action by the British Operations Research Service (ORS) and are highly reliable. Estimates of the retreating Germans' prior

strength, by contrast, are much less so, hence percentage loss figures are inherently soft. The ORS estimated that 30,000 German vehicles undertook the withdrawal, implying a net loss rate of 33 percent. This estimate indicated that 250 armored vehicles escaped the pocket, yet German records report only 72 on hand immediately afterward, implying that the ORS had overestimated German escapees by over a factor of three, and suggesting that German loss rates might have been as high as 80 percent if armored vehicle results were representative of German experience overall: ibid., p. 119. Note that many German vehicle losses were simply abandoned under air attack, rather than destroyed by the aircraft directly. Some vehicle losses counted by the ORS were also attributed to Allied ground forces, though many of these were presumably due to the Germans' uncustomary exposure in their haste to escape the pocket.

83. Given $\tau_R = 4.22$; $\tau_B = 4.03$; $R = 208,000$; $B = 91,800$; $w_{th} = 128$ (i.e., 80 miles); $w_a = 8.5$; and constants per table A. 1 (save that $k_5 = k_6 = 0$, since the calculation here focuses on losses in a single offensive sector, rather than theaterwide). As noted below, w_a could plausibly be coded either as 2 km or as 15 given the British dispositions' nonuniformity across the Second Army assault frontage; a 2 km coding would overestimate offensive penetration in GOODWOOD given the model's structure (which assumes uniform troop allocations across the assault frontage and does not penalize over-narrow fronts); a 15 km coding would underestimate it. Given this, I split the difference with a value of 8.5. For these conditions, the lower bound w_a of 2 implies 16 km of attacker ground gain; the upper bound of 15 implies only 3 km.

84. Specifically, $G = 4.42$; $t^* = 0.44$; $C_R = 180,030$; $C_B = 2,120$.

85. *BOHN*, map: The GOODWOOD Battle.

86. British troop losses came to 5,537: D'Este, *Decision in Normandy*, pp. 385–86. On British armor losses, see ibid.; *AOHN*, p. 193. Alexander McKee refers to the battle as "the death ride of the armoured divisions": *Caen*, chap. 17. Note that many of these losses were recovered from the battlefield and subsequently repaired. (For a much lower estimate based on very restrictive criteria, see Sweet, *Mounting the Threat*, pp. 114–16.) German losses, whether tanks or personnel, are unknown and can only be estimated. Some units were hit very hard: 16th Luftwaffe Feld Division, for example, was reduced to "wreckage" (*Trummer*) and by July 23 held an infantry strength of just two battalions: NA RG 242 T-313-420, Anlage 174 zu KTB PzW, 23.7.44. Hellmuth Reinhardt, commander of LXXXVI Corps, estimated his corps' personnel losses in GOODWOOD as up to 50 percent: NA RG 338, FMS MS P-157 (unfinished), Generalmajor a.D. Hellmuth Reinhardt, Das LXXXVI Armeekorps in der Zeit von Juni bis Nov. 1944, Pt. 2.IV.2. If one assumes comparable loss rates for those elements of I SS Corps exposed to the bomb carpet (i.e., 272d Infantry Division and 101st SS Panzer Battalion), and perhaps one-third of that for I SS Corps elements initially in reserve beyond the bombers' reach but heavily engaged early in the battle (i.e., 1st and 12th SS Panzer divisions), this implies 7,000–8,000 German troops killed and wounded, given prebattle strengths in TDRC-7725, pp. A6 to A7, and TDRC-5041, p. 6. I estimate 120–30 German tanks lost in the battle, based on the differences in tank strengths reported before and after the battle by 1st SS and 21st Panzer divisions, which I assume to be generally representative: TDRC-5041, p. 6; NA RG 242 T-313-420, Anlage 135 zu KTB PzW, Nachtrag zur Tagesmeldung, 15.7.44; Anlage 172 zu KTB PzW, Nachtrag zur Tagesmeldung vom 20.7.44; and Anlage 193 zu KTB PzW, Nachtrag zur Tagesmeldung, 23.7.44. By this estimate, British tank losses thus exceeded the Germans' by at least 3:1, and perhaps by 4.2:1 or more.

87. D'Este, *Decision in Normandy*, chap. 22: "The Furor over GOODWOOD"; *BOHN*, pp. 351–58.

88. Quoted in D'Este, *Decision in Normandy*, p. 394.

89. The battle dragged on for two days, though almost all the British advance occurred on the first morning; once 11th Armoured Division's lead units reached the base of the Bourguebus Ridge about noon on July 18, the British had reached their high-watermark for the battle: ibid., pp. 378–79; TDRC-5041, p. 10.

90. Specifically, $r_0 = 189,145$ and $C_R = 180,030$, given the parameters noted above.

91. *BOHN*, pp. 333, 535, appendix 4, pt 2; D'Este, *Decision in Normandy*, p 385.

92. By contrast, the model gets German losses about right. It predicts about 2,100 German combat arms casualties for the operation overall. In actuality, German aggregate personnel losses were probably around 7,000–8,000 troops of all branches (per note 86), of which perhaps 1,900–2,200 were in the direct-fire combat arms (per note 30). Note that the carpet bombing spread casualties more uniformly across German combat and non-combat branches at GOODWOOD than would be typical elsewhere.

93. See, e.g., *BOHN*, pp. 225–326; *AOHN*, pp. 53–203.

94. The model permits attackers to *misuse* that infantry (e.g., via poor cooperation with armor), but not to leave it out of harm's way.

95. Some British infantry did see action on July 18, but largely in mop-up actions against bypassed villages struck hard by the carpet bombing (especially Cuverville and Demouville); while this took time (and prevented the infantry from supporting the armored advance on the primary objectives), it incurred few casualties: *The 1st and 2nd Northamptonshire Yeomanry, 1939–1946* (Brunswick, Germany: J. H. Meyer, 1946), pp. 119–20.

96. *BOHN*, pp. 537–39.

97. Alvin D. Coox and L. Van Loan Naisawald, *Survey of Allied Tank Casualties in World War II* (Ft. Leslie McNair: Operations Research Office, Johns Hopkins University, March 31, 1951), ORO-T-117, declassified March 27, 1978, pp. 33, 42.

98. Some argue that the British offensive's radical tank-heaviness was a deliberate effort to conserve British infantry in the face of dwindling replacements: e.g., D'Este, *Decision in Normandy*, pp. 252–70, 337–90.

99. The model assumes that high-velocity, non–modern-system attackers will be unable to use infantry effectively, but the result is assumed to be unusually heavy infantry losses given their consequent exposure. Attackers, like the British at GOODWOOD, who simply leave the infantry behind lose their services but do not expose them to fire and thus do not suffer disproportionate infantry losses per se. The model is not designed to accommodate the casualty implications of such employment.

100. By focusing on the VIII Corps corridor per se, I isolate a sector of uniform attacker concentration and unit composition.

101. This assumes exogenous values of 14,450 for r_0 and 37.5 for b_0 (i.e., 300 forward German direct-fire combat arms soldiers per km in I SS and LXXXVI Corps, on a 2-km front, over 16 km of depth) rather than the endogenous formulations for r_0 and b_0 as given in equations 9 and 10 of the appendix, and assumes other values for independent variables and constants as noted above. Figures for forward German soldiers per km are from TDRC-7725, p. A-7, and TDRC-5041, p. 6, given a 26-km front for the two corps as noted above.

102. On German depth and tactical skill, see *BOHN*, pp. 332–33, 336; D'Este, *Decision in Normandy*, pp. 376–77, 387; Keegan *Six Armies*, p. 218; Hastings, *Overlord*, pp. 170–86;

Belfield and Essame, *Battle for Normandy*, p. 140; Maule, *Normandy Breakout*, p. 88; Von Luck, *Panzer Commander*, p. 151. On poor British combined arms coordination, see *BOHN*, p. 352; D'Este, pp. 291–6, 388–89; Belfield and Essame, pp. 144–45; McKee, *Caen*, pp. 250, 280; Maule, p. 82; Von Luck, p. 150. On congestion, see *BOHN*, pp. 335, 345, 352; D'Este, pp. 376–78, 380; Keegan, pp. 218–19; Belfield and Essame, p. 135; McKee, pp. 251, 255; Maule, pp. 82–83; Martin Blumenson, *The Duel for France, 1944* (Boston: Houghton Mifflin, 1963), p. 70. On the related issues of separation between British maneuver elements and fire support, and German ability to observe British staging areas (which contributed to British congestion by inducing Dempsey to delay VIII Corps' deployment until the last minute in an attempt to preserve surprise), see *BOHN*, p. 335; McKee, p. 256; Belfield and Essame, p. 135.

103. In fact, the Germans' chief lesson from the battle was that they should place even greater emphasis on defensive depth in the future. In particular, von Kluge concluded that forward garrisons should be thinned even further: NA RG 242, T-354-147, Anlage 165 zu KTB PzW, Besprechung in Anwesenheit des Gen.Feldm.v.Kluge am 20.7.44. Note that some German commanders felt their forward infantry divisions in Normandy were unevenly trained: NA RG 338 FMS MS B-526, Generalleutnant Kurt Badinski, 276th I.D. (1.1.44–20.8.44), p. 21; NA RG 338, FMS MS B-630, Oberstleutnant l.G. Horst von Wangenheim, 277.I.D. (Januar bis 24. Juli 1944), pp. 21–22, 24–25, 30; NA RG 338 FMS MS B-441, Generalleutnant Edgar Feuchtinger, 21.Pz.Div. (1942 bis Juli 1944), p. 38. If so, this offers another contributing explanation for the model's tendency to overestimate British losses: were f_e to increase modestly from 0 to 0.25, for example, reflecting uneven forward infantry training, British casualties would fall to 2,500 for the exogenous b_0, r_0 case discussed above (relative to the 3,370 figure estimated above), holding ground gain constant. Results in the endogenous b_0, r_0 case would be little different: the attack would be contained after a 6-km advance (rather than 4) in 0.6 days (rather than 0.5).

104. Hastings, *Overlord*, pp. 186–95; Belfield and Essame, *Battle for Normandy*, p. 140.

105. The overwhelming majority—about 83 percent—of the Tigers and Panthers in the I SS and LXXXVI Corps were held in the two reserve divisions, 1st and 12th SS Panzer, and the 503rd Heavy Tank Battalion: NA RG242, T-313-420, KTB PzW 15.7.44, Anlage 135; KTB PzW 10.7.44, Anlage 105; TDRC 5041, p. 6. None saw action on the morning of July 18. The lead elements of 1st SS tank regiment did not make contact with the British 11th Armoured until 1430 on the 18th; 12th SS did not make contact until the afternoon of the 19th; while the 503d was caught in the carpet bombing and rendered combat ineffective until noon on the 18th, when it got about six to eight Tigers into action for a counterattack from Emieville: TDRC-5041, pp. 12–13; Heywood, "Goodwood," at p. 175; Keegan, *Six Armies*, p. 208. Even then, the few Tigers the 503d did get into action were largely ineffective, as the bombing had thrown their gunsights out of alignment, making it impossible to lay the main guns accurately: Heywood, p. 176. By contrast, the lead elements of the British 11th Armoured Division had been halted at the foot of the Bourguebus ridge by around 1100 on the 18th and made negligible progress thereafter: Sweet, *Mounting the Threat*, p. 84. (Although published accounts by British sources make periodic references to Panther and Tiger fire on the morning of the 18th, German sources show no operable Panthers or Tigers actually present until the afternoon, with few present until mid-to-late afternoon; the great majority of German antitank fire on the battle's first morning were from 75-mm and 88-mm towed antitank guns. Tiger- and Panther-obsessed Allied tank crews had a tendency to mistake almost any German tanks or

antitank fires for Tigers and Panthers, and this presumably accounts for the erroneous reporting: see, e.g., Keegan, *Six Armies*, p. 177, on Allied soldiers' fixation with Tigers and
Panthers.)

106. The 88-mm battery in Cagny was initially without *any* supporting infantry; later
that day, a single platoon from Von Luck's staff company arrived to provide local security,
but even then the 88 battery was under orders to destroy its guns and withdraw if British
infantry appeared: Von Luck, *Panzer Commander*, pp. 154–57. Had British infantry been
operating in conjunction with the lead tanks, the guns at Cagny (and elsewhere) that
wrought so much damage on the morning of the 18th could have been easily silenced.

107. Belfield and Essame, *Battle for Normandy*, p. 137; Maule, p. 110.

108. See, e.g., D'Este, *Decision in Normandy*, pp. 338, 368; Martin Blumenson, "Reflections," p. 215.

109. *BOHN*, p. 351; Belfield and Essame, *Battle for Normandy*, p. 139; McKee, *Caen*, p. 261.

110. *Military Operational Research Unit Report No. 23: Battle Study, Operation "Goodwood,"*
p. 14; on the fate of the Fifes and Forfars and Guards Armoured at Cagny, see R. J. B. Sellar,
The Fife and Forfar Yeomanry, 1919–1956 (London: Blackwood, 1960), pp. 168–71; Captain
the Earl of Rosse and Col. E. R. Hill, *The Story of the Guards Armoured Division* (London:
Geoffrey Bles, 1956), pp. 39–40.

111. On German defensive depth and carpet bombing effectiveness more generally, see
Gooderson, *Air Power*, chap. 6, esp. pp. 146, 158.

112. The 88-mm battery that caused such havoc at Cagny had just *four* surviving guns:
Von Luck, *Panzer Commander*, p. 153.

113. E.g., Sweet, *Mounting the Threat*, pp. 108–16; Belchem, *Victory in Normandy*, p. 155;
John North, *North-West Europe 1944–5: The Achievement of 21st Army Group* (London: Her
Majesty's Stationery Office, 1953), pp. 59–60.

114. See note 6.

115. The phrasing is D'Este's: *Decision in Normandy*, p. 388. See also Blumenson, *Duel
for France*, p. 70; Von Luck, *Panzer Commander*, pp. 158–59. This view was shared by some
in the Allied High Command; for Air Marshal Tedder's views, for instance, see Keegan,
Six Armies, p. 217. Conversely, others argue that Goodwood failed because it was too
bold: e.g., McKee, *Caen*, p. 250; Hastings, *Overlord*, p. 238. The latter is more consistent
with my findings.

116. *BOHN*, p. 340.

Chapter Seven
Operation Desert Storm

1. A total of 540,000 of the troops and 148 of the fatalities were Americans. Total
American and allied casualties (killed and wounded) came to 1,116: Freedman and Karsh,
The Gulf Conflict, p. 409; Atkinson, *Crusade*, pp. 491–92.

2. Cordesman and Wagner, *Lessons of Modern War*, Vol. 1, pp. 15, 18, 150; Addington,
Patterns of War, pp. 182, 184, 237; Karber et al., *Correlation of Forces*, pp. 2–3; Bruce, ed.,
Harbottle's Dictionary, p. 95.

3. See references in chapter 1, n. 1.

4. See, e.g., Andrew Krepinevich, *The Bottom-Up Review: An Assessment* (Washington,
DC: Defense Budget Project, February 1994), pp. i, 22, 25–26, 49; Lawrence J. Korb, "The

Impact of the Persian Gulf War on Military Budgets and Force Structure," and Bobby R. Inman, et al., "U.S. Strategy after the Storm," in Joseph S. Nye, Jr., and Roger K. Smith, eds., *After the Storm: Lessons from the Gulf War* (New York: Madison Books for the Aspen Strategy Group, 1992), pp. 221–40 and 267–89, respectively; Rep. Les Aspin, *An Approach to Sizing American Conventional Forces for the Post-Soviet Era: Four Illustrative Options* (Washington, DC: House Armed Services Committee, Feb. 25, 1992); Christopher Bowie et al., *The New Calculus* (Santa Monica: RAND, 1993); Michael O'Hanlon, *Defense Planning for the Late 1990s* (Washington, DC: Brookings, 1995), e.g., pp. 30–32; Philip Finnegan, "War Emphasizes Stealth Need, Says Cheney," *Defense News*, February 11, 1991, p. 10; U.S. House Armed Services Committee, *Defense for a New Era: Lessons of the Persian Gulf War* (Washington, DC: US GPO, 1992), hereafter HASC; John Collins, *Desert Shield and Desert Storm: Implications for Future U.S. Force Requirements* (Washington, DC: Congressional Research Service, 1991); Scales, et al., *Certain Victory*, p. 364; Gordon and Trainor, *The Generals' War*, p. 470.

5. Note that DESERT STORM provides a stronger test of dyadic technology per se than either MICHAEL or GOODWOOD, as the technological imbalance here was among the greatest on record (see below). While DESERT STORM is not critical in Eckstein's terms for the gross outcome of breakthrough vs. containment, the extreme technological imbalance suggests that the case's details should be as consistent with dyadic technology theory's predictions as any case ever will be—that they are not is thus unusually strong disconfirmatory evidence for dyadic theory.

6. *GWAPS*, vol. 2, pt. 1, pp. 102, 120–58, 264–66; Summary Report, pp. 7, 11–13, 40–52.

7. U.S. Department of Defense, *Conduct of the Persian Gulf War*, Final Report to Congress Pursuant to Title V of Public Law 102–25 (Washington, DC: US GPO, April 1992), hereafter Title V, pp. 251–58. While the Guard's performance was certainly not "elite" by Western standards, they were clearly Iraq's best troops.

8. These were the Tawakalna, Medina, and Adnan Republican Guard divisions, and the 52d, 12th, and 10th Armored: Scales, *Certain Victory*, pp. 232–36, 266; Richard M. Swain, *"Lucky War": Third Army in Desert Storm* (Ft. Leavenworth, KS: U.S. Army Command and General Staff College, 1994), pp. 244, 247; Gordon and Trainor, *The Generals' War*, p. 387; U.S. News and World Report, (USNWR), *Triumph without Victory* p. 335; Lieutenant Colonel Peter S. Kindsvatter, "VII Corps in the Gulf War: Ground Offensive," *Military Review* 72, 2 (February 1992), p. 34.

9. U.S. armored cavalry regiments (ACRs) have three ground squadrons of three cavalry troops and one tank company each. Each troop is roughly equivalent to a reinforced tank or mechanized infantry company with twenty to thirty armored vehicles. "The Battle of 73 Easting" thus pitted less than half the 2d ACR against a brigade (the 18th) of the Tawakalna: Jesse Orlansky and COL Jack Thorpe, eds., *73 Easting: Lessons Learned from Desert Storm via Advanced Distributed Simulation Technology* (Alexandria, VA: Institute for Defense Analyses, 1992), IDA D-1110, pp. I-114, I-121 to 125.

10. Orlansky and Thorpe, *73 Easting*, pp. I-111 to I-136; Krause, *73 Easting*; J. R. Crooks et al., *73 Easting Re-Creation Data Book* (Westlake, CA: Illusion Engineering, 1992), IEI Report No. DA-MDA972-1-92, appendices, shoot history by vehicle for Eagle, Ghost, Iron Troops; "The Battle of 73 Easting," briefing slides prepared by Janus Gaming Division, TRADOC Analysis Command, White Sands, NM, March 30, 1992, henceforth TRAC brief, esp. slide 3 text, slide 16 text.

11. Scales, *Certain Victory*, pp. 292–300; Gordon and Trainor, *The Generals' War*, pp. 407–8; Atkinson, *Crusade*, pp. 465–67; USNWR, *Triumph without Victory*, pp. 377–86.

12. Scales, *Certain Victory*, pp. 282–84; USNWR, *Triumph without Victory*, pp. 357–70.

13. Scales, *Certain Victory*, pp. 267–70.

14. Kindsvatter, "VII Corps," p. 17.

15. Systemic technology theory is ambiguous on the Gulf War. On one hand, deep strike and ground-attack air technologies were clearly very advanced and very plentiful in 1991 (especially for the Coalition), and the U.S. M1A1 tank was history's most advanced. These characteristics would conduce to offensive advantage. On the other hand, precision-guided antitank technologies were also very advanced and very plentiful; firepower in general was prevalent and lethal. These characteristics would conduce to defensive advantage. It is thus unclear how DESERT STORM should be coded. An important shortcoming of orthodox offense-defense theory is its absence of clear, operational criteria for coding the offense-defense balance; while extrema like MICHAEL and GOODWOOD enable unambiguous characterization, many other cases do not: Jack Levy, "Offensive/Defensive Balance"; Biddle, "Rebuilding the Foundations," pp. 741–74.

16. *GWAPS*, vol. 2, pt. 1, p. 87n; Scales, *Certain Victory*, p. 295. As the U.S. shouldered the bulk of the war's close combat, I focus on U.S. technology here.

17. Scales, "Accuracy Defeated Range," pp. 473–81; Alex Vernon, *The Eyes of Orion* (Kent, OH: Kent State University Press, 1999), p. 204.

18. Gordon and Trainor, *The Generals' War*, pp. 353, 475; Scales, *Certain Victory*, p. 254; *GWAPS*, vol. 2, pt. 1, pp. 58–59.

19. *GWAPS*, Summary Report, pp. 223–34, vol. 2, pt. 2, pp. 109–11; Title V, p. 164; Perry, "Desert Storm," pp. 66–82.

20. Scales, *Certain Victory*, p. 216.

21. *GWAPS*, vol. 2, pt. 2, pp. 168, 220. Other estimates have ranged from a high of 540,000 (the wartime CENTCOM figure) to a low of 183,000: HASC, pp. 29–34.

22. This assumes a roughly Normandy-equivalent figure of 15 percent of total in-theater soldiers for the Coalition, and 30 percent for the Iraqis: see chapter 6 n. 30.

23. Congressional Budget Office, *Strengthening NATO*, pp. 11–13, appendix C; and *Army Ground Force Modernization*, pp. 30–31.

24. Cordesman and Wagner, *Lessons of Modern War*, vol. 1, p. 17; vol. 3, p. 261.

25. Local FFRs in key battles, on the other hand, were highly variable. At VII Corps' initial point of attack, the 1st Infantry Division probably enjoyed a local numerical advantage of at least 3 or 4:1 over the Iraqi 26th Infantry (assuming 18,000 soldiers for the 1st Infantry, and fewer than 5,000 for the 26th, per *GWAPS*, vol. 2, pt. 2, pp. 166, 212). Other later battles occurred at sometimes much lower local FFRs: see below.

26. On the other hand, local FSRs in key battles, like FFRs, were highly variable. The 26th Infantry Division at VII Corps' point of attack probably deployed about 200 troops per km and perhaps 10–15 forward troops per square km: Scales, *Certain Victory*, p. 231; troop strength is estimated following *GWAPS*, vol. 2, pt. 2, p. 168. Other later battles occurred at sometimes much higher local FSRs: see below.

27. Scales, *Certain Victory*, fig. 5–1.

28. See, e.g., Thompson and Gantz, *Conventional Arms Control*, p. 12; Davis et al., *Central Region Stability*, p. 31; Mearsheimer, *Conventional Deterrence*, p. 181; William Mako, *U.S. Ground Forces and the Defense of Central Europe* (Washington, DC: Brookings, 1983), p. 37; using troop counts per division and brigade per Mako, p. 113.

29. Cordesman and Wagner, *Lessons of Modern War*, vol. 1, pp. 17, 118.

30. I focus here on the Americans (and to a lesser extent, the British) as these shouldered the great bulk of the fighting.

31. Scales, *Certain Victory*, p. 67.

32. Peter Allen, *The Yom Kippur War* (New York: Scribner's, 1982), pp. 68, 118.

33. Scales, *Certain Victory*, pp. 91, 95.

34. MG Barry McCaffrey, Testimony before the Senate Armed Services Committee, May 9, 1991, slide 11; MAJ Jason Kamiya, *A History of the 24th Mechanized Infantry Division Combat Team during Operation DESERT STORM* (Ft. Stewart, GA: 24th Mechanized Infantry Division, nd), p. 3.

35. Scales, *Certain Victory*, pp. 91, 95.

36. *GWAPS*, vol. 2, pt. 2, p. 163.

37. *GWAPS* reports prewar manning levels ranging from 57 to 85 percent for Iraqi divisions but very conservatively assumes upper-bound manning levels for all divisions other than the eleven frontline units known to be in the worst shape (ibid., p. 168); this implausibly assumes that Republican Guard and conscript army infantry units had the same manning levels prior to the air war. I instead assume an intermediate manning level of 65 percent for the remaining fourteen forward infantry divisions (with army heavy and Republican Guard units assumed to be manned at 85 percent of nominally authorized levels, per *GWAPS*). I further assume that all desertions during the air war were from forward divisions, but that actual casualties from air attack were distributed evenly (in fact, forward divisions were harder hit). Given *GWAPS*' figures for overall desertions and pre–groundwar Iraqi casualties (p. 220), this implies that about 70 percent of Iraqi divisional troop strength was in mobile reserve on the eve of the ground war.

38. Scales, *Certain Victory*, p. 95.

39. See, e.g., Title V, pp. 251–53.

40. See, e.g., Lupfer, *Dynamics of Doctrine*, p. 15. On the Coalition's ability to locate such entrenchments with precision, see Scales, *Certain Victory*, p. 228.

41. See, e.g., Title V, pp. 251–53; Murray Hammick, "Iraqi Obstacles and Defensive Positions," *International Defense Review* 24, 9 (1991), pp. 989–91. The Iraqis had dug a shallow trench in front of their forward infantry positions that was to be filled with oil and ignited, but this depended on an uninterrupted supply of oil; the latter was denied by air attack on the pumping system. A sand berm covered much of the Iraqi infantry's front, but this was poorly covered by defensive fires and thus was easily breached by U.S. engineers. The "Saddam Line" at the Saudi border was thus haphazard at best; Republican Guard positions to its rear, however, were little better, and in some ways even worse (often lacking even the rudimentary obstacle systems of the forward defenses): Robert Zirkle, "Memorandum for the Record: Information Obtained during West Point/IDA Janus 73 Easting Session, 8–10 April 1992," Institute for Defense Analyses, April 15, 1992, pp. 1, 2.

42. Orlansky and Thorpe, *73 Easting*, p. I-54; Gordon and Trainor, *The Generals' War*, pp. 407–8; Scales, *Certain Victory*, pp. 210, 261, 269, 294; Steve Vogel, "Metal Rain," *Army Times*, September 16, 1991, p. 22.

43. In fact, it was standard operating procedure in the 2d ACR to fire at any berm, whether a target had been positively identified behind it or not: Zirkle, "Memorandum for the Record," p. 2. On berms, see, e.g., TRAC brief, slide 10 text.

44. See, e.g., Orlansky and Thorpe, *73 Easting*, p. I-54; Peter Tsouras and Elmo C. Wright, Jr., "The Ground War," in Bruce W. Watson, ed., *Military Lessons of the Gulf War*

(Novato, CA: Presidio Press, 1991), pp. 81–120; *Operation Desert Shield/Desert Storm, Hearings Before the Committee on Armed Services, United States Senate* (Washington, DC: USGPO, 1991), S. Hrg. 102–326, henceforth SASC, p. 115. Solid earth in sufficient depth can stop any current tank gun, but this requires digging into the ground, not perching above it behind piles of sand.

45. Scales, *Certain Victory*, p. 118; Gordon and Trainor, *The Generals' War*, pp. 352–3; James Pardew, "The Iraqi Army's Defeat in Kuwait," *Parameters* 21, 4 (Winter 1991–92), pp. 17–23.

46. A one-word radio message is enough to sound the alarm. Even less can be accommodated if commanders agree in advance that failure to check in at specified times will be taken as warning of attack. The brevity of the message makes it virtually impossible to jam; the procedural back up of interpreting silence as warning means that even a dead observer can still provide an alert: see, e.g., Kenneth Macksey, *First Clash* (New York: Berkeley Books, 1988), p. 102.

47. Steve Vogel, "A Swift Kick: 2d ACR's Taming of the Guard," *Army Times*, August 5, 1991, p. 30; see also Krause, *Battle of 73 Easting*, p. 32. Other examples from elsewhere in the KTO are commonplace: see, e.g., Vogel, "Metal Rain," p. 16: "Iraqi prisoners [taken at Medina Ridge] later said they thought the artillery was an air attack, and many had abandoned their vehicles for bomb shelters . . . in their thermals, the U.S. crews could see Iraqi soldiers leaving their bunkers and reboarding tanks and BMP infantry fighting vehicles. 'A lot of them were mowed down trying to get back to their vehicles,' said [Major Chess] Harris, the 3d Brigade's executive officer." See also Title V, pp. 139–40; Atkinson, *Crusade*, p. 466; Gordon and Trainor, *The Generals' War*, p. 359; USNWR, *Triumph without Victory*, p. 384; Steve Vogel, "Hell Night: For the 2d Armored Division, It Was No Clean War," *Army Times*, October 7, 1991, p. 15; Krause, p. 19, describing 2d ACR engagements prior to 73 Easting.

48. Krause, *Battle of 73 Easting*, pp. 21, 32; Orlansky and Thorpe, *73 Easting*, p. I-117; Turrell interview. Note that in Ghost troop's sector, for example, some eighteen minutes elapsed between the time U.S. attackers made initial contact with the Tawakalna main line of resistance and the first observed return fire by the Iraqis: Krause, p. 16. Properly manned defending vehicles would ordinarily return hostile fire immediately (indeed, defenders ordinarily get the first shot in tactical mechanized combat). Not all Tawakalna vehicles were empty; at least some 2d ACR crews reported receiving Iraqi fire or observing tank turret movement from the beginning of the battle: interview, CPT H. R. McMaster, USA, January 1994. Nevertheless, considerable evidence suggests that Iraqi warning failures frequently provided Coalition attackers with opportunities to engage empty targets. In fact, the Marine Corps has estimated that the majority of all Iraqi armored vehicles destroyed on the Marines' front were unoccupied when killed: U.S. Marine Corps Battlefield Assessment Team, *Armor/Antiarmor Operations in Southwest Asia* (Quantico, VA: Marine Corps Research Center, July 1991), Research Paper No.2-0002, henceforth USMC BAT, p. 18. Most had moved from their pre–groundwar locations into the positions encountered by the Marines; pre-attack desertion thus cannot explain the crews' absence when the tanks were killed, suggesting that failure to obtain timely warning was probably a major contributing cause.

49. See, e.g., Krause, *Battle of 73 Easting*, p. 28; Scales, *Certain Victory*, pp. 117–18, 257, 293; Atkinson, *Crusade*, p. 212; Gordon and Trainor, *The Generals' War*, pp. 287, 360; Scales, "Accuracy Defeated Range," pp. 473–81.

50. Krause, *Battle of 73 Easting*, pp. 17–18. As the Iraqis proved unable to implement evasive "shoot and scoot" tactics, U.S. counterfire quickly silenced the Iraqis' one, abortive, attempt to provide fire support: Orlansky and Thorpe, *73 Easting*, p. I-145.

51. Krause, *Battle of 73 Easting*, pp. 17–18.

52. See, e.g., Freedman and Karsh, *The Gulf Conflict*, p. 437; Norman Friedman, *Desert Victory: The War for Kuwait* (Annapolis: Naval Institute Press, 1991), pp. 235, 246, 252–53; James Blackwell, *Thunder in the Desert: The Strategy and Tactics of the Persian Gulf War* (New York: Bantam, 1991), pp. 220–23; Harry G. Summers, Jr., *On Strategy II: A Critical Analysis of the Gulf War* (New York: Dell, 1992), pp. 155, 265.

53. Scales, *Certain Victory*, p. 149. The plan also called for a frontal assault by the 1st and 2d U.S. Marine divisions near the coastal highway, though this was intended as a secondary attack to draw Iraqi reserves forward and render them more vulnerable to the primary effort by VII Corps: Gordon and Trainor, *The Generals' War*, p. 374.

54. On operational maneuver as an explanation of radically low losses, see the discussion below.

55. Scales, *Certain Victory*, p. 229. In Operation GOODWOOD, by contrast, just the first of the three armored divisions massed on the VIII Corps corridor placed over 300 tanks on just a 2-km front—or about the same number of armored vehicles as in 1st Infantry's breach effort but on only one-third the frontage: TDRC-7725, pp. A-4 to A-5; Sweet, *Mounting the Threat*, p. 112. And the British at GOODWOOD expected to commit all three of VIII Corps' armored divisions on that frontage in the initial assault, a design calling for about three times the DESERT STORM breakthrough effort's vehicle count on one-third of its frontage. While the DESERT STORM frontage was narrow enough to enable tremendous differential concentration, it was thus not nearly so narrow as the logistically asphyxiating frontage at GOODWOOD.

56. Scales, *Certain Victory* (p. 229), estimates the local FFR at the point of attack as "battalions against platoons," or at least 9:1.

57. For an overview, see *GWAPS*, vol. 2, pt. 1, pp. 249–326. Not all of the Coalition air effort was in direct support of the breakthrough effort; much of it was either explicitly strategic in nature, or implicitly strategic (in the sense that much of the pre-invasion air targeting of Iraqi ground forces was at least partly intended to induce concession without requiring a ground invasion). Once the ground campaign began, however, the bulk of the Coalition air effort turned to supporting—and exploiting—its effects.

58. Scales, *Certain Victory*, pp. 232–36, 266; Swain, *"Lucky War,"* pp. 244, 247; Gordon and Trainor, *The Generals' War*, p. 387; USNWR, *Triumph without Victory*, p. 335; Kindsvatter, "VII Corps," p. 34.

59. Haste in the breakthrough phase would be inconsistent with the modern system; haste in the exploitation phase is not. The whole purpose of breakthrough is to provide the opportunity to accelerate in exploitation, substituting hasty attacks on hastily prepared rearward defenses for deliberate assaults on the deliberately prepared forward defenses typically encountered in the initial breakthrough effort. A fast-moving exploitation is part and parcel of modern system operations. See the discussion of "Breakthrough and Exploitation" in chapter 3, and "Increased Mobility" in chapter 4.

60. Scales, *Certain Victory*, pp. 226–32.

61. For similar examples from elsewhere in the theater, see ibid., pp. 233–320; Charles Cureton, *U.S. Marines in the Persian Gulf, 1990–1991: With the 1st Marine Division in Desert Shield and Desert Storm* (Washington, DC: History and Museums Division, Headquarters U.S. Marine Corps, 1993), pp. 26–121.

62. Gordon and Trainor, *The Generals' War*, pp. 346–48, 357–61; SASC, pp. 66–68.

63. Krause, *73 Easting*, pp. 11–12; interview, CPT H. R. McMaster, USA, January 1994.

64. At 73 Easting, for example, the 2d ACR transitioned directly into the assault from a 17-km approach march: Krause, *73 Easting*, p. 15; for combat formations at 73 Easting, see ibid., pp. 51–55.

65. Scales, *Certain Victory*, e.g., pp. 237–40, 247, 253, 259, 261, 265, 273, 276, 281.

66. Ibid., pp. 267–70, 273–84.

67. Ibid., pp. 224–32. Note that as the VII Corps action against the Republican Guard occurred during the exploitation phase following successful breakthrough, it was thus waged at a significantly higher velocity than the initial breakthrough per se. V_a as specified in the formal model pertains only to the breakthrough phase.

68. Given $\tau_R = 7.39$; $\tau_B = 6.19$; $R = 120,000$; $B = 60,000$; $w_{th} = 750$; $w_a = 6$; and constants per table A-1 (save that $k_5 = 0$, per the logic in chapters 4 and 5); which implies attacker losses of $d * C_a = 1157.3$ (recall that C_R as given in equation 20 of the appendix pertains only to contained offensives). $V_r = 50$ assumes reserve movements restricted to nighttime hours, as the Iraqis appear to have done: *GWAPS*, vol. 2, pt. 2, pp. 192, 200. The model actually predicts breakthrough under these conditions for any values of V_r and f_e. To prevent breakthrough under such numerical and technological inferiority, a defender would require radically greater depth: even for $f_e = 0.05$, $V_r = 15$, and $f_r = 0.7$, for example, $d \geq 145$ is required to prevent breakthrough for $V_a = 3$ and $w_a = 6$. (Recall that d for the Coalition defense in DESERT SHIELD exceeded 150.)

69. See, e.g., Gordon and Trainor, *The Generals' War*, p. 474; Perry, "Desert Storm," pp. 66–82; Inman, et al., "U.S. Strategy after the Storm," p. 284; HASC, p. 7; Richard Hallion, *Storm over Iraq: Airpower and the Gulf War* (Washington, DC: Smithsonian Press, 1992), pp. 241–68; Dilip Hiro, *Desert Shield to Desert Storm: The Second Gulf War* (New York: Routledge, 1992), pp. 320, 441.

70. In principle, even a historically large Iraqi armor residual could still inflict historically low Coalition losses if the ratio of Iraqi survivors to Coalition attackers were historically low, or if the Iraqi loss rate were so high as to render their survivors ineffective (though numerous). Neither exception holds here. For the former, see the discussion under "Iraqi Numerical Inferiority" below. For the latter, the causal mechanism is typically held to be the loss of will to fight: Leonard Wainstein, *The Relationship of Battle Damage to Unit Combat Performance* (Alexandria, VA: Institute for Defense Analyses, 1986), IDA P-1903, pp. 1–2. As argued below, however, this cannot explain the result here.

71. *GWAPS*, vol. 2, part 2, pp. 170, 214, 218–19; Summary Volume, p. 106.

72. See, e.g., Krause, *73 Easting*, pp. 11, 12, 13, 15, 16, 19, 21, 22; also LTC Douglas A. Macgregor, "Closing with the Enemy," *Military Review* 73 2 (February 1993), p. 65; 1st Lt. Daniel L. Davis, "The 2d ACR at the Battle of 73 Easting," *Field Artillery* (April 1992), pp. 48–53; SSgt. William H. McMichael, "Iron Troop's Trial by Fire," *Soldiers* (June 1991), pp. 8–12.

73. Krause, *73 Easting*, p. 12; see also 2d Lt. Richard M. Bohannon, "Dragon's Roar: 1–37 Armor in the Battle of 73 Easting," *Armor* (May–June 1992), p.16.

74. 73 Easting Data Base. See also Krause, *73 Easting*, pp. 12, 16, 17, 22.

75. In fact, some participants reported numerous small-scale counterattacks at various points in the battle: see, e.g., Krause, *73 Easting*, pp. 12, 16, 20, 22; also Lt. John Hillen, "2d Armored Cavalry: The Campaign to Liberate Kuwait," *Armor* (July–August 1991), p. 11. Not all of these, however, can be unambiguously identified as deliberate attacks—confusion

over the location of U.S. and Iraqi forces, for example, may account for some movements of small, isolated Iraqi units toward U.S. forces. The analysis above is conservative in crediting as a true counterattack only the action repelled by Ghost troop after nightfall, which can be clearly distinguished as a deliberate counterattack by the behavior of the Iraqi units conducting the action (e.g., dismounting infantry, returning fire, and continuing to close with U.S. forces when taken under fire—such behavior is inconsistent with any interpretation other than deliberate counterattack): interview, LTC Robert C. Turrell, USA ret'd., IDA, April 11, 1995. U.S. participants in the action were quite emphatic on this point. As Lt. Keith Garwick of Ghost Troop reports: "We just couldn't understand it. I still don't understand it. Those guys were insane. They wouldn't stop. They kept dying and dying and dying" (Krause, p. 15).

76. Krause, *73 Easting*, p. 14.

77. TRAC brief, slide 3 text, slide 16 text. In Eagle Troop's sector, for example, no Iraqis were taken prisoner until after the battle when a U.S. psychological warfare team was brought forward to broadcast surrender appeals in Arabic: personal communication, MAJ H. R. McMaster, September 8, 1995. The Eagle Troop commander described the 73 Easting battlefield as "covered with enemy dead": Krause, *73 Easting*, p. 15.

78. Scales, *Certain Victory*, pp. 232–36; Swain, "*Lucky War*," pp. 244, 247; Gordon and Trainor, *The Generals' War*, pp. 387–88.

79. Scales, *Certain Victory*, pp. 232–36.

80. See, e.g., Nigel Pearce, *The Shield and the Sabre: The Desert Rats in the Gulf, 1990–91* (London: Her Majesty's Stationery Office, 1992), pp. 101, 102, 166; Swain, "*Lucky War*," pp. 247, 254; Gordon and Trainor, *The Generals' War*, e.g. pp. 359, 363–68; Atkinson, *Crusade*, pp. 441–81; USNWR, *Triumph without Victory*, e.g., pp. 332–98; Scales (who overstates the point), *Certain Victory*, e.g., pp. 257, 268, 358, 359, 368; Freedman and Karsh, *The Gulf Conflict*, p. 397.

81. *GWAPS*, vol. 2, pt 2, p. 169.

82. And of course, this lower bound excludes any other Iraqi forces—such as the Iraqi armor known to have fought in the Burqan counterattack or the brigade-level engagement between the U.S. 24th Mechanized Division and the Hammurabi Guard Division on March 2 (see, e.g., Gordon and Trainor, *The Generals' War*, pp. 363–68; and Scales, *Certain Victory*, pp. 312–14, respectively). This bound is thus highly conservative.

The estimate itself is derived from standard vehicle counts for Republican Guard and army heavy division organizations as found in Friedman, *Desert Victory*, p. 294; MAJ John Antal, "Iraq's Armored Fist," *Infantry* (January–February 1991), pp. 27–30; and Richard Jupa and James Dingeman, "The Republican Guards," *Army* (March 1991), pp. 54–62; average air attrition for Guard divisions as of February 23 as given by *GWAPS*, Summary Report, p. 106; specific air attrition for the 12th and 52d Armored divisions as derived from interviews with captured Iraqi officers and reported in *GWAPS*, vol. 2, pt. 2, p. 214; and Iraqi divisional dispositions as reported, e.g., in Gordon and Trainor, *The Generals' War*, p. 388. Note that although personnel and weapon strengths were significantly below nominally authorized levels in Iraqi Army infantry divisions, tank strength in Guard and army heavy divisions closely approximated nominal authorization: *GWAPS*, vol. 2, pt. 2, p. 169. Note also that the estimate above is consistent with an analysis conducted by the 3d U.S. Armored Division staff, as reported in Orlansky and Thorpe, *73 Easting*, p. I-51, which identified 374 destroyed Iraqi tanks and 404 other armored vehicles on the battlefield in excess of air force battle damage assessment claims in the sector assigned to them during their engagement with the Iraqi blocking force. Their estimate excludes the Medina and 52d divisions (which were outside the 3rd Armored sector) and overestimates air kills by including all pilot claims as kills. Using the Iraqis' own air damage reports for the 52d and 12th divisions as reported in *GWAPS*, and *GWAPS*'s figure for Guard air attrition for the Tawakalna and Medina, the 3d Armored's analysis implies at least 727 active tanks and 572 active armored vehicles in the Iraqi blocking positions. Note also that the Adnan Division, while nominally part of the blocking force, has been excluded from the totals above as there is less evidence it actively resisted: e.g., Atkinson, *Crusade*, pp. 465–66.

83. Blumenson, *Breakout and Pursuit*, pp. 30, 700; Playfair, *Mediterranean, vol. 3*, p. 220; Playfair and Molony, *Mediterranean, Vol.4*, pp. 9–10, 78, 290, 334; F. W. von Mellenthin, *Panzer Battles* (1956; reprint New York: Ballantine, 1984), pp. 63, 111; Addington, *Patterns of War*, pp. 187, 197; Cordesman and Wagner, *Lessons of Modern War*, pp. 15, 18.

84. To cite two extrema for historical casualty infliction, in the 1967 Arab-Israeli War, an Arab defending army with 2,250 tanks killed about 300 Israeli tanks; while in mid-July 1944, a German force with under 320 tanks killed over 400 British and Canadian tanks in defeating Operation GOODWOOD. Of course, the comparison is a crude one, but similar results for the Feburary 24 Iraqi armored force would imply Coalition armor losses of perhaps 160 to 5,125 vehicles—versus the actual total of only 15 tanks and perhaps 25 other armored vehicles. For 1967 data, see Cordesman and Wagner, *Lessons of Modern War*, vol.1, pp. 15, 18; for GOODWOOD, see chapter 6; for Coalition tank losses, see Title V, p. xiv; for ratio of, e.g., M1 to Bradley losses, see Kindsvatter, "VII Corps," p. 17.

85. As *GWAPS* put it: "Ironically, the loss of equipment, a key index of bomb damage assessment used during the war, was not decisive in any direct way. The Iraqi army did not run out of tanks, armored personnel carriers, or artillery" (Summary Report, p. 117). See also Biddle, "Victory Misunderstood," pp. 149–52; Daryl Press, "The Myth of Air Power in the Persian Gulf War and the Future of Warfare," *International Security* 26, 2 (Fall 2001), pp. 5–44.

86. See, e.g., Atkinson, *Crusade*, pp. 443–48, 467; USNWR, *Triumph without Victory*, p. 409; Scales, *Certain Victory*, pp. 364–67; Daryl Press, "Lessons from Ground Combat in the Gulf: The Impact of Training and Technology," *International Security*, 21, 2 (Fall 1997), pp. 137–46.

87. Note that Marine tank losses were lower both in absolute terms and as a fraction of total strength (though of course, both Army and Marine losses were very low): SASC, pp. 79–80; USMC BAT, pp. v, 15. Note also that an Army brigade equipped with M1A1s (the "Tiger" brigade) was attached to support the Marine offensive, but most of the combat activity was borne by the Marines' organic M60A1s: USMC BAT, p. A-2.

88. SASC, pp. 66–68; Molly Moore, *A Woman at War: Storming Kuwait with the U.S. Marines* (New York: Charles Scribner's Sons, 1993), pp. 239–41, 245–48; Gordon and Trainor, *The Generals' War*, pp. 363–68.

89. Alternatively, the key ground force technology has sometimes been described as superior night fighting equipment, which would pertain to Army M2s and M3s as well as M1s: see, e.g., Scales, *Certain Victory*, pp. 366–67. Marine LAVs and most Marine M60s, however, lacked thermal sights—the army had loaned the Marines a small number of M60A3s with better night-vision equipment, but the great majority of Marine armor lacked this: Moore, *Woman at War*; p. 200; Title V, p. 747; Gordon and Trainor, *The Generals' War*, p. 359. Its absence did not cause heavier losses to the Marines.

90. For a particularly germane example, see Lt. (P) John A. Nagl, "A Tale of Two Battles: Victorious in Iraq, an Experienced Armor Task Force Gets Waxed at the NTC,"

Armor (May–June 1992), pp. 6–10. On the National Training Center (NTC) and the record of the resident OPFOR, see, e.g., Anne Chapman, *The Origins and Development of the National Training Center, 1976–1984* (Ft. Monroe, VA: Office of the Command Historian, U.S. Army Training and Doctrine Command, 1992), pp. 89–90; Bolger, *Dragons at War*.

91. Gordon and Trainor, *The Generals' War*, p. 407; USNWR, *Triumph without Victory*, p. 380.

92. For the upper bound frontage, see GEN Galvin, "Conventional Arms Control," p. 103, and assuming, for the upper bound, three brigades abreast at Galvin's maximum divisional frontage. For the lower bound, see, e.g., Mearsheimer, "Numbers, Strategy," pp. 174–85, and assuming two brigades forward.

93. Scales, *Certain Victory*, pp. 267–70.

94. 73 Easting project database.

95. For other examples, see Pearce, *Shield and Sabre*, pp. 102, 110.

96. Cf. Press, "Lessons from Ground Combat," which holds that either technology or force employment is sufficient to explain the DESERT STORM loss rate, but that neither is necessary. Press further holds that Iraqi force employment was not radically unlike that of previous Arab armies; yet one cannot explain a historically unprecedented loss rate without identifying some unprecedented causal agent. For the theory advanced above, that unprecedented agent is the Coalition's technology. While not sufficient, it is necessary—in interaction with force employment.

97. See, e.g., Freedman and Karsh, *The Gulf Conflict*, p. 437; Friedman, *Desert Victory*, pp. 235, 246, 252–53; Blackwell, *Thunder in the Desert*, pp. 220–23; Summers, *On Strategy II*, pp. 155, 265.

98. See, e.g., Swain, *"Lucky War,"* pp. 244, 246. Many of the individual engagements that made up these actions were likewise simple frontal assaults. The Iraqi defenses at 73 Easting, for example, were clearly oriented to meet an attack from the west; the 2d ACR's axis of advance was a straight line almost due west to due east: Krause, *73 Easting*, pp. 1–15; Orlansky and Thorpe, *73 Easting*, pp. I-121 to 136; 73 Easting database. The Battles of Norfolk, Medina Ridge, and Wadi al Batin were also direct frontal assaults: Scales, *Certain Victory*, pp. 267–70, 282–84, 292–300; Gordon and Trainor, *The Generals' War*, pp. 407–8; Atkinson, *Crusade*, pp. 465–67; USNWR, *Triumph without Victory*, pp. 377–86.

99. Scales, *Certain Victory*, pp. 224–32; Gordon and Trainor, *The Generals' War*, pp. 379–80, 382–83.

100. See, e.g., Gordon and Trainor, *The Generals' War*, pp. 341, 358.

101. See, e.g., John Mueller, "The Perfect Enemy: Assessing the Gulf War," *Security Studies* 5, 1 (Autumn 1995), pp. 77–117; Michael J. Mazarr, Don M. Snider, and James A. Blackwell, Jr., *Desert Storm: The Gulf War and What We Learned* (Boulder: Westview, 1993), pp. 113–17, 177–78; Jeffrey Record, *Hollow Victory* (Washington, DC: Brassey's, 1993), pp. 6, 135; Pardew, "The Iraqi Army's Defeat," pp. 17–23; Moore, *Woman at War*, e.g., pp. 224, 275–76, 292, 302.

102. Cordesman and Wagner, *Lessons of Modern War*, vol. 1, pp. 15, 18; vol. 3, pp. 255–56, 261, 267; Bruce, ed., *Harbottle's Dictionary*, p. 232.

103. In fact, no systematic attempt has yet been made to show that the 1991 skill differential was unusually large in historical terms. On the contrary, Mueller, for example, actually implies that the incompetence he ascribes to the Iraqis is typical of other defeated armies in previous Mideast wars ("The Perfect Enemy," p. 79n). While this seems quite plausible, it poses important difficulties for the Iraqi incompetence argument as an explanation of a historically unprecedented outcome.

104. In 1967 an Arab force with 2,250 tanks killed about 300 Israeli tanks; in 1991, the active residual of Iraqi armor that remained after accounting for air-induced attrition numbered at least 600 tanks and 600 other armored vehicles but killed only 15 Coalition tanks and perhaps 25 other armored vehicles. Even if we assume *no* Israeli air-induced attrition of Arab vehicles, the result thus implies a difference in kill rates for defending armor of at least a factor of four [i.e., $(2,250/300)/(1,200/40)$] that must then be accounted for by 1967–91 differences in ground technology, skill, motivation, or numerical imbalance. Of course, this is a crude comparison; weapons other than armored vehicles can kill tanks, for example. But if non-armored-vehicle-based antitank weapons were considered, this would likely increase the difference to be explained by the latter three effects above, since such weapons' effectiveness has generally increased since 1967 (making the Iraqis' inability to kill more than 40 Coalition armored vehicles still more surprising). And of course, if we reduce the 1967 Arab tank total to reflect air-induced attrition (providing a more parallel comparison with the 1,200-vehicle Iraqi residual figure above), or assume a larger Iraqi armor residual than the lower bound given above, then the result would again increase the difference in performance. For 1967 results, see Cordesman and Wagner, *Lessons of Modern War*, vol. 1, pp. 15, 18. For 1991 figures, see discussion above.

CHAPTER EIGHT
STASTICAL TESTS

1. Force employment as I define it *can* be measured—see chapters 5–7. No appropriate large-*n* dataset, however, is yet available.

2. Ron Cowen, "Searching for Other Worlds," *Science News* 148 (November 18, 1995), pp. 332 ff.

3. COW dataset.

4. Helmbold, *Rates of Advance*, CAA-RP-90-04.

5. The original CDB90 dataset contains 419 twentieth-century battles, the cleaned version I use here deletes 37 double-counted data points and thus contains 382 (see below).

6. Data are available from the author; for documentation, see chapter 2.

7. *Systemic* technological theories, by contrast, can be tested using the COW data by treating time as a proxy for technological progress: see below. Some use military expenditure per soldier as a measure of unit-level "technological sophistication" derived from the COW data; for my purposes, however, this is inappropriate: see chapter 2 n. 50. I thus use the explicit MILTECH data for such assessments rather than the expenditure/capita proxy.

8. Note, however, that most wars in COW are short; in a very short war, major offensives by both sides are less common than in long conflicts with multiple turning points. The median duration of twentieth-century wars in COW, for example, is only 5.1 months; only a third exceed 9 months. While I cannot exclude bias stemming from COW's unit of analysis, its magnitude and importance are thus unclear.

9. This difficulty pertains only to theories of capability at the operational level or below; orthodox theories specified at the strategic level are testable directly using COW (see chapter 2).

10. This unit of analysis also fits the causal logic of most orthodox theories, which implicitly assume that strategic outcomes are straightforward aggregates of tactical and

operational ones: tanks, for example, are seen as offensive at the strategic level because they facilitate assaults at the tactical level: Jonathan Shimshoni, "Technology, Military Advantage, and World War I," *International Security* 15, 3, (Winter 1990/91), pp. 187–215. For orthodox theories, consistency with observed outcomes for both battles and wars is thus necessary for validity.

11. George Kuhn, *Ground Forces Battle Casualty Rate Patterns* (McLean, VA: Logistics Management Institute, 1991), LMI FP703TR3.

12. This review was directed by the author; documentation is provided in memoranda for the record available from the author.

13. *Combat History Analysis Study Effort (CHASE): Progress Report for the Period August 1984–June 1985* (Bethesda, MD: U.S. Army Concepts Analysis Agency, 1986), CAA-TP-86-2, p. I-2; Trevor Dupuy, *Analysis of Factors that have Influenced Outcomes of Battles and Wars* (Dunn Loring, VA: Historical Evaluation and Research Organization, 1984), CAA SR-84-6, Vol. 1; also John Mearsheimer, "Assessing the Conventional Balance: The 3:1 Rule and Its Critics," *International Security* 13, 4, (Spring 1989), pp. 54–89 at 65–67. Cf. Joshua Epstein, "The 3:1 Rule, the Adaptive Dynamic Model, and the Future of Security Studies," *International Security* 13, 4, (Spring 1989), pp. 90–127 at 104–6; Michael Desch, "Democracy and Victory: Why Regime Type Hardly Matters," *International Security* 27, 2, (Fall 2002), pp. 5–47. Desch, however, incorrectly rejects all uses of CDB90 on grounds of statistical inefficiency (p. 40). *Bias* would invalidate findings—inefficiency does not. Efficient estimators drawn from error-free data are obviously preferable, but even very noisy data—if unbiased—can yield important insight, especially where findings attain statistical significance in spite of the noise, as here. As Desch notes, there is no reason to expect bias in these data.

14. The latter data were derived from I.S.O. Playfair, *The Mediterranean and Middle East* (London: Her Majesty's Stationery Office, 1954–60), vol. III, 1960, pp. 383–4, 391, map 39; David M. Glantz, *From the Don to the Dnepr* (London: Cass, 1991), pp. 225, 230 (while Glantz is not literally an official historian, he is employed as a historian by the U.S. Army and his work is of at least comparable authority).

15. Rather than using dummy variables, Dan Reiter and Allan Stam instead randomly select single data points for each state in each war and drop the remaining data, creating a subset with equal representation for each state in CDB90: "Democracy and Battlefield Military Effectiveness," *Journal of Conflict Resolution* 42, 3, (June 1998), pp. 259–77. This radically reduces the amount of information in the dataset, however (with their focus on single sides rather than two-sided battles and their inclusion of the entire 1600–1982 timespan, the pre-selection n is 1,094; the post-selection n is only 82), and poses unaddressed issues of sampling variance. Using dummy variables, by contrast, retains a much larger n, preserves more of the information in the data, and poses no issues of sampling beyond those inherent in the dataset's original construction.

16. 50 of the 419 data points in the original dataset were double counted; deleting subunit references removed 37 of these, leaving a dataset of 382 battles.

17. Data are available from the author.

18. Assuming that measurement errors in the dependent and independent variables are uncorrelated: Potluri Rao and Roger Miller, *Applied Econometrics* (Belmont, CA: Wadsworth, 1971), pp. 179–84.

19. A very strong causal effect, however, should emerge even from noisy data. Hence materiel's empirical failure in chapter 2 is important in itself, since capability is so widely

attributed to materiel per se. Nevertheless, null findings are less powerful given substantial measurement error than they would be without it.

20. This is true as long as there is no reason to assume that the measurement errors systematically favor one theory over another. Since these data were obviously not collected with the new theory in mind (the data do not even consider its primary explanatory variable), there seems little reason to assume that the coders systematically mismeasured the data to suit its terms.

21. Note that this does not imply a constant mean over time. Defensive depth, for example, may well have increased in all armies since 1900, though without eliminating differences between states who choose relatively more or relatively less depth around the contemporary mean.

22. Note the frequency of suboptimal (i.e., non–modern-system) force employment in the case studies reported in chapters 5–7.

23. More specifically, it follows from the basic Lanchester differential equations that the attacker:defender loss exchange ratio (dR/dB) will be given by:

$$\frac{dR}{dB} = \frac{bB}{rR}$$

(where R is the number of Red shooters, B the number of Blue shooters, b the number of Red shooters killed per Blue shooter per unit time, and r the number of Blue shooters killed per Red shooter per unit time), which declines nonlinearly in R/B, the FFR. Lanchester, *Aircraft in Warfare*.

24. This can be shown to follow from equations 20 and 21 of the appendix. All hypotheses deduced from the new theory assume constant force employment, per the assumptions noted above.

25. See the discussion under "Why Does Force Employment Vary" in chapter 3.

26. Official theater combat models, for example, typically treat territorial gain as directly proportional to the FFR; national variations in force employment as defined here are excluded: see, e.g., Battilega and Grange, eds. *Military Applications of Modeling*, pp. 104–20; Rex Goad, "The Modeling of Movement in Tactical Games," in Reiner Huber, ed., *Operational Research Games for Defense* (Munich: R. Oldenbourg, 1979), pp. 190–214.

27. This can be shown to follow from equation 18 of the appendix.

28. The Lanchester Square Law, for example, implies that battle duration, d, will be given by:

$$d = \frac{1}{2\sqrt{rb}} \log\left(\frac{B\sqrt{b}+R\sqrt{r}}{|B\sqrt{b}-R\sqrt{r}|}\right)$$

which is asymptotic at $\frac{R}{B} = \sqrt{\frac{b}{r}}$ and decreasing in $\frac{R}{B}$ for $\frac{R}{B} > \sqrt{\frac{b}{r}}$; $\frac{R}{B} > \sqrt{\frac{b}{r}}$ is the attacker victory condition for the Square Law (i.e., the minimum FFR at which a fight to the finish annihilates Blue rather than Red), hence for attacker preponderances sufficient to win, duration falls nonlinearly with increasing preponderance. Conversely, Square Law durations *increase* nonlinearly as the FFR increases for cases where the attacker is *defeated* (i.e., d will increase in $\frac{R}{B}$ for $\frac{R}{B} < \sqrt{\frac{b}{r}}$). Karr, *Lanchester Attrition Processes*, p. 6, with battle duration defined as the time at which the loser is annihilated.

29. This can be shown to follow from equation 17 of the appendix.

30. See the discussion under "Why Does Force Employment Vary" in chapter 3.

31. See chapter 2.

32. Per the logic underlying hypothesis 2b above.

33. See, e.g., Mearsheimer, *Conventional Deterrence*, pp. 181–83.

34. This can be shown to follow from equation 17 of the appendix.

35. See chapter 2.

36. Stephen Van Evera, "Offense, Defense, and Causes of War," *International Security* 22, 4 (Spring 1998), pp. 5–43.

37. Hence hypotheses 13a–15a are testable.

38. Lynn Jones, "Offense-Defense Theory," p. 668.

39. Note the absence of any specific weapon-type variables in the formal model (see appendix).

40. Absent a systematic decrease over time in force employment's variance across dyads, which there is no prima facie reason to expect. On the new theory's hypothesized increase in variance, see figure 4.1; LER displays a similar increase. By contrast, orthodox offense-defense theory sees one-sided effects to technological change: new technologies shift all outcomes in one direction—either to the attacker's benefit if the technology is offensive or to the defender's benefit if not. This logic implies systematic secular shifts in mean outcomes, but no systematic change in either within-era or across-era variance over time.

41. The chief difference is that I test no hypotheses on periodicity or across-vs.-within period variance for territorial gain or duration. For casualties, periodicity hypotheses allow offense-defense theory to be tested using COW even though COW contains no specific weapon counts: the periods act as surrogates for more specific information on tank, aircraft, and artillery holdings. Neither territorial gain nor battle duration hypotheses can be tested via COW, however, since COW lacks these dependent variables. Hence there is no reason to consider periodicity with respect to territorial gain or duration; such tests would be redundant to the weapon-type claims in hypotheses 19–21 and 23–25.

42. See chapter 2.

43. Note the absence of specific weapon-type terms in the formal model (see the appendix). The new theory does imply that success in *exploitation* will increase with mobility and deep strike capability (and thus with tank and aircraft availability), which would increase territorial gain, but such effects should only obtain following breakthrough, which is uncommon. See chapter 3.

44. Per the logic presented for hypothesis 17b above.

45. Glaser and Kaufmann, "Offense-Defense Balance," pp. 62–63.

46. See chapter 2.

47. Note the absence of any specific weapon-type terms in the formal model (see appendix).

48. Per the logic presented for hypothesis 17b above.

49. LERs for wars (as in COW) rather than battles (as in CDB90) can be misleading if used to test theories specified at the tactical or operational level and distinguishing attack from defense, since in a long war a single state will often be both attacker and defender at different times (see above). For dyadic technology theory, however, this is moot, inasmuch as dyadic technology theory does not rest on distinctions between attack and defense: it holds only that superior weapons should convey superior capability. Even orthodox offense-defense theory can still be tested meaningfully using war-level LER data

(see chapter 2), inasmuch as orthodox offense-defense theorists explicitly argue that the war is the appropriate unit of analysis (see, e.g., Glaser and Kaufmann); it is appropriate to test a theory on its own terms.

50. Hypotheses on territory and duration cannot be examined given territorial gain's absence from COW and technological sophistication's absence from CDB90. Whereas COW contains duration data, these concern wars rather than operations, whose duration will obviously be very different; the new theory makes claims only for the latter.

51. Of course, this statistical model does not correspond directly to the formal model presented in the appendix, since available datasets lack many of latter's key variables. Instead, this model (and the two others presented in equations 8.2 to 8.4) presents an indirect test of the formal model's provisions based on variables observable in the available data.

52. Troop counts for FFR and FSR are ration strengths, per the available data in CDB90 and COW.

53. Weapon counts per capita give the sum of attacker and defender weapons of that type divided by the sum of attacker and defender troops. The greater the value, the more prevalent the weapon type. To disaggregate separate values for attacker and defender weapons would blur the distinction between offense-defense theory and preponderance theory: for offense-defense theorists, tanks are offense-conducive whether held by attackers or defenders; separate measures of attacker and defender tanks per capita would reflect the sides' relative weight of materiel, not the offense-defense balance as such. As presented here, these variables thus account for offense-defense theory's explanation of capability.

54. The 58th pair—the United States attacking Germany in World War II—is dropped to avoid collinearity.

55. The smallest datum is (-28.3).

56. To avoid collinearity, no dummy for army-group level and above is included.

57. To avoid collinearity, no dummy for wars fought between 1973 and 1992 is included. Note that periodization dummies are unecessary for CDB90 analyses, since CDB90 provides explict values for tank, aircraft, and artillery counts.

58. More formally, $techedge = \tau_r - \tau_b$.

59. See Bennett and Stam, "Duration of Interstate Wars," pp. 239–57; William H. Greene, *Econometric Analysis*, 4th ed. (New York: Macmillan, 1999), pp. 937–51.

60. The dummy variable *win* and the interaction term log(*FFR*) *win* are included in a jackknife specification to test the Lanchestrian prediction that duration should increase with FFR for attacker ("Red") losses but decrease with FFR for attacker victories. Specifically, the Lanchester prediction implies $\beta_3 < 0$, $|\beta_3| > \beta_1$, and $\beta_2 > 0$. Failure to satisfy any of these inequalities contradicts the Lanchester prediction. On jackknife models, see, e.g., Rao and Miller, *Applied Econometrics*, pp. 98–99.

61. On the Goldfeldt-Quandt test, see, e.g., Robert Pindyck and Daniel Rubenfeld, *Econometric Models and Economic Forecasts*, 2d ed. (New York: McGraw-Hill, 1981), pp. 148–50.

62. Note that the log(FFR) and log(FSR) formulations assume nonlinearity in the relationship between log(LER) and preponderance, per hypotheses 1a and 7a. A variety of other nonlinear and linear functional forms were tested, including (1/FFR), a quadratic in FSR, and raw FFR and FSR; none improved the results significantly.

63. A complete set of interactions between national identity dummies and materiel variables would pose a prohibitive cost in degrees of freedom, but to assess the possibility of meaningful interactions I performed several analyses limited to datapoints from single

attacker-defender pairs. The results frequently displayed sizeable differences in estimated materiel coefficients, but few were significant.

64. The smallest FSR in CDB90 is 40.5; the minimum artillery per capita is zero. With other variables at their means, setting FSR at 40.5 and artillery per capita at zero reduces log(LER) from 0.15 to -0.21; the predicted log(LER) for German attacks on U.S. defenders in World War II (the dummy variable with the smallest absolute value of those which were statistically significant) is -0.59 with all other variables at their means. (FSR and artillery per capita are the only materiel variables whose signs are as predicted by orthodox theory, and hence the only variables for which sensitivity analysis makes sense.)

65. Given MILTECH's limited coverage, only the difference between the 1946–72 and 1973–92 periods can be evaluated; the 1973–92 dummy is dropped to avoid collinearity.

66. The systemic technology variables' insignificance is more dispositive, since the key difference between the new and orthodox theories' predictions here is significance per se. For FFR, the theories predict different signs. Hence a theory that predicts the sign correctly offers relatively stronger performance than one that does not, even if the coefficient falls somewhat short of ordinary significance standards.

67. This finding is not sensitive to the particular periodization adopted here; no periodization available in these data materially changes the results.

68. Of course, not all within-era variance is attributable to force employment. Some of the variance both within and across eras is due to nonsystematic random factors rather than either technology or force employment; moreover, at least some of the systematic components of within-era variance are presumably attributable to non-force-employment-related unit-level influences. The results strongly suggest that systemic technology's influence on LER is weak, and that some unit-level factor (or factors) are exerting powerful influence (nonsystematic random effects are unlikely to account for all or most of the within-era variance when the across-era variance, on which random effects also operate, is smaller by orders of magnitude). The only unit-level theory of capability to date emphasizes force employment, hence these results favor it over the orthodox alternative of systemic technology, but the results cannot uniquely identify force employment as *the* unit-level factor responsible for high within-era variance. This limitation is inherent given the absence of either force employment or technology from available large-*n* ex post datasets. To observe these variables' effects directly requires either small-*n* ex post or ex ante simulation techniques, as presented in chapters 5–7 and 9.

69. As with the casualty analyses, I performed several calculations limited to datapoints from single attacker-defender pairs by way of evaluating possible dummy-materiel interactions; again the coefficients were frequently different but rarely significant.

70. Here again, the systemic technology variables' failure to attain significance is more problematic than for preponderance variables, since significance per se is the whole difference between the new and orthodox theories' predictions for systemic technology.

71. Here, too, analyses limited to datapoints from single attacker-defender pairs showed different but rarely significant coefficients on the materiel variables.

72. No other outcome in table 8.7 is as sensitive to a handful of data points: none switches from corroboration to contradiction (or from significance to insignificance) with removal of even the four most extreme values; for all but one case (corps-level duration), the eight most extreme values can be removed without materially altering the findings.

73. These findings are broadly consistent with prior efforts to test pieces of orthodox theory. The few empirical tests of offense-defense theory typically focus on the offense-defense

balance's consequences rather than its causes and are thus inapposite: Hopf, "Polarity," pp. 475–94; Fearon, "Offense-Defense Balance." Neither FSRs nor dyadic technology theory have received any prior large-n attention. The most extensive prior empirical literature concerns FFRs in Lanchester theory. While none controls for the offense-defense or FSR variables above, and of course none addresses force employment, the results nevertheless tend to reinforce the disconfirmatory thrust of the findings above: see references in chap. 2, n. 24. Note that Robert Helmbold finds a significant relationship between FFR and *fractional* loss exchange ratios (the attacker's percentage casualties divided by the defender's), though not between FFR and LERs (attacker casualties per defender casualty): *Personnel Attrition Rates.* Helmbold also finds a significant relationship between the probability of victory and a complex parameter he calls "advantage": "The Defender's Advantage Parameter: Final Thoughts," *Phalanx* 30, 3 (September 1997), pp. 27, 29. These results are not necessarily inconsistent with my findings above, though the differing structure of controls and dependent variables clouds the relationship between the analyses.

CHAPTER NINE
EXPERIMENTAL TESTS

1. For model documentation, see *Janus(A) 2.0 User's Manual*, Janus(A) 2.0 Model, prepared for the Department of the Army, HQ TRADOC Analysis Command ATRC-2D, Ft. Leavenworth, KS, by TITAN Corporation, Ft. Leavenworth, KS. On Janus validation, see L. Ingber, H. Fujio, and M. S. Wehner, "Mathematical Comparison of Combat Computer Models to Exercise Data," *Mathematical and Computer Modeling* 15, 1 (1991), pp. 65ff; L. Ingber, "Mathematical Comparison of Janus (T)," in S. E. Johnson and A. H. Lewis, eds., *The Science of Command and Control, Part II* (Washington, DC: AFCEA International Press, 1989), pp. 165–76.

2. On the battle itself, see chapter 7.

3. For these purposes, the DARPA/IDA Simnet system was used; for the counterfactual experiments, Janus was used, given the latter's greater flexibility and quicker turnaround time, and the reduced need for visual fidelity in counterfactual analysis. On Janus and Simnet in the 73 Easting Project, see W. M. Christenson and Robert Zirkle, *73 Easting Battle Replication* (Alexandria, VA: Institute for Defense Analyses, 1992), IDA P-2770. For a more detailed description of 73 Easting Project methodology, see Orlansky and Thorpe, eds., *73 Easting*, pp. I-65 to I-79; II-1 to II-118; on the criteria by which the battle was selected for simulation, see pp. I-70, I-71.

4. In all excursion scenarios, historical deployments and movement tracks were retained (though in scenario G, some U.S. arrivals were delayed to create a strung-out formation). Note that the mean base case simulation results (two U.S. vehicle losses) closely approximate the historical outcome (one). For a more detailed discussion of correspondence between Janus results and the historical outcome, see Christenson and Zirkle, *73 Easting Battle Replication.*

5. By contrast, none of the controlled variations examined here could be expected to have changed other aspects of the battle: neither U.S. nor Iraqi movements were predicated on thermal sights, air supremacy, or poor Iraqi covering force discipline or position preparation—thus there is no reason to assume that these movements would have differed for any of the given excursion scenarios. At least one of 2d ACR's company grade

officers has stated explicitly that his plan of maneuver would have been the same with or without the changes embodied in the excursions here: interview, Captain H. R. McMaster, USA, January 1994. Moreover, Iraqi position preparation and covering force discipline can be improved in Janus to modern-system standards without altering the geographic distribution or movement tracks of their forces (either of which would otherwise require speculative modification of the historical U.S. maneuver plan). On the requirements of valid counterfactual inference, see Philip Tetlock and Aaron Belkin, eds., *Counterfactual Thought Experiments in World Politics* (Princeton: Princeton University Press, 1996).

6. As a stochastic model, Janus outcomes for the same scenario vary from run to run. An important advantage of stochastic simulation experimentation is its ability to distinguish systematic from nonsystematic random variation by running the cases multiple times and observing the resulting variance.

7. In a "turret-down" or "turret-defilade" position, the entire vehicle is below grade and thus masked from hostile observation or fire; only the commander's hatch is above grade. Thus, a turret-down tank cannot fire its main gun (or be fired upon by opposing tanks), but the vehicle commander can search for targets by standing in the open hatch and scanning the surroundings with binoculars. In a "hull-down" or "hull-defilade" position, the vehicle's hull is below grade, but the turret is exposed. A hull-down tank can thus fire and be fired upon, though the defilade reduces vulnerability by reducing the vehicle's presented area. In Western practice, prepared tank positions are ordinarily dug as a ramp, connecting a deeper, turret-down position and a shallower, hull-down location; above-ground revetments are avoided: Headquarters, Department of the Army, *FM 5-103*, pp. 4–14 to 4–15; Richard Simpkin, *Tank Warfare* (New York: Crane Russak, 1979), pp. 97, 112, 160, 167.

8. It should be emphasized, however, that 73 Easting was a hasty attack at a very disadvantageous local FFR. Although it would be difficult to study the effects of a deliberate attack at a favorable local FFR in 73 Easting without doing violence to the ceteris paribus assumptions underlying the analysis, the ex post facto tests in chapters 5–8 give reason to expect that a deliberate attack with more aggressive implementation of modern system methods could have reduced U.S. casualties considerably relative to those suffered in excursion A. Iraqi losses, by contrast, could be expected to fall significantly regardless.

9. See, e.g., Scales, *Certain Victory*, pp. 261–62; Atkinson, *Crusade*, p. 443; USNWR, *Triumph without Victory*, p. 409.

10. Note, again, that the real Iraqis made many more mistakes than just the two considered here; the single errors in excursions B and C thus imply a dramatic (though still incomplete) increase in Iraqi modern-system adherence relative to their historical performance.

11. Though, again, the incomplete offensive implementation of modern-system methods inherent in an exploitation phase hasty attack presumably increased the attacker's putative losses in the excursion: see note 8.

CHAPTER TEN
CONCLUSION

1. Wohlforth, *Elusive Balance*; Aaron Friedberg, *The Weary Titan Britain and the Experience of Relative Decline, 1895–1905* (Princeton: Princeton University Press, 1988); Wesley

Wark, *The Ultimate Enemy* (Ithaca: Cornell University Press, 1985); Herrmann, *Arming of Europe*; Ernest May, ed., *Knowing One's Enemies* (Princeton: Princeton University Press, 1984); Williamson Murray and Alan Millett, eds., *Calculations: Net Assessment and the Coming of World War II* (New York: Free Press, 1992); Williamson Murray, *The Change in the European Balance of Power, 1938–1939* (Princeton: Princeton University Press, 1984); Rosen, "Net Assessment," pp. 283–301; Pickett, Roche, and Watts, "Net Assessment," pp. 158–88.

2. Critiquing this view is McKeown, "Limitations of 'Structural' Theories," pp. 43–64. On modern states' death rates, see Karen Ruth Adams, "State Survival and State Death: International and Technological Contexts" (Ph.D. diss., University of California, Berkeley, 2000).

3. See, e.g., Kenneth Waltz, *Theory of International Politics* (Reading, MA: Addison-Wesley, 1979), p. 127.

4. On Iraqi 1991 force employment, see chapter 6; for the Iran-Iraq War, see Cordesman and Wagner, *Lessons of Modern War*, Volume 2: *The Iran-Iraq War*.

5. On German force employment at GOODWOOD, see chapter 5; for COBRA, see Blumenson, *Breakout and Pursuit*, pp. 224–28, map 5.

6. Nor would a selection argument resolve the inconsistency: whereas Nazi Germany left the international system by its defeat in World War II, neither Britain nor Iraq was removed. Much depends on the opponent's force employment and the war's stakes.

7. One can thus simultaneously conclude that force matters in international politics, but that unit-level phenomena are important. On unit-level variables' role in generating military power, see also Rosen, *Societies and Military Power*; Stam, *Win, Lose or Draw*; Reiter and Stam, *Democracy and War* (Princeton: Princeton University Press, 2002); Biddle and Zirkle, "Technology," pp. 171–212.

8. Glaser, "Realists as Optimists," pp. 50–90.

9. To this end, see Biddle, "Rebuilding the Foundations."

10. Theories of perception will predict decisions more accurately than theories that use reality as a proxy for perceptions, however strong the theories' understanding of reality. Theories using flawed understandings of reality, however, will be worst of all. The strongest case for using military reality as a proxy for perception is that leaders who misperceive it will be removed by natural selection—i.e., by military defeat. Theories built on flawed understandings of military reality will mispredict defeat and hence will undermine the selection logic that justifies reality's use as a proxy in the first place. For any theory using reality as a proxy for perception, getting reality right is crucial; the discussion below aims at this goal.

11. The modern system, moreover, is not a viable unidimensional proxy for a multidimensional concept of capability. It may at first seem otherwise: after all, the modern system is militarily preferable to non–modern-system force employment for almost all states; perhaps its presence or absence could be taken as an approximation of capability as a whole across all three dimensions of capability for all states. But this does not make the modern system a sufficient proxy. The breadth of the modern system's military appeal stems significantly from its role in breakthrough. Breakthrough is central for capability because it is the only way for attackers to maximize all three dimensions of capability simultaneously (see chapter 3). For defenders, preventing breakthrough is thus necessary for high capability in *any* dimension (hence the modern system's importance for defensive capability)—but preventing breakthrough alone is not *sufficient* for high capability in *all* dimensions. As the appendix demonstrates, for contained offensives the dimensions of capability trade off against one another for both attackers and defenders. This is irrelevant

if a defender allows breakthrough, but it looms much larger otherwise: a defender can fail in all dimensions simultaneously if it permits breakthrough, but against a modern system attacker it cannot succeed equally in all dimensions simultaneously even if the defender adopts the modern system. The modern system is thus an essential first step in any assessment of capability, but it cannot be the last step for any analysis of international politics that turns on capability. Hence the analysis here treats the respective dimensions of capability as distinct variables that cannot be aggregated (absent the special condition of breakthrough) without specification of a state's preferences across dimensions.

12. In the new theory, for example, Israel (which could otherwise implement the modern system but whose geography precludes modern-system defensive depth) might be able to conquer its neighbors' territory but not defend its own. Conversely, two fully modern-system opponents of comparable size would each be able to hold most of their own territory but unable to conquer much of their opponent's.

13. Or recover decision makers' actual perceptions rather than relying on objective proxies. The effort needed to characterize perceptions accurately, however, suggests that large-n research will probably rely on objective proxies for the foreseeable future.

14. Whereas force employment per se is absent from the major IR datasets, likely covariates such as civil military relations, regime type, or human capital are included. An auxiliary theory specified in the latter (or similar) terms would thus permit easier statistical testing of IR propositions involving capability. This would be particularly helpful for assessing peacetime capability. Actual force employment can be observed only in war; theories predicting wartime force employment from causal variables observable in peacetime would be necessary to assess military potential ex ante. Similarly, theories of force employment's determinants could assist theorists working at levels of analysis other than the operation: to address capability at the level of wars rather than operations, for example, requires assessment of how force employment will change (if at all) across theaters and campaigns as a function of observable characteristics.

15. See, e.g., Ellis, *Brute Force*; Parker, *Struggle for Survival*, pp. 86, 131–50; Pointing, *Armageddon*, p. 163.

16. Richard Overy, *Why the Allies Won* (London: Jonathan Cape, 1995). See also Niall Ferguson, ed., *Virtual History* (New York: Basic Books, 1999), pp. 228–347.

17. See, e.g., Bidwell and Graham, *Firepower*; Prior and Wilson, *Command on the Western Front*; Griffith, *Battle Tactics*; Lupfer, *Dynamics of Doctrine*; McInnes, *Men, Machines*; Bailey, *First World War*; Sheffield, *Forgotten Victory*.

18. The RMA literature is voluminous. Seminal works include Krepinevich, "Cavalry to Computer," pp. 30–42; Tofflers, *War and Anti-War*; Cohen, "Revolution in Warfare," pp. 37–54; James R. Blaker, *Understanding the Revolution in Military Affairs* (Washington, DC: Progressive Policy Institute, 1997); Michael Vickers, *Warfare in 2020: A Primer* (Washington, DC: Center for Strategic and Budgetary Assessments, 1996); Mazarr, *Military-Technical Revolution*; James R. Fitzsimonds and Jan M. Van Tol, "Revolutions in Military Affairs," *Joint Force Quarterly*, no. 4 (Spring 1994), pp. 24–31; Daniel Goure, "Is There a Military-Technical Revolution in America's Future?" *The Washington Quarterly* 16, 4 (Autumn 1993), pp. 175–92; Jeffrey Cooper, *Another View of the Revolution in Military Affairs* (Carlisle Barracks, PA: U.S. Army War College Strategic Studies Institute, 1994); Bracken, "The Military after Next," pp. 157–74. For a critical review, see Biddle, "Past as Prologue."

19. See, e.g., Bradley Graham, "Battle Plans for a New Century," *Washington Post*, February 21, 1995, pp.1ff; John Barry, "The Battle over Warfare," *Newsweek*, December 5,

1994, pp. 27ff; Jeff Erlich, "One on One: Interview with Secretary of Defense William Perry," *Defense News*, May 1–7, 1995, p. 38; "Deutch Gets Report Card Letter on the Revolution in Military Affairs," *Inside the Navy*, October 24, 1994, p. 11. The George W. Bush administration, for example, campaigned on the claim that the United States should respond to revolutionary change in warfare by skipping a generation of incremental weapon modernization to focus on more advanced systems: Thomas E. Ricks, "For Rumsfeld, Many Roadblocks," *Washington Post*, August 7, 2001, p. 1.

20. Elsewhere I have considered the case for RMA in more detail: Biddle, "Past as Prologue"; "Victory Misunderstood"; and *Commentary on Victory Misunderstood* (Alexandria, VA: Institute for Defense Analyses, 1997), IDA D-2014, available at www.ida.org/DIVISIONS/ sfrd/crp/commentary_on_vm.htm (accessed February 3, 2003). The discussion below supplements but is not meant to supercede the more detailed treatment therein.

21. See Biddle, "Past as Prologue," figs. 2–5.

22. Nicholas Halasz, *Nobel: A Biography of Alfred Nobel* (New York: Orion Press, 1959).

23. Jean de Bloch, *The Future of War*, trans. R. C. Long (New York: Doubleday and McClure, 1899).

24. Theodore Ropp, *The Development of a Modern Navy: French Naval Policy, 1871–1904*, ed. Stephen S. Roberts (1937; reprint Annapolis: Naval Institute Press, 1987); William McNeill, *The Pursuit of Power: Technology, Armed Force, and Society since A.D. 1000* (Chicago: University of Chicago Press, 1982), pp. 262–65; Van Creveld, *Technology in War*, pp. 204–5.

25. Michael Paris, *Winged Warfare: The Literature and Theory of Aerial Warfare in Britain, 1859–1917* (Manchester: Manchester University Press, 1992); Robert Wohl, *A Passion for Wings: Aviation and the Western Imagination, 1908–1918* (New Haven: Yale University Press, 1994); Timothy Travers, "Future Warfare: H. G. Wells and British Military Theory, 1895–1916," in Brian Bond and Ian Roy, eds., *War and Society* (New York: Holmes & Meier, 1975), pp. 67–87.

26. T. Biddle, *Rhetoric and Reality*, pp. 69–76; Sir Charles Webster and Noble Frankland, *The Strategic Air Offensive against Germany, 1939–45*, Vol. 1 (London: Her Majesty's Stationery Office, 1961), pp. 52–64, 144–54; Malcolm Smith, *British Air Strategy between the Wars* (Oxford: Clarendon, 1984); Richard Overy, "Air Power and the Origins of Deterrence Theory before 1939," *Journal of Strategic Studies* 15, 1 (March 1992); Anthony Verrier, *The Bomber Offensive* (London: Batsford, 1968), pp. 33–78.

27. Caroline Ziemke, "In the Shadow of the Giant: USAF Tactical Air Command in the Era of Strategic Bombing, 1945–1955" (Ph.D Diss., Ohio State University, 1989); Andrew Bacevich, *The Pentomic Era* (Washington, DC: National Defense University Press, 1986); Robert Doughty, *Tactical Doctrine*.

28. Alternatively, RMA advocates sometimes hold that even incremental technical advances will nevertheless bring radical change in outcomes by analogy to phase changes in physics: just as a gradual, continuous reduction in water temperature eventually yields discontinuous transformation into ice, so some say that incremental increases in lethality or information can eventually accumulate into discontinuous transformation in the nature of warfare. This argument is hard to assess in the absence of any explicit logic for identifying a threshold, but there is nevertheless ample evidence to suggest we are probably nowhere near any such point yet. Technology in 1991, for example, was insufficient to induce a revolutionary effect on Coalition loss rates in the Gulf War. As chapter 6 demonstrates, 1991 is far more consistent with the new theory's account than it is with a model of revolutionary discontinuity brought about by new technology. The 1999 air war over

Kosovo offers another case in point. Seventy-eight days of bombing with over 38,000 combat sorties killed only some 30–93 Serbian tanks, up to 153 other armored vehicles, and as many as 389 artillery pieces, mortars, and antiaircraft weapons—less than 9, 20, and 9 percent of Serbia's holdings overall, respectively: Cohen and Shelton, "Joint Statement," p. 1; Gen. Wesley Clark, "Kosovo Strike Assessment," NATO Headquarters, Brussels, Sept. 16, 1999; International Institute for Strategic Studies, *Military Balance, 1998/99*, pp. 99–100; Barry Posen, "The War for Kosovo: Serbia's Political-Military Strategy," *International Security* 24, 4 (Spring 2000), pp. 64–5n; Daniel Byman and Matthew Waxman, "Kosovo and the Great Air Power Debate," *International Security* 24, 4 (Spring 2000), pp. 5–38. Nor did Afghanistan in 2001–2 bring a revolutionary discontinuity: see below. Overall, there is little basis in the evidence for concluding that a phase change in the nature of war is likely any time soon.

29. See, e.g., Thomas Ricks, "Bulls-Eye War," *Washington Post*, December 2, 2001, pp. 1ff; Jim Hoagland, "All Aboard in Afghanistan," *Washington Post*, November 20, 2001, p. 23; John Barry, "A New Breed of Soldier," *Newsweek*, December 10, 2001; John Diamond, "Pentagon Plumbs Lessons from War," *Chicago Tribune*, January 14, 2002.

30. As observed in excursion D from the counterfactual analysis: when the U.S. technological portfolio was reduced to air supremacy alone, partial Iraqi modern-system implementation proved sufficient to reduce their losses by over a factor of two, and increase U.S. casualties by a factor of twenty: chapter 9.

31. MHI, Tape 032602p, CPT M. int.; Tape 032802p, CPT D. int.

32. MHI, Tape 032602p, CPT M. int. This quickly became widespread throughout the theater: see, e.g., MHI, Tape 032802a, MAJ D. int.; Tape 032602a, CPT H. et al. int.; Tape 032602p, MAJ M., MAJ K. int.

33. MHI, Tape 032602p, CPT M. int.; Tape 032602p, MAJ M., MAJ K. int.

34. MHI, Tape 032602a, CPT H. et al. int.

35. MHI, Tape 032802a, MAJ D. int.

36. MHI, Tape 041902p, LTC Briley int.; Tape 042002p, LTC Gray int.; Tape 041802p, LTC Lundy int.

37. See, e.g., MHI, Tape 032802a, MAJ D. int.; Tape 041902a, CPT Lecklenburg int.; Tape 041902a, CPT Murphy int.; Tape 041902a, MAJ Busko int. Al Qaeda's implementation of the modern system in Afghanistan was nevertheless superior in many ways to the Republican Guard's in the 1991 Gulf War: compare, for example, the descriptions of al Qaeda fighting positions in Biddle, *Afghanistan*, pp. 19–21, 26–33, with those of Republican Guard positions in chapter 7.

38. On Allied Afghan capabilities, see esp. MHI, Tape 032602p, CPT M. int.; Tape 032602a, CPT H. et al. int.; Memorandum for the Record, CPT H. int., July 2, 2002; Memorandum for the Record, COL J. int., July 2, 2002.

39. MHI, Tape 032602p, CPT M. int.; Tape 032602p, MAJ M., MAJ K. int.; Tape 032602a, CPT H. et al. int.; Tape 032802a, MAJ D. int.; Tape 041902p, LTC Briley int.; Tape 042002p, LTC Gray int.; Tape 041802p, LTC Lundy int.

40. MHI, Tape 032602a, CPT H. int.; Memorandum for the Record, CPT H. int., July 2, 2002.

41. MHI, Memorandum for the Record, COL J. int., July 2, 2002.

42. For a more detailed account of the Afghan campaign, see Biddle, *Afghanistan*.

43. For 2003 Coalition troop strength and casualties through May 1, see dior.whs. mil/mmid/casualty/OIF-thru-20030501.pdf and usinfo.state.gov/regional/nea/iraq/text2003/

318 • Notes to Chapter 10

0329dod.htm; for geographical statistics, see *CIA World Factbook 2002*, available at www.cia.gov/cia/publications/factbook; each was downloaded July 17, 2003. For the Coalition loss rate in 1991, see chapter 6.

44. As described in Goure, "Military-Technical Revolution," p. 178; Johnson and Blaker, "1997–2001 Defense Budget," pp. 3–4. See also, e.g., Richard J. Newman, "Warfare 2020," *U.S. News and World Report*, August 5, 1996, pp. 34–41; Jim Hoagland, "Ready for What?" *Washington Post*, March 28, 1996, p. A27; Bracken, "The Military after Next"; Frank Kendall, "Exploiting the Military Technical Revolution: A Concept for Joint Warfare," *Strategic Review* 20, 2 (Spring 1992), p. 29.

45. See, e.g., Vickers, *Warfare in 2020*, pp. 1, 8, 9, 14; Blaker, *Understanding the Revolution*, pp. 16, 19–20, 22; Cohen, "A Revolution in Warfare," p. 45; Mazarr et al., *Military-Technical Revolution*, pp. 34–53; MAJ Terry New, "Airpower Enters Decisive Era," *Defense News*, May 6, 1991, p. 28.

46. Some now argue that heavy armor's success in Baghdad in Operation IRAQI FREEDOM of 2003 undermines the orthodox view of urban warfare as demanding lighter, more dismount-intensive forces. Heavy armor's survivability in Baghdad, however, may have had much to do with the shortcomings of Iraqi force employment in 2003; it is far from clear that a more skilled opponent could have been defeated in any urban battle with so little reliance on dismounted infantry by the attacker. As this book goes to press, the complete story on urban warfare in IRAQI FREEDOM has yet to be written; for the time being, however, it may be wise to exercise caution in generalizing the Baghdad experience to potential future battles against enemies with a better grasp of modern-system principles than the Iraqis displayed in either 1991 or 2003.

47. As GEN Eric Shinseki, U.S. Army chief of staff, has recently proposed: www.house.gov/hasc/testimony/106thcongress/99-10-21shinseki.htm (accessed February 3, 2003).

48. See, e.g., Richard Newman, "After the Tank," *U.S. News and World Report*, September 18, 2000.

49. This does not imply that any given force design is the best choice; "lighter" surely makes sense, but just how much lighter is a question beyond the scope of the current inquiry.

50. See, e.g., James Cooke, "Admiral W. A. Owens Issues Challenge to Military Operations Research Community," *Phalanx* 28, 1 (March 1995), pp.1ff; Charles Marshall and Randy Garrett, "Simulation for C4ISR: Command, Control, Communications, Intelligence, Surveillance, and Reconnaissance," *Phalanx* 29, 1 (March 1996), pp.1ff; Cohen, "A Revolution in Warfare," p. 53.

51. See Prosser, "JWARS Role."

52. Recent JWARS briefings, for example, make no reference to the effects of variations in force employment: e.g., Prosser, "JWARS Role."

53. See references in notes 18–19 above.

54. House, *Combined Arms Warfare*, p. 89; Robert Citino, *Armored Forces: History and Sourcebook* (Westport, CT: Greenwood, 1994), pp. 49–50.

55. Post–World War II U.S. Army doctrines, for example, include combined arms maneuver, the Pentomic Division and associated doctrine, the Reorganized Armor Division and associated doctrine, the Active Defense, and AirLand Battle: see Doughty, *Tactical Doctrine*; Romjue, *Active Defense*.

56. Though there are exceptions: on the study of war in political science, see, e.g., references cited in chapter 2, nn. 8–12, 35, 37; on operational military history, see, e.g., references cited in chapter 1, n. 37; on military theory in operations research, see, e.g., DuBois,

Hughes, and Low, *Concise Theory of Combat*; on empiricism in operations research, see, e.g., references cited in chapter 2, n. 24; also Helmbold, *Rates of Advance*; Helmbold, "Defender's Advantage Parameter," pp. 27, 29.

57. Thomas Schelling, *The Strategy of Conflict* (1960; reprint Cambridge: Harvard University Press, 1980) pp. 8–9; Bernard Brodie, "Strategy as a Science," *World Politics* 1 (July 1949), pp. 467–88.

58. On the current status of strategic studies in academia, see Richard Betts, "Should Strategic Studies Survive?" *World Politics* 50 (October 1997), pp. 7–33.

Appendix

A Formal Model of Capability

1. I employ the traditional naming convention of referring to the theater invader as "Red" (R) and the theater defender as "Blue" (B); this convention dates to the mid nineteenth century and is standard usage in the American defense planning community. "Direct-fire combat arms" include infantry, armor, cavalry and air defense. This focus on combat maneuver personnel is not meant to suggest that support functions are not critically important—rather, it is meant only to simplify the casualty calculations, inasmuch as combat maneuver personnel suffer the great bulk of combat losses.

2. Empirically, τ_R and τ_B can be computed using the procedure outlined in chapter 2:

$$\tau_i = \frac{1}{2}\left(\frac{\sum_a y_{a_i} n_{a_i}}{\sum_a n_{a_i}} + \frac{\sum_t y_{t_i} n_{t_i}}{\sum_t n_{t_i}}\right)$$

where:

y_{a_i} = year of introduction for aircraft type a for side i
n_{a_i} = number of aircraft of type a on side i
y_{t_i} = year of introduction for tank type t for side i
n_{t_i} = number of tanks of type t on side i

3. "Velocity" is used as an index measure for modern-system tactical implementation by moving units. As noted in chapter 3, high velocity implies limited opportunity to employ modern-system exposure reduction methods, and low velocity implies greater opportunity; thus the higher the velocity, the lower the degree of possible modern-system implementation. Velocity is measured as the distance between jumpoff and objective (or, for defenders, from assembly area to deployed fighting positions), divided by the elapsed time from the initiation of preparatory actions (e.g., reconnaissance or artillery fire) to planned arrival of the initial troops at the destination.

4. See note 3.

5. I assume that forward defenses are uniformly distributed front-to-rear, predeployed throughout the depth of the defense from the outset of the attack, and that the garrisons of overrun positions are destroyed. As the attacker advances into depth, it thus encounters a series of fresh defenses whose strength grows monotonically as reinforcing reserves arrive at the point of attack (until the entire reserve has arrived) even though the defender's troop strength theaterwide declines with losses suffered.

6. This treatment thus follows Clausewitz's analysis of the culminating point of an attack: Clausewitz, *On War*, pp. 194–97, 204, 528–29. For similar perspectives, see Jomini, *Art of War*, esp. pp. 67–70; and Sun Tzu, *The Art of War*, trans. Samuel B. Griffith (London: Oxford University Press, 1963), esp. p. 98, verses 13 and 14. For more recent discussions along similar lines, see, e.g., Richard Betts, "Conventional Deterrence: Predictive Uncertainty and Policy Confidence," *World Politics* 37, 2 (January 1985), pp. 153–79; and Basil Liddell Hart, *Europe in Arms* (London: Faber and Faber, 1937), pp. 83, 334.

7. For asymmetrically distributed technology, the measures thus reflect both the absolute sophistication of one's own equipment, and it's relative standing vis-à-vis the opponent: ceteris paribus, T_C and T_ρ both increase whenever one's own technology improves but decrease whenever the opponent's technology improves (whereas a simple ratio, $\tau_R : \tau_B$, for example, would reflect only relative standing and not the absolute sophistication of either side). T_C and T_ρ thus account for both systemic and dyadic conceptions of technology's effects on capability.

8. I assume that the invader's forces will be echeloned at the point of attack, with troops in excess of local density limits withheld in assembly areas immediately to the rear awaiting commitment to the battle when the engaged echelon reaches exhaustion. Since local density limits are independent of troop strengths, and since attackers' initial strength will ordinarily exceed these, the effects of variance in local preponderance on casualties from the fighting at the point of attack will be determined only by the defender's local strength (the invader's engaged strength being a density-limited constant until and unless the invader's total strength in the sector falls below the density limit). Only the defender's local strength is thus included explicitly in the expression here; the attacker's (constant) engaged strength is treated implicitly via the constant, k_7. On density limits at the point of attack, see Biddle et al., *Defense at Low Force Levels*, P-2380.

9. This model assumes that maximum munition load per sortie is not the limiting constraint on ground target kills—target acquisition is.

10. It is never in the defender's interest to increase f_e, hence it was not necessary to consider the defender's exposure fraction for the purposes of the game.

11. These information and move-sequence assumptions are very conservative with respect to a modern-system defender's ability to prevent breakthrough: more realistic assumptions are likely to imply more effective defenses than those seen in the comparative statics below. Since the modern system's effectiveness in denying breakthrough over a wide range of materiel conditions (and even against modern-system attackers) is among my more important findings, these assumptions are thus also conservative with respect to my argument's viability overall.

12. Relevant parameter ranges are: for f_r, 0–1; for d, 1 to whatever value needed to preclude breakthrough; and for V_r, 0–100 (100 km/day is taken as the practical maximum given the time needed to plan a major movement and dig in upon arrival).

13. More formally, figure A.2 assumes ground-gain-maximizing velocity choices for the invader as a function of the defender's choice of depth and reserves. An alternative assumption of constant velocity choice would imply a larger containment zone (for a defensive depth of 15 km, for example, a constant velocity choice of 1 km/day would yield contained offensives given defender reserve allocations of 0.3–0.99, as opposed to the containment range of 0.4–0.85 in figure A.2); the assumption used here is thus worst-case from the defender's standpoint.

14. More generally, increased reserve withholds spread the forward defense more thinly without increasing the distance the invader must travel to break through. While

modest defensive garrisons are sufficient to compel attackers to reduce their speed dramatically relative to the potential speed of their conveyances, any reduction in the size of the forward garrison does enable some increase in offensive velocity, ceteris paribus. Very small garrisons thus eventually enable a velocity increase too great for the defender's larger reserve to counter in time, and the invader breaks through before the larger reserve can arrive. By contrast, increased defensive depth increases the distance the attacker must travel in order to break through (as well as reducing the density of the forward garrison). This in turn increases the attacker's troop requirements to defend lengthening flanks and affords the defender more time to move reserves to the threatened sector. These effects compensate for the associated reduction in forward troop density and enable arbitrarily deep defenses to preclude breakthrough—albeit at the cost of allowing invaders increasingly deep penetration distances before the offensive can be brought to a halt (see figure A.5 and accompanying discussion below).

15. See figure 5.9.

16. Jukes, *Kursk*, p. 53.

17. David G. Gray, *IDA Unclassified Conventional Forces Database* (Alexandria, VA: Institute for Defense Analyses, 1989), IDA D-708.

18. This represents a rather mild relaxation of modern-system tactical norms; for more extreme examples, see chapters 5 and especially 7.

19. Specifically, f_r is fixed at 0.45, per table A.1.

20. See figure 5.7.

21. Figure A.5 assumes ground-gain-minimizing choices of reserve fraction and reserve velocity for defenders, and ground-gain-maximizing velocity choices for the invader as a function of the given defensive depth. This procedure is adopted here to avoid the artificialities associated with fixing choices in what is inherently a strategic interaction. In particular, astute attackers would exploit a defense of extreme depth by increasing their velocity and thereby increasing their net territorial gain; to hold the attacker's velocity constant while increasing defensive depth would thus overstate the advantages of depth. In effect, the figure thus assumes that both sides will choose rationally (subject to a priority goal of maximizing territorial control), given exogenously constrained defensive depth. An alternative assumption of constant reserve fraction and closure velocity would yield a shallower increase in territorial gain (to a maximum of only 14 km at a defensive depth of 50 km), a steeper decline in attacker losses (to a minimum of 353,000 at a depth of 50 km), a decline in LER (to a minimum of 1.7 at a depth of 50 km), and an increase in duration (to 3.4 days for a depth of 50 km), assuming a constant reserve fraction of 0.45 and a constant closure velocity of 4 km/day.

22. LER is depicted in preference to raw defender casualties to facilitate comparison of attacker and defender performance; raw defender casualties are computed by the model and are implicit in the combination of LER and attacker casualty data shown.

23. This is because the increased depth is purchased at the cost of decreased density for the garrison of the prepared forward defenses; this thinned-out garrison has less stopping power and imposes fewer casualties on the attacker per kilometer gained. Attackers can exploit this opportunity in different ways. They can maintain the same velocity they would have chosen against a denser defense (thus reducing casualties) and thereby extend the advance's duration (a larger surviving attack force requires a larger defensive reserve arrival to halt; to assemble this larger reserve takes more time) and thus its total penetration depth. Or they can maintain the same casualties they would have suffered against a denser defense by increasing velocity, thereby penetrating further in the same (or less)

time. Figure A.5 assumes that the attacker chooses the velocity that maximizes ultimate penetration depth; the net result of this criterion is a modest increase in velocity, affording some reduction in both casualties and campaign duration. A different attacker preference among the dependent variables of territorial gain, casualties, and duration (e.g., an attacker criterion of minimizing casualties or duration for a given penetration depth) would yield different specific values for these variables at any given depth, but regardless of the attacker's preferences, increased defensive depth implies increased offensive capability at the margin. Note, however, that defensive depth increases the distance attackers *must* advance to break through even as it increases the distance they *can* advance—and it systematically increases the former more than the latter: the penetration distance needed to break through increases linearly with increasing depth (for a depth of 20 km, a 20-km advance is needed to break through; for a depth of 30 km a 30-km advance is needed, and so on), but as figure A.5 shows, the penetration distance achievable by the attacker is non-linear and diminishing (penetration distance increases by 3.2 km when depth increases from 10 to 20 km, but only by 1.6 km when depth increases from 40 to 50 km). Increased defensive depth thus enables attackers to gain more ground in limited aims attacks but leaves attackers further and further from breakthough in the process.

24. For a discussion of additional costs, see chapter 3.

25. Assumptions are per figure A.5, save that the defender is assumed to adopt ground-gain-minimizing choice of depth and reserve velocity (subject to the constraint that the attack be contained short of breakthrough) for the given reserve fraction.

26. This is because neither extreme (no reserves or all reserves) allows the counterconcentration so essential for modern-system defensive operations. Defenses with no (or nearly no) reserves lack the wherewithal to counterconcentrate; defenses with no (or nearly no) forward garrison cannot compel the attacker to slow down, and thus such defenses lack the time needed to counterconcentrate. In both cases, attackers are allowed to retain their initial numerical advantage too long, yielding excessive ground gain. To some extent, defenders can compensate for radically high or radically low reserve fractions by radical increases in depth: by compelling the attacker to expose (and defend) extended flanks, very deep defenses eventually halt an attack via excessive diversion of assault forces into flank defense duty. This effect is stronger at very high than very low reserve fractions, since the latter affords the defender only a small reserve force to use in counterattack: this smaller counterattack force is less threatening and requires smaller diversions of the attacker's forces to thwart. For very high reserve fractions, deeper defenses also help compensate for high attacker penetration speed by increasing the distance attackers must travel to break through, affording the (large) reserve more time to deploy at the cost of allowing attackers to take more ground in the meantime. For these reasons, very low reserve allocations are more damaging to defenders than very high ones. In either case, however, radical increases in depth can prevent breakthrough for the entire range of reserve fractions considered here, though the depths needed can be very great (30 km for a reserve fraction of 0.1, and 18 km for a reserve fraction of 0.9, as opposed to only 8 km for a reserve fraction of 0.4), and the resulting increase in the territorial gain available to a limited aims attacker is substantial.

27. Assumptions are per figures A.5 and A.6, save that the defender is assumed to adopt ground-gain-minimizing choices of depth, reserve velocity, and reserve withhold (subject to the constraint that the attack be contained short of breakthrough) for the given exposure level.

28. Figure A.8 assumes a constant defensive depth of 10 km, a constant reserve fraction of 0.5, a constant reserve velocity of 100 km/day, and a defensive exposure fraction of zero. Whereas attackers with the initiative can observe defensive force employment before choosing their assault velocity, defenders must anticipate the attacker's tactics when designing and preparing their defenses; hence defensive force employment is held constant here, rather than varying with attacker velocity. The defender choices assumed here ensure that the offensive will be contained regardless of the attacker's velocity choice and embody a modest safety margin against miscalculation (for the conditions assumed here, a defensive depth of as little as 8 km and a reserve withhold of 0.45 would suffice to preclude breakthrough). Were the defender able to anticipate the specific attacker velocity choices given in the horizontal axis, territorial gain would fall off much more rapidly for velocities below or above 4.5 km/day, attacker casualties and LER would be higher for such points, and campaign duration would be shorter.

29. This is because near-zero-velocity assaults move so slowly that the defender has time to counterconcentrate completely before any significant penetration can be made; such cautious tactics minimize attacker casualties but confront the attackers with such heavily reinforced defenses that little headway can be made. While such methods minimize casualties, they thus cannot maximize mission accomplishment—the latter requires attackers to balance casualty containment with the need to move quickly enough to deny the defender time to react fully. Conversely, moving *too* quickly means accepting very high exposure levels, which increases casualties to the point where mission accomplishment is again compromised. Offensive velocity thus has an internal optimum with respect to territorial gain: neither minimum nor maximum velocity maximizes penetration depth.

30. Note, however, that even outnumbered attackers can still gain some territory against even a modern-system defense: for an attacker:defender troop balance of 0.75:1, the attacker can still penetrate to a depth of about two kilometers.

31. Note, however, that attacker casualties increase less rapidly than attacker troop strength as preponderance increases (troop strength rises by 50 percent between 1:1 and 1.5:1, yet casualties increase by only 41 percent, for example). The attacker's loss *rate* (losses as a fraction of total troop strength) thus declines as preponderance increases, even as absolute casualty figures grow. Similarly, although defender casualties grow less rapidly with increasing preponderance than do attacker losses (hence the increase in LER), the defender's casualty rate (losses as a fraction of total troop strength) increases as preponderance increases.

32. Attackers can thus always do equal or better—in all dimensions—with greater numerical preponderance, but to do very much better in any one dimension against a modern-system defender requires accepting a penalty in reduced performance elsewhere. To do significantly better in all dimensions of capability simultaneously requires breakthrough, and this cannot be accomplished against a modern-system defense.

33. This is essentially what happened to the German defenders in late summer and autumn of 1918, where a series of contained limited-aims offensives by the Allies pushed the Germans nearly out of France and Belgium: see chapter 3.

34. The defender is assumed to deploy roughly 1970-era equipment; hence an attacker-defender gap of fifteen years implies that the attacker deploys 1985-era equipment, and so on. For other parameter values, see table A.2.

35. Available data extend back only to 1956, however: see chapter 8.

36. Similar results obtain when modern-system attackers strike technologically superior modern-system defenses: a thirty-year defender lead implies about a 60 percent reduction in territorial gain, a 4 percent increase in attacker casualties, and a 5 percent increase in LER relative to an assumption of technological parity at the 1970 state of the art (campaign duration, however, falls by about 4 percent). While these effects are nontrivial, modern-system attackers are thus still able to take and hold ground against defenders with weapons even thirty years more advanced than their own.

37. A *non*–modern-system defense would enable clean breakthrough by a modern-system attacker with a thirty-year technological edge (though it would also enable breakthrough by a modern-system attacker at technological parity).

38. Reserve fractions can be held constant at 0.6.

39. And/or the possibility that we might be willing to wait much longer in the aftermath of the Cold War, with lower stakes and lower risks of delay. Nevertheless, in both the Gulf War and the Kosovo campaign, decision makers were clearly unwilling to wait indefinitely for the air campaigns to succeed: in the Gulf, a land invasion followed six weeks of bombing; in Kosovo, it has been reported that the Clinton administration was preparing for a possible land invasion when Milosevic conceded: see, e.g., O'Hanlon and Daalder, *Winning Ugly*, pp. 155–64.

40. The use of a Kosovo-scale kill rate approximates the effects of modern-system concealment on ground-attack air effectiveness: the Serbs may not have completely exploited the potential of modern-system methods, but the unusually covered nature of the terrain made concealment readily available to them. Hence, few of their forces were exposed on any given day: Cohen and Shelton, "Joint Statement," pp. 11–12; Clark and Corley, "Press Conference on the Kosovo Strike Assessment," p. 2.

41. A total of 606 Americans were killed or wounded in action in the Gulf War (148 killed, 458 wounded), or about one out of every 1,000 U.S. military personnel in the theater: Atkinson, *Crusade*, pp. 491, 492.

42. Against exposed defenses, by contrast, much shorter air campaigns can still produce radically low attacker loss rates.

43. Assumptions are per figures A.2–A.13, save that defensive depth is fixed at 8 and 15 km in the 1910s and 2000s cases, respectively; reserve withhold is fixed at 0.45 and 0.7, and reserve velocity is fixed at 100 and 20 km/day: see table A.2.

44. The "modern-system" and "non–modern-system" cases are as defined for figures 4.1–4.3; a midcentury technology level corresponding roughly to the 1940s is assumed. Other parameter values are per figures A.13 and A.14.

45. Again, the "non–modern-system" defense assumed here is only a modest departure from modern-system principles; a more substantial departure yields breakthrough rather than containment even with a 200-km ground gain.

46. Values for all other variables are per figures A.9, A.10, and A.8, respectively: see tables A.1–A.2.

47. With the exception that the relationships between assault velocity and casualties or campaign duration remain fundamentally similar even for halved constants, and that the relationship between systemic technology and invader casualties varies very slightly from the baseline for very early century technology (when the constants are halved) and very recent technology (when the constants are doubled).

Index

magnifies effect of force employment, 142, 146, 149, 188–89. *See also* policy

nighttime: and air attacks in World War II, 263n.12; and attacks, 105; and Operation DESERT STORM, 141; and troop movements, 125

Nobel, Alfred, 198

non-modern system opponents, 57, 63; and attacker territorial gain, 73, 270n.89; and casualties during Operation MICHAEL, 101–2; and deep strikes, 42, 62; and dyadic technology gap, 67; and numerical preponderance, 69

Northern Alliance, 7

North Korea, 64–65

North Vietnamese army, 3

numerical preponderance, 3, 4, 5, 14–15; and attacker territorial gain, 76–77, **76**; combined with dyadic technology theory, 16–17; and conflict with technology viewpoint, 19–20; and defense against modern-system attack, 70, 269n.81; effects of determined by force employment, 190–91; and exclusion of force employment viewpoint, 20; and force-to-force and force-to-space ratios, 71–72; and formal model, 227–28, **227**; and "human wave" tactics, 69, 269n.80; and hypotheses of statistical performance vs. new theory, **155**, 157–58; impossibility of breakthrough against modern system defense, 69–70; and international relations theory, 18, 193; and lethality of modern weapons, 69; and loss-exchange ratio (LER), 22–23, **22**; new theory operationalization of, 287n.30; and non-modern system vs. modern system force employment, 69; and Operation DESERT STORM, 135, 145–46, 149; and Operation GOODWOOD, 108, 114–19, 287n.30; and Operation MICHAEL, 86–94, 100–101; as predictor of victory or defeat, 20–22, **21**; and security, 20; and sensitivity analysis, 236, **237**; usefulness of in era of modern force employment, 54, 69–72. *See also* force-to-force ratio; force-to-space ratio

Objective Norfolk, 135, 141

offense-defense theory, 15, 19, 241n.13, 245n.8; and arms control negotiations, 16; and international relations theory, 194, 195; and lack of systematic empirical work, 17; and Operation GOODWOOD, 112; and Operation

MICHAEL, 79, 100, 271n.3; and World War II, 284n.3. *See also* systemic technology theory

offensive military capability: definition of, 6; distinguishing from defensive, 194, 195

offensive operations, 39–44; modern system as adaptation of traditional methods, 41; and assault frontage in World War I, 95–96; and breakthrough and exploitation operations, 40–42; and deep strikes, 42, 62; and differential concentration, 40–41, 42, 43; drawbacks of modern system, 43–44; limited aims "bite and hold," 42–43; and Operation DESERT STORM, 139–40; and Operation GOODWOOD, 120–21; and Operation MICHAEL, 95–96; and opportunities for counterattack, 42, 43–44

offensive tactics, 35–39; and activities before attack, 60–61; and assault velocities in World War I, 95, **95**; and attack velocity, 226–27, **226**; and combined arms integration, 37, 38–39; complexity as drawback of modern system, 38–39; cover and concealment, 35–36, 38, 39; and deep battle doctrine, 41–42; dispersion and independent small-unit maneuver, 36, 38, 257n.45; and formal model and breakthrough, 222–23, **222**; and Operation DESERT STORM, 140–41; and Operation GOODWOOD, 121–22; and Operation MICHAEL, 94–95, 101; speed limitations of, 39; and suppressive fire, 31–32, 36–37, 38

Office of Net Assessment of Defense Department, 249n.30

Omar, Mullah, 7

operation, definition of, 6

operational art, 252–53n.57

operational level of war, 26

operational planning, 63

Operation ANACONDA, 7, 68, 201, 266n.52; and al Qaeda hiding from aircraft, 58, 200; and cover, 56–57, 59; and wrong interpretation of reconnaissance imagery, 65

Operation BARBAROSSA, 258n.47

Operation COBRA, 109, 119, 120, 122, 127, 130; first day objectives in, 291n.67; German defenses during, 194; and Operation GOODWOOD as breakthrough or limited aims attack, 284n.6

Operation DESERT SHIELD, 137

Operation DESERT STORM, 12, 132–49; and armored vehicle losses, **185**, 186; and breaching effort by 1st Infantry Division, 139, 140;

Operation DESERT STORM (*cont.*)
and defensive operations and tactics, 136–39;
failure of Iraqi independent small-unit
defense, 138, 147; and force-to-force and
force-to-space ratios, 136; initial air campaign,
133–34; and Iraqi active resistance, 143–44;
and Iraqi armor force size in historical
context, 144; and Iraqi equipment that
survived air war, 142–43, 304n.85; and Iraqi
incompetence, 147–48, 305n.103; and lack of
warning of attack, 139–40, 146–47, 186–87,
300nn.47, 48; and linear combination of
causes explanation of Coalition losses,
148–49, 188–89; and low Coalition loss rate,
133, 147–48; and "Maneuver Warfare"
conception of Coalition offense, 147; and
new forms of ground technology, 144–45,
149; and numerical preponderance, 145–46;
and offensive operations and tactics, 139–41;
overview of events, 1991, 133–35; and process
tracing, 141–47; and technology, 132, 135,
185–88, 305n.96; and theory of superior
coalition air technology, 142; why chosen,
132–33. *See also* Battle of 73 Easting;
experimental tests; Gulf War of 1991; Iraq
Operation GOODWOOD, 12, 103–31; and
argument that offensive succeeded, 130; as
breakthrough attempt vs. limited-aims attack,
120, 284–85n.6; and British as overcautious,
130–31; and British lack of modern system
offensive tactics, 121–22, 129, 194; and CDB90
dataset, 153, 154; and defensive operations
and tactics, 122–25; and depth of prepared
defenses and reserves, 122–24, **123, 124**; and
forest cover, 56, 264n.27; and German use of
modern-system defense tactics, 124, 125,
295n.103; historical explanations for British
failure, 128–31; map of attack of Second
British Army in July 1944, **111**; and map of
Normandy beachhead, **110**; and offensive
operations and tactics, 120–22; and orthodox
theory predictions, 108, 126–28; overview of
events, July 1944, 109–11; and predictions by
new theory including contained offensive,
108–9, 126–28, 131, 191, 293n.83, 294n.92;
preparatory air bombardment, 111, 112, 113,
121, 291n.60; and preponderance, 108, 114–19,
287n.30; and systemic technology advantage
for offense, 108; and troop numbers, 114–15;
weapon technology in, 112–14; why chosen as
case method test, 108–9

Operation IRAQI FREEDOM, 201–2, 318n.46
Operation MICHAEL, 12, 78–107; and aircraft,
85–86; and alternative explanations of
German breakthrough, 102–6; breakthrough
without decisive exploitation, 99–100,
279–80n.97; British defensive forces, 82–83,
96–99, 278n.86, 279n.93; British Official
History of, 102; casualties in, 100–102; and
CDB90 dataset, 153, 154; and defensive tactics
and operations, 96–99; fog as explanation of
German breakthrough, 104–6; force
employment in, 94–99, 281n.113; and force-
to-force ratios, 87–89, **88**, 94, 103, 275nn.45,
49; and force-to-space ratios, 90–96, **91–93**,
103, 118, 277n.70; German numerical
strength, 86–87, 103–4, 106; historical interest
of, 79, 82; map of first three German drives
on Western Front, 1918, **80**; map of Somme
Offensive (First German Drive) 1918, **81**; and
new theory's predictions and explanations,
99–102, 106–7, 191; and numerical imbalance,
86–94; and offensive tactics and operations,
94–96; overview of events, March to April
1918, 82–83; and troop training, 89; and use
of tanks, 34; weapon technology in, 83–86,
271n.2; why chosen as case method test,
78–82, 271n.2. *See also* Second Battle of the
Somme
organizational adaptability, 26, 27, 253n.59
organizational problems in adopting modern
system force employment, 48–51
Overy, Richard, 195
Owens, William, 72

Pakistan, 8
Panther tanks, 113, 114, 128–29, 295–96n.105
Pashtun militia, 68
Passchendaele, 87, 93, 95, 96, 105, 255n.19,
277n.69
Patton, George, 267n.59
peacekeeping, 5, 241n.13
Persian Gulf War. *See* Gulf War
"Plan 1919," 42
platform speed, 266n.47
Plumer, Hubert, 254n.9
Poland, Germany's invasion of in 1939–40,
43, 133
policy, implications of new theory of capability
for, 196–208; and defense budget priorities,
203; and force structure, 203–5; and future
research, 206–8; and research, development